PIMLICO

702

THE FOURTH CRUSADE

Jonathan Phillips is a Senior Lecturer in Medieval History at Royal Holloway, University of London. He is the author of *Defenders of the Holy Land: Relations between the Latin East and the West, 1119–1187* (1996), and *The Crusades, 1095–1197* (2002). He has also written articles for *BBC History* and *History Today*, and has published in the *Independent*. He has made a number of radio broadcasts on Radio 3, Radio 4 and the BBC World Service, and has contributed to several television programmes for Channel 4, the BBC and the History Channel USA.

THE FOURTH CRUSADE

And the Sack of Constantinople

JONATHAN PHILLIPS

PIMLICO

Published by Pimlico 2005

2 4 6 8 10 9 7 5 3 1

Copyright © Jonathan Phillips 2004

First published in Great Britain by
Jonathan Cape 2004

Pimlico edition 2005

Pimlico
Random House, 20 Vauxhall Bridge Road,
London SW1V 2SA

Random House Australia (Pty) Limited
20 Alfred Street, Milsons Point, Sydney,
New South Wales 2061, Australia

Random House New Zealand Limited
18 Poland Road, Glenfield,
Auckland 10, New Zealand

Random House South Africa (Pty) Limited
Endulini, 5A Jubilee Road, Parktown 2193, South Africa

Random House UK Limited Reg. No. 954009

A CIP catalogue record for this book
is available from the British Library

ISBN 1-8441-3080-0

Printed and bound in Great Britain by Bookmarque Ltd, Croydon, Surrey

Contents

For Tom
and for
my parents

Acknowledgements

IN THE COURSE of writing this book I have been fortunate to receive the assistance of a great number of people. During my research I benefited from the generous hospitality and knowledge of Dr Christoph Maier in Basel and Professor Isin Demirkent and Dr Ebru Altan in Istanbul, and the organisational help of Fusun Ersak and Claire Lillywhite-Pinch. Discussions with Matthew Bennett, Dr Linda Ross, Dr Merav Mack, Natasha Hodgson, Dr Marcus Bull, Neil Blackburn, Dr Penny Cole and Professor Jonathan Riley-Smith proved important in formulating my ideas and tracking down various elusive references. Dr Thomas Asbridge has offered sound and cheerful advice from the start of this project. Dr Jonathan Harris, Edwin Fuller and Dr Christoph Maier read all, or part, of the manuscript and their observations and corrections have been invaluable. Any mistakes that remain are, of course, my own. I am grateful to Dr Emmett Sullivan for his skill in producing some of the photographs used here. Sally Tornow, Caroline Campbell, Suzanne Tarlin and David Watkinson, along with Austen and Janice Rose, Dr Ian and Diane Jenkins, Andy and Jackie Griffiths, and Lisa and John Barry, have all provided much encouragement and an important counterbalance to academic life. I am very pleased to acknowledge the perceptive guidance and constant support of my agent, Catherine Clarke, the efforts of her US counterpart, Emma Parry, and the good faith of Wendy Wolf at Viking Penguin. Will Sulkin, my editor at Jonathan Cape, has been enormously helpful, patient and constructive during the writing of this book; the work of Jörg Hensgen, Chloe Johnson-Hill, Ros Porter, Hilary Redmon and Mandy Greenfield was also invaluable. My greatest debt is to Niki for her wholehearted love and commitment to our special life together. I am very happy to dedicate this book to my dear parents and to my wonderful son, Tom.

List of Illustrations

Count Hugh of Vaudémont and his wife Aigeline of Burgundy, twelfth-century sculpture from the priory of Belval in Lorraine (*Conway Library, Courtauld Institute of Art*).

Pope Innocent III, church of San Speco, Subiaco (*Scala*).

A devil pours molten metal down the throat of a false moneyer, twelfth-century tympanum, Conques (*author's photograph*).

Early tournament (*British Library*).

Thirteenth-century silver *grosso* (*Emmett Sullivan*).

A Venetian ship, Venetian Maritime Code of 1255 (*author's photograph*).

Early-fifteenth-century plan of Constantinople (*Bibliothèque Nationale de France*).

A knight receives communion from a priest, Rheims Cathedral, early thirteenth century (*Bridgeman Art Library*).

Land walls of Constantinople (*author's photograph*).

Crusaders attack Constantinople, from a later manuscript of Geoffrey of Villehardouin (*Bodleian Library*).

Interior of Hagia Sophia (*author's photograph*).

Late-eleventh or early-twelfth-century icon of St Michael (*AKG London*).

A Note on Nomenclature

THE MAJORITY OF the crusading army that set out from Venice in October 1202 originated from areas within France. It included men from Blois, Champagne, Amiens, Saint-Pol, the Île-de-France and Burgundy. However, several other regions of Europe sent substantial contingents as well. For example, the count of Flanders, who was subject to the overlordship of the king of France, commanded a large force. Similarly, the leader of the crusade, Marquis Boniface of Montferrat, headed men from his northern Italian homelands. Other notable groups came from the German Empire, including the men under Bishop Martin of Pairis and Bishop Conrad of Halberstadt. Given the polyglot nature of this army it is impractical to set out this list every time these crusaders are mentioned. For reasons of style and brevity, therefore, I have used the word 'French' as a blanket term to cover all of the crusaders listed above. If a specific contingent is under discussion, this will be made clear. Large numbers of Venetians also took the cross, but because they formed a distinct group, they are (where appropriate) distinguished from the 'French' crusaders noted above. Simple references to 'crusaders' or 'westerners' can be taken to refer to the army as a whole, both French and Venetian forces alike. The term 'Franks' refers to those who settled in the Holy Land after the First Crusade (1095–9), and their descendants.

The Coronation of Emperor Baldwin

16 MAY 1204 marked a defining moment in medieval history – a seismic change in the accepted world order. For more than eight centuries successive Byzantine emperors had dominated an enormous and sophisticated empire, but this had been swept aside by the armies of the Fourth Crusade – the holy warriors of the Catholic Church. Now a northern European sat on a throne in the great cathedral of the Hagia Sophia, acclaimed by a packed congregation of western knights and traders; the Greeks were far away from their mother city, fleeing from the horrors inflicted by the ruthless warriors who had so brutally sacked their great metropolis. To the westerners, however, God had approved of their fight and now they sought His blessing. Under the soaring dome of the Hagia Sophia, the closing words of the Catholic mass faded away to end the coronation ceremony of Baldwin of Flanders, the first crusader emperor of Constantinople.

Baldwin himself was transformed: as a powerful noble he was accustomed to a position of authority, but now he ascended to a higher, almost divine, status. Earlier in the day the leaders of the western army had collected the count from the Bucoleon palace and escorted him to a side chapel of the cathedral. There, Baldwin exchanged his woollen hoşe for a pair made of the finest red samite and donned shoes covered in rich gemstones. He then put on layer after layer of the most dazzling robes. First, a splendid coat with golden buttons at the front and back; then a long cloak, studded with jewels, that came down to his feet at the front and had to be wound round his middle and brought up over his left arm.

As if this were not enough – in terms of weight alone it must have been a remarkable costume to bear – he wore one further gown. This too sparkled with precious stones and carried designs of the imperial eagle; it was so richly embellished that eye-witnesses reported that the garment shone as if it were aflame. Accompanied by his senior colleagues, Baldwin walked to the altar of the Hagia Sophia – partially damaged during the conquest, it was originally an exquisite piece of workmanship, 29 feet long, studded with gold and precious stones and surmounted by a solid silver canopy. The nobles carried his sword, his crown and the imperial standard; and they were followed by the crusader bishops whose task was to crown the new emperor. At the altar, after Baldwin had knelt in prayer to give thanks for the crusaders' victory, the bishops stripped him to the waist to signify his humility before God. They anointed him, re-dressed him and, finally, gathered around him. Each held the crown with one hand and then they blessed it, made the sign of the cross, and placed it on his head. For an instant the knot of churchmen, themselves dressed in their finest vestments, masked the figure bearing the fearsome imperial eagle on his back, but then they withdrew to reveal the new emperor of Constantinople in all his magnificence – a tangible manifestation of the power and riches that the crusaders had seized. In tribute the bishops immediately presented the emperor with one of the hundreds of treasures pillaged from the imperial palaces: an enormous ruby, the size of an apple, to clasp the front of his robes.

Baldwin sat on a high throne, holding in one hand a sceptre and in the other a golden orb. One can only imagine his feelings and thoughts as he faced the huge crowd, all magnificently attired in jewelled and silken robes. As the congregation chanted the mass, Baldwin's mind perhaps turned to his northern European home: the cold, marshy lands of Flanders; he may have thought of the wife he would now summon to be his empress; he could have reflected upon his illustrious crusading ancestors; and he may have remembered the suffering and sacrifice of his fellow-men as they fought to capture Constantinople. Finally, amidst all the opulence and excitement at the dawning of a new era, he may have remembered that the Fourth Crusaders had first set out to recapture the holy city of Jerusalem, and not to destroy, as they had, the greatest civilisation in Christendom.

Introduction

IN APRIL 1204 the armies of the Fourth Crusade conquered and sacked Constantinople. An eye-witness wrote of the crusaders' lack of humanity, of 'madmen raging against the sacred', of murderous men who refused to 'spare pious maidens' and of 'these forerunners of Antichrist, chief agents of his anticipated ungodly deeds' who smashed altars and plundered precious objects.[1]

Almost 800 years later, in the summer of 2001, Pope John Paul II issued an extraordinary statement – an apology to the Greek Orthodox Church for the terrible slaughter perpetrated by the warriors of the Fourth Crusade. He said: 'It is tragic that the assailants, who set out to secure free access for Christians to the Holy Land, turned against their brothers in the faith. That they were Latin Christians fills Catholics with deep regret.' The fact that the pope felt the need to issue such a document – rare in its acceptance of culpability – reveals just how deep a wound had been left by this long-distant campaign.

The purpose of this book is to tell the remarkable story of the Fourth Crusade – an episode coloured by brutality and determination; depravity and avarice, political intrigue and religious zeal.[2] Several modern accounts of the Fourth Crusade have been written by Byzantine scholars whose primary concern has been its impact on the Greek Orthodox world. Unsurprisingly, perhaps, they have expressed hostile judgements on the motives of the French and the Venetians and, in some cases, their sense of outrage overshadows a broader critical approach.[3] This volume, however, is written by an historian of the crusades – a viewpoint that has encouraged me to provide a western European context for the expedition, as well as considering the situation in Byzantium. This work also seeks to explain why the crusade followed the course it did, to identify some of the underlying causes of these disturbing events and to consider how the westerners achieved their victory.

As a movement that advocated violence in the name of Christ, the crusades have elicited many hostile judgements.[4] The eighteenth-century Scottish historian, William Robertson, described the crusades as a 'singular monument of human folly', and Edward Gibbon's *Decline and Fall of the Roman Empire* opined that the idea had 'checked rather than forwarded the maturity of Europe'.[5] Steven Runciman's *History of the Crusades* concluded that 'seen in the perspective of history the whole crusading movement was a fiasco'. He lamented that 'the Holy War itself was nothing more than a long act of intolerance in the name of God, which is a sin against the Holy Ghost'.[6]

Historians and commentators have lambasted the Fourth Crusade in particular. In the eighteenth century Voltaire wrote that 'the only fruit of the Christians on their barbarous crusades was to exterminate other Christians'.[7] Runciman concluded that 'the harm done by the crusaders to Islam was small in comparison with that done to the Eastern Christians'.[8]

Yet, however unpalatable the ideas and actions of the crusaders seem today, it is undeniable that for several hundred years they represented – according to the beliefs, values and understanding of the medieval age – a hugely popular and enduring institution. Almost as soon as the First Crusade was launched in 1095, it exerted a pervasive influence across all levels of society and precipitated a new intensity of contact – and conflict – with the peoples and lands outside the Catholic world.

In the general perception, crusading is inextricably linked to a conflict with Islam. This connection is perpetuated to the present day with Usama bin Laden drawing a parallel between the crusaders fighting Muslims and American action in Afghanistan in 2001–2. He claimed that 'This war is similar to the previous crusades, led by Richard the Lionheart, [Frederick] Barbarossa [of Germany] and [King] Louis [IX] of France. In the present age they rally behind [George W.] Bush.' Al-Qa'ida propaganda also suggests that Israel is the successor to the Crusader States of the twelfth and thirteenth centuries.[9] Some in the West have looked back to the medieval period, too. In the immediate aftermath of the terrorist attacks of 11 September 2001, the notion of a holy war was inadvisedly employed by President George W. Bush, who called for a crusade against al-Qa'ida. At the time he was trying to secure support from Egypt and Syria – two countries directly affected by the original crusades – yet he invoked a concept still viewed in the Middle East as a pretext for western imperialism.[10]

The outcome of the Fourth Crusade clearly represents a dramatic distortion of the basic idea of the Catholic Church fighting the infidel. Contemporaries and modern historians alike have been fascinated by how a movement that began with the object of reclaiming the Holy Land for Christianity could, in just over a century, develop into a vehicle for the destruction of the most magnificent city in the Christian world.

The crusaders themselves expressed delight and relief at their achievement. Count Baldwin of Flanders, one of the leaders of the campaign, wrote that 'we might safely say that no history could ever relate marvels greater than these so far as the fortunes of war are concerned'. He saw divine approval for the crusaders' actions: 'This was done by the Lord, and it is a miracle above all miracles in our eyes.'[11] Once the details of their savagery seeped out, however, others – even in the West – were less complimentary. Pope Innocent III (1198–1216), the man who had launched the expedition, thundered against the crusaders thus: 'You vowed to liberate the Holy Land ... [but] you rashly turned away from the purity of your vow when you took up arms not against Saracens but Christians ... The Greek Church has seen in the Latins nothing other than an example of affliction and the works of Hell so that now it rightly detests them more than dogs.'[12]

The most vivid way to explore the crusade is through the wealth of contemporary accounts. This material conveys a remarkable range of emotions: fear, pride, exhilaration, self-justification and, at times, an engaging sense of awe at what the expedition was trying to achieve and at the new sights, peoples and landscapes the participants encountered. The actions of medieval military leaders are often adequately recorded and those engaged in the Fourth Crusade are no exception. We are fortunate, however, in that accounts by men of more humble rank have also survived for 1204. To complement these narratives this book employs a broad swathe of analogous crusading texts and images in order to give some impression of the hopes and fears of all the crusaders (and their families) as they embarked upon their extraordinary adventure.

In the case of the Fourth Crusade there is, compared with some other expeditions, a generous selection of source material to choose from. Part of this was the work of eye-witnesses (warriors and churchmen), and part was composed by European-based monastic chroniclers who recorded the stories of returning crusaders. Prior to the twelfth century, literacy was almost exclusively the province of churchmen. Most narratives of the First Crusade (1095–9) were written by churchmen who imbued their texts with a heavy emphasis on divine will and theology. During the twelfth century the growth of courtly life led to the patronage of troubadours and the writing of *chansons de geste* – great epic tales, often based on oral tradition, but sometimes written down by laymen. Within such a culture it was a relatively small step to the idea of the educated layman (usually a nobleman) writing down or dictating his own heroic experiences. This mixture of evidence, from both ecclesiastical (clerical) and secular (lay) authors better represents a true cross-section of society and also allows the reader to follow the crusade through the eyes and minds of knights and nobles whose priorities and motives were, at times, different from those of their ecclesiastical colleagues.

Amongst the most revealing of all evidence are the contemporary letters written by those who participated in, and directed, the crusade. These texts can show how attitudes and policies developed as events unfolded. While they are not immune from attempts to justify or give a particular slant to certain episodes, they provide a degree of detail and an immediacy that later narratives sometimes lack. In addition, the sermons delivered by churchmen trying to gather support for the crusade provide a useful insight into the possible motives of the men who took the cross.

Two other important sources are troubadour songs and official documentary material. The former do not necessarily provide factual information, but offer an expressive insight into the preoccupations of the knightly classes who so dominated crusading at this time. The latter encompasses the commercial agreements faithfully preserved by Italian mercantile communities and, from the archives of countless monasteries, the contracts of sales and mortgages of land and rights made to departing crusaders seeking to finance their campaigns.

The history of the Fourth Crusade is not just recorded from the perspective of the Catholic West, however. Several contemporary Byzantine writers witnessed the campaign and their observations survive in the highly ornate and learned style of classical authors, so beloved by the court of Constantinople.[13] Alongside these accounts, travel writings are another important resource. Just as today's tourist looks to a plethora of guide-books, so too did the medieval traveller, and the commentaries of these individuals – be they Muslim, Jewish, Greek Orthodox or Catholic – are often interesting and evocative supplements to the main narratives.

Finally, an indispensable and exciting sort of information is in a visual form. Sometimes this survives as buildings (ruined, or modified through the ages) or figurative sculptures, wall paintings, coins, as well as manuscript illuminations of people, events or objects (such as ships) connected with the crusades.

Although there are some tantalising gaps in the evidence – for example, there are no extant contemporary Venetian accounts – there remains a remarkably broad palette from which to write the history of the Fourth Crusade. To explain why it sacked Constantinople we must first sketch out the emotional, spiritual and political landscape of the early thirteenth century.

The world of the crusaders was, in many respects, fundamentally different from the society of today. Learning, communications, centralised authority and healthcare were, at best, rudimentary. Travelling times, for example, were measured in weeks and not hours, and knowledge of the world outside the Catholic West was clouded by fear, prejudice and lack of information.[14]

The two most dominant factors in medieval life were violence and religion.[15] Violence took the form of both national-level conflicts and, more commonly, local warfare where the limited power of central authority allowed small-scale feuding between neighbouring lords.

Probably the greatest difference between the secularised western world of the early twenty-first century and the Middle Ages was the importance of the Christian faith. Religion saturated the medieval period in a way that is hard for us to comprehend. The sermons and imagery of the churches ceaselessly reminded men and women of their sinful lives and luridly depicted the eternal tortures of hell that awaited them if they failed to repent. The pressure to make good the consequences of those sins through penitential prayers and devotional acts, such as pilgrimage, was an integral part of the relationship between the Church and its flock. People also looked to God and His saints for protection against enemies, for cures from sickness, for good harvests, for judgement of legal cases (through Trial by Ordeal) or battles. In a modern context some of this can seem little more than superstition, yet to begin to understand the context of the Fourth Crusade it is vital to accept, for example, medieval man's belief in the ability of saints to perform miraculous cures, or to intervene in warfare.

When, on 27 November 1095, Pope Urban II stood up to speak at the Council of Clermont in central France, he fused the familiar ideas of pilgrimage, violence and the need for penance to create a new and enduring concept – the crusade. He argued that the knights of France should march to the Holy Land and reclaim it from infidel hands. In doing so the warriors would undertake a penitential act of such an arduous nature that it merited a spiritual reward of an unprecedented magnitude: the remission of all penance. This meant that the sins accumulated through a life of violence would be wiped clean and the fires of hell would be avoided – the perfect opportunity for people so concerned with their spiritual welfare. Guibert of Nogent, a contemporary observer, described this most eloquently: 'In our time God instituted holy warfare, so that the arms-bearers and the wandering populace . . . should find a new way of attaining salvation; so that they might not be obliged to abandon the world completely, as used to be the case, by adopting the monastic way of life . . . but might obtain God's grace to some extent while enjoying their accustomed freedom and dress, and in a way consistent with their own station.'[16]

The knight was being offered a chance to do what he excelled at – fighting and killing – yet because he fought for a cause judged by the pope to be just, he would be rewarded. As Urban finished his speech, the crowd roared their approval and one reporter claimed they shouted, '*Deus vult! Deus vult!*' – 'God wills it! God wills it!' – before rushing forward to be signed with the cross.

The response to Urban's appeal was incredible. News of the call to arms spread rapidly across Europe and over the next four years more than 60,000 people from all areas and every level of society set out to march the 2,500 miles (the distance from northern France) to the Holy Land. After an extraordinarily arduous journey they took Jerusalem on 15 July 1099 to secure Christ's city for the Catholic faithful.

The capture of Jerusalem released an horrific tension within the crusaders and they massacred the Muslim and Jewish defenders of the city. A later Frankish writer described the terrible scene: '. . . everywhere lay fragments of human bodies, and the very ground was covered with the blood of the slain. Still more dreadful was it to gaze upon the victors themselves, dripping in blood from head to foot.' Yet, alongside this horror, 'Clad in fresh garments, with clean hands and bare feet, in humility they [the crusaders] began to make the rounds of the venerable places which the Saviour had deigned to sanctify and make glorious with his bodily presence.'[17] The people of Christendom were overjoyed at the news – truly God had blessed the crusaders and, by their success, He had signified divine approval for their cause.

Most of the crusaders returned home having completed their vow, but a small core remained to cement the Frankish hold on the Levant (Frank is a generic contemporary term used by both Europeans and Muslims for the settlers, notwithstanding their heterogeneous origins across the West). Over the next few decades, thousands of Europeans came to settle in the eastern Mediterranean as farmers, traders, churchmen and nobles. Many more took advantage of the Catholic hold on the holy places to visit as pilgrims. The needs of these pilgrims led to the formation of the Military Orders – organisations of warrior-monks, sworn to protect Christ's patrimony and to look after visitors. The Knights Hospitaller had a dual military and medical function (and survive today in the guise of the St John's Ambulance Brigade) while the Templars were a purely military force. The First Crusade had crossed the rubicon of religiously directed violence and allowed the formation of bodies of men sworn to the service of God, fighting the Devil in the world, rather than in the cloister. Holy war and crusading thus showed a remarkable flexibility that would enable the concept to expand and adapt to many different situations.

The reaction of the Muslim world to the First Crusade was one of incomprehension. They had no way of knowing that this ferocious band of warriors was bent upon a war of religious colonisation and, in any case, the Muslims of Syria were distracted by intense internal feuding, which meant they offered little concerted opposition to the invaders. Yet, over time, the Muslims began to fight back and through the *jihad*, the Islamic holy war, their leaders started to take the struggle to the Franks.[18]

In 1144, the Muslims of Aleppo took the city of Edessa in northern Syria and this led to the call for what we know as the Second Crusade (1145–9). This numbering system is actually a creation of eighteenth-century French historians and applies only to the largest of the crusades, although we can now identify several smaller campaigns between (for example) the Second and Third Crusades that fulfil the criteria of a papally authorised holy war. In outcome the Second Crusade proved a disastrous failure. Abbot Bernard of Clairvaux had inspired participants with the promise that they were a lucky generation who had been given a special opportunity to reap divine rewards. His assurances fell flat, however, as the armies of the kings of France and Germany suffered terrible losses on their journey through Asia Minor and then abandoned the siege of Damascus after only four days – a terrible humiliation. Nonetheless, the Second Crusade was important in that it saw a formal expansion in the compass of crusading.

Back in the eighth century the Iberian peninsula had been conquered by the Moors of North Africa. Over time the Christians had pushed back the invaders, and with the advent of crusades to the East the idea was adopted in Spain to give the struggle there a new and sharper edge. Since 1113–14 the wars against the Spanish Muslims had been accorded the same status, and given the same spiritual rewards, as campaigns in the Holy Land. In 1147–8 the papacy drew explicit parallels between the simultaneous expeditions to the Levant and crusading activity in Iberia. The pope also accorded crusading status to the wars against the pagan tribes of the Baltic region, on the grounds that it would extend the frontiers of Christianity and serve to revenge the murder of Christian missionaries in times past.[19] By 1150, therefore, crusading was developing far beyond its origins as a war against the infidel in the Holy Land, to become a wide-ranging instrument of Catholic defence and expansion.

During the 1170s Saladin emerged as the leader of the Muslim world and he gathered the forces of Egypt, Syria and the Jazira (northern Iraq) to create the biggest threat that the Franks in the East had ever faced. The settlers appealed for support from the Greek Orthodox Christians of the Byzantine Empire and the Catholics of western Europe.

The Byzantine Empire was the successor to the Roman Empire, and Constantinople (modern Istanbul) was the seat of the ecumenical patriarch, the head of the Church within these lands. In 1054, however, there was a clash between the papacy and the patriarch of Constantinople that led to the declaration of a formal schism between the two churches, which remains in place to the present day. The dispute arose over liturgical and doctrinal differences, plus the vital matter of who possessed the supreme authority: the successor of St Peter (the pope) or the pentarchy of the five patriarchs of the Christian Church (Rome, Antioch, Alexandria, Jerusalem and Constantinople). In theory, therefore, after 1054 the Catholics viewed the Greeks as schismatics and heretics and as enemies of the faithful. By the time of the Fourth Crusade this long-standing crack in the relationship between Byzantium and the West would do much to enable the crusaders to justify the final attack on Constantinople in 1204.

Contact between Byzantium and the West was complex and, on occasion, seems contradictory. Attempts to end the schism sometimes brought the two sides closer, and in 1095 a request by Emperor Alexius I (ruled 1081–1118) for help against the Turks of Asia Minor was another reason why Pope Urban II called for the First Crusade. The notion of the two Christian forces joining together against Islam was an attractive one, but in the course of the major crusading expeditions of the twelfth century there was serious ill-feeling between the western armies and their Greek hosts. The latter saw the crusaders as poorly disciplined barbarians who posed a real danger to Constantinople; indeed, some on the Second Crusade advocated an assault on the city. The crusaders were always suspicious of their hosts. They mistrusted Greek promises to provide food and supplies and blamed them for failing to keep such agreements or, in the case of the Second Crusade, for allegedly betraying them to the Turks in Asia Minor. Prior to the Fourth Crusade, this history was another element of tension in relations between Constantinople and the West.

At times, however, the Greeks and the Catholics were on good terms. Contacts between Emperor Manuel Comnenus (1143–80) and the kings of Jerusalem were very positive, with intermarriage between the royal houses and the submission of King Amalric (1163–74) to Byzantine overlordship in 1171. Manuel also used western administrators and officials in his government and was friendly with King Louis VII of France (1137–80). After the emperor's death, however, there was a dramatic change of attitude towards westerners in Constantinople, largely engendered by the rise to power of Andronicus Comnenus (1183–5).

In May 1182 a group of his supporters, in conjunction with the Constantinople mob, targeted the merchant communities who lived close to the city's main harbour on the shores of the Golden Horn.[20] Some of the traders, who were mainly Genoese and Pisans, managed to flee, but the old and the infirm were caught and slain. Property was destroyed, churches burned and, showing the darker side of Catholic–Orthodox relations, churchmen were captured and tortured. Most notoriously, a hospital run by the Knights Hospitaller was attacked and the sick slaughtered in their beds. A papal legate was seized and killed: his head was cut off and tied to the tail of a dog to emphasise the insult to the Catholic Church. Many other westerners were taken prisoner and sold into slavery under the Turks. The viciousness of this episode horrified commentators on all sides. Eustathios of Thessalonica, a contemporary Byzantine observer, wrote: 'This was a bestial act and cannot be compared with any other form of madness.'[21] William of Tyre, who composed his *Historia* before 1185, commented: 'In such a fashion did the perfidious Greek nation, a brood of vipers, like a serpent in the bosom . . . evilly requite their guests – those who had not deserved such treatment and were far from anticipating anything of the kind.'[22] While trade between the Italians and Byzantium soon resumed, there is no doubt that such a hideous incident added another drop of poison to the swelling undercurrent of ill-feeling between the Greeks and the West.

The death of Manuel Comnenus meant that the Frankish settlers could no longer hope for help from the Greeks, and their efforts to secure support from Europe were hardly more successful. England and France were locked in decades of acrimonious feuding and skirmishing and, in spite of the impassioned pleas of Frankish envoys, their kings were unwilling to settle their differences to help defend the Holy Land and offered only financial assistance.

In the kingdom of Jerusalem the reign of the leper-king, Baldwin IV (1174–85), weakened the Franks further because his slow and terrible decline encouraged plotting and feuding amongst those trying to succeed him.[23] In spite of these problems, the settlers' military prowess held off Saladin until 1187 when the pendulum swung firmly in favour of the sultan. He crushed the Christians at the Battle of Hattin and soon captured Jerusalem to leave the Franks with barely a fingerhold on the coast. Now, belatedly, western Europe had to act.

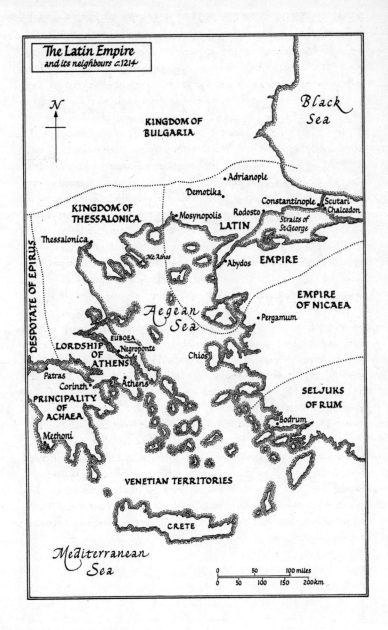

The Latin Empire
and its neighbours c.1214

N

Black Sea

KINGDOM OF BULGARIA

• Adrianople

Demotika •

KINGDOM OF THESSALONICA

• Mosynopolis

Constantinople • Scutari
Rodosto • Chalcedon

Thessalonica •

LATIN

Straits of St. George

Mt Athos

• Abydos

EMPIRE

Aegean Sea

EMPIRE OF NICAEA

• Pergamum

DESPOTATE OF EPIRUS

EUBOEA
Negroponte

LORDSHIP OF ATHENS

Chios

Patras
Corinth • • Athens

PRINCIPALITY OF ACHAEA

SELJUKS OF RUM

Methoni •

• Bodrum

VENETIAN TERRITORIES

CRETE

Mediterranean Sea

0   50   100 miles
0   50   100   150   200km

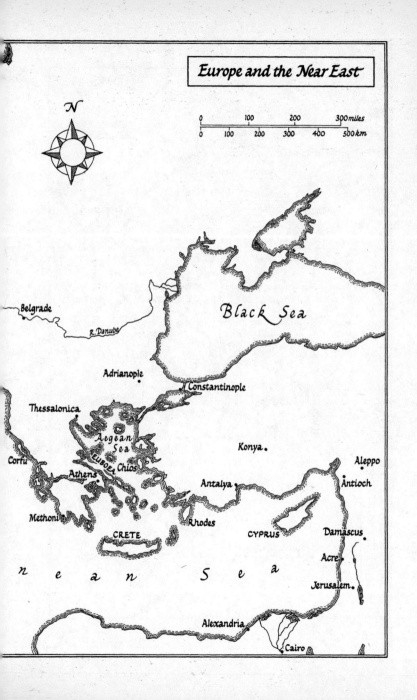

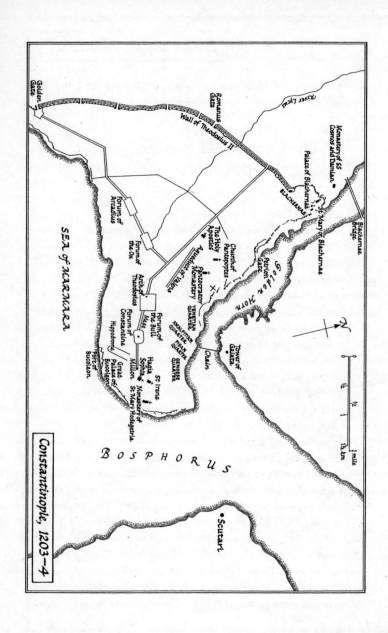

Constantinople, 1203–4

Golden Gate
Romanus Gate
Wall of Theodosius II
River Lycus
Monastery of SS Cosmos and Damian
Palace of Blachernae
St Mary of Blachernae
Blachernae
Blachernae Bridge
Forum of Arcadius
The Holy Apostles
Church of Pantepoptes
Pantocrator Monastery
Petrion Gate
Golden Horn
Forum of the Ox
Amenhicanum Monastery
St Saviour in Chora
VENETIAN QUARTER
Forum of Theodosius
Arch of Theodosius
Forum of the Bull
AMALFITAN QUARTER
PISAN QUARTER
GENOESE QUARTER
Chain
Tower of Galata
Hippodrome
Forum of Constantine
Mese
SEA OF MARMARA
Port of Bucoleon
Great Palace of Bucoleon
Hagia Sophia
St Irene
Milion
St Mary Hodegetria
Monastery of St Mary Hodegetria
BOSPHORUS
Scutari
N
0   ½   1 mile
0   ½   1½ km

CHAPTER ONE

'Oh God, the Heathens are come into thine inheritance'

The Origins and Preaching of the Fourth Crusade, 1187–99

On hearing with what severe and terrible judgement the land of Jerusalem has been smitten by the divine hand . . . we could not decide easily what to do or say: the psalmist laments: 'Oh God, the heathens are come into thine inheritance.' Saladin's army came on those regions . . . our side was overpowered, the Lord's Cross was taken, the king was captured and almost everyone else was either killed by the sword or seized by hostile hands . . . The bishops, and the Templars and Hospitallers were beheaded in Saladin's sight . . . those savage barbarians thirsted after Christian blood and used all their force to profane the holy places and banish the worship of God from the land. What a great cause for mourning this ought to be for us and the whole Christian people![1]

With these powerful and anguished words, Pope Gregory VIII lamented the defeat of the Christian army at the Battle of Hattin on 4 July 1187. Within three months of his victory the great Muslim leader, Saladin, had swept through the Frankish lands and achieved the climax of his *jihad*, with the capture of Jerusalem.

The loss of Christ's city provoked grief and outrage in Europe. The rulers of the West, temporarily at least, put aside their customary disharmony and in October 1187 the papacy launched the Third Crusade to recover the Holy Land. Emperor Frederick Barbarossa of Germany (1152–90), the most senior figure in Christendom, led a huge contingent of up to 100,000 men, but as he waded across a river in southern Asia

Minor he suffered a fatal heart attack and died. The German force broke up and it was left to the armies of King Philip II Augustus of France (1180–1223) and Richard I of England (1189–99) to take the fight to the armies of Islam. In the West, these two men were bitter enemies and their relationship on the crusade hardly improved. In theory, Philip was Richard's overlord, but in practice the English king's energy and military skills meant that everyone recognised him as the dominant figure. The contemporary Muslim writer Beha ad-Din noted: 'the news of his coming had a dread and frightening effect on the hearts of the Muslims . . . He had much experience of fighting and was intrepid in battle, and yet he was, in their [the Franks'] eyes below the royal status of the king of France, although richer and more renowned for martial skill and courage.'[2]

The two kings arrived in the Levant during the early summer of 1191. Philip soon departed to deal with urgent political matters in northern France, but Richard remained in the East for another 18 months. His victories in battles at Arsuf and Jaffa did much to undermine Saladin's reputation, but the crusaders were unable to make a serious attempt to retake Jerusalem itself. Richard did, however, do much to re-establish the Crusader States along the coastline (stretching from northern Syria to Jaffa in modern Israel) and to restore them as a viable political and economic entity. News of intrigues between Philip and Prince John eventually forced him to leave the eastern Mediterranean, but, as he sailed, a contemporary English crusader quoted him as saying: 'O Holy Land I commend you to God. In his loving grace may He grant me such length of life that I may bring you help as He wills. I certainly hope some time in the future to bring you the aid that I intend.'[3]

Richard had gained a heroic reputation, but during his journey home he was captured by political rivals and spent 15 months in prison at the hands of the duke of Austria and then the emperor of Germany. King Philip exploited his absence to take large areas of Richard's territories in northern France, which meant that once the English ruler was free, he was much preoccupied with re-establishing his authority. In these circumstances Richard could do little, in the mid-1190s, to fulfil his promise to help the Holy Land.[4]

Richard's departure could have been disastrous for the Franks in the Levant, but to their great good fortune, just six months after the king sailed, Saladin died, worn out by decades of warfare. The unity of the

Muslims in the Middle East was shattered and a series of factions emerged in Aleppo, Damascus and Cairo, each more concerned to form alliances to defeat the other than with fighting the Franks. The Christians were able to continue their recovery and Frederick Barbarossa's son, Emperor Henry VI (1190–7), hoping to fulfil his father's vows, launched a new crusade (known to historians as the German Crusade). This seemed to offer a real opportunity to exploit the Muslims' disharmony, yet once again the Franks' hopes were to be dashed. In the early winter of 1197 came news that the emperor had died of a fever at Messina in southern Italy. The German forces returned home and, with Henry's son Frederick aged only two, the empire was thrown into a civil war between rival claimants for the imperial title. Pope Celestine III – by this time well into his nineties – tried to mediate, but with little success.

On 8 January 1198 Celestine died, and later that same day the cardinal-bishops and bishops of the Catholic Church in Rome made an inspired choice as his replacement. They elected Lothario of Segni as Pope Innocent III, the man who would become the most powerful, dynamic and revered pontiff of the medieval period. Innocent provided the vision and drive that the papacy had lacked for generations. His pontificate saw crusades against Muslims in Spain and the Holy Land, against heretics, renegade Catholics, Orthodox Christians, as well as the pagan people of the Baltic. He permitted the foundation of the Franciscan and Dominican friars; excommunicated kings and princes; and revitalised the administration of the papal court, enabling the authority of Rome to reach ever more widely across Catholic Europe.[5]

Elected pope at the age of 37, Innocent was one of the youngest men ever to ascend the throne of St Peter. He was born in 1160 or 1161 into a landowning family at Segni, about 30 miles south-east of Rome, and his early education was at the Benedictine abbey of St Andrea al Celio in Rome itself. In the early 1180s he travelled north to Paris University: the intellectual hub of medieval Europe and the most admired centre of theological study. Here Innocent received the best education available in his age and formed many of the spiritual and philosophical ideas that would shape his conception of the papacy. He bolstered this theological background with a legal training and for three years (1186–9) studied at the law school of Bologna – again the most prestigious institution of its sort in the West. Around this time the papacy became increasingly legalistic in its procedures, and Innocent's intellectual capabilities, allied with his deep spirituality and personal presence, were perfectly tailored to the needs of the Curia.[6]

Written sources indicate that the pope was of average height and good-looking. A mosaic portrait from about 1200 is the most contemporaneous image that we have and it shows a man with large eyes, a longish nose and a moustache. A fresco from the church of San Speco, Subiaco, depicts him in full papal dignity, complete with the ceremonial mitre, pallium (a length of material draped around the neck that symbolised high ecclesiastical office) and mantle (see plate section). Innocent was known for his skills as a writer and as a persuasive public speaker: his ability to compose and deliver sermons was exceptional. He had a sharp sense of humour, too: the envoy of one of his most bitter political opponents sought an audience and was greeted with the comment: 'Even the devil would have to be given a hearing – if he could repent.'[7]

A great corpus of papal letters provides some insight into Innocent's mind. Over-familiar as we are today with endless layers of paperwork, one might expect the papacy to have been a cradle of bureaucratic complexity, but prior to the thirteenth century this was not always so. While earlier popes had preserved copies of some important documents, it was not until the time of Innocent III that a systematic archive was kept. Of the thousands of letters sent out from, and received by, the papal secretariat, the most significant were copied into specially bound volumes (known as registers), arranged by pontifical year, dating from the date of coronation (not election), which in Innocent's case was 22 February. It is true that some of these letters were redrafted before being placed in the register; that many were probably written by secretaries, rather than the pope himself; and that much of year three and all of year four of the record (1200–2) have been lost. Nonetheless, it remains an invaluable body of material, which enables us to follow Innocent's planning of the crusade and his reactions to its progress.[8]

Innocent provided a massive injection of spiritual vigour into the leadership of the Catholic Church and very quickly revealed his agenda for the papacy and his aims as the pastor of Catholic Europe. He saw an intimate link between the moral reform of (what he regarded as) a sinful society and a successful crusade to the Holy Land. The latter would free God's city from the infidel and this in itself would be a sign of divine approval for the spiritual regeneration of His people. Evangelical preachers were to urge churchmen and laymen alike to mend their ways and earn God's favour again.

Innocent's passion to free the holy city became the dominant and consuming issue of his pontificate. A contemporary account of his life recorded that 'In the midst of all his work, he quite fervently longed for the relief and recovery of the Holy Land and anxiously mulled over how he could achieve this more effectively.'[9]

In 1197 Saladin's successors disregarded their differences to confront the German Crusade and the following spring the Germans withdrew, leaving the Franks feeling particularly vulnerable. In response to this situation the settlers dispatched the bishop of Lydda to the West to convey an appeal for help. In late June 1198 Innocent wrote of the need for the Christian faithful to assist the Holy Land, and on 15 August he issued his first call for a new crusade.[10] The tone was far more intense than Pope Gregory VIII's document of 1187 and clearly reflects Innocent's ardent desire to defeat the infidel. More than 800 years later, the fervour of his appeal still reaches out from his letter:

Following the pitiable collapse of the territory of Jerusalem, following the lamentable massacre of the Christian people, following the deplorable invasion of that land on which the feet of Christ stood and where God, our King, had deigned before the beginning of time, to work out salvation in the midst of the Earth, following the ignominious alienation from our possession of the vivifying Cross . . . the Apostolic See, alarmed over the ill-fortune of such calamity, grieved. It cried out and wailed to such a degree that due to incessant crying out, its throat was made hoarse, and from incessant weeping its eyes almost failed . . . Still the Apostolic See cries out, and like a trumpet it raises its voice, eager to arouse the Christian peoples to fight Christ's battle and to avenge the injury done to the Crucified One . . . The Sepulchre of the Lord, which the Prophet foretold would be glorious, has been profaned by the impious and made inglorious.[11]

After this dramatic exposition on the condition of the Holy Land and his own personal grief, Innocent turned his attention to the political realities of 1198. He wrote of the rulers of western Europe giving themselves over to luxurious embraces and wealthy living, and railed against their ceaseless in-fighting. Innocent then introduced a common rhetorical device into his appeal, pretending to quote a Muslim who insulted the Christians thus:

> Where is your God, who can deliver neither Himself nor you from our hands? Behold! We now have profaned your holy places. Behold! We now have extended our hand to the objects of your desire, and in the initial assault we have violently overrun and hold, against your will, those places in which you pretend your superstition began. Already we have weakened and shattered the lances of the Gauls, we have frustrated the efforts of the English; we have now, for a second time, held in check the might of the Germans; we have tamed the proud Spaniards. And although you took steps to rouse up all your powers against us, you have, thus far, scarcely made progress in any way. Where then is your God?[12]

In reality, such a speech was unlikely, but the words served Innocent's purpose perfectly. The description of recent military setbacks was true and the insults to each western crusading nation, along with the fundamental questioning of God's power, were intended to shame the audience into action, to inspire them to regain lost honour and to avenge the insults to their own name and that of Christianity itself. He challenged his audience to respond: 'Therefore, take up, O sons, the spirit of fortitude; receive the shield of faith and the helmet of salvation. Trust not in numbers, but rather in the power of God . . . come to the aid of Him through whom you exist, live and have being.'[13]

Innocent urged Christ's warriors to set out with the right frame of mind, unclouded by sins such as vanity, greed or pride. He criticised the arrogance of some earlier crusaders and attacked the moral degeneracy of those living in the Levant whose behaviour had allegedly descended into drunkenness and gluttony.

The pope then turned to practicalities: he directed the expedition to set out in March 1199. Nobles and cities alike were to provide appropriate numbers of men 'to defend the land of the Lord's birth' for at least two years. The emphasis on cities providing crusaders reflected the rising importance of urban centres in western Europe at the end of the twelfth century. Agricultural life remained dominant, but a growth in trade, learning and population was a stimulus to the slow rise of towns and cities, each proud to secure its own civic identity and, where possible, independence from central control. From Innocent's perspective their wealth and status meant they could offer valuable support for the expedition.

Innocent's concern for the crusade was also made plain in his appointment of two senior churchmen to act as his representatives (or legates) in the recruitment and direction of the army. Once under way, both the Second (1145–9) and Third (1189–92) Crusades had experienced only limited influence from papal legates, and Innocent planned to take a much closer interest in his own campaign. One legate (Peter Capuano) was to travel to England and France to make peace between Richard and Philip, and another (Soffredo) was to seek Venetian support for the enterprise. He also directed other churchmen to preach and support the crusade. Many people in western Europe had criticised the Church – with its obvious prosperity – for not providing sufficient assistance in earlier crusades, but Innocent commanded, under pain of suspension of office, that the clergy should outfit and finance knights for the expedition as well. Finally, he identified local churchmen to lead the recruitment in each particular area.[14]

This passionate and uncompromising appeal was sent out to the kingdoms of France, England, Hungary and Sicily. As Innocent himself was aware, however, its timing was not propitious. Neither Germany nor Spain could be approached: the former was gripped by civil war and the latter was fully occupied in the reconquest of Iberia from the Muslims. Furthermore, England and France were still locked in conflict. Because, ultimately, the Fourth Crusade was led by nobles rather than kings, it might appear that Innocent had chosen to ignore monarchs as he gathered support for the expedition. After all, as pope, might he not find it easier to direct nobles, rather than kings? Furthermore, it was the pride and enmity of Richard and Philip that had, in part, caused the Third Crusade to fail to recover Jerusalem. Yet Innocent recognised that the combined resources, prestige and experience of the two kings would be invaluable to the Christian cause. Richard and Philip represented his best opportunities to muster a strong army and he realised that the two men (or, indeed, just one of them) would not take the cross again unless peace was firmly established between them.

In view of his record as a crusading hero, Richard was probably the man most worth pursuing. Since the king's release from captivity in February 1194 he had spent years trying to recover the northern French lands lost to Philip during his incarceration. Recent military engagements had given Richard considerable momentum in this quest and at a battle at Gisors in northern France in late September 1198 King Philip was unseated from his horse and pitched into the nearby river. 'I hear that he was forced to drink from the river' was Richard's satisfied report of the engagement.[15] As well as being a great warrior, Richard was a well-educated individual and an astute politician. His personality was a volatile mixture of a music-loving and quick-witted man of arms and a sharp-tempered, brutal pragmatist: in the course of the papal legate's efforts to convince him to crusade, it was the latter aspect of this mercurial character that he would display to greatest effect.

In December 1198, Peter Capuano reached northern Europe. The source for the meeting between Richard and Peter is the *History of William Marshal*, a vernacular history composed in the 1220s and based on the memories of one of northern Europe's leading noblemen.[16] In spite of this time gap, William vividly recalled the legate's appearance: his complexion was likened to the yellow of a stork's foot and his efforts at humility were grossly overplayed for his northern European audience, because both the king and the marshal found the man's obsequiousness nauseating. The legate's message was hardly any more palatable, as he tried to remind Richard that his continued hostility to Philip harmed the Christian presence in the Holy Land. Richard is known to have had a truly vile temper (on one occasion, unable to defeat one of his knights in a mock fight, he completely lost his composure and ordered the man never to appear before him again), and on this occasion he unleashed an epic performance. Just when, he asked Peter, had Philip taken the lands at issue in the first instance? The answer was in the aftermath of the crusade. While Richard had been risking his life on behalf of Christendom, Philip had (as the Lionheart saw it) slunk back to Europe, unable to tolerate the rigours of the campaign, and had treacherously stolen his lands: 'If it had not been for his malice, forcing me to return, I would have been able to recover the whole of Outremer. Then, when I was in prison, he conspired to keep me there so that he could steal my lands.' Richard demanded that all of these territories should be returned; only then would he make peace.

Peter's platitudinous response was this: 'Ah, sire, how true it is that no one can have everything that he wants.' Again he made the case for the needs of the Holy Land and insisted upon peace between England and France. Richard grumpily offered a five-year truce which would enable Philip to retain the castles, but not the surrounding lands, that he held. This was the best deal he was prepared to make.

Perhaps, at this point, Peter might have sensed that the royal blood pressure had already reached an unhealthy level and he should have left while the mood was merely tense. Unfortunately he pressed onwards and made a further stipulation: the release of 'one of the men Richard hated most in all the world', Bishop Philip Beauvais — recently taken captive by the English ruler. This cousin of the French king was the man responsible for encouraging Richard's jailers to treat him harshly and was known as a warlike individual, often seen in full armour at the head of a contingent of fighting men. Peter claimed it was wrong to detain a person who was both anointed and consecrated. This was a demand too far; the king roared:

> By my head, he is deconsecrated for he is a false Christian. It was not as a bishop that he was captured, but as a knight, fighting and fully armed, a laced helmet on his head. Sir Hypocrite! What a fool you are! If you had not been an envoy I would send you back with something to show the pope which he would not forget! Never did the pope raise a finger to help me when I was in prison and wanted his help to be free. And now he asks me to set free a robber and an incendiary who has never done me anything but harm. Get out of here, Sir Traitor; liar, trickster, corrupt dealer in churches, and never let me see you again!

As the legate retreated before this torrent of rage, Richard threatened to have him castrated. Peter fled, preferring to preserve the clerical dignity intact. Richard himself, said to be as angry as a wounded boar, stormed off to his bedchamber, slammed the shutters closed and refused to speak to a soul.[7]

With the collapse of this particular diplomatic effort, peace between Philip and Richard seemed more unlikely than ever and the crusade even further from reality. Then, on 26 March 1199, as he besieged the small castle of Chalus-Chabrol, south of Limoges, Richard was hit by a crossbow bolt in the shoulder. One source recorded that the king himself tried to remove it, but it snapped off and left the barb in his flesh. Night had fallen and in the flickering torchlight a surgeon tried to dig out the metal, but he only succeeded in butchering Richard even more. Over the next few days, as his wound began to blacken and as gangrene set in, the king feared the worst. He summoned his mother, the indomitable Eleanor of Aquitaine, now aged 77, and she hastened to his side. Richard also made provision for his succession. With no legitimate children of his own (he probably had one bastard son), he named his brother John as his heir. Some reports indicate that he engaged in carnal pleasures too, indulging heavily in the 'joys of Venus', before his strength finally ebbed away. On his deathbed Richard ordered that his heart should be placed in Rouen cathedral, the centre of his Norman lands; his brains and entrails should be given to the abbey of Charroux in Poitou, his spiritual homeland; and his body should be taken to the abbey of Fontevrault, to join that of his father. Nothing was to be sent to England, the land of his birth and the place where he had spent barely six months of his reign.

Richard pardoned the crossbowman who had fired the fatal bolt, confessed his sins and received extreme unction. He passed away in the early evening of 6 April 1199. In spite of the dying king's wishes, his associates failed to share his chivalric attitude towards the royal killer and the unfortunate crossbowman was flayed alive and then hanged.[18]

King John needed to establish himself in power, while Philip of France had to adjust to the fact that his most formidable opponent had gone, a situation that left him free to contemplate making further inroads into English territory. From Pope Innocent's perspective, in spite of the poor relations between Rome and the English crown, Richard's death meant the end of the greatest crusading warrior of the age, a man who struck fear into the hearts of the Muslims and a monarch who could have been a potent figurehead in the effort to reclaim Jerusalem. Innocent's first and preferred vision for the new crusade had, therefore, proven stillborn.

Philip of France was a very different sort of man from Richard the Lionheart. Eight years younger than his arch-rival, he had come to the throne in 1180 aged only 15. After a difficult decade imposing his authority in France, Philip had taken the cross to fight in the Third Crusade. He was not a particularly enthusiastic warrior and brought a smaller force of knights than Richard to the Levant, yet he played some role in the successful capture of Acre in 1191. After only three months in the East, however, Philip chose to return home. To many – particularly Richard's propagandists – this was a sign of cowardice and Philip was heavily crit-icised. Over time he matured into a clever, thoughtful ruler who did much to enhance the economic and administrative structures of the French crown. He was responsible for developing the city of Paris and it was early in his reign that the first college of the University of Paris – the finest university of the medieval period – was founded. Philip also under-took to extend the walls of the city: the existing structure protected just 25 acres; he enclosed 675. He ordered the streets to be paved for the first time and decreed that the abattoirs should be situated downriver from the city. Commercial life flourished: the market at Les Halles was enlarged and important French nobles began to recognise the prestige of Paris and saw that it was important to have a presence there, rather than remaining on their rural estates.

As a man, Philip was said to be earnest, pious, highly strung and fond of wine, food and women. In some ways he hosted a rather austere court, with legislation against swearing (a 20-sous gift to the poor for blas-phemy, or a dip in the River Seine for those who refused to pay), and he displayed little interest in the patronage of music or literature. The king was described as a tall, fresh-faced man, balding by his mid-thirties and becoming ruddy with drink. It was his personal life that was to bring him the greatest difficulty, however, one consequence of which – poor relations with Pope Innocent – undoubtedly contributed towards his failure to take part in the Fourth Crusade. Philip's first marriage took place when he was aged 15 and his bride, Isabella of Hainault, was 10. Seven years later, in 1187, a son, Louis (later King Louis VIII, 1223–6), was born, but Isabella died in childbirth in 1190. After the Third Crusade, Philip decided to marry again and settled upon Princess Ingeborg of Denmark. She offered a large dowry and a good strategic alliance against the German Empire. Eighteen-year-old Ingeborg was said to be 'a lady of remarkable beauty', yet during the wedding ceremony on 14 August 1193 the king is reported to have gone deathly pale and started to tremble. He sent his wife away and refused to sleep with her.

There is no clear explanation for this turn of events but, in any case, Philip soon chose another woman, Agnes of Méran, as his preferred partner. Some blamed Agnes for bewitching Philip so that he turned against Ingeborg, which may suggest an existing liaison with Agnes. He soon sought a divorce. The French bishops agreed and nullified the marriage, leaving Philip free to wed Agnes in 1196. Ingeborg resisted and claimed the new marriage to be adulterous, bigamous and incestuous (Agnes and Philip were distantly related); the papacy agreed and urged the king to take his wife back. Philip steadfastly refused, and Ingeborg spent much of the next 20 years as a shadowy figure, confined to prisons, convents and generally out of public view. In 1203 she wrote an anguished letter to Innocent: 'no one dares visit me, no priest is allowed to comfort my soul. I am deprived of medical aid necessary for my health. I no longer have enough clothes and those that I have are not worthy of a queen . . . I am shut in a house and forbidden to go out.'

Five years earlier, in May 1198, Innocent had written to the king to condemn his actions and to threaten ecclesiastical sanctions against France. An interdict, or ban on public prayer, was proclaimed, but Philip resisted it strongly. In fact he lambasted the clergy who obeyed it, saying that they had no heed for the souls of the poor who were deprived of spiritual consolation. Philip made several promises that he would set Agnes aside and bring Ingeborg to his bed, but invariably broke his word. In the autumn of 1201, however, Agnes died and a way forward could be seen. Ingeborg was treated marginally better, although it was not until 1213 that she was restored to court; Philip, meanwhile, sought comfort in the arms of a prostitute from Arras. In short, the tensions caused by the king's personal life, combined with the enduring conflict with England, meant that the second of Pope Innocent's original choices to lead a new crusade would not, and could not, countenance taking the cross.[19]

If the rulers of Europe were unable to fight for the Holy Land, the responsibility fell to the senior nobility. This was less significant than it may seem: the First Crusade had triumphed without the involvement of kings — it was made up of counts and dukes, and of substantial contingents of knights and foot-soldiers.

When a man took the cross and had the clothing on his shoulder marked with Christ's sign, what was required of him in emotional, physical and financial terms? What questions did the crusaders ask themselves and what effect did their decisions have upon their families?

On the eve of the Fourth Crusade, exactly 100 years had passed since the capture of Jerusalem (July 1099) by the armies of the First Crusade.

There was, therefore, a large body of knowledge accumulated from the journeys of previous generations, passed down through families and told and retold in the courts, taverns, squares and households of Europe. Innocent's crusaders would not be stepping into the unknown in the way that the knights of 1095 had done. Whether an insight into crusading was a positive stimulus to take the cross might, to modern eyes at least, be open to debate. Even in as tough an age as the twelfth century, crusading was a particularly stark and brutal experience that would stretch physical and mental capabilities to extremes.

First of all there was the journey itself. From northern France to the Holy Land was almost 2,500 miles, a distance that had to be covered on horseback or, in part, by sea; or, most likely when one's horse died of starvation, on foot. While many of the nobility were accustomed to moving around the courts of Europe, few foot-soldiers of peasant stock had ever left the area close to their villages. For nobles and lesser men alike, the crusade represented easily the greatest adventure of their lives.

From the end of the twelfth century seaborne crusading expeditions became more common because they were deemed faster and safer than the land march. Most of the holy warriors had travelled by river because, given the dismal condition of many medieval roads, it afforded a highly effective method of communication. The experience of the deep, open sea was, however, an entirely different matter. Fifty years after the Fourth Crusade, Jean of Joinville, a knight on the first crusade of King (St) Louis IX of France, eloquently expressed the fears of the landlubber when he described the prayers and hymn-singing of his fellow-crusaders:

> We saw nothing but sea and sky around us, while each day the wind carried us farther and farther from the land in which we were born. I give you these details so that you may appreciate the temerity of the man who dares, with other people's property in his possession, or in a state of mortal sin himself, to place himself in such a precarious position. For what can a voyager tell, when he goes to sleep at night, whether he may be lying at the bottom of the sea the next morning?[20]

The duration of a crusade was another issue for those considering taking part in the holy war. Pope Innocent asked for a two-year commitment, although many previous campaigns, such as the First Crusade, had lasted longer. Aside from royal or noble households, this was before the age of the professional soldier and conscription (although emergency levies might be implemented in times of crisis). Knights were accustomed to the idea of rendering a period of service to their lord, but this tended to be fixed at 40 days per year: the Lord Almighty, however, required a far lengthier commitment. While crusading was, in theory, a strictly voluntary exercise, there is little doubt that if a noble decided to take the cross, then barring old age or physical impediment, his household knights were duty bound to share their master's enthusiasm.[21]

The most pressing emotion for the crusaders – as the majority of soldiers throughout history have experienced – was a fear of death or captivity. The mortality rates for earlier expeditions were truly terrible, with losses from illness and starvation compounding those inflicted by enemy forces. Even with the limited amount of information at our disposal we have hard evidence of death rates at around 35 per cent on the First Crusade and up to 50 per cent on the German crossing of Asia Minor during the Second Crusade.[22] Figures for the medieval period obviously lack the precision of modern records, and sources tend to concentrate on the nobility, rather than the ordinary men, although in the case of the latter one may suppose even heavier casualties, given their inferior armour and weaker diet, as well as their minimal value as captives. It is sobering that the authorities who sanctioned the crusades were willing to tolerate such appalling levels of mortality. For a crusader, fear of death was muted by the promise of martyrdom: a guaranteed place in paradise. The brutality of medieval warfare would have been familiar in the West, but the hardships of a crusade – the distance, the climate, the unknown enemy and problems of food supply – would have held additional terrors.

The stories of survivors from previous crusades must have brought this home to those who prepared to take the cross in 1199 and 1200. Fulcher of Chartres's account of the First Crusade, written around 1106, described the fear in the Christian camp during the Battle of Dorylaeum (in Asia Minor) on 1 July 1097: 'We were all huddled together like sheep in a fold, trembling and frightened, surrounded on all sides by enemies so that we could not turn in any direction.'[23] Another chronicler recorded: 'the Turks burst into the camp in strength, striking with arrows from their horn bows, killing pilgrim foot-soldiers . . . sparing no one on the grounds of age'.[24]

Raymond of Aguilers was chaplain to Raymond of Saint-Gilles, count of Toulouse, during the First Crusade and his account of a battle at the siege of Antioch (1098) conveys a little of the confusion of battle:

> The boldness of the enemy grew . . . our men, relying on their favourable and lofty location, fought against the enemy and at the first attack overthrew them; but, forgetful of the threatening battle and intent upon plunder, they [in turn] were most vilely put to flight. For more than one hundred men were suffocated in the gate of the city, and even more horses. Then the Turks who had entered the fortress wanted to go down into the city . . . The battle was waged with such force from morning to evening that nothing like it was ever heard of. A certain frightful and as yet unknown calamity befell us, for amidst the hail of arrows and rocks and the constant charge of javelins, and the deaths of so many, our men became unconscious. If you ask for the end of this fight, it was night.[25]

Almost 50 years later the French contingent on the Second Crusade suffered even more grievously when their forces were slaughtered by the Turks in southern Asia Minor: Odo of Deuil, a participant in the expedition, described the feelings in the camp as survivors slowly straggled back to their comrades and regathered: 'There was no sleep that night, during which each man either waited for one of his friends who never came, or joyously, and with no regard for material loss, welcomed one who had been despoiled.'[26]

Alongside the risk of death was the danger of captivity. Ordinary soldiers might be butchered on the battlefield, or else sold in the slave markets of Aleppo, Damascus or Cairo and often condemned to a life of arduous labour. Men of greater standing, if recognised as such, were imprisoned and then, eventually, ransomed. Conditions for prisoners were inevitably poor. Ibn Wasil, an early thirteenth-century Muslim writer, described the prison at Ba'albek as a pit with no windows: 'there was no difference between night and day in there'. Ironically, Ba'albek is the same town where the western hostages John McCarthy, Brian Keenan, Terry Waite and Frank Reed were incarcerated during the Lebanese civil war in the 1980s. Another prison is described at the castle of Beth Guvrin, where a captive was kept in solitary confinement for a year until the trap-door was opened and a second prisoner lowered into the cell. In spite of these grim conditions, survival was possible: in the 1160s the ruler of Aleppo freed German prisoners taken captive on the Second Crusade back in 1147–8.

Sometimes, however, important prisoners were not ransomed, as was the case of the unfortunate Gervase of Bazoches, seized by the Damascenes in 1101. King Baldwin I of Jerusalem resisted paying for him and Gervase's captors urged him to convert to Islam or face death. A contemporary describes Gervase's fate: 'Splendidly obdurate, he rejected such criminal behaviour, and was horrified even to hear such a suggestion. This praise-worthy man was immediately seized, tied to a tree in the middle of a field and was torn by arrows from all sides. The crown was then sawn from his head, and the rest was made into the form of a cup, as though to hold drinks for the ruler of Damascus, by whose orders these acts had been done, to frighten our men.'[27]

Even if a crusader managed to avoid death or imprisonment, for most participants the expedition was an unbelievably gruelling experience. The most likely causes of hardship were lack of food and water. Only limited supplies could be carried with the armies and, once they moved out of friendly territories, it might prove impossible to secure provisions from a scared or hostile local population. As the writer of the *Gesta Francorum* understood from first-hand knowledge, the warriors of the First Crusade were forced to go to extreme lengths to survive: 'Our men were so terribly afflicted by thirst that they bled their horses and asses and drank the blood; others let down belts and clothes into a sewer and squeezed the liquid into their mouths; others passed water into one another's cupped hands and drank; others dug up damp earth and lay down on their backs, piling the earth upon their chests because they were so dry with thirst.'[28] At the siege of Jerusalem in July 1099 the same author wrote: 'we suffered so badly from thirst that we sewed up the skins of oxen and buffaloes, and we used to carry water in them for the distance of nearly six miles. We drank water from these vessels, although it stank, and what with foul water and barley bread we suffered great distress every day, for the Saracens used to lie in wait for our men by every spring and pool, where they killed them and cut them to pieces.'[29] Earlier in the crusade an eight-month siege at Antioch in northern Syria tested men's endurance to the limits: 'So terrible was the famine that men boiled and ate the leaves of figs, vines, thistles and all kinds of trees. Others stewed the dried skins of horses, camels, asses, oxen or buffaloes, which they ate.'[30] Unsurprisingly, these arduous conditions caused many thousands of men to desert. By the time of the Third Crusade, however, better organisation and stricter discipline meant that fewer fled the campaign, although the problem of food and water supply remained a potential hazard for all medieval armies.

Closely associated with such deprivation was, of course, illness and disease. The army of the First Crusade was ravaged by an outbreak of (probably) typhoid in late 1098 and participants in the Third Crusade were endlessly riven by a variety of debilitating illnesses. A particularly dreadful plague hit the camp besieging Acre in 1190-1 and thousands perished, both rich and poor alike. The author of the *Itinerarium Peregrinorum et Gesta Regis Ricardi*, an account of the Third Crusade, commented:

> a recital of the enormous number of all those who died in the army in that short time would seem beyond belief. The total of the magnates alone, according to one writer, can be set out as follows, but that writer declared that it was impossible to discover the losses amongst the masses. In the army died: six archbishops and the patriarch of Jerusalem, twelve bishops, forty counts, 500 great nobles as well as a great crowd of priests, clergy and people whose number cannot be known.[31]

Emergency medical care was, unsurprisingly, minimal. The Knights Hospitaller had field hospitals for the battles in the Holy Land, but the chances of dying from injury or infection of wounds remained considerable.

Because of the punishing physical demands of warfare and the conventions of medieval society, most crusaders were male. But some women also hoped to benefit from the offer of spiritual reward. Orderic Vitalis, writing in Normandy in the early twelfth century, reported: 'wives, lamenting, longed passionately to leave their children and all their riches behind to follow their husbands'.[32] Although some women are known to have taken the cross, usually these were ladies of high birth, such as Queen Eleanor of France (best known today as Eleanor of Aquitaine, later the wife of Henry II of England). Unfortunately, she became embroiled in one of the great scandals of the medieval period when allegations of an affair with her uncle, Prince Raymond of Antioch, did much to confirm the prejudices of many churchmen that women could only bring trouble to a crusading army through their natural inclination to provoke the vices of lust and envy. Ordinary women might be present on a crusade as pilgrims, accompanying the expedition, or else they took on lowly, menial roles, such as washerwomen or – in spite of the spiritual character of a crusade – as prostitutes. The majority of crusaders' wives chose to stay at home, however, where their presence was arguably more valuable as the guardian of family lands and of the next generation of the nobility.[33]

Some women might actually encourage men to take the cross. As a chronicler of the Third Crusade wrote: 'Brides urged their husbands and mothers incited their sons to go, their only sorrow being that they were not able to set out with them because of the weakness of their sex.'[34] On the other hand, women might also prevent men from going on crusade. Gerald of Wales had recruited a knight for the same expedition, only for the man's wife to 'put a sudden stop to his noble intentions by playing upon his weakness and exercising her womanly charms'.[35]

Given the strong possibility that a crusader would die, the emotional pressure on those taking the cross must have been intense. In theory, a married man had to get his wife's agreement before he became a crusader. Whether this stricture had any real effect is hard to tell: a man swept up by the enthusiasm of a sermon, or feeling pressured by peers or family traditions, may have had scant regard for the views of his spouse. In a few cases, however, it must have hampered recruitment because, in order to maximise support for his crusade – and contrary to canon law – in a letter of 1201 Pope Innocent indicated that a man need not seek his wife's consent.

Regardless of marital status, many crusaders willingly set aside the comforts and security of home and family. A participant in the Second Crusade eloquently outlined the sacrifices made: 'Yet it is a fact that they [the crusaders] have exchanged all their honours and dignities for a blessed pilgrimage in order to obtain an eternal reward. The alluring affection of wives, the tender kisses of sucking infants at the breast, the even more delightful pledges of grown-up children, the much desired consolation of relatives and friends – all these they have left behind to follow Christ, retaining only the sweet but torturing memory of their native land.'[36]

The thought of leaving a wife, children, parents, family and friends must surely have weighed heavily on all those who took the cross. Given the rudimentary nature of medieval communications, even sending letters home was a difficult task. For the elite, and those with access to a literate cleric, this was an option, however. In early 1098 Count Stephen of Blois was able to address greetings to Adela, 'his sweetest and most amiable wife, to his dear children and to his vassals of all ranks' and report good progress for the First Crusade. Events could change quickly, though, and by the time Adela received the letter a couple of months later, Stephen's optimism, along with his courage, had evaporated and the count had deserted the expedition.[37] Given the restricted levels of literacy, messages to religious houses were often the main conduit of news to the West and the clerics in turn would pass on information to the local people. In the light of these handicaps, all those in Europe could do was to pray for the safety of the crusaders; indeed, they were positively encouraged to do so by the papacy. In one case at least, an even more devout course was taken when one Walter of Treione joined the monastery of St Peter at Chartres to pray for his father as the latter set out on the Second Crusade in 1147.[38]

As the men fought and marched their way to the Holy Land, their thoughts must often have strayed back to their native lands. A sense of homesickness emerges from some sources, particularly at moments of crisis. As the first Frankish settlers struggled to establish their control over the Holy Land they faced hostile armies far larger than their own. At times such as this the outlook seemed grim, as Fulcher of Chartres wrote: 'On all sides we were besieged by our enemies . . . That day nothing went well; we had no rest, nor were our thirsty beasts even watered. Indeed, I wished very much that I were in Chartres or Orléans, and so did others.'[39] One can sense his yearning for the security of the familiar sounds and smells of northern France – and feel the fatigue and fear of an army in trouble and far from home. One advantage later crusaders held over the pioneers of 1095–9 was the presence of fellow-Franks in the Levant. The shared faith, language and, in many cases, family ties represented a bridgehead that could help to soften the cultural shock of the journey to the East.

The safety of family and property were important concerns, too. On a personal level, some may have feared for a partner's fidelity. The Muslim defenders at the siege of Lisbon in 1147 enjoyed baiting their attackers: 'they taunted us with the idea of numerous children about to be born at home in our absence, and said that on this account our wives would not be concerned about our deaths since they would have bastard progeny enough. And they undertook that if any of us should survive, we would return to our home lands in poverty and misery; and they mocked us and gnashed their teeth against us.'[40]

One way to try to ensure a woman's safety, and her sexual purity, was to place her under the close care of a religious house. The First Crusader Gilbert of Aalst actually founded the monastery of Merhem for his sister Lietgard as he prepared to leave for the Levant.[41]

The protection afforded by the great religious institutions of the time was important in dealing with another serious worry faced by a departing crusader and his family. Because of the turbulence of the medieval age, the absence of a noble and probably many of his knights presented a (literally) heaven-sent opportunity for a less scrupulous neighbour to exploit. The papacy had tried to pre-empt such a possibility by promising that crusaders' lands were under ecclesiastical guardianship and threatening heavy penalties for anyone who transgressed. In fact, the welter of legal cases after the First Crusade seems to indicate that, even so, many knights and nobles suffered losses of land or rights in the course of their absence.[42] In order to prevent this a crusader would appoint someone – often a close relative – to look after his property. Hostile incursions were sometimes resisted as a result. Sibylla of Flanders took control of the county when her husband Thierry left on the Second Crusade in 1146. Two years later, when the neighbouring count of Hainault tried to seize Flemish territory, Sibylla herself led the opposition and forced the invaders to flee. Sibylla was by no means the only woman left in charge when her husband went on crusade, but such moments represented rare opportunities for women to exercise real political power in the medieval age.[43]

Another consideration before taking the cross was the cost of the campaign. To equip a knight, his squires and servants required a considerable outlay. Chain mail, weapons and, most of all, horses were extremely expensive. It was also essential to take large sums of money to purchase food, although nobles sometimes carried valuables with them to barter, exchange or use as gifts as required.

The funding of a crusade obliged men to mortgage or sell their land

and property rights, usually to the Church, because it was the only institution with sufficient resources to buy or lend large sums of money. Thousands of transactions, recorded in documents known as charters, survive from the medieval period and a significant proportion of them are connected with financing crusades. In a few cases we can see two or three documents made by the same man as he sought to organise the disposal of various property rights and to raise the cash he needed. At times, particular churches could not cope with the demand for money and were compelled to melt down valuables. They might also give gifts to an individual crusader in the form of money or useful items such as pack animals. Doubtless families offered whatever backing they could, although the disposal of land and rights often led to interminable arguments as to the validity of particular promises or deals.

It has been estimated that a knight needed to spend four times his annual income to pay for a crusade – yet his family still needed to survive at home and there had to be provision for them in case he did not return. Many crusaders seem to have run out of money in the course of their journey to the East, which meant that they relied on the patronage of the most senior nobles, or on securing booty from the campaign. If either of these was not forthcoming, destitution loomed; there was still the need to pay for a passage back to the West, too. It is not surprising to find crusaders expressing concern over financial matters. Hugh of Saint-Pol was one of the leading figures on the Fourth Crusade and in July 1203 he wrote to friends in northern Europe: 'I am quite anxious about my lands and my loans because, if I return (God willing), I will return burdened with many debts, and it is in my interest that they be paid off from my lands.'[44]

As people have discovered following recent episodes such as the Vietnam War and the 1991 Gulf conflict, it is easy to overlook the mixture of emotions generated in the aftermath of a crusade. For some families the homecoming brought fame and joy. Men's achievements were enshrined in oral verse and literature. William of Malmesbury, writing in the 1120s, rhapsodised about the achievements of Godfrey of Bouillon and Tancred of Antioch:

> . . . leaders of high renown, to whose praises posterity, if it judge aright, will assign no limits; heroes from the cold of Europe plunged

into the intolerable heat of the East, careless of their own lives . . .
they overwhelmed so many enemy cities by the fame and operation
of their prowess . . . Let poets with their eulogies now give place,
and fabled history no longer laud the heroes of Antiquity. Nothing
to be compared with their glory has ever been begotten by any age.[45]

In the 1130s the Anglo-Norman monk, Orderic Vitalis, described why
he included the story of the First Crusade in his *Ecclesiastical History*: 'a
noble and marvellous theme for exposition is unfolded for writers to
study . . . Never, I believe, has a more glorious subject been given . . .
than the Lord offered in our own time to poets and writers when He
triumphed over pagans in the East through the efforts of a few Christians
whom He had stirred up to leave their homes . . .'[46] The Flemish historian Lambert of Ardres wrote of the deeds of his own lord, Arnold the
Old: 'It ought to be known, however, that in this fight at Antioch [June
1098], Arnold the Old was reputed to be the best amongst the many
nobles of many nations and peoples, because of the strength of his spirit
as much as the skill in knighthood of his outstanding body.'[47] Crusaders
such as Count Robert II of Flanders became known as '*Jerosolimitanus*' in
recognition of their exploits in the East.

Against the prospect of fame and admiration other, more negative
features emerge. Most crusaders returned in relative poverty, although
Guy of Rochefort came home from the 1101 campaign 'renowned and
rich', according to a contemporary.[48] More commonly, a journey to the
Holy Land opened up the possibility of bringing back relics – objects
of inestimable value – to present to a local ecclesiastical institution. In
part this was to give thanks for a safe return; in part to acknowledge a
church's financial support. Churchmen carried back relics for their own
religious houses. In 1148–9, Bishop Ortlieb of Basel presented the
monastery of Schönthal with a piece of the True Cross along with stones
from Gethsemane, Calvary, the Holy Sepulchre, the tomb of Lazarus and
Bethlehem: all objects sanctified by their association with the holy places.
Aside from relics, one crusader found an altogether more bizarre souvenir
to commemorate his experience: Gouffier of Lastours brought a tame
lion home with him; its fate is unknown.[49]

Yet for crusaders whose campaigns foundered there was the burden of
defeat. Expeditions that had, in theory, been divinely blessed at their

outset must have failed for a reason and the explanation given usually represented either a practical or a spiritual angle. In the course of the Second Crusade, as the French army crossed Asia Minor, it lost formation and was decimated by the Turks. One man, Geoffrey of Rancon, was consistently mentioned and the chroniclers made it plain that he was held fully responsible for the huge losses. Odo of Deuil was present at the battle and wrote: 'Geoffrey of Rancon . . . earned our everlasting hatred . . . the entire people judged that he should be hanged because he had not obeyed the king's command about the day's march; and perhaps the king's uncle, who shared the guilt, protected Geoffrey from punishment.'[50] Bernard of Clairvaux, the churchman who had led the preaching of the Second Crusade, preferred to identify the participants' thoughts of greed and glory as the cause of their defeat.

Some families, of course, had to learn the tragic news of the loss of one of their kin. Aside from the effect this had on dynastic and political affairs, we have very limited insight into the human and emotional cost of such a loss, although a few rare examples do survive. We know that Ebrolda, the widow of Berengarius, a knight who died on the First Crusade, withdrew from the world and became a nun at the priory of Marcigny. More difficult still were the cases where no one knew for certain whether a man had been captured or killed. In 1106, Ida of Louvain took the remarkable step of making a journey to the East in the hope of finding her husband, Baldwin of Mons, count of Hainault, who had gone missing in Asia Minor in 1098. A local chronicler wrote that 'out of love for God and her husband, with great effort and expense, she travelled to the Levant, where, unfortunately, she found no comfort or certainty'.[51] Another contemporary wrote: 'Whether he was killed or captured, no one knows to this day.'[52]

Even if a crusader returned safely to the West, he had to deal with the psychological impact of years of warfare and suffering, as well as memories of the loss of friends and relatives in the course of the fighting. Men had to become reaccustomed to their homelands, rather than sharing in the routine labours of the crusade. Sometimes relatives would have died in their absence; on occasion their lands would have been reduced or threatened by the actions of a local rival, which in turn led to negotiations, warfare or a difficult legal case in order to regain lost territory or rights. The crusader's family and household also had to readjust to an individual whose absence they had compensated for during the time of the crusade. Medieval sources are not especially attuned to providing such information, but in one or two instances the participants' behaviour hints at what a terrible ordeal they had been through, both physically and mentally. King Conrad III of Germany received a head wound in battle in Asia Minor in 1147 and, although he recuperated at Constantinople before returning to the crusade the following year, the injury troubled him for the remainder of his life. Conrad may also have contracted malaria in the East, because for several years after his crusade he was plagued by a debilitating illness, not connected with his head wound. Another crusader, Guy Trousseau of Montlhéry, suffered what appears to have been a nervous breakdown. He had deserted from the First Crusade during the siege of Antioch and, as Abbot Suger recorded, 'he had been broken by the stress of a long trip and the irritation that comes from various afflictions, and by guilt for his behaviour at Antioch . . . Now wasting away and devoid of all bodily strength, he feared that his only daughter might be disinherited.' In such a status-conscious military society it seems that Guy could not bear the dishonour of his actions and he was, literally, dying of shame.[53]

Another glimpse of the human cost of a crusade can be had in a contemporary statue in the Musée des Beaux Arts in Nancy (see plate section). It is believed that the couple are Count Hugh of Vaudémont and his wife Aigeline of Burgundy. The sculpture was originally placed in the abbey of Belval, a priory supported by the Vaudémont family, and it was probably commissioned by Aigeline when her husband died in 1155. Hugh had taken part in the Second Crusade, and the statue shows his wife greeting him on his return. The sculpture conveys genuine emotion and intimacy and is a moving and powerful reminder of the feelings of separation and fear generated by a crusade. The couple cling tightly to each other with Aigeline's left hand protectively clasped around her husband's waist, just below his crusader's cross, while her right hand tenderly rests on his right shoulder and touches his neck. Her head rests against his bearded face, nestling on his left shoulder, determined to feel his warmth and closeness. Aigeline is clearly relieved to see Hugh again, yet her pleasure is mixed with tension and the way she clings to him so closely gives the impression that she never wants to let go of him; after the years of being apart, she cannot bear the thought of losing him again.

On Hugh's part, the strain of completing the journey is apparent in the fixed expression on his face; the count stares straight ahead, exhausted, but resolute and unbowed at the completion of his vow. He grips his pilgrim's staff tightly (there was a close overlap between the ideas of pilgrimage and crusading at this time, hence the pilgrim's staff and wallet) and his shoes are in tatters, showing the hardship of the trip. Yet he too reveals his feelings for Aigeline, with his left hand placed protectively around her left shoulder and his fingers just squeezing her for reassurance. Hugh and Aigeline were fortunate in that they were reunited and their mutual devotion still shines through, but for many others, of course, the outcome of a crusade was not so happy.[54]

In essence, a crusade was known to be a highly dangerous, expensive business. It could bring fame and honour to an individual and his family; it could also bring death, insecurity and financial ruin. The reasons why generations of westerners chose to engage in this most hazardous of ventures are complex and powerful.

CHAPTER TWO

'Now, therefore, brothers, take the triumphal sign of the Cross'

Abbot Martin's Crusade Sermon, Basel Cathedral, May 1200

I N LATE 1199 and early 1200 the papacy redoubled its efforts to raise support for the Fourth Crusade. News of the planned expedition rippled across the Catholic West and passed the lips of traders, pilgrims, diplomats and soldiers. Preachers tirelessly worked the courts, market places and cathedrals of France, Germany, the Low Countries, England and Italy. Regardless of language, politics and status, the call to the crusade permeated everywhere: an insistent, relentless reminder to everyone of their Christian duty to regain the Holy Land.

One particularly eminent preacher was Fulk of Neuilly.[1] He had risen from a simple parish priest to become a familiar figure in the schools of Paris and to the public at large. He was described as stern-voiced and rigorous in his rebukes to sinners, especially adulterous women and usurers. He was responsible for many miracles and healings, too. 'In every place he was received with the greatest reverence as an angel of the Lord,' wrote the contemporary Cistercian chronicler, Ralph of Coggeshall. Fulk was, in one way, however, a worldly individual. Not for him the grim asceticism of some religious men. He was known to eat very well and never refused food, an enthusiasm that provoked surprise amongst those who preferred their holy men to fast and suffer in their cause.[2]

Pope Innocent had heard of Fulk's skills as an orator and asked him to preach the new crusade.[3] The cleric went to a meeting at the abbey of Cîteaux to persuade the Cistercian monks to help him, but they were unwilling to assist, in spite of their long record of involvement in crusade preaching. Fulk was outraged and marched over to the gates urging a crowd assembled for the occasion to make the journey to Jerusalem. Such was his reputation that people flocked to join the campaign. 'From all points they hasten in large numbers: rich and poor, nobles and the base alike, the old along with the young, an innumerable multitude of both sexes. And they eagerly receive the sign of the Cross from him,' reported Ralph of Coggeshall.[4]

Fulk called upon several co-preachers from amongst his contacts in Paris, but these men proved largely ineffectual. It seems they were too fixated upon ideas of spiritual purity and moral reform (which were particularly important in contemporary Church thinking) to make an effective link to the call for a new crusade.[5]

In the spring of 1200 one region yet to be visited by an official preacher was the city of Basel and the Upper Rhineland, an area already rich in crusading history. Finally, an announcement was made: on 3 May, the feast-day of the Discovery of the True Cross, Abbot Martin of Pairis, a Cistercian monastery in Alsace, was to deliver a sermon in St Mary's cathedral in Basel.[6] At last – an opportunity for the faithful to take the sign of the cross and to carry Christ's emblem into holy war. Historians usually rely on the contents of chronicles, papal bulls, contemporary letters and charters to piece together the motivation of crusaders. In the case of the Fourth Crusade, however, the narrative of Gunther, a monk from Pairis, contains the text of a crusade sermon that provides a vivid insight into the workings of a crusade appeal.[7]

Gunther wrote his *Historia Constantinopolitana* before the end of 1205 and based much of his work on the account of the expedition given to him by his abbot. Martin was later an enthusiastic participant in the sack of Constantinople and was to bring back a rich haul of relics to the abbey. Gunther wrote his work to justify this holy theft and he explained it in terms of God's benevolent direction of mankind. It is a complex piece of writing, artfully constructed to display its themes to their best advantage.[8] The crusade sermon itself is prefaced by the words: 'He [Martin] is reported to have spoken in these or similar words.' Gunther is in effect admitting, therefore, that his text is not a verbatim replica of the speech, but is heavily based on the abbot's original with (probably) a little shaping from the author. In spite of this caveat, this is one of the earliest and most complete contemporary records of a crusade sermon and its general tenor reflects the papacy's appeal to the motives, hopes and beliefs of a crusader.

The city of Basel dates back to Roman times and the name comes from the Greek word *basileus*, meaning emperor, and was adopted in honour of Emperor Valentinian I (364–75). It stands on the Rhine, the great arterial waterway running through Germany and central Europe. The cathedral of St Mary's is positioned on a hill about 100 feet above the river and provided Martin with a large auditorium for his speech: it is more than 160 feet long and the nave is almost 45 feet wide.[9] A fire in 1185 had badly damaged the church, and the slow pace of reconstruction meant that it is unlikely that the nave was properly roofed by 1200. To some extent, therefore, the western side of the church was a building site and may well have been partially open to the elements. By the time of Martin's speech, however, the series of solid, but stately, arches that extend down the body of the church were probably in place. At its apex each arch was slightly pointed, in what we now call the early Gothic style, and this represented the most modern architectural thinking of the age. Today we can see little other than the pale pink-white sandstone from which the cathedral is largely constructed. This gives the building a rather austere aspect, but in Martin's time the completed section of the church would have been covered in brightly coloured paintings and decorations, depicting biblical scenes and events from saints' lives. Complex and intricate sculptures adorned the pillars and tombs of the cathedral and some of these still survive: the same fallen Christians, Old Testament heroes and fierce, mythical animals stare down at today's tourists and worshippers as scowled and grimaced at Martin and his audience 800 years ago.

In the ambulatory of the crypt there survives an image of Lütold of Aarburg, the bishop of Basel who took part in the Fourth Crusade. Lütold's head and feet have been uncovered from beneath later plasterwork and building modifications, although his body is destroyed. Remarkably this constitutes the only contemporary, or near-contemporary picture of a participant in the expedition, although it was as a distinguished bishop, rather than as a crusader, that he was memorialised. The north transept of St Mary's contains one particularly vivid series of panels designed to show the sacrifice and suffering of St Vincent, an early Christian martyr. The panels depict his trial, his torture by beating, by fire, by incarceration and by drowning, and then his burial: a lesson in the sacrifice of a true Christian. For Martin's potential crusade recruits, the ideas of suffering and death would have provided stark reminders of their possible fate, although the reassuring images of angels would have been a sign of heavenly reward to the faithful.

Medieval churches were often the focus of urban life. Today they are frequently quiet, ordered and austere places, but to envisage them in the Middle Ages we must imagine something quite different: places of noise, chaos and colour. Food-sellers, money-changers and other tradesmen milled around outside the building, hawking their wares and their skills to the curious, the needy and the unwary. Performers looked for a chance to draw in an audience for their songs, or to hear tales of heroism and the exotic. The sounds and smells of cooking, the cries of merchants and the shouts and cheers of people gathered around games of dice all formed part of the ambience. The crowds outside the cathedral buzzed with passing news as they swapped tales and related the latest gossip and intrigues. Such gatherings were by far the best source of news and information, and stories of a scandal or a disaster spread like wildfire. We should also imagine a real mix of languages: in the heart of Europe on such a pivotal communication route as the Rhine, French, German, Occitan (the language of southern France) and Latin would be common; and perhaps Danish, Spanish, English or Russian might be heard from the more adventurous travellers. The turmoil around the cathedral would spill inside, with pilgrims and visitors mixing with guides and local clerics. The sick, the crippled and the destitute would be there, begging for alms and support, and trying to scratch a living from the charity of others. Some churches had sloped floors so that the filth and rubbish produced by this mass of humanity could be washed out onto the street at the end of every day. At Basel the focus of this tumult was, of course, the launch of the crusade and the prospect brought great crowds to the cathedral.

For Abbot Martin this would be the biggest meeting of all on his preaching tour. We know little of his previous career, but this was probably the largest audience he had ever addressed; it must have been a daunting prospect. He bore the responsibility for accomplishing God's work and for this reason – and with as stern a taskmaster as Pope Innocent III behind him – the pressure to succeed was tremendous. In planning his sermon Martin must have weighed up many different, and sometimes conflicting, considerations. The abbot had to ensure that his appeal was pitched at just the right level; his audience was a public gathering, not an assembly of educated churchmen or a small group of local lords whom he knew well from the day-to-day business of his monastery. There had to be clear messages running through his speech: he had to stress the urgent need for the crusade and the inestimable rewards for those taking the cross. Too much complex theology or a lack of clarity might take the sting from his words. Martin had to provoke a range of emotions: anger, sorrow, the desire for vengeance – feelings that would be born out of a wish to save the Holy Land from the infidel. There was also a need for a closer, more personal focus to the appeal: he had to prick an individual's desire to atone for his sins, to avoid the torments of hell and to save his soul through a penitential journey (in other words, the crusade). He could light upon the more secular values of family honour, crusading traditions and a desire for worldly gain. In essence, of course, if someone took the cross they were making an enormous commitment and probably one of the most significant decisions of their lives. To travel almost 2,200 miles from Basel to the Holy Land, to risk illness and injury, to fight a fierce and successful enemy – not to mention bearing the huge expense of equipment, transport and food – was a profoundly serious undertaking. Martin was also urging people to part from their families, to leave wives and children without their protector and to hope they remained safe in the men's absence.

Against these negative factors, Martin could set a number of hugely attractive incentives. His prime card was to play upon the essential religiosity of the time: the deep-rooted devotion that permeated Christian Europe in this period and which had been the dominant motive for crusaders since the start of the movement in 1095. Furthermore, because there had been several crusades by 1200, a tradition of crusading had grown up in many families and areas, and this was something else for the abbot to exploit. Such traditions created a sense of expectation and honour that each generation would play its part in the fight for the Holy Land. Martin could also hold out the prospect of material advantage. To some churchmen the idea of profiting from a religious war seemed incongruous, but the papacy had recognised the reality of the situation and reconciled itself to the practice of crusading. At the very least, booty was required to cover the costs of the campaign and there was also a need to pay the wages of knights, squires and other soldiers. There was sound canon law (a mixture of biblical precedent and the decisions of previous popes) to support the payment of adequate wages in Christian warfare. Excess was to be frowned upon, however – if an army took too much booty it would commit the sin of greed, thereby incurring God's disfavour and leading the expedition to fail.[10]

As Abbot Martin pondered the exact words to use, he most probably consulted, or remembered, examples of earlier crusade preaching. In the international hierarchy of Cistercian abbeys, the house of Pairis was connected to the house of Morimond – the intellectual centre of the order – and Martin may have turned there for information. Its library held histories of the First Crusade, as well as letters and texts written by other Cistercians such as Bernard of Clairvaux (d. 1153). Bernard, who was later canonised, had been one of the most powerful crusade preachers of the twelfth century and was known as 'the mellifluous doctor' on account of his honeyed words. Quite wisely, Martin seems to have borrowed some of these ideas and images. Bernard himself preached for the Second Crusade at Basel on 6 December 1146.[11]

What little information we have about Abbot Martin's personality suggests that he was well equipped to deliver the sermon. Although our evidence comes solely from Gunther, his fellow-Cistercian, and could be open to charges of bias and exaggeration, it appears that the abbot was an engaging and gregarious man. He was described as being cheerful, humble (always an appropriate attribute for a good churchman) and popular. He was praised for his maturity, his gentleness amongst his monks, yet he also carried genuine authority with lay people of all ranks and was, according to Gunther, 'regarded by both clerics and laity as lovable and easy to deal with'. As the abbot started his preaching tour, some monks were concerned that his constitution – probably weakened by years of ascetic practices such as fasting and vigils – would not withstand the rigours of a recruitment campaign. Decades earlier, St Bernard had performed such debilitating devotional routines that his digestive system was all but destroyed and he was sick so frequently that he needed a special hole in the ground next to his pew in the church to vomit into. Martin was a rather more robust individual, however, and he seems to have been galvanised by his task; with 'energetic self-confidence' he set about his work.[12]

News of the sermon was trailed well in advance to attract the maximum audience. While many of Martin's listeners came from the city itself, others would have journeyed specially to hear him. In late April and early

May, Basel must have seemed to possess a magnetic attraction. The roads became markedly busier as potential crusaders, traders and those who were simply curious to listen were pulled towards the cathedral. People would have travelled together in carts, bartered, begged and bought food; they must have felt a shared bond of brotherhood and adventure as they moved into the city. The visitors had much to discuss. They exchanged news of the situation in the Holy Land and of the legendary ferocity of their Muslim enemies; they debated the choice of route to the East; they discussed possible arrangements for lands and families and the problem of raising money. Some may have been on pilgrimage or earlier crusades to the East, and their anecdotes and experiences were doubtless relayed and generously embellished. The exploits of crusading heroes would also have been talked of. Since the time of the First Crusade, the events of that divinely blessed expedition had been told and retold, with its leaders' deeds and reputations glossed and ampli-fied. The troubadour songs of the chivalric courts, epic stories (the *chansons de geste*) and the monastic chroniclers of the age all recalled the deeds of their predecessors.

Finally, on 3 May 1200, the great day arrived and large numbers were said to be 'hungrily' waiting for the preacher to begin. The altar in Basel cathedral stands on a raised area above the crypt, placing Martin a few feet above his audience and giving him a good platform from which to address the church. When the abbot stood up to deliver his sermon the seething crowd in front of him fell silent. Martin felt huge anticipation, 'his whole being afire with celestial devotion', and as the moment of his oration approached, he offered up a silent prayer. Fortified by divine inspiration, the abbot prepared to speak. To a modern reader many of the words and images he used appear highly exaggerated; equally the powerful reaction of the audience strikes us as unnatural. Today, displays of open emotion by a public figure tend to arouse special comment. In medieval times, crying, close physical contact and prostrating oneself on the ground in an act of devotion were not so unusual. They might be noted by observers, but were not regarded as extraordinary. We should recall the scale of the commitment that the abbot was seeking. To persuade people that the huge sacrifices of a crusader were worthwhile would require the performance of a lifetime.

At the start of his sermon Martin employed a truly striking device.

He suggested that the words were not his own, but that Christ was speaking through him. 'Heed my word to you, my lords and brothers; heed my word to you! Indeed, not my word, but Christ's. Christ himself is the author of this sermon; I am his fragile instrument. Today Christ addresses you in his words through my mouth. It is he who grieves before you over his wounds.' Immediately, therefore, his sermon was imbued with a divine authority and a spiritual presence. From the outset the audience was pressed to respond as the Lord wished.

Very quickly the abbot came to the heart of his message: 'Christ has been expelled from his holy place – his seat of power. He has been exiled from that city which he consecrated to himself with his own blood. Oh, the pain!' Images of the loss of Jerusalem and the spilling of blood (Christ's blood, shed on behalf of mankind) were expertly coupled with Martin's exclamation of hurt. With the claim that, through him, Christ addressed the congregation, the abbot had created a sense that Christ himself – there in Basel cathedral – cried out in agony. In other words, Martin had brought Christ's suffering and loss directly to his listeners.[13]

The abbot developed the idea of the injury suffered by Christ through the Christians' expulsion from Jerusalem. He also outlined the life of Christ, the resurrection and His work with the apostles. He emphasised that Christ Himself had instituted the sacrament of the holy body and blood (the Eucharist), something that was familiar to all present through regular religious observance. After this succinct overview, inexorably tying Christ's presence on earth and His gifts to mankind to the loss of the physical Jerusalem, Martin brought his audience starkly back to the present: 'this land is now dominated by the barbarism of a heathen people. Oh the misery, the sorrow, the utter calamity! The Holy Land . . . has been given over to the hands of the impious. Its churches have been destroyed, its shrine [the Holy Sepulchre] polluted, its royal throne and dignity transferred to the gentiles.' The image of the heathen polluting and defiling the Holy Land dated back to the time of the First Crusade and was a well-used message in crusading sermons. Clearly this would provoke a sense of outrage in the audience: an unclean and ungodly race was occupying Christ's lands. Connecting the damage to the churches of the Holy Land – buildings that some in the audience may have visited on pilgrimage themselves – he again returned the focus to the present.

Alongside the destruction of churches, the abbot mentioned the loss of the True Cross: 'That most sacred and venerable Cross of wood, which was drenched with the blood of Christ, is locked and hidden away by persons to whom the word of the Cross is foolishness, so that no Christian might know what was done with it or where to look for it.'

The True Cross was probably the most important single relic of the age and was believed to be part of the cross upon which Christ was crucified. Because His body was assumed into heaven, there were no bones left as relics, and items closely associated with Christ's presence on earth were, therefore, highly prized. The True Cross, as the object upon which Christ had suffered for all mankind, was obviously a relic imbued with enormous spiritual significance. It had been found in Jerusalem in the fourth century by Helena, the mother of Constantine, the first Christian emperor, and the feast-day to commemorate that event was 3 May.[14] Martin had, therefore, cleverly tied Christ's suffering, this important historical event and the feast-day to his own crusade preaching. The relic itself had been split into two pieces: one part was sent to Constantinople, the other one remained in Jerusalem. The piece at Jerusalem was removed by the Persians, but was rediscovered by Patriarch Heraclius of Jerusalem in the seventh century. Following the Arab invasions later that century it was divided again and a large section was found by the crusaders soon after the capture of the holy city in 1099. The complicated history of the relic, or indeed its authenticity, is in many ways irrelevant, because the crusaders believed absolutely in its veracity.

The wood was mounted in a large metal cross, decorated with gold and silver; it was kept in a special chapel in the church of the Holy Sepulchre and was carried into battle by the Franks who regarded it as a protective talisman. In July 1187, however, at the Battle of Hattin, Saladin had captured the cross and it had not been seen since. Its recovery was a central preoccupation for the Church and there had been unsuccessful attempts to negotiate its return. Martin incited his audience to help regain this relic so intimately connected with Christ's presence on earth. The fact that he had chosen to deliver his oration on the feast-day of the True Cross added even greater potency to his appeal and shows again how carefully calculated his entire approach to the sermon was.[15]

The abbot then shifted his focus and commented on the military situation in the Levant: 'virtually all of our people who used to inhabit that frontier have been eliminated'. The abbot noted that the survivors, centred upon the city of Acre (today in the far north of Israel), were subject to repeated enemy attacks and for this reason as well, 'such is Christ's plight, which forces him today to appeal to you through my mouth'. In reality the circumstances in the Levant were not quite as Martin described. Although the Frankish lands were massively truncated after Saladin's conquests of 1187, the work of the Third Crusade meant that they had a reasonably firm hold on the coastal strip. Furthermore, because the Muslim world had disintegrated into a bitter struggle between Saladin's heirs, it was not in a position to mount a serious assault on the Christians. In the context of a crusade sermon, however, strict accuracy was not essential. It is unlikely that either Martin or his audience knew the full facts and it was fundamentally true that the Franks were weak and did not hold Jerusalem. In any case, exaggeration and hyperbole were staples of crusade preaching from the very start. In 1095 Urban II's descriptions of Christians in the Holy Land being tied to posts and used as archery practice by the infidel, or else being eviscerated, were absolutely groundless. But, true or false, they served a purpose and succeeded in whipping up his listeners into a frenzy of religious fervour and a wish to revenge themselves on the Muslims. People had to believe that they were risking their lives for good reason and the perilous position of their fellow-Christians in the Holy Land formed a substantial part of that cause.[16]

After this powerful exposition of the need to perform God's work, the abbot appealed directly to his audience: 'And so now, true warriors, hasten to help Christ. Enlist in His Christian army. Rush to join the happy ranks. Today I commit you to the cause of Christ, so that you might labour to restore Him to His patrimony, from which He has been so unmercifully expelled.' This brought home the urgency of the situation. It also touched upon a theme familiar to the knighthood of western Europe, namely the notion of the rightful inheritance of property. There were endless disputes over land succession, and the idea of losing land that was properly due to an individual would strike a strong chord; if the dispossessed individual was Christ Himself, then the need to restore the proper order would be even greater.

Abbot Martin then acknowledged an awareness of the dangers that faced crusaders and the worries that confronted them, and he tried to fortify his audience by remembering the deeds of their predecessors. 'Lest you be frightened by the fact that presently the heathens' savagery against our people has greatly increased in its fury, I want you to remember the accomplishments of . . . that famous expedition led by Duke Godfrey . . . [the first Frankish ruler of Jerusalem].'

This history lesson was designed to appeal to the knights' sense of honour and a wish to emulate the deeds of their forefathers, as well as to fulfil their Christian duty. Martin also offered encouragement by pointing out that the First Crusaders succeeded without having any base in the Levant. In 1200, on the other hand, the Christians held Acre and Antioch and many other castles, and these could provide a springboard for the recovery of Jerusalem.

The final section of the sermon focused on the rewards for a crusader. After putting the case for a moral commitment to the cause, the abbot backed this up with a simple and direct appeal to two of medieval man's greatest interests: the afterlife and money. The crusade was God's work, and Martin promised 'absolutely' that 'whoever takes the sign of the Cross and makes sincere confession will be totally absolved of every sin and when he leaves this present life, no matter where, when, or by what happenstance, he will receive life eternal'. It is difficult to overstate the medieval preoccupation with making good the consequences of sin and avoiding the eternal torments of hell. One historian has described it as 'the most guilt-ridden age in history', where sins of violence, lust, greed and envy were never far from the thoughts and deeds of its people. One glance at the graphic and terrifying sculptures surviving over the doorways of churches such as Autun, Conques or Arles demonstrate unmistakably the horrors of hell (see plate section). Fearsome devils, with terrible teeth and claws, draw hapless sinners towards a variety of grim and eternal torments; promiscuous women have serpents attached to their breasts; those guilty of minting false coins have molten metal poured down their throats; a sinful knight is slowly roasted on a spit, while another is simply pushed into the jaws of a huge monster. Yet a crusader could – if he confessed his sins – be absolved from all his misdeeds. It was a bargain: performing the work of God on a crusade was such an arduous act of penance that the participant would receive a reward of appropriate generosity. This deal lay at the heart of the offer that had proven so attractive to generations of crusaders, dating back to the launch of the First Crusade in 1095. Incidentally, the statements making plain that the time of death made no difference to the crusader receiving his heavenly reward were designed to address a specific and important concern. The audience would be aware that many could die on the way to the Holy Land, through shipwreck, by enemy action or, most likely of all, from illness. Martin was reassuring crusaders that once they had taken their vow and confessed their sins, their place in heaven was certain. In other words, if his intentions were proper, a crusader would not be denied his heavenly rewards through failing to complete his journey to the Holy Land.[17]

Alongside the offer of this spiritual jackpot, Martin buttressed his case by holding out the hope of secular rewards as well. Some reports of Urban II's sermon at the Council of Clermont in 1095 mention the pope describing a 'land of milk and honey' to which the crusaders were travelling. Few preachers from the Second and Third Crusades were so explicit in their use of secular gains as a lure to take the cross. Martin, however, was not at all coy. He said: 'Now I shall not even mention that the land to which you are headed is by far richer and more fertile than this land, and it is easily possible that many from your ranks will acquire a greater prosperity even in material goods there than they will remember enjoying back here.' The cynic might argue that Gunther was preparing his readers for events later in his account when Martin – on behalf of the Church, of course – had gathered great riches. The writer may have been suggesting that the crusaders had been encouraged towards such acts by the preaching of the expedition, which here, we must remember, was said to have Christ's endorsement. Equally, given the lack of surviving sermons from the time, such a message might have been no more than routine. In fact, because so many Frankish knights had been killed or captured at the Battle of Hattin in 1187, if the Fourth Crusade did succeed in retaking the Holy Land, then there would have been quite genuine possibilities to secure lands and wealth.

Martin rounded off this section of his appeal with a reminder: 'Now, brothers, look at how great a guarantee comes with this pilgrimage. Here, in the matter of the kingdom of Heaven, there is an unconditional pledge; in the matter of temporal prosperity, a better than average hope.' Who could resist such an attractive proposition?

As he moved towards the end of his oration, Martin pulled off one final flourish: 'I, myself, vow to join in both the journey and the labour and, insofar as it is God's will, I hope to share in all your successes and trials.' Many crusade preachers did not actually take part in the expedition, but here Martin fervently assured his audience that he was prepared to suffer and to face the same risks as they. Once again, therefore, he added a new ingredient to the power of his words and the pressure of his arguments.

After this rousing exhortation, in the last moments of the sermon he demanded that his audience should act. 'Now, therefore, brothers, take the triumphal sign of the Cross in a spirit of joy, so that, by faithfully serving the cause of Him who was crucified, you will earn sumptuous and eternal pay for brief and trivial work.'

By this time Martin was emotionally and physically exhausted. He had to strain his voice in so large a space and he had put every ounce of concentration and energy into his message. His own tears and cries peppered the performance, such were the depths of feeling he brought forth. His audience, too, was deeply affected by his words. In the course of his sermon, 'You could see tears . . . from everyone . . . you could hear groans, and sobs, and sighs, and all manner of similar signs that gave an indication of personal remorse.' The careful construction of the speech and the astutely chosen messages were designed for maximum impact upon the listener. Coupled with Martin's compelling delivery, they ensured that all those present had shared in Christ's suffering, had appreciated the danger of the Christians in the East, had been reminded of the heroes of the First Crusade, and were offered substantial spiritual and material rewards. 'When, with compressed lips, the wise man fell silent, the mob roared on every side, stung by sweet pain; they hurry to assume cruciform tokens and divine service, to enlist in the ranks of the Leader, who leads us to the stars by way of the cross.'

In spite of his fatigue, Martin must have felt elated. Crowds surged forward to commit themselves to God's work. While many had probably decided to take the cross beforehand, his words would have turned these thoughts into reality and almost certainly persuaded others to join the crusade. Once the tumult had died down, Martin could turn to practical matters: he set a date by which all were to have put their private affairs in good order. They were to reassemble at the cathedral and then 'take up with him the path of holy pilgrimage'.[18]

CHAPTER THREE

'The Tournament was a fully pitched battle and never
was there a better seen'

The Tournament at Écry, November 1199

A BBOT MARTIN'S HEARTFELT appeal touched sharply upon the
hopes and aspirations of his audience in Basel. Other preachers
delivered powerful and passionate sermons across western Europe
through 1199 and 1200 and a growing number of people came forward
to join the expedition. One particular occasion brought recruitment for
the crusade to life, yet intriguingly this was not a sermon or religious
assembly, but a much more worldly event: a tournament, the dramatic
and glamorous playground for the knightly classes of northern Europe.[1]

On 28 November 1199, at the castle of Écry-sur-Aisne, Count Thibaut
of Champagne and his cousin, Count Louis of Blois, assembled the elite
of northern French knighthood for a great festival to celebrate prowess
at arms, to offer a forum for social advancement and to entertain. Today
the castle has all but disappeared and only a few foundations remain in
the village of Asfeld on the River Aisne, around 16 miles north of the
city of Reims, the seat of the duchy of Champagne.

Tournaments were a spectacular and integral part of courtly life during
the Middle Ages and some aspects of the purpose and ethos of such
events help to explain why many at Écry chose to enlist in the crusade.
At the time of the Fourth Crusade, however, tournaments were very
different from the familiar images provided by television and film. We
are accustomed to a formal setting: two knights facing one another in a
joust; they couch lances under their arms, hunch behind their shields,
then charge at top speed; a crash, and the splintering of wooden lances
as they hit each other, the thump as one hits the ground; cheers for the

victor. Grandstands full of brightly costumed admirers applaud, while at each end of the lists cluster the knights' tents, topped with banners fluttering in bright sunlight. By the fourteenth century this picture may hold true, but earlier on the reality of an event such as that at Écry was far more chaotic and considerably more brutal.

Tournaments were rambling, anarchic occasions, laced with bloodshed and vengeance. They were not held in the enclosed setting of a jousting list, but ranged over many acres of land; the arena was usually defined by two designated villages or castles. In 1199 the tournament ground lay between Écry and the village of Balham, 2½ miles to the north-east. A long, gentle slope leads out of Écry towards Balham. To the left runs the Aisne, a broad, swift-running channel that loops gently along a shallow valley. Outside of this the wide, chalky plains of the region provided ample ground for a fast and free-ranging contest.

Such an open space was needed because men rarely participated in single combat, but gathered into two contingents, with up to 200 knights on each side. The formation of the groups often reflected real political alliances and this could generate razor-sharp tensions. On the signal of a herald the tournament began with a lance-charge. The two forces hammered towards each other at maximum speed, the bellowing of the men blended with the thundering of hooves and the rattle of harness. Then, the seismic impact of two fully armed contingents of knights in collision, the thud of bodies, the clash of metal on metal, flesh absorbing the momentum of a charge; the first cries of the injured. Hand-to-hand fighting would break out and helmets would ring from the blows that crashed down upon them. Amidst the fury of clashing steel, men were often wounded; occasionally they died. There were few rules and no referees. At times a mêlée or a scrum would develop and the scene frequently descended into near-mayhem, with the group that preserved better order the more likely winner. Little regard was given to the physical surroundings: orchards, vineyards and crops were damaged or trampled underfoot; the knights might use a barn or other farm building in which to hide or prepare an ambush; and the streets of a village might suddenly become the location of a full-scale clash between rival parties.

The purpose of these savage confrontations was to rehearse and train for real warfare, the only difference being that the aim was to capture the opponent, rather than to kill him. Of course, in the heat of the engagement –

and perhaps, if one came across an old adversary – a sword might be swung a little too hard and lives could be lost. Inevitably accidents also happened: Count Geoffrey of Brittany, a younger brother of Richard the Lionheart, died at a tournament in 1186; six years later Duke Leopold of Austria was killed when his horse fell upon him in a 'warlike game'. Others might be crippled; or misfortune could see a man trapped in his armour. After one particularly fierce encounter William Marshal, the greatest warrior of his day, could not be found. At last he was located in the local smithy, bent over a forge, submitting to the blows of the local blacksmith who was trying to remove a helmet so bent that it could not be taken off the knight's head. Eventually William was freed. In some ways, the more violent the tournament, the better: as Roger of Howden, an English writer of the late twelfth century, commented: 'he is not fit for battle who has never seen his own blood flow, who has not heard his teeth crunch under the blow of an opponent, or felt the full weight of his adversary upon him'.[2] The fast-moving combat of a tournament provided by far the most realistic preparation for actual warfare that could be imagined; the *History of William Marshal* described one such occasion as 'a fully pitched battle'.[3]

Tournaments were immensely popular in northern Europe (strangely, they hardly occurred in southern France or Italy) and the nobility acquired a genuine taste for these spectacular pageants. Newly knighted youths were sent off to take part in the dozens of events that took place over the tournament season. They would learn to work with their fellow-knights and could practise the use of the lance, as well as closer exchanges with the sword and the mace. One of the attractions of the tournament circuit was the prospect of making money. Captured opponents had to pay to be released and their horses and equipment might also be forfeit. In 1177 William Marshal and his partner, Roger of Jouy, claimed to have taken 103 knights, a feat that did much to make their reputations.[4] A young knight from a relatively lowly background might achieve social advancement through his skill at arms, and it was known that the great nobles of the day often visited tournaments to identify the most talented newcomers and try to persuade them to join their households. So alongside military training there was the chance, as a twelfth-century Flemish writer remarked: 'to live gloriously and to attain secular honour'.[5]

If a young knight was successful as a warrior there was another prize to be gained: he might also win the favour of a lady at court. At the edge of the tournament area there were special refuges where knights rested or tended their wounds, but also where spectators could gather. We hear of people watching tournaments from town or castle walls, safely above the action. Embedded in chivalric culture was the idea of courtly love: a knight would seek the admiration and patronage of a lady and, if he succeeded in proving his skill in battle, she would bestow a token upon him: a lock of hair, a piece of cloth or a trinket of some kind. The knight would become her champion and, in return for her love and esteem, he would try to perform bold deeds in her name. The *History of William Marshal* reported that the arrival of the ladies at a tournament at Joigny left the knights 'convinced that they had become better men'. Once the contest began, 'those who had been in the company of the ladies continually got the better of the other side'.[6] The growing body of courtly literature celebrated this erotic interplay between a lady and the knight. Geoffrey of Monmouth, who wrote a semi-fictional *History of the Kings of Britain* in the early 1130s, provides this account of events at the court of King Arthur: 'Every knight in the country who was in any way famed for his bravery wore livery and arms showing his own distinctive colour; and women of fashion often displayed the same colours. They scorned to give their love to any man who had not proved himself three times in battle. In this way the womenfolk became chaste and more virtuous and for their love the knights were ever more daring.'[7]

In many cases, such a relationship was limited to the bearing of tokens or a kiss for the victor. Moral constraints and the need to preserve a dynastic line usually dictated caution on the part of a noblewoman. Married women of the highest rank were wary of becoming involved with a knight, no matter how brave he was, not least because the penalties for adultery were severe. In some lands it was death; in others, terrible mutilation such as nasoctomy – the slitting of the nose. On occasion, of course, illicit relationships did take place – sometimes with disastrous consequences. In 1182 Count Philip of Flanders discovered one of his retinue in bed with his wife. The knight was given summary justice: he was beaten by the household butchers and then he was hung head-down in a sewer until he suffocated. Sometimes rumours alone were enough to result in a scandal. William Marshal allegedly dallied with the wife of the Young King Henry (Henry II's eldest son, who died in 1183, six years before his father) and when this became public her husband forced William to leave the court. Nonetheless, some clandestine arrangements did survive and, for the unmarried at least, flirting and innuendo were *de rigueur*. We must imagine the great ladies of the day, dressed in their finest silks, or shrouded in furs and mantles in winter, as essential players in the ritual of a tournament.[8]

Social display was a vital aspect of chivalric society. The best knights were not just daring warriors, but also patrons of music and literature and generous in the giving and making of entertainments. As tournaments became a central part of this culture, the great literary epics of the age celebrated and reinforced their importance. While these fictional writings have to be treated with some caution, when they concerned as familiar an event as a tournament they had to relate fairly closely to reality for the intended audience to feel properly involved.[9] Chrétien de Troyes was one of the leading writers of the age and his patron was Count Philip of Flanders, a man known for his huge enthusiasm for tournaments. Chrétien described a tournament in his story '*Érec and Énide*':

A month after Pentecost the tournament gathered and was engaged in the plain . . . There were many bright-red banners, and many blue and many white, and many wimples and many sleeves given as tokens of love. Many lances were brought there painted azure and red, many gold and silver, many of other colours, many striped and many variegated. On that day was seen the lacing on of many a helmet . . . some green, some yellow, some of bright red, gleaming in the sunlight. There were many coats of arms and many white hauberks, many swords at the left-hand side, many good shields, fresh and new, of azure and fine red, and silver ones with golden bosses. Many fine horses . . . all came together at a gallop.

The field was entirely covered with armour . . . the tumult grew. Lances were broken and shields were pierced, hauberks dented and torn apart, saddles were emptied, knights fell, horses sweated and foamed. Swords were drawn above those who fell to the ground with a clatter. Some ran to accept the pledges of the defeated and others to resume . . .

Érec was not intent upon winning horses or taking prisoners, but on jousting and doing well in order to make evident his prowess.

He made the ranks tremble before him; his skill excited and encouraged those on whose side he fought.[10]

With so many knights and nobles gathered in one place, a tournament was a wonderful opportunity to display other, non-military, attributes such as hospitality and largesse. Gifts were given in the form of patronage, money and valuable objects, horses or even land. The lords' desire to outdo each other meant that the cost of staging such events could be enormous. Knights and their entourages had to be accommodated; squires, grooms and servants to be fed; horses stabled. Huge feasts were organised: jongleurs, magicians, dwarves, tumblers and story-tellers were hired and the finest food prepared. Gold and silver vessels were used to carry the food and drink and complex seating arrangements reflected hierarchy and status. Musicians were engaged and the cacophony of tambourines, drums, flutes, panpipes, trumpets and reed pipes resonated around a castle's Great Hall.

There was also dancing. The Joigny tournament recorded by William Marshal was attended by many beautiful women. As the ladies arrived, the men rose to meet them. One said: 'Come on, let us dance'; William himself provided a song and the knights took the ladies by the hand and danced.[11] The halls would be decked in banners and shields, while some chambers were covered in frescos showing scenes from great battles of the past. In the mid-thirteenth century Henry III of England had Westminster Hall and rooms in the Tower of London, Winchester Castle and Clarendon Palace embellished with images of the deeds of his crusading ancestors, Duke Robert of Normandy and Richard the Lionheart.[12] The doge's palace in Venice contained frescos of the capture of Tyre in 1124. The castle at Écry may have been too humble for decoration on such a lavish scale, but the presence in November 1199 of men such as Thibaut and Louis almost certainly ensured that splendid feasts and entertainments accompanied the tournament.

The depiction of crusading deeds in a lord's castle reveals a link from this most secular of settings to holy war. The relationship between tournaments, the crusades and the Church was one of mutual tensions and contradictions. In theory, the papacy deeply disapproved of tournaments. In 1139 Pope Innocent II decreed: 'We entirely forbid, moreover, these abominable jousts and tournaments in which knights come together by agreement and rashly engage in showing off their physical prowess and daring, and which often result in human deaths and danger to souls.'[13] For the Church, tournaments promoted nothing but sin: the vices of pride, hatred and vanity; feasts led to gluttony and the knights were aroused to lechery as they sought to impress wanton and immoral women. Given the reality of these events, there was a considerable degree of truth in such arguments. Knights were indeed directing their energies to self-serving ends; there was also the disorder and destruction caused by such contests. Yet in spite of repeated legislation against tournaments (1130, 1139, 1148, 1179), the knights and nobles of northern Europe became ever more enthusiastic about them.

In truth, because the tournament was such an ideal practice for warfare and provided the optimum outlet for display, advancement and patronage, it could not be suppressed. For example, in spite of the papal prohibitions, the great tournament organised by Emperor Frederick Barbarossa at Mainz in 1184 was attended by several important churchmen. Many of these men were relatives of the senior nobility and their close family ties and shared cultural and geographic milieu meant that it was quite natural for them to become involved. More importantly for the history of the crusades, in spite of the opportunities – as the papacy saw it – to commit sin, many of the men who took part in, or supported, tournaments were also well known for their piety. Count Philip of Flanders went on crusade in 1177–8 and then died at the siege of Acre during the Third Crusade in 1191. Count Henry 'the Liberal' of Champagne (so called because of his generosity) was known as a lavish benefactor of religious houses and was also an experienced crusader. In fact, Flanders and Champagne, the real heartlands of the tournament, were committed and enduring supporters of the crusading cause.[14]

The close relationship between crusading and chivalry was plain to see. The military experience acquired at a tournament was also applicable to a holy war. The need for contingents of knights from different regions to meet up and learn how to co-ordinate operations with each other could prove invaluable on crusade. Furthermore, chivalry had a strong religious aspect as well. The idea of serving a lord, the notion of honour, the ritual of dubbing and the blessing of weapons have strong ecclesiastical over-tones. Notwithstanding the papacy's deep mistrust of these events, rather than being a barrier to a crusade, the shared values and comradeship of the tournament circuit would, by the start of the thirteenth century, prove a genuine stimulus to the movement. Later in the thirteenth century some in the Church came to look upon tournaments more positively and saw their worth as a training ground for crusaders. Humbert of Romans, a leading churchman, even described these events as 'like going to fight the Saracens'.[15]

Undoubtedly the need to achieve honour through one's deeds in battle was a powerful incentive to the chivalric knight. What better forum for this than in God's work? We have seen how earlier crusaders could be fêted for their bravery: Richard I of England's reputation was made during the Third Crusade where his boldness in battle won admirers on all sides. A Muslim observer wrote: 'never had we faced a bolder or more subtle opponent'.[16] Western writers described him as 'the finest knight on earth' and it was on the crusade that Richard acquired his sobriquet of 'Lionhearted'. Even before his feats of valour in the East, just taking the cross doubled his worth, according to a contemporary writer.[17]

Conon of Béthune was a Flemish knight who took part in the Fourth Crusade and who also wrote romantic verse. He linked the most worldly aspect of chivalry to the crusades by observing that no amount of success in a tournament could win a knight such admiration from fair ladies as the taking of the cross. His contemporary, Guy of Coucy, expressed his feelings more directly: 'May God raise me to that honour that I may hold her, in whom I dwell with all my heart and thought, naked in my arms once before I cross the sea to Outremer.'[18] The crusade became, therefore, a forum in which to prove all aspects of chivalric, as well as Christian, virtue. The preaching of the crusade in 1198–9 presented an opportunity for a pious, ambitious and chivalric knight. It may be no coincidence that a new generation had just emerged at the head of the major noble houses of northern France – a group ready to step forward and fight for the Lord and to secure their reputations.

At some point during the tournament at Écry, Count Thibaut and his cousin, Count Louis, halted the proceedings and took the cross, committing themselves to God's service.[19] The two men must have been moved to this by a private sermon of which we have no record. Tournaments were often held in conjunction with major religious or family festivals and in 1199 the presence of a churchman preaching the cross would not have been unlikely. This, set against the background of Innocent's appeal, would have prompted Thibaut and Louis to consider the matter. Both men were too powerful and had too great a set of responsibilities to have acted completely spontaneously. Their family heritages were rich in crusading ancestry and both would have known that their vows were binding before God. The two counts would have been aware of the profound undertakings they had made; to try to avoid them would bring upon themselves ecclesiastical sanctions and great shame. In fact, along with the essential religiosity of the time and the chivalric ethos, the family background of both these young men was almost certainly a fundamental element in their decision to take the cross.

Thibaut was the younger, aged only 20, but he had already ruled Champagne for three years. His lands comprised one of the largest, richest and most prestigious lordships in western Europe; the counts of Champagne were, along with the counts of Flanders, probably the most senior figures of the realm behind the king of France. Thibaut's grand-parents included King Louis VII of France (1137–80) and Eleanor of Aquitaine (both crusaders as well), and he was also a nephew of Richard the Lionheart, King John of England and King Philip of France. As well as having this superior family tree, Thibaut's crusading pedigree was highly impressive: his father, Henry, had participated in the Second Crusade and had made an expedition of his own in 1179–80. Thibaut's brother, Count Henry II, had taken the cross for the Third Crusade and had commanded the French contingent before the arrival of King Philip. To add partic-ular distinction to the family's achievements, when Conrad of Montferrat, the man designated as the next ruler of Jerusalem, was murdered in 1192, it was Henry who was selected to take his place. On 5 May that year he became ruler of Jerusalem, a position of enormous prestige even though the city itself remained in Muslim hands. Henry reigned until 10 September 1197 when his dwarfish entertainer toppled from a balcony and pulled him down to his death. Henry's wife Isabella remained the titular ruler of Jerusalem, and Thibaut became the count of Champagne. One can see how Thibaut had a strong incentive to uphold his family's crusading traditions and to help regain the city that his father had once ruled. He had reached the age of majority in 1198 and now, as a grown man, he could live up to his heritage.[20]

Louis of Blois was aged 28 when he took the cross. He too was a grandson of Louis VII and Eleanor and a nephew of King John and

King Philip. In spite of his young age he already had crusading experience. His father, Thibaut the Good, had taken part in the Third Crusade and there is evidence that Louis had accompanied him. Thibaut the Good was amongst the many nobles who died at the siege of Acre in 1191, but his son survived and prospered. Louis's wife, Catherine, brought the county of Clermont to him; her first husband, Raoul, had also perished at Acre and so Louis ruled over a considerable territory.[21]

The actions of Thibaut and Louis ignited recruitment for the Fourth Crusade. At last Innocent's project had attracted men of real authority. The pope must have been delighted that nobles of such distinguished rank were prepared to take part in the expedition. It was, after all, more than a year since he had first launched the appeal and, with the collapse of his efforts to persuade the kings of England and France to fight for Christ, there was a very real possibility that the whole plan might fade into oblivion: a dismal start to the pontificate of a man of such spiritual fire. The events at Écry were pivotal. As Thibaut's marshal, Geoffrey of Villehardouin (the author of one of the most important accounts of the Fourth Crusade), wrote: 'People throughout the country were greatly impressed when men of such high standing took the cross.'[22]

Once Thibaut had signified his intention to participate in the crusade, there was a huge pressure on many of his vassals – or at least those of fighting age – to join. Geoffrey of Villehardouin provides lists of the nobles and knights who followed Thibaut and Louis and they feature many men with crusading ancestors, including the author himself. Geoffrey was a man in his early fifties and, as the marshal of Champagne, he was the count's most senior military adviser and officer. Geoffrey took part in the Third Crusade, but on 14 November 1190 he was outside the Christian camp at the siege of Acre when he was ambushed by Muslim soldiers and imprisoned. It would be four years until he returned to Champagne, where he featured prominently in courtly life as an arbitrator of justice and as a key presence at most important events.

Before his death in 1212 or 1213 he narrated his story, probably relying on contemporary notes to support his memory. As a member of the elite inner circle of the crusade leadership, Geoffrey was party to most of its key meetings and his memoir provides an unparalleled insight into its workings. He boldly proclaimed the veracity of his text: 'the author of this work . . . has never, to his knowledge, put anything in it contrary to the truth'.[23] Some historians have been less convinced and view him as an apologist, concealing facts that could reflect badly on the crusade (such as the full details of the sack of Constantinople) and covering up any hint that there was a possible plot to divert the crusade to Byzantium. More commonly, however, he is regarded in a more positive light and as a man saturated in the values of his warrior class. As a result he may express distorted judgements and omit certain episodes, but he is generally judged to be without any sinister purpose.[24]

Others who took the cross at Écry included Reynald of Montmirail, a cousin of Thibaut and Louis, and Simon of Montfort, a man who would later gain notoriety as the leader of the vicious crusade against the Cathar heretics of southern France in 1208–9. Simon had already fought in the Holy Land in 1198–9 and was now prepared to pledge himself to the crusading cause a second time.[25]

Another contingent came from the Île-de-France region around Paris; its leader was Bishop Nivelo of Soissons. The involvement of leading churchmen in a crusade was commonplace throughout the movement. Such men were often close relatives of the major nobles and they were needed to provide spiritual direction to the troops through regular worship and the confession and absolution so essential before a major battle.

Enthusiasm for the crusade began to filter across northern Europe. On 23 February 1200, Ash Wednesday, Count Baldwin of Flanders and his wife Marie took the cross in the city of Bruges. Above all other noble houses in the West, it was the counts of Flanders who could boast the longest and most intense commitment to the crusades. Count Robert II had been one of the heroes of the First Crusade; Count Charles the Good had fought in defence of the Holy Land for a year in around 1108; Count Thierry had made no fewer than four crusades to the Levant in 1139, 1146–9, 1157–8 and 1164 – a unique record of endurance and piety; Count Philip had been to the Levant in 1177–8 and died at Acre in 1191. With this background, one suspects that Baldwin's decision to become a crusader was merely a question of timing.[26]

The count himself was aged 28; his wife Marie was aged 26. She was the sister of Thibaut of Champagne and therefore had the same impressive crusading traditions and ties to the ruling house of Jerusalem. Baldwin and Marie had been betrothed as infants and married at the ages of 14 and 12 respectively, but unlike many arranged marriages from the medieval period, their relationship was (as far as we can tell) genuinely very close. Gislebert of Mons, a contemporary chronicler, wrote of Baldwin's 'burning love' for Marie and praised him for spurning all other women in a way few other nobles of the day did. The count was said to be deeply contented with his wife and did not turn to the usual collection of prostitutes and casual partnerships often found around the loveless marriages in the higher levels of medieval society. Even in official documents Baldwin chose to compliment Marie; instead of simply naming her as a witness to a charter, he described her as 'my beautiful wife', 'my adored wife' or 'my most loving wife'; hardly the language of dry diplomacy. This was not mere convention, but a sign of Baldwin's deep devotion. His love for Marie was widely recognised; the Byzantine writer Niketas Choniates, usually hostile towards those westerners who had sacked his beloved Constantinople, wrote of Baldwin: 'He was, furthermore, devout in his duties to God, and was reported to be temperate in his personal conduct; for as long as he was separated from his dear wife, he never so much as cast a glance at another woman.' It seems that Baldwin expected his fellow-crusaders to follow an equally continent code of behaviour because, as Niketas continued: 'Most important, twice a week in the evening he had a herald proclaim that no one who slept within the palace was to have sexual intercourse with any woman who was not his legal wife.'[27]

At the time Baldwin and Marie took the cross she was heavily pregnant, expecting their first child, a daughter, Joan, who was born in late 1199 or early 1200. The presence on the crusade of the wives of leading men was not unknown. Marie's grandmother, Eleanor of Aquitaine, provided an obvious (if infamous) precedent, and Richard the Lionheart had married his bride Berengaria of Navarre on Cyprus as he travelled east on the Third Crusade. Alongside personal feelings for one another – a wish to be together – it was religious devotion, the need to continue trying to provide heirs, and the crusader lord's ability to protect and feed his own family that explained why women such as Marie could go on crusade. Many other Flemings, including Baldwin's brother, Henry, took the cross for the Holy Land as well, and they formed a strong, experienced contingent that contained several veterans of the Third Crusade, as well as numerous men with strong crusading traditions stretching back through the twelfth century.

After the Flemings had joined the expedition, Villehardouin recorded that Count Hugh of Saint-Pol, Count Peter of Amiens and Count Geoffrey of Perche, three other important noblemen from northern France, also pledged themselves to the crusade, along with large numbers of their knights and men-at-arms. One particular recruit from the second of these contingents is of great significance for historians of the Fourth Crusade: numbered amongst the vassals of Peter of Amiens was a humble knight, Robert of Clari, who wrote a record of his experiences on the campaign that provides us with one of the most vivid and exciting of all crusade narratives. He returned from the expedition in 1205 and in 1216 wrote up, or dictated, his work, in Old French, rather than the Latin used by the clergy. Robert produced an account from the perspective of an ordinary knight who, unlike Villehardouin, was not privy to the highest decision-making levels. His work is full of ideas and opinions as to how and why the crusade developed and his front-line experiences at Constantinople and his engaging sense of marvel at the size and scale of the great city add true vigour and value to his authority as a first-rate historical source. Like Villehardouin, Robert named many individuals from the French contingents who took the cross and 'carried banners' to indicate their status as wealthy knights.[28]

In the spring of 1200 the leading nobles chose to assemble at the town of Soissons in the north of Champagne. In spite of the encouraging involvement of these important men, there was still some concern that overall the crusaders were too few in number. Another meeting was scheduled to take place at Compiègne two months later and here some serious planning took place.[29]

Perhaps by this time news had reached northern France that the crusade was attracting support in the German Empire. Abbot Martin's sermon in Basel and the work of other preachers had led to men such as Conrad, bishop of Halberstadt (in Saxony), joining the crusade with a sizeable contingent. In any case, the nobles at Compiègne settled down to debate the essential framework of the crusade. Presumably they discussed financial matters and how each proposed to finance his expedition. They stated the projected numbers in each of their retinues, and probably debated who else might follow them. Most crucially, they had to decide how to reach the eastern Mediterranean. The First and Second Crusades had chosen to march across Europe, through the Byzantine Empire, and had then fought their way over Asia Minor to northern Syria. Since 1182, however, the Byzantines had been resolute opponents of their fellow-Christians and were bitterly hostile to any western incursions. Emperor Frederick Barbarossa had managed to muscle his way past Constantinople and to defeat the Seljuk Turks in battle in 1190, but Richard and Philip had chosen to sail to the Levant. It was this latter course of action that the French nobles decided to follow. In reality it was the only realistic option open to them, on account of their relatively limited numbers and the continued enmity of the Greeks.

Many of the crusading ancestors of the Flemings – a seafaring people – had sailed from northern Europe, down the English Channel, around the Iberian peninsula and on to the Holy Land.[30] But for most on the Fourth Crusade the prospect of sea travel was profoundly terrifying, though it offered a quicker and, in military terms, safer route to the Levant than any other. The landbound expeditions could take at least eight months; by sea it was possible to sail from Italy to the eastern Mediterranean in four to six weeks.[31] Because the northern French crusaders were not seafarers, and the Flemings lacked the ships to transport an army of the size now recruited, it was necessary to seek the services of the Italian maritime cities of Venice, Genoa or Pisa.

These three cities represented the most developed commercial powers in western Europe and their merchant fleets sailed extensively across the Mediterranean basin, even to trade with Muslim North Africa and Spain. All of these cities had taken part in crusades to the Holy Land and against the Muslims in the Balearics and the Iberian peninsula. The intense sense of religious devotion that permeated western Europe did not, of course, stop at the gates of the great trading centres, and the Italians possessed a potent mix of religious zeal and driving commercial ambition.[32] Each of these commercial centres was deeply imbued with a sense of Christian duty and was drawn to take part in the holy wars for spiritual reward; crusaders from all of the cities were as determined and delighted to secure the Holy Land for the faithful as their fellow-Catholics elsewhere in Europe. They were also keen to bring back relics from the East to venerate in their churches: the treasury of the cathedral of St Lawrence in Genoa still houses a piece of the True Cross, a plate believed to have carried the head of John the Baptist, and a beautiful emerald-green bowl from Caesarea, once thought to be the Holy Grail itself. The Venetians acquired the body of St Nicholas on the First Crusade and in the 1123–4 crusade to Tyre they brought back a block of stone from which Christ was said to have preached.[33] Irrevocably entwined with this religious zeal and acute business sense was a growing feeling of pride in the achievements of their respective cities. The Italians did not view spiritual advance, commercial enterprise and civic prestige as the unhappy combination that it may seem today. A Genoese chronicler described the taking of the important southern Spanish trading port of Almeria in 1147 thus: 'they captured the city for the honour of God and all of Christendom and determined to remain in control of it out of necessity of all Christians and the honour of Genoa'.[34]

Devout Christians the Italians undoubtedly were, but their support for the crusading movement had always come at a substantial price. In the early years of the Frankish conquest of the Holy Land there was a need to capture many of the coastal towns and cities of the Levant. The crusaders could not provide the ships to transport westerners to take part in these campaigns, nor the naval skills necessary to mount seaborne attacks on places such as Caesarea, Beirut, Acre and Sidon. In return for their expertise, the Italians gained streets and houses in these cities and secured highly profitable rights to use the harbours and trading points within each port. They also had their own churches, dedicated to the patron saint of their home city. Thus we find a church of St Lawrence in the Genoese quarter of Acre, and a church of St Mark's in the Venetian district. They were also given the right to administer their own justice to their own people – a notable prerogative in that it cut across the authority of the local lord or monarch. In essence, little Pisan, Genoese or Venetian colonies grew up in the Crusader States, manned by personnel sent out from each mother city. Traders and administrators would probably serve for a two- or three-year term before returning home.

The Italians provided the Frankish settlers with an essential lifeline to the West. Twice a year, in March and September (for Easter and Christmas), great fleets set out from Italy to transport pilgrims, new crusaders and new settlers to the Levant. They would also carry items such as cloth, wood and metal, and would trade these for spices, silks, oils and sugar to bring back to their homelands. The most important port of the eastern Mediterranean was, however, the Egyptian city of Alexandria. The fact that it was a Muslim-held city did not prevent the Italians from having outposts there and from engaging in normal trading relations. Obviously at times of crisis the position of those in Alexandria was perilous and they might be expelled by the rulers or, on one rare occasion (1174) killed. Yet the requirements of the commercial world were not delineated by faith. Saladin himself had to justify the Italians' presence in Egypt to his spiritual overlord, the caliph of Baghdad, and he explained that the trade in metals and military equipment was essential to his cause. In parallel, Muslim traders moved freely through the Crusader States, bringing their goods from Damascus and Aleppo to ports such as Acre and Beirut. They had to pay heavy taxes, but equally Frankish traders who ventured inland into their territories were required to pay dues as well. Ibn Jubayr, a Spanish Muslim who made a pilgrimage to the Holy Land in 1184, was amazed by this state of affairs and wrote:

> One of the astonishing things is that although the fires of discord burn between the two parties . . . yet Muslim and Christian travellers will come and go between them without interference. The sultan [Saladin] invested [the castle of Kerak, in Transjordan], but still the caravans passed successively from Egypt to Damascus, going through the lands without impediment from them. In the same way the Muslims continuously journeyed from Damascus to Acre and likewise not one of the Christian merchants was stopped or hindered in Muslim territories . . . Security never leaves them [the merchants] in any circumstance, neither in peace nor war.

The lengthy siege of Acre (1189–91) brought trade to a halt for a time, but once relative calm returned, so too did the commercial traffic as the world of business crossed and recrossed the lines drawn by the conflict between Christianity and Islam.[35]

The three Italian cities were bitter competitors and on many occasions their rivalry spilled over into outright conflict; indeed, at the time of the Fourth Crusade, Genoa and Pisa were engaged in a period of intense feuding. In spite of papal attempts to mediate, their continuing struggle made it difficult for them to contemplate transporting a large army to the Holy Land.[36] Furthermore, disputes concerning the Genoese transportation of King Philip's army during the Third Crusade meant that the French were less willing to engage the Genoese again on an exclusive basis.

It was, therefore, to Venice that the envoys turned. In his crusade bull of August 1198 Innocent had explicitly mentioned the dispatch of his legate Soffredo to Venice 'in search of aid for the Holy Land', and, with Pisa and Genoa at odds, he had little or no alternative anyway.[37]

Villehardouin reported that when the crusade leaders assembled in council at Compiègne they decided to appoint six envoys to negotiate a sea passage on behalf of the crusading army. They were given charters; documents sealed by all the principal nobles who promised to abide by whatever arrangements were settled upon by their representatives. This was obviously an enormous responsibility and the six men were chosen with great care: two each from the contingents of Thibaut, Louis and Baldwin. Amongst these was Geoffrey of Villehardouin, whose presence here gives his chronicle a unique insight into the decision-making process.[38]

The terms that these men negotiated were amongst the most important influences on the outcome of the crusade. The circumstances fostered by their deal shaped and directed the armies' actions in ways no one foresaw and did much to draw the crusade towards its terrible conclusion. Villehardouin and his colleagues, of course, could not have anticipated the outcome of the campaign and set out in complete good faith to secure passage for the army of Christ to regain His patrimony. In the early months of 1201 they passed across the Alps and into northern Italy, probably though Piacenza, and thence to Venice itself, reaching the city in the first week of Lent, March 1201.

CHAPTER FOUR

'Our lords entreat you, in God's name to take pity
on the land overseas'

The Treaty of Venice, April 1201

SET UPON A clutch of islands in the lagoon at the head of the
Adriatic, the city of Venice was a powerful and independent force
in the medieval world and boasted a proud and distinctive history.[1]
The islands had been inhabited by fishermen since Roman times when
the region was part of the great empire. In those days the lagoons were
far more extensive, both inland and stretching to the north and south of
the area that would later become Venice. With the decline of the Roman
Empire in the fourth and fifth centuries most of Italy came under the
rule of Germanic tribes. One exception was the territory known as Venetia.
This remained under the control of officials sent out from
Constantinople, which, since 331 as the emperors sought a safer base further
east, had been the 'new Rome'. This link with Byzantium was fundamental in shaping the development of Venice over the next few centuries.

The Lombard invasion of Italy in 580 forced many refugees from the
mainland to seek safety on the islands deep amongst the lagoons. Several
settlements grew up and in 697 the Byzantine officials appointed the
first *dux* (or doge) to rule the area. In 810, Charlemagne's son, Pepin,
attempted to conquer the region on behalf of the Frankish Empire, but
was unable to cross to the Rialto island that already formed the hub of
the settlement.

A subsequent peace treaty made plain that Venice was part of the
Byzantine Empire, although the islanders soon began to assert their independence. This was vividly symbolised in 829 with the theft of the relics
of St Mark from Alexandria and the adoption of the apostle in place of

Theodore, a Greek warrior saint, as the patron saint of the city. However, a loosening of political ties did not mean a complete break from Constantinople, and trading links remained strong, as did Greek influence on cultural matters, such as architecture.

Around this time the Venetians concentrated their sailing skills on the myriad river valleys that ran into the broad natural basin that lay below the Dolomites in northern Italy. Their bargemen became great traders, selling salt and fish from their own region, as well as products brought up from the Mediterranean by Byzantine merchants (spices, silk and incense) in return for staple foodstuffs including grain, which they were unable to grow on their own small, sandy islands.

Neighbouring regions such as the Po river valley became increasingly peaceful during the ninth and tenth centuries, the economy prospered and the Venetians started to travel further afield to satisfy a rising demand for luxury products. Their ships sailed into the Mediterranean with ever-greater frequency, trading with Muslim North Africa as well as Asia Minor and the Levant. Slaves from the Slavic lands and timber from the plains and mountains to the north of Venice became important exports. The slaves and wood were sold to North Africa in return for gold and this, in turn, was spent in Constantinople to obtain luxury goods to sell in the West. This growth in trade, combined with the ready availability of timber, meant that the Venetian shipbuilding industry emerged to help sustain the city's commercial ascendancy.

In 1082 Emperor Alexius I of Byzantium favoured the Venetians by granting them complete exemption from tariffs across the Byzantine Empire – another substantial boost to the islanders' economy.[2] By the eleventh century Venice was a strong, wealthy and vigorous political and economic force. Unlike its rivals Pisa and Genoa, it had managed to remain independent from the German emperor who ruled over much of northern Italy. At the time of the Fourth Crusade, the city had grown to be one of the largest urban centres in Europe with a population estimated at about 60,000 people based on the islands centred around the Rialto.

In early 1202 the envoys halted their horses at the eastern edge of the Veneto plain and transferred to small barges for the last leg of their journey. Their boats passed through the lush vegetation of the lagoons and on to stretches of green, open water where they caught their first sight of Venice. They saw a skyline unlike that of any other city in northern Italy. Centuries of rivalry meant that places such as Siena, Genoa, Bologna and Perugia were marked by a forest of tall stone towers. These structures were built by families and kin groups as statements of wealth and power and as defence against aggressive neighbours both inside and outside the city. Venice had no such high towers, in part because it had suffered few political upheavals – the non-hereditary system of election for the doges worked well – and, more practically, because the sand upon which it was built could not support buildings of this sort. The clay lagoon floor (beneath the sand), combined with wooden piles, offered some sort of foundation, but this underlying weakness and a lack of local stone meant that it was hard to construct tall buildings. Today the Venetian skyline remains remark-ably low, broken principally by the *campanile* (bell-tower) of St Mark's Square. First constructed in 1173, the present structure originates from the sixteenth century, although a collapse in 1902 led to it being rebuilt.

Soon after the envoys' arrival, the ruler of Venice, Doge Enrico Dandolo, came to welcome the Frenchmen. This remarkable individual was to be one of the central players in the Fourth Crusade.[3] By this time he was already a most venerable man, probably aged over 90 years old; he was also blind. To survive to such an advanced age indicated a hardy consti-tution and was a comparative rarity in the medieval period, although genetics seems to have favoured the Dandolo family because several other members of the clan lived into their eighties and beyond.[4] Enrico had been blind since the 1170s and he told Villehardouin personally that he had suffered the disability as the result of a severe blow to the head. Later rumours suggested that the wound had been inflicted by Emperor Manuel Comnenus during an embassy to Constantinople in 1172. Manuel had realised that Dandolo was a dangerous opponent and had had him bound and then blinded by using glass to reflect the sun's rays into his eyes. Thus, the story went, Dandolo swore to be avenged on the Greeks; hence the diversion of the Fourth Crusade to Constantinople. Sadly, this neat reasoning does not tally with the evidence because, as well as his account to Villehardouin, we know that the doge could still see in 1176. Thus, however attractive it is, the idea of a long-standing personal grudge against the Greeks based upon Dandolo being blinded by Manuel Comnenus cannot be sustained.[5]

In spite of his handicap, Dandolo was a man of incredible energy, drive and determination, dedicated to securing wealth and honour for his people. Some contemporaries such as Innocent III (as well as later historians) have criticised him for his greed and ambition, but, equally, many of the crusaders themselves spoke highly of his qualities.[6] Gunther of Pairis described him thus: 'He was, to be sure, sightless of eye, but most perceptive of mind and compensated for physical blindness with a lively intellect and, best of all, foresight. In the case of matters that were unclear, the others always took every care to seek his advice and they usually followed his lead in public affairs.'[7] Baldwin of Flanders wrote of the high esteem in which all the crusaders held him.[8] Robert of Clari regarded Dandolo as 'a most worthy man'.[9]

Dandolo was elected doge in 1192 and very quickly set about emphasising both personal and civic prestige. One way he did this was to reform the city's coinage from the standard silver penny to a new denomination that included a large silver *grosso* worth no less than 24 pennies. There was no standardised coinage at national (let alone international) level in the Middle Ages and each city or county would have its own particular currency, which created a huge and complex exchange market.

Aside from their financial function, coins could also signal the manner in which a city or region wanted to be perceived. In the days before mass media, coins were one of the few items to receive widespread circulation and the design could transmit an image of a particular area and its rulers far beyond its homeland. Some rulers, such as the kings of France, did not engage in this practice and minted fairly unimaginative coins adorned only with their name, title and a simple cross; others, such as the emperors of Germany, chose to depict their monarch in full regalia upon a throne. In 1194, Dandolo decided to recast the Venetian coinage and his *grosso* was a masterpiece of political and religious imagery, as well as a statement of his city's financial power (see plate section).

On one side sits a beautifully executed depiction of Christ on his throne; on the other, the patron saint of Venice, St Mark, blesses the doge himself, who is actually named in person towards the edge of the coin. In other words, the *grosso* shows divine approval for the doge and emphasises the link between his authority and the saint's protection of the city's leader. This coin became the highest-denomination currency in Europe and was praised for its fineness and purity: it was no less than 98.5 per cent silver, far superior to anything else in the West.

Given the Venetians' international trading position, Dandolo was not simply concerned with western European markets, but also with the Byzantine and eastern Mediterranean worlds. The Venetians had earlier made much use of coinage from the kingdom of Jerusalem and, in the latter half of the twelfth century, the Byzantine coinage as well. In recent decades, however, this had declined in purity and, coupled with the unstable relations between the Greeks and the Venetians, it was unwise for the latter to rely on the Byzantine currency. The new *grosso* would give the Venetians more independence and it was soon internationally recognised as the most important silver coinage in both Europe and the Mediterranean. The fact that it was Enrico Dandolo who had introduced it reveals him as a man of considerable political and economic acumen.[10]

The crusaders' envoys met, therefore, a formidable and highly experienced leader, familiar in the ways of commerce and diplomacy and confident in the capabilities of his great city. Dandolo listened to the embassy's credentials and their letters of introduction and acknowledged their high standing; he then asked them to speak concerning their mission. Villehardouin reported that the Frenchmen wanted to address the city council to lay before it their lords' message. He hoped this could be done the following day, but Dandolo replied that he would need four days to call the assembly to order.

The crusaders duly appeared in the doge's palace next to the church of St Mark's on the Rivo Alto, the central island of Venice. Villehardouin described the palace as 'a most beautiful building and very richly furnished'. There the leading men of Venice, the doge and a group of judges known as the Small Council, awaited the embassy. One of the envoys addressed his audience:

My lords, we have come to you on behalf of the great nobles of France, who have taken the cross to avenge the outrage suffered by our Lord, and, if God so wills, to recapture Jerusalem. And since our lords know that there is no people who can help them so well as yours, they entreat you, in God's name, to take pity on the land overseas, and the outrage suffered by our Lord, and graciously do your best to supply us with a fleet of warships and transports.

The embassy delivered, therefore, a plain request for military assistance, couched in the familiar terms of a holy war to regain Christ's patrimony. The Venetians were well aware of Pope Innocent's call for the crusade from the visit of legate Soffredo and, through their commercial networks, would have had a clear appreciation of the political and strategic realities of the situation in the Levant.[11]

'How can this be done?' asked the doge. 'In any way that you care to advise or propose, so long as our lords can meet your conditions and bear the cost,' came the reply. Perhaps taken aback by the scale of the request, the doge asked for a week to deliver his response: 'do not be surprised at so long a delay, since such an important matter demands our full consideration'. Dandolo was right to ask for a period of grace. If he agreed to the envoys' proposition – and some sense of the projected size of the force *must* have been given at this stage – he would be asking his people to embark upon the most ambitious step in their commercial history. To transport the French crusaders to the Holy Land necessitated a level of commitment unprecedented in medieval commerce. The number of ships required would absorb almost the entire Venetian fleet and would entail the construction of many new ships as well. To devote the manpower of the city to one project was a breathtaking idea; in fact, it would require the suspension of practically all other commercial activity with the outside world. A modern comparison might entail a major international airline ceasing flights for a year to prepare its planes for one particular client, and then to serve that client exclusively for a further period afterwards. To us, the level of risk seems fearfully high; only the firmest assurances – and the greatest rewards – could produce such an agreement. In the case of the Fourth Crusade, the two engines of faith and commerce should be borne in mind. The Venetians' motivation as Christians, along with their hopes of securing unparalleled long-term economic advantages in the eastern Mediterranean, were powerful lures.

As well as building the ships, the Venetians would also sail the fleet and participate in the expedition. Collectively, these responsibilities would draw in far more men than the city had ever previously committed to a crusade. It must also involve their doge, as befitted the ruler of a maritime state. In 1122–4 Doge Domenico had led a crusade to Tyre, and now Enrico Dandolo wanted to do the same. The idea that a man of his age was prepared to submit himself to the rigours of a sea voyage and a holy war showed incredible devotion and determination. As an aside, several leaders on the First Crusade had been men of relatively advanced years and there is a suggestion that their intention was to end their days in the Holy Land and to be buried in the very earth sanctified by Christ's presence; perhaps Dandolo intended the same fate for himself.[12] Given the extraordinary level of commitment required, Dandolo and his fellow-citizens must have wanted the most watertight of guarantees that their labours would be rewarded in full. If the deal collapsed, then Venice faced ruin – and Dandolo himself would have to bear the enormous responsibility for that disaster.

A week later the envoys returned to the palace and, after further discussions, Dandolo announced the terms of the Venetians' offer to the crusaders, subject to the approval of the Grand Council and the assembly of the commons. Villehardouin provides this information:

> We will build transports to carry 4,500 horses and 9,000 squires, and other ships to accommodate 4,500 knights and 20,000 foot sergeants. We will also include in our contract a nine months' supply of rations for all men and fodder for all the horses. This is what we will do for you, and no less, on condition you pay us [four] marks per horse and two marks per man. We will, moreover, abide by the terms of the covenant we now place before you for the space of one year from the day on which we set sail from the port of Venice, to act in the service of God and of Christendom, whichever it may be. The total cost of all that we have outlined here amounts to 85,000 marks. And we will do more than this. We will provide, for the love of God, fifty additional armed galleys, on condition that so long as our association lasts we shall have one half, and you the other half, of everything that we win, either by land or sea. It now remains for you to consider if you, on your part, can accept and fulfil our conditions.[13]

The treaty itself survives in full and its key terms are those related by Villehardouin, although it includes further details such as the provision of foodstuffs for the crusaders – wheat, flour, fruit, vegetables, wine and water, and, likewise, adequate provision for their horses.[14]

The envoys asked for a day to consider the offer and, after discussions deep into the evening, they agreed to the terms. The following morning they formally accepted. The matter was still not closed, however, because the doge needed to persuade his fellow-citizens to endorse the plan. First he had to sway the Grand Council, a group of the 40 most senior men of the city. According to Villehardouin, Dandolo gradually argued them around to his position and convinced them that they should approve the contract. Villehardouin conveys a slight sense of reluctance on the part of some Council members and, given the scale of the proposal, it is unsurprising that a few took time to be won over. Afterwards the common people of Venice had to agree. For them, Dandolo realised that a more emotional appeal was required and he chose a powerful but calculated setting to secure the outcome he desired.[15]

Along with a recognition of the commercial advantages to Venice, Dandolo, as a pious medieval man, was stirred by the idea of freeing the Holy Land. This was, after all, the purpose underlying the entire crusading movement and – with Villehardouin and his companions as visible representatives of that hope, and as men sworn to fight and, if necessary, to die for God – it was important to exploit the basic religiosity of the Venetian people. Dandolo invited 10,000 of the common people to hear a mass of the Holy Spirit in the church of St Mark's, and to pray for divine guidance concerning the envoys' request for help.

The church of St Mark's began life as the private chapel of the doge, whose palace was (and still is) located next door.[16] The first church was built to house the relics of St Mark, stolen from Alexandria in 828. Fires and subsidence necessitated several reconstruction programmes. The underlying shape of St Mark's is that of a Greek cross (the four arms are of the same length) and the replacement of the wooden roof with five new brick domes in the latter half of the eleventh century formed the basis of the building we see today. These domes remain in place, although from the outside they are now hidden under the later lead-covered onion lanterns that dominate the present skyline. In other words, to picture the church in Villehardouin's day we must imagine a much lower, flatter outline. To support these domes huge, thick walls were added, along with various apses and a porch. The shape and decoration of the church demonstrate the cultural affinity between Venice and Byzantium, because St Mark's was deliberately modelled on the church of the Holy Apostles in Constantinople (destroyed in 1453). The massive central piers are pierced by archways to give a greater sense of light, and the central dome with its ring of small windows seems almost to hover over the mighty vaults. The tomb of St Mark is in a crypt under the high altar; it lies, therefore, at the end of a long arena suitable for the great processional ceremonies of the church and the doge.

Some of the surviving mosaics, sculpture, flooring and marble date from after the sack of Constantinople, but in the spring of 1201 the Frenchmen still went into a sumptuously decorated church. Several mosaics were already in place and others extant now, such as the main Christ figure over the east apse, are copies of twelfth-century work. Below this great image of Christ are depictions of four patron saints, clad in beautiful blue and ivory robes and bearing gifts; these date from around 1106.[17]

On entering the church, the visitor is faced by an array of brown, gold, green and blue mosaics. The eye is caught by a bewildering variety of divine beings and sacred events and there is an impressive opulence and intensity in the overall decorative effect. The last of the three arches of the short nave merges into the central supporting pillars. These stretch above to the three central domes, which then step away down the church to the main focus of the building, the east apse containing the figure of Christ overlooking the tomb of St Mark.

Villehardouin and his colleagues walked into the church. All those inside knew of the envoys' presence in the city and the nature, if not the details, of their business. With the crusader cross emblazoned on their shoulders, the Frenchmen strode down the aisle, watched intently by those at ground level and by the people staring down from the galleries above the porch and along the nave. It must have been an intimidating moment. The envoys had settled on the deal that would enable their crusade to take place; now they had to clear the last obstacle that might otherwise stop them from realising their purpose. Opposition to the scheme would certainly end all possibility of launching the crusade.

Dandolo introduced the Frenchmen, and Villehardouin himself, presumably through an interpreter, addressed the crowd. He made an emotional appeal to the Venetians, flattering them that, as the greatest seafaring power, it was to their city that the nobles of France looked. He asked them to take pity on Jerusalem and begged them, in God's name, 'to avenge the insult offered to our Lord . . . They [the nobles of France] have commanded us to kneel at your feet, and not to rise until you consent to take pity on the Holy Land overseas.' He drove home the familiar messages of civic pride and fundamental religious fervour: the envoys believed passionately in their cause and, as Villehardouin drew to a close, they all began to shed tears and fell to their knees in front of the assembled congregation. The call to help the holy places brought the doge and his associates to tears as well and everyone in the church cried out: 'We consent! We consent!'

The shouts of the audience echoed up to the divine figures adorning the walls and domes, as though the Venetians were determined to convince their spiritual guardians of their enthusiasm and sincerity. The popular piety of the crowd had been harnessed; 'this great surge of piety', as Villehardouin expressed it, carried the concept of the crusade into reality. The expedition was acclaimed and the people of Venice were committed to the holy war. The doge returned to the lectern and, brimming with pride and emotion, said: 'Behold the honour God has paid you in inspiring the finest nation in the world to turn aside from all other people and choose you to join with them in so high an enterprise as the deliverance of our Lord!' Regardless of their relentless commercial drive, it is important to remember that the core spiritual appeal of the crusade had profoundly moved the Venetians.

The deeds of the agreement were duly drawn up. They embodied both the spiritual reasons for the crusade and the terms of the commercial contract. The following day these were confirmed: the two parties were now locked into a crushing contractual embrace of honour, huge financial outlay and high risk. The Venetians were to be paid in four instalments by April 1202 and the fleet would be prepared to set sail later that year on 29 June, the feast-day of Sts Peter and Paul.[18]

The signed and sealed charters were brought to Dandolo's palace and there, in the presence of his Grand Council, he prepared to hand over the documents to the envoys. It was a momentous occasion: the sight of the full covenant was too much for Dandolo and, as he presented the Frenchmen with the charters, the aged doge fell to his knees and began to weep. With tears streaming down his face, he swore on the Bible to hold firm to the terms of the contract. Moved by the emotion of their leader, the Venetian councillors gave their oath and then the crusaders followed suit. They too felt the enormity of the moment and shed tears as well. Perhaps at this moment the Venetians and the Frenchmen realised that their plans were moving decisively from theory into reality and that they were now irrevocably bound to the crusade.[19]

While the scale of this agreement was unprecedented, the basic principles of the transportation of a body of crusaders at a fixed cost per man and horse were familiar. The most recent example was the contract of 1190 between the Genoese and the French. This specified the conveyance of 650 knights, 1,300 horses and 1,300 squires at a rate of nine marks per unit – that is to say, one knight, two horses and two squires for eight months – equivalent to 13½ marks per year. The Venetian charge was 14 marks per year, a similar enough rate.[20]

In the case of the 1201 covenant, however, the key difference was the size of the army. The crusaders had sworn to bring 33,500 men to Venice by April 1202 and it was the failure to reach this figure that created a fundamental fault-line that proved critical in determining the fate of the entire expedition. It was as if here, at the moment the deal was conceived, a genetic flaw was introduced that had the capability of distorting or crippling the whole project as it grew towards fruition.

Tied to the number of crusaders required at Venice was the huge cost of transport for these men. The sum of 85,000 marks was equivalent to 60,000 pounds sterling, around twice the annual income of King John of England or of King Philip of France. On one hand, this demonstrates the massive outlay needed by the Venetians to prepare the fleet, but it also makes one pause at the scale of the commitment.[21] In the case of King Philip's contract with the Genoese, he must have been certain that he would have 650 knights to accompany him: as the ruler of France he knew the size of his army from his advisers and from basic feudal obligations. With regard to the envoys in 1201 there was no such firm template to work from. They presumably had a clear idea of the number of men from Flanders, Champagne and Blois who had taken the cross; they may also have had some estimates of the size of some of the groups likely to join from Germany or Italy. Yet 33,500 was a substantial number to aim for in the contemporary political climate and was probably many more than the recruits already enlisted. By way of comparison, although we have no accurate figures for any earlier crusading expeditions, historians have estimated that 7,000 knights and 50,000 others took part in the First Crusade. The biggest crusader army to date had been Frederick Barbarossa's huge force, said to have comprised about 20,000 knights and up to 80,000 other participants.[22]

A key problem for the envoys in 1201 lay in their reliance on many men taking the cross in the future, rather than basing their figures on firm commitments already made. They were, in essence, making an educated guess. Yet these men were highly experienced crusaders and diplomats – they should have been able to arrive at a reasonably accurate figure for such a crucial agreement. Villehardouin himself had participated in the Third Crusade, as had Conon of Béthune, Milo of Brabant and John of Friaise; in other words, four of the six men had actually seen for themselves the size of the forces that could be assembled. They must have made a reasoned and carefully considered calculation to engage in the deal with Venice. Time alone would reveal whether their estimates reflected blind optimism, calamitous misjudgement or plain realism.

Aside from the provisions outlined in the sealed pact there was one further element introduced into the planning of the expedition – a secret agreement that the crusade would initially sail to Egypt, rather than to the Holy Land.[23] On the face of it, this seems illogical; if the objective of the campaign was to reclaim Jerusalem, why should it try to conquer other Muslim-held lands? In fact, the idea of an invasion of Egypt was, in strategic terms at least, an excellent and familiar solution to the problem of capturing the holy city. There was a long history of the crusaders and the Frankish settlers in the Levant trying to seize Egypt in order to compel the Muslims to surrender Jerusalem. The extraordinary wealth of the Nile Delta and the trade routes from North Africa across to the Middle East would give the Christians unparalleled military and economic strength to bring true stability to their hold on the Holy Land. Furthermore, it would end the Franks' position as a fragile regional power clinging to the Mediterranean coast and surrounded on almost every landward side by the forces of Islam.[24] If they were to immediately capture Jerusalem, this would be acclaimed as a great triumph and would certainly weaken morale in the Muslim world, but the overall balance of power would simply return to the position created by Saladin before he invaded Jerusalem in 1187. The Muslims and the Franks had long recognised that control of Egypt led to possession of the Holy Land, and a later writer commented that 'the keys to Jerusalem are to be found in Cairo'.

The prosperity of Egypt was a source of wonder to a Frankish visitor in the 1160s; Archbishop William of Tyre (d. 1185), the chancellor of the kingdom of Jerusalem and author of a history of the Latin East, wrote of 'the marvellous abundance of all good things there and of each individual commodity; the inestimable taxes belonging to the ruler himself; the imposts and taxes from the cities both on the coast and farther inland; and the vast amount of annual revenue . . . The people there, devoted to luxurious living and ignorant of the science of war, had become enervated through a period of long-continued peace.'[25] After Saladin had taken the country in 1169, William lamented that 'he draws an inestimable supply of the purest gold of the first quality'.[26]

The Frankish settlers had expended enormous energies in their attempts to conquer the land they called Babylon. The first king of Jerusalem, Baldwin I (1100–18), died en route home from an expedition to Egypt; further campaigns were fought there in the 1120s and the 1140s. Between 1163 and 1169 King Amalric (1163–74) invaded the country no fewer than five times and during one incursion his royal flag fluttered over Alexandria, though ultimately his efforts failed. Later, as the consummate general of the age, Richard the Lionheart appreciated the need to take Egypt to ensure a long-term future for the Crusader States. Twice during the Third Crusade he tried to persuade the army to march southwards, rather than go towards Jerusalem, yet on both occasions opposition from the rank and file, who were determined to focus upon the object of their devotion rather than the bigger military picture, meant that he was unable to realise his plans. Richard had also opened contacts with the Genoese, proposing to engage their naval skills in any future invasion of Egypt in return for commercial advantages.[27]

The essential components of the 1201 agreement can be seen in Richard's experiences: a need for naval expertise to attack Egypt (Amalric had used Pisan and Byzantine fleets); the offer of trading benefits to the provider of this force; and an awareness of the potential pressure from the bulk of the crusader army to go to Jerusalem rather than first to Cairo. Villehardouin and his colleagues had experienced such tensions at first hand between 1191 and 1193 and they had few qualms about keeping this aspect of their plan hidden. As the marshal wrote: '[this part of the plan] was kept a closely guarded secret; to the public at large it was merely announced that we were going overseas'.[28] As the land in which Christ had lived and walked, Jerusalem had a spiritual potency that nowhere else could rival. As yet, the massive outbreak of popular enthusiasm needed to generate a viable crusade and to persuade men to risk their lives and leave their loved ones could not be shifted elsewhere. Regardless of the best long-term motives of the crusade leadership, a call to attack Egypt would not capture the popular imagination in western Europe. Villehardouin's careful choice of the word 'overseas' was a clever deceit because, to the average knight, squire or foot-soldier, it automatically meant the Holy Land and would encourage him to take the cross in good heart.

It also made sound strategic sense to conceal the destination of the crusade. The Muslim world was in some disarray after the death of Saladin, with the rulers of Cairo, Aleppo and Damascus each seeking to dominate their rivals. The Franks were well aware of these difficulties and knew that it was a situation worth exploiting. A clearly signalled attack in one area might cause the Muslims to put their differences aside and prepare a strong defence against the invaders. Furthermore, Egypt itself was in a particularly fragile position at the turn of the thirteenth century because the Nile flood had failed for five consecutive years and had brought poverty and famine to the country.

Finally, there was a diplomatic consideration: the existence of a five-year truce between the kingdom of Jerusalem and the Muslims of Syria. Gunther of Pairis mentioned this agreement as a part of their motivation for attacking Egypt rather than Jerusalem. 'They [the crusaders] had decided to . . . sail in a direct assault against Alexandria, an Egyptian city. They chose this destination because at this time a truce between our people and the barbarians was in effect in the regions beyond the sea. Our people could not violate what they had pledged in good faith.'[29] In the early thirteenth century the Christians and Muslims of the Holy Land were both militarily under strength and needed a period to recover and regroup. The two sides tended to observe such truces, because to continually break them reduced their value in future. An invasion of Egypt did not, however, enter this category and would enable Christian aggression to fall outside the letter of the agreement.

Alongside this diplomatic factor, the superiority of western seapower was another reason to target Egypt. The Muslim navy was, compared to the maritime strength of Venice, relatively weak. The Syrian Muslims, who had ruled the country since the late 1160s, were from a landlocked equestrian culture who regarded seafaring as a dangerous activity best undertaken by common criminals; indeed, many sailors in the Muslim fleets were convicts. The Arab proverb, 'It is preferable to hear the flatulence of camels than the prayers of fishes', expresses this sentiment concisely. Saladin did try to develop a navy, but limited resources and poor seamanship rendered his efforts largely worthless. The bulk of his fleet was captured at the siege of Acre in 1191 and such was the scale of this disaster that his successors were still struggling to rebuild it by the time of the Fourth Crusade.[30]

From the perspective of the Venetians, of course, the prospect of a dominant position in Alexandria was a truly tantalising one. Without doubt this was the commercial jewel of the eastern Mediterranean and would open up the markets of North Africa and the Middle East in an unprecedented way. Egypt was a major source of alum, sugar, spices and wheat and was an important market for wood and metals. The Venetians had a limited foothold in the country and conducted only around 10 per cent of their eastern Mediterranean business in Alexandria. This compared to about 65 per cent with Byzantium and 25 per cent with the Crusader States.[31] By contrast, the Genoese and the Pisans were much more active in Muslim ports.[32] Papal directives forbade trade with the Islamic world and, in response to Innocent's attempts to enlist Venetian help at the start of the Fourth Crusade, the city sent envoys to ask for dispensation to deal with Egypt. The pope complained of Venetian sales of materials for war (weapons, iron, galley timbers) and threatened them with excommunication if this continued. He did, however, acknowledge that the Venetians — as a trading, rather than agricultural economy — gained their entire livelihood through commerce, and in order to encourage this help for the crusade he gave them grudging licence to continue supplying non-military items. This was a calculated, pragmatic move from Innocent as he tried to satisfy the conflicting diplomatic, religious and economic pressures created by the Venetians' activities.[33]

Dandolo himself had been to Egypt in 1174 and he had seen its magnificent trading power, but also its declining defensive strength — something that even Saladin had failed to fully address. William of Tyre provides a vivid description of the city from around this period:

Alexandria is most conveniently situated for carrying on extensive commerce. It has two ports that are separated from one another by a very narrow stretch of land. At the end of that tongue rises a tower of marvellous height called the Pharos. By the Nile, Alexandria receives from upper Egypt an abundance of food supplies of every kind and, indeed, a wealth of almost every commodity. If there is anything that the country itself lacks, it is brought by ships from the lands across the sea in profuse abundance. As a result Alexandria has the reputation of receiving a larger supply of wares of every description than any other maritime city. Whatever this part of the world lacks in the matter of pearls, spices, Oriental treasures, and foreign wares is brought hither from the two Indies; Saba, Arabia, and both the Ethiopias, as well as from Persia and other lands nearby . . . People from East and West flock thither in great numbers, and Alexandria is a public market for both worlds.[34]

Ibn Jubayr, while on pilgrimage to Mecca in 1184–5, lavished praise on the buildings of Alexandria:

We have never seen a town with broader streets or higher structures, or more ancient and beautiful. Its markets are also magnificent. A remarkable thing about the construction of the city is that the buildings below the ground are like those above it and are even finer and stronger, because the waters of the Nile wind underground beneath the houses and alleyways . . . We also observed many marble columns of height, amplitude and splendour such as cannot be imagined.[35]

The Venetians too, therefore, had good reason to encourage the attack to focus on Alexandria. In comparison, the ports of the Frankish East, although not insignificant (particularly Acre), were relatively second-rate. While the enormous scale of the Venetians' commitment to the crusade cannot be doubted, the stakes they were playing for were equally vast. The basic terms of the contract with the crusaders must have been enough to cover their initial investment in shipping and men. What really helped to convince Dandolo to sell the idea to his senior councillors was the expectation of commercial dominance of the most important port in the Mediterranean. This was a unique opportunity for the Venetians, and one they had never had sight of before. For Dandolo, it would be a chance to crown his time as doge with a dual triumph: to help retake Christ's patrimony for the faithful and to establish his home city as the greatest commercial force in the Mediterranean.

There was one further connection between Venice and Alexandria and, while this was a comparatively minor issue compared to the grander commercial and strategic matters, it is worth noting. The patron saint of Venice was Mark the Evangelist, a companion of St Peter and St Paul, who eventually resided in Alexandria and was martyred there around AD 74. In the ninth century two Venetians had brought Mark's body from Alexandria – hidden in a consignment of pork to deter the Muslim port officials from examining their cargo too closely – and it was housed in the doge's private chapel, the building that eventually developed into St Mark's. This link between their patron saint and the immediate target of their crusade may have given a further edge to the Venetians' involvement in the expedition.[36]

With the formal contract and the secret deal agreed, the Frenchmen borrowed some money to make a down payment on the sum owed. The first instalment was not due until August, but the envoys wanted the Venetians to start work on the fleet immediately and paid over 5,000 silver marks. Afterwards they left for home, riding across the north Italian plain to Piacenza where the party divided. Villehardouin headed northwards to France, and the others turned west and south to visit the other Italian mercantile cities of Pisa and Genoa to discover if they were prepared to provide any help for the crusade. Given the dominant position established by the Venetians, this seemed unlikely, but perhaps the envoys thought that some crusaders might, for reasons of convenience, prefer to travel from western Italy and they therefore wanted to see if any travel arrangements might be offered.[37]

Back in Venice, work on the great fleet began. The Venetians had 13 months to make ready their existing ships and to build the new vessels required. Dandolo and his advisers sent out the appropriate orders; the focus on the crusader fleet was to be total: all commercial activity was to be suspended. Thousands of sailors would be used to man this huge fleet; they had to be enlisted and trained. Vast supplies of foodstuffs needed to be assembled – representatives went out to the farmers of northern Italy and contracted to buy their crops in hitherto unimagined volume; they engaged regional centres such as Padua and Piacenza, as well as Ravenna and Rimini further south. Corn and pulses were gathered for men and horses, along with 16,775 amphorae of wine for the crusaders, plus at least the same amount again for the Venetian soldiers and sailors. After the autumn harvest of 1201 the roads towards the Venetian coast, and the ferry-boats and barges moving over the lagoon, teemed with labourers, ceaselessly hauling victuals into the storehouses as the city drew in foodstuffs with a seemingly unquenchable appetite.

Dandolo must have summoned the master shipbuilders of the city and laid before them the full requirements of the contract, although he had presumably sought some kind of advice from them before setting out the terms of the offer in the first instance. Such was the vast cost of this construction programme that a later Venetian writer reported that the doge had to mint extra silver *grossi* to give as wages to the masters because there were insufficient small pennies to pay them.[38]

The heart of the Venetian shipbuilding industry was known as the Arsenal. This was (and still is) located about 750 yards east of St Mark's in the adjacent Castello district. It was established in 1104 as an official shipyard of the Venetian state and its task was to produce and maintain a fleet. Quite naturally, this created an institution of enormous technical expertise and was a major reason for the Venetians' maritime strength. Specialised ships for warfare, for the carrying of horses and for troop transportation could be conceived and created, and the Arsenal also carried the spares and supplies to maintain such vessels. Dandolo was plainly confident that the Arsenal could design and produce the necessary shipping to fulfil his own needs and those of the crusaders.[39]

The number of ships required was immense. The 4,500 knights, the 9,000 squires and the 20,000 foot-soldiers were to travel on *naves* or large sailing ships, often converted cargo carriers. The names of some of the biggest of these ships were recorded in the sources and are known from the particular role they played in later events. The size of these vessels varied: the greatest, called *World*, and others, such as *Paradise* and *Pilgrim*, had masts tall enough to reach the towers of Constantinople in 1204. Most would have been rather smaller and it is estimated that around 60–70 of these vessels were needed to transport the crusaders (see plate section).

To us, these ships would appear ugly and ungainly; they were short, rounded tubs. Some surviving visual evidence, such as mosaics, ceramics and manuscript illustrations, along with details from mid-thirteenth-century shipping contracts, allow estimates to be made of their size and capacity. Three-decked versions of the round ship were approximately 110 feet long and 32 feet wide. In comparison, a modern aeroplane such as an Airbus A320 is 120 feet long and its fuselage is about 16 feet wide. It carries up to 150 passengers and eight crew on flights of (usually) no more than four-and-a-half hours' duration. By the end of such a flight, most passengers are cramped and fidgety. As we look over a medieval ship, perhaps the equivalent of a jet as the main mode of transport, and consider that journeys lasted many weeks, such figures are sobering.[40]

At each end of the medieval ship were wooden structures known as castles that brought the overall height of the hull to more than 40 feet. On both sides at the back of the vessel were huge steering oars, slung in wooden 'wings' to keep them attached to the ship. These great paddles were then connected by a series of pivots and tackle to the tiller, which was manned by the helmsman on top of the rearward castle. Rudders were not found on Mediterranean ships until the fourteenth century. The knights' cabins were in the rearmost tower and offered what passed for luxury accommodation, affording at least some privacy. On top of the solid superstructure was a more lightly built apartment that provided some protection from the elements and was again available to the most important passengers. The bulk of the men were housed in the central section of the ship and were cramped into the smallest possible space each – as little as two feet by five feet according to one mid-thirteenth-century statute. On one of these big vessels a crew of 80–100 men joined up to 600 passengers (most ships would have carried fewer). The noise of creaking wood and snapping sails, the smell of sea and sweat, and the sheer proximity of so many people must have produced an incredibly intense experience.

Medieval people were used to sharing sleeping quarters in the Great Hall of a castle, but here was added the unfamiliarity of sea travel and the fact that the sailors had to carry out their tasks amidst the crusaders. As they huddled below decks, rolling from side to side in the dark, dank underbelly of the ship, many a passenger must have regretted ever leaving dry land. The fear and chaos of a storm terrified the crusaders; the sudden squalls that can whip up in the Mediterranean induced trepidation, prayer and promises to repent for a lifetime's sins. Above them, the masts towered more than 96 feet high, carrying immense sails, cracking and whipping in the wind under a yard-arm up to 150 feet long. Speeds were slow by today's standards and the voyage from Venice to Acre — a distance of about 1,800 miles if all went well — was anticipated to take four to six weeks. On a typical journey, after sailing down the Adriatic, Crete was a vital port of call, then Rhodes, the bay of Antalya off the southern coast of Asia Minor, Limassol on Cyprus, the Levantine coast at Beirut, before moving down to Acre. Each ship pulled along two or three small rowing boats that were used to go ashore to collect fresh water. It must have appeared like a mother duck and her chicks as the big, round ships trailed their 'offspring' behind them.

The transport of horses by sea was a difficult and dangerous affair.[41] Horses were essential to enable the western knights to deliver their feared charge and they were expensive status symbols of the military elite. The horse ships, known as *tarida*, probably carried up to 30 animals. Each beast had to be suspended in a sling to prevent sudden movements of the ship causing them to lose their footing and injure themselves. Large amounts of food and water had to be stored in these vessels and there was also the need to muck out each horse and throw the dung overboard. The animals were carried deep in the boat, with the main entrance falling below the waterline when fully loaded. When beached on shore and ready for battle, this door could then be opened and the horses, saddled up with their riders already mounted and fully armed, could cross a ramp and pour out of the ship, straight into the fray. With the numbers of knights the crusaders planned on recruiting, the deployment of their shock troops directly from the sea into a battle situation would have given the Christians' invasion force a formidable edge and one that might have created an immediate and overwhelming tactical advantage. To carry the 4,500 crusader horses would have needed around 150 ships. More importantly, these vessels were powered primarily by oarsmen. More than 100 men plus perhaps 30 other crew would be required to propel the ship, bringing a further 19,500 Venetians into the campaign.

Finally, there was the Venetian fleet of 50 battle-galleys, led by the doge's own vermilion-painted ship. Again, just over 100 oarsmen were needed, with a crew of warriors, officers and sailors. These galleys were roughly 125 feet long, but only about 12 feet wide (compare this 1:10 width/length ratio to the 1:3½ width/length ratio of the round ships). They were only about 14 feet high at the stem and 11 feet tall at the stern. Oarsmen usually worked two men per bench, each with a 22-foot oar.

They could move the boat along at an average speed of around three knots an hour in daylight, but unlike sail-powered vessels they needed to rest at night. Another problem with the galleys was that they sat very low in the water in order to make the most effective use of the oars, yet this made them hopelessly susceptible to swamping in heavy seas and difficult to turn quickly. Furthermore, they also carried a large volume of water – well over a gallon per day per man – to keep the crew hydrated in the summer heat. In spite of these disadvantages, the galley was the main attacking vessel in the navies of the medieval Mediterranean and its oarsmen could reach speeds of up to 10 knots in short bursts. Their main weapon was a pointed, metal-tipped beak that projected beyond the prow, above the waterline, unlike the ram of a Roman galley that ran below the surface. This was intended to damage the oars of an enemy vessel and cripple it before the ship's soldiers used grappling irons and ropes to snare their quarry, board it and seize it. Galleys would be essential to defeat any seaborne opposition that the Muslims chose to direct against the crusaders and on many occasions in the past, such as the sieges of Tyre (1124) and Acre (1191), victories at sea had done much to pave the way for a subsequent success on land. At the start of the thirteenth century the recovering Egyptian fleet contained a number of battle-galleys. It was, therefore, essential for the crusade to possess the ability to engage with and defeat these vessels.[42]

From these crude estimates it is apparent that the Venetians needed to employ or provide at least 30,000 men – probably over half the adult population of the city itself – to sail a fleet of the size proposed in the contract. Thousands of local mariners from the Adriatic shores must have come to join the crusade as the Venetians strove to fulfil their side of the bargain. Meanwhile, as Villehardouin rode northwards carrying the news of a successfully negotiated deal, he must have wondered how recruitment for the crusade was progressing and which great nobles planned to join him on the expedition. By chance, as he crossed Mount Cenis in northern Italy, he met Walter of Brienne, a leading French lord who had taken the cross with Villehardouin and Count Thibaut of Champagne. Walter was heading towards Apulia in southern Italy to regain some lands belonging to his new wife, a member of the Sicilian royal family. He and his companions praised Villehardouin for what he had achieved and promised to join the army in Venice once they had completed their business in the south. In good heart, therefore, the marshal continued his journey. Little did he know, however, that the crusade was about to suffer its first, tragic setback.[43]

CHAPTER FIVE

'Alas, Love, what a hard parting I shall have to make'

Final Preparations and Leaving Home, May 1201–June 1202

A S VILLEHARDOUIN REACHED the southern regions of the county of Champagne in May 1201 he heard deeply disturbing news. His master – one of the three leaders of the crusade – Thibaut of Champagne, lay seriously ill at the town of Troyes. The count was in low spirits when Geoffrey arrived, but he was greatly heartened to learn of the treaty with Venice. We do not know the nature of Thibaut's illness, but he was sufficiently invigorated by these developments to ride his horse – something that he had not done for weeks. Sadly, this burst of energy was to be shortlived and he soon plunged into a terminal decline. Thibaut's sickness was all the more poignant for the fact that his wife, Blanche, was approaching the ninth month of her pregnancy.

The count realised that his last days were drawing near and he made his final testament. According to Robert of Clari he had raised 50,000 livres, some of it extracted from the Jewish community of Champagne. The Jews were a common target for those seeking funds for the crusades because they were a wealthy section of society whose profits often derived from the practice of usury – the lending of money for interest – which was viewed as deeply sinful by the Catholic Church. The twelfth century saw a dramatic expansion in the economy of western Europe and this raised a number of moral questions: should a Christian society seek profit at all? Was it right to make a profit (from interest on a loan) without seeming to perform any work? As churchmen railed against the deadly crimes of avarice and fraud, usury began to be compared to theft. One aspect of this disapproval was the notion that usurers were selling time

— the longer the loan, the greater the interest paid; yet time was not theirs, but belonged to God. The Book of Psalms described the righteous man as one 'who does not put out his money at interest' (Ps. 15:5). Deuteronomy ruled: 'Thou shalt not lend to thy brother money to usury, nor corn, not any other thing: But to the stranger. To thy brother thou shalt lend that which he wanteth, without usury: that the Lord thy God may bless thee in all thy works in the land, which thou shalt go into to possess' (Deut. 23:19–20).[1]

The Jews, operating outside these strictures, were the main practitioners of usury, which formed a central element in the blossoming economy. For many in western Europe, however, the Jews had a much more sinister legacy as the killers of Christ, a record that rendered them suitable targets for holy war. In 1096, the ill-disciplined rabble of the People's Crusade (sometimes known as the Peasants' Crusade) visited terrible acts of violence and murder on the Jewish communities of the Rhineland. Similarly, 50 years later, the Second Crusade provoked another outbreak of anti-Semitism in the same region. In simple terms, it was argued that if the crusade was intended to eradicate non-believers, then one should start at home and remove the impure from Christian lands. In 1146, Peter the Venerable, abbot of Cluny, wrote: 'But why should we pursue the enemies of the Christian faith in far and distant lands while the vile blasphemers, far worse than any Saracens, namely the Jews, who are not far away from us, but who live in our midst, blaspheme, abuse and trample on Christ and the Christian sacraments so freely, insolently and with impunity.'[2] In fact, the Bible stated that the Jews should not be killed in order that they may be punished on earth and, ultimately, be saved. In the same year as Peter's pronouncements, Abbot Bernard of Clairvaux wrote: 'Is it not a far better triumph for the Church to convince and convert the Jews than put them to the sword?'[3] Bernard's views prevailed and he did much to halt the persecution of Jews.

In the late 1190s, Thibaut of Champagne had sufficient control over his lands to prevent any outbreaks of anti-Semitism, and he chose the Jews as a suitable source of finance for his own expedition. By the late twelfth and early thirteenth centuries secular rulers were able to exploit formal church legislation against the Jews and usury to impose special levies on Jewish communities; indeed, it was from a tax of this sort that Thibaut had secured part of his crusade funding. In his will the count stipulated that this money should be divided amongst those who had taken the cross, although individual beneficiaries had to swear to sail from Venice – an early recognition of the need to try to channel men and resources in that direction. A further proportion of the funds was to be allocated to the common purse of the army and spent as seen fit.

On 24 May the count finally passed away, greatly mourned by all. The death of such a prominent figure was a public affair. Villehardouin, who was almost certainly present, wrote that Thibaut died 'surrounded by a great crowd of relations and vassals. As for the mourning over his death and at his funeral, I dare not venture to describe it, for never was more honour paid to any other man . . . no man of his day was ever more deeply loved by his own people.'[4] In part this is the tribute of a loyal retainer, but there is also a strong sense that Thibaut was genuinely loved and admired by his people. His widow, Blanche, commissioned a magnificent memorial for her husband in the church of Saint-Étienne in Troyes, where Thibaut was interred at the foot of his father's grave. The tomb did not survive the French Revolution, but in 1704 a priest of the church wrote a highly detailed description of the monument. The plinth was decorated with 28 enamels, 34 columns of silver, and numerous niches that contained figures of relatives such as Louis VII of France (1137–80), who took part in the Second Crusade, and Henry II of Champagne, who ruled Jerusalem in the late twelfth century. The priest recorded a splendid image of a man holding a pilgrim's staff and, on his right shoulder, bearing a cross made of the finest silver and decorated with gemstones. Such powerful imagery was, of course, linked to Thibaut's unfulfilled crusade vow and the inscription on his tomb sought to draw a connection between the count's planned expedition and the divine reward that his admirers felt was his due:

> Intent upon making amends for the injuries of the Cross
> and the land of the Crucified
> He arranged the way with expenses, an army, a navy.
> Seeking the terrestrial city, he finds the celestial one;
> While he is obtaining his goal far distant, he finds it at home.[5]

In other words, in death Thibaut had gone to the heavenly Jerusalem, rather than the earthly one he hoped to reach on crusade. Around a week after the funeral, Blanche gave birth to a son, also named Thibaut, who would later succeed to the comital title and lead a crusade of his own to the Holy Land in 1239–40.[6]

Aside from the loss of a close friend, Thibaut's death raised serious issues for the leadership of the crusade. A group of Champenois nobles turned to the duke of Burgundy and offered him all of Thibaut's money and their loyalty if he would take the count's place as their leader, but he declined. Soon afterwards, the count of Bar-le-Duc, Thibaut's cousin, rejected a similar approach. Although it is difficult to assess the precise impact of the count's passing, the demise of such an inspirational and popular figure, whose taking of the cross had done much to spark the initial enthusiasm for the crusade in northern France, must have had a significant effect on recruitment and morale. Thibaut had the charisma and pedigree to pull many other nobles and knights along with him and, as his will revealed, he was committed to going to the Holy Land via Venice and fulfilling the contract negotiated by Villehardouin. The marshal wrote that the crusaders were 'greatly disheartened' when Thibaut died.[7] It is possible that worries over the succession to the county of Champagne may also have discouraged some of his nobles from leaving on crusade: a female regency (Thibaut had no other children) or the arrival of an outsider chosen to take charge of the area were recipes for instability and it might be more prudent to stay at home.[8]

In early June or July the senior crusaders met at Soissons in an attempt to resolve the growing crisis. The situation had become intensely serious and the counts of Flanders, Blois, Perche and Saint-Pol all joined the assembly to discuss how best to fill the vacuum caused by Thibaut's death. Villehardouin credits himself with suggesting the solution: he proposed that Boniface, the marquis of Montferrat (in northern Italy), take overall charge of the crusade. Boniface was a man of truly international standing whose family was closely related to the Capetian kings of France and to the Hohenstaufen claimants to the imperial throne of Germany. The wealthy, fertile lands of Montferrat spread across Piedmont and included Turin, Casale and Tortona. Such was Boniface's eminence that he was to be offered full control of the entire army, whereas previously it seems that Thibaut, Louis of Blois and Baldwin of Flanders had formed an unofficial triumvirate, each leading his own contingent.

Like Thibaut, Boniface came from a well-established crusading line with a long tradition of holy war. Unlike the northern French crusade leaders, he was an older man, aged about 50, who had ruled Montferrat since 1183, although he had not yet been on crusade. Over the latter half of the twelfth century, Boniface's father, William the Old, and his (Boniface's) three brothers, William Longsword, Conrad and Renier, had carved an indelible impression on the political landscape of western Europe, Byzantium and the Crusader States. William the Old fought on the Second Crusade and returned to the Holy Land in 1185, where he was captured by Saladin at the Battle of Hattin in 1187. Eleven years previously his son, William Longsword, had married Sibylla, the heiress to the throne of Jerusalem. The contemporary chronicler, William of Tyre, gives an incisive portrait of the qualities and failings of this member of the clan:

> The marquis was a rather tall, good-looking young man with blond hair. He was exceedingly irascible, but generous and of an open disposition and manly courage. He never concealed any purpose but showed frankly just what he thought in his own mind. He was fond of eating and altogether too devoted to drinking, although not to such an extent to injure his mind. He had been trained in arms from the earliest youth and had the reputation of being experienced in the art of war. His worldly position was exalted – in fact, few, if any, could claim to be his equals.[9]

Unfortunately, a mere three months after the marriage, he became seriously ill – possibly with malaria – and very soon, in June 1177, he died, leaving his wife pregnant with the future King Baldwin V of Jerusalem (1185–6).

In 1179 the house of Montferrat began to extend its influence into the Byzantine world. Such was the family's standing that Emperor Manuel Comnenus offered Renier the hand in marriage of Maria, second in line to the imperial throne. William of Tyre was present at the ceremony in 1180 and he enthused over the magnificent nuptial splendour and the generous gifts that the emperor lavished on his own people as well as strangers:

> We may mention the games of the circus which the inhabitants of Constantinople call hippodromes, and the glorious spectacles of varied

nature shown to the people with great pomp during the days of the celebration; the imperial magnificence of the vestments and the royal robes adorned with a profusion of precious stones and pearls of a great weight; the vast amount of gold and silver furniture in the palace of untold value. Words would fail to speak in fitting terms of the valuable draperies adorning the royal abode, to mention the numerous servants and members of court . . .'[10]

The union of the 17-year-old westerner with the 30-year-old Byzantine princess proved deeply unhappy. The Byzantine writer Niketas Choniates, no admirer of Maria, described the couple thus: 'The maiden [Maria], a princess wooed by many, was like Agamemnon's daughter, Electra, raving long in the palace and, stately as a white poplar wet with dew, longing for the marriage bed. Later . . . she became the consort of [Renier] of Montferrat, who was fair of face and pleasant to look upon: his well-groomed hair shone like the sun and he was too young to grow a beard, while she had passed her thirtieth year and was as strong as a man.'[11]

The emperor may also have granted Renier rights of overlordship to the city of Thessalonica in northern Greece, a considerable gift and one that later attracted the attention of Boniface.[12]

In 1181–2 Constantinople was the scene of plot and counter-plot and when the anti-western usurper – Andronicus Comnenus – triumphed, both Renier and Maria were poisoned. For Boniface this episode created a grudge for the Montferrat family against the Byzantines, which was to prove an unhealthy background to later events. Andronicus became emperor in September 1183, but he was brutally removed after just two years. His successor, Isaac II Angelos (1185–95), wanted to rebuild a relationship with the Montferrats so he offered Boniface the hand in marriage of his sister, Theodora. Boniface already had a wife, but his brother Conrad was proposed as an alternative and the pair were duly married.

Once at Constantinople, Conrad took charge of the imperial army and fought off yet another revolt. His bravery won him the plaudits of local commentators: Niketas Choniates described him as one who 'so excelled in bravery and sagacity that he was far-famed . . . graced as he was with good fortune, acute intelligence and strength of arm'.[13] Conrad used a number of western mercenaries in his army but a mistrust of outsiders provided a pretext for many in the political hierarchy to delay the true rewards of his status and position. Judging that the anti-western attitude still prevalent among some factions in the city posed a threat, Conrad decided to fulfil a crusade vow that he had made before accepting the offer to marry Theodora. This was in the summer of 1187 – the very moment when Saladin was destroying the Frankish armies in the Holy Land. Conrad sailed to the Levant and arrived at the port of Tyre (in the south of modern-day Lebanon) on 13 July, unaware of the Christians' terrible defeat at Hattin. Saladin swept through the Crusader East until he reached the walls of Tyre. The citizens thanked God that 'He had sent them a ship [Conrad's] at such a moment of crisis'.[14] The marquis led a valiant last-ditch defence of the city and his success in fending off the Muslims gave the Christians a crucial, solitary bridgehead on the coast of southern Palestine. Such was his determination that even when Saladin paraded Conrad's captured father, William the Old (taken at Hattin), in front of the walls of Tyre and threatened to kill him if the marquis did not surrender, Conrad was defiant. He shouted: '"Tie him to a stake and I shall be the first to shoot at him, for he is too old and is hardly worth anything." They brought him [William the Old] before the city and he cried out and said, "Conrad, dear son, guard well the city!" And Conrad took a crossbow in his hand and shot at his father. When Saladin heard that he had shot at his father, he said, "This man is an unbeliever and very cruel."'[15] Then Saladin sent messengers to convince Conrad that he really did mean to kill his prisoner, but the marquis responded that he wished his father to die, because after all William's shameful deeds such a wicked man would have a noble end and he, the marquis, would have a martyr as a father![16]

As well as being an uncompromising negotiator, Conrad was a great soldier and an extremely ambitious man.[17] With King Guy of Jerusalem in captivity, the marquis began to act as the *de facto* ruler of the Holy Land. Even when Guy was released, Conrad refused to cede authority to a man whom he viewed as discredited by the loss of Jerusalem. Guy was only king by virtue of his wife Sibylla's royal blood and, when she died at the siege of Acre, his claim to the throne was weakened. A period of rivalry saw the energetic newcomer emerge as the stronger candidate for the crown and in 1191 Conrad married Sibylla's sister, Isabella, the sole heiress to Jerusalem. This was a move of breathtaking political opportunism: his own marriage to Princess Theodora remained in place; Isabella too was married; and if this were not enough, Conrad and Isabella were distantly related. The union therefore possessed the rare distinction of being both incestuous and doubly bigamous. Protests against its legitimacy, however, were scarcely under way when, on 28 April 1192, Conrad fell victim to the Assassins' knife in the coastal city of Acre.

Isabella was at the town baths and, to pass the time before she returned for supper, the marquis went to see his friend, the bishop of Beauvais. Unfortunately for Conrad, the bishop had already eaten and so the marquis set out for home again. As he rode along the narrow alleyways of the city, he passed two men clothed in monastic habits who gestured, as if to present him with a letter. Suspecting nothing, Conrad greeted them both and held out his hand, whereupon they stabbed him in the stomach. The marquis collapsed, mortally wounded, and died within the hour.[18] There was confusion as to who had hired members of the Shi'i sect – the master murderers of the age – to carry out this task. Some blamed Saladin, while many others felt Richard the Lionheart was responsible because he had long opposed Conrad's candidacy for the throne.

A few months earlier William the Old had died as well. The eastern Mediterranean had claimed the lives of four members of the Montferrat family. Perhaps this contained a warning, but the new crusade offered Boniface the opportunity to add even greater glory to his dynasty's legacy and to lead an expedition to the land that his brother should have been ruling over.

Boniface was the cultured and dynamic patron of a brilliant chivalric court, and many knights and troubadours clustered around such a generous and stimulating figure. Raimbaut of Vaqueiras, who was both a troubadour and a knight, became a close companion of the marquis. He originated from the Orange region, deep in southern France, but took service with Boniface at Montferrat around 1179–80. He wrote to the marquis thus: 'In your court reign all good usages: munificence and services of ladies, elegant raiment, handsome armour, trumpets and diversions and viols and song, and at the hour of dining it has never pleased you to see a keeper at the door.'[19]

To the leadership of the Fourth Crusade, Boniface and his family brought an impressive combination of prestige, military experience and crusading connections to the Levant and the eastern Mediterranean. In this respect he was a clever choice, although as a northern Italian involved with Genoa and imperial Germany he carried with him a number of political tensions that affected the predominantly northern French complexion of the crusade.

It is thought likely that Villehardouin visited the marquis on his way home from Venice in 1201, so Boniface must have known at an early stage about the crusade's plans, including the invasion of Egypt. Once Villehardouin had persuaded the French nobles gathered at Soissons to agree to his recommendation, envoys were dispatched to Montferrat. The marquis's response was promising. In the late summer he travelled north across the Alps, via the Great St Bernard Pass, towards Soissons, accompanied by other Lombard nobles and the Cistercian churchman Abbot Peter of Lucedio, who was later to become patriarch of Antioch. En route Boniface made a detour to visit King Philip in Paris. The *Gesta* (Deeds) of Pope Innocent III suggests that it was Philip who put forward Boniface's name in the first instance. Whether or not this is true, it was good politics for the marquis to pay his respects to his cousin, the French monarch, as he passed through royal lands and as he contemplated leading many of Philip's subjects overseas.[20]

The meeting with the French nobility was arranged to take place in an orchard next to the abbey of Notre-Dame of Soissons. In late August the trees were heavy with apples, and the orchard provided a peaceful, shady setting for such serious business. The French crusaders spared no effort in their bid to convince the marquis that he should be their leader. They offered Boniface full command of their army, half of Thibaut's crusading money and the commitment of the count's men. 'We sent for you as the most worthy man that we knew . . . be our lord and take the cross for the love of God.'[21] They implored the marquis to agree to their request and fell at his feet in tears. Given his presence in northern France and his visit to King Philip, it is obvious that Boniface was already highly receptive to the proposal. After hearing out the Frenchmen, he knelt before them and solemnly agreed to lead the army of Christ.

There must have been delight and relief amongst the leadership. It still remained for Boniface to take the cross and the marquis, along with Bishop Nivelo of Soissons (already a crusader himself), Abbot Peter of Lucedio and Fulk of Neuilly (the man who had led much of the crusade preaching around northern Europe over the previous two years) walked the short distance from the orchard to the church of Notre-Dame.

The rite for taking the cross was a fairly simple process, according to the first surviving liturgical text to describe the event. There was a blessing and then the presentation of the cross, accompanied by the words 'Lord, bless this ensign of the Holy Cross that it may help forward the salvation of Thy servant'. The crusader then attached the cross to his shoulder. He was also given the traditional pilgrim's insignia of a staff and a scrip (wallet) to emphasise the close links between crusade and pilgrimage.[22]

Before leaving the church itself, the crusaders may well have paused at one particular tomb to ask for divine help. The abbey contained a splendid, sculptured sarcophagus (surviving today in the Louvre) that contained the remains of St Drausius, a seventh-century bishop of Soissons. Drausius was famed for his ability to confer success in battle on all those who spent the night in vigil at his tomb. Generations of Soissons crusaders had venerated this site and there was a strong belief in the protection accorded by the saint. One writer from the 1160s reported that so widespread was the conviction in Drausius's powers that men from Burgundy and Italy travelled to the tomb to ask for his intervention. Perhaps Boniface himself, as a northern Italian, was pleased to undertake the vigil and to seek all possible divine help as he contemplated the burden of leadership.

The following day Boniface prepared to leave Soissons. If he was to depart for the Levant in the spring (1202), he had much to do to set his affairs in order. He urged his fellow-crusaders to do the same and bade them farewell, knowing that their next meeting would be in Venice. As he turned southwards, the achievements of his family must have loomed large in the marquis's mind; this was his chance to emulate, exceed and, possibly, take revenge for some episodes in their past. He must also have been very proud; to have such powerful French nobles turn to him and to have the cachet of undisputed leadership of the crusade were marks of great distinction. His troubadour friend, Raimbaut of Vaqueiras, was not present at Soissons, but he was moved to write a song in praise of his lord and to outline the noble task of the crusaders:

Now men may know and prove that for fair deeds God gives a fair reward, for He has bestowed on the noble marquis a recompense and a gift, granting him to surpass in worth even the best, so that the crusaders of France and Champagne have besought God for him as the best of all men, to recover the Sepulchre and the Cross whereon lay Jesus, who would have him in His fellowship; and God has given him true vassals and land and riches and high courage in abundance, so that he may better perform the task.

. . . With such honour he has taken the cross that no further honour seems wanting, for it is with honour that he would possess this world and the next, and God has given him the power, the wit and the wisdom to possess both, and for this he strives his utmost.

. . . May Saint Nicholas of Bari guide our fleet, and let the men of Champagne raise their banner, and let the marquis cry 'Montferrat and the lion!' and the Flemish count 'Flanders!' as they deal heavy blows; and let every man strike then with his sword and break his lance, and we shall easily have routed and slain all the Turks, and will recover on the field of battle the True Cross which we have lost . . .

Our Lord commands and tells us all to go forth and liberate the Sepulchre and the Cross. Let him who wishes to be in His fellowship die for His sake, if he would remain alive in Paradise, and let him do all in his power to cross the sea and slay the race of dogs.[23]

On leaving Soissons, Boniface did not ride directly home, but chose to make his way about 175 miles southwards to the abbey of Citeaux, the fulcrum of the Cistercian order of monks. Every year, on 13 September, the Feast of the Holy Cross, the abbots of this huge international organisation assembled to discuss the affairs of their brotherhood.

The Cistercians were founded at the end of the eleventh century and their order was based on the principles of poverty, simplicity and separation from the evils of the world. They wore undyed white habits and liked to contrast their austere lifestyle with that of other monastic orders, such as the Cluniacs, whose splendour and wealth were well known. The Cistercian monasteries were simple, undecorated buildings, strikingly beautiful in their starkness. With Bernard of Clairvaux as a charismatic and compelling spokesman, the order attracted thousands of recruits and was given numerous donations of land. By the end of the twelfth century there were 530 Cistercian houses across the Christian world, stretching from Palestine to Spain and from Norway to Sicily.[24] Such remarkable success led to phenomenal institutional wealth. The Cistercians were expert farm managers and were known to turn rough rural regions they had been given by pious patrons into highly profitable farmlands. This wealth also enabled them to finance many individual crusaders.

Notwithstanding these riches, the personal integrity of the Cistercians was highly esteemed by the papacy and the white monks were often commissioned to preach crusades. Over time, the Cistercian General Chapter (as the annual gathering was known) had evolved into something more than an internal business meeting: it was an important focus for the intersection between Church and secular society. The news that Boniface would be present added an extra attraction to the event and members of the Burgundian nobility and crowds of other lay people were reported in attendance as well.

Fulk of Neuilly took advantage of the opportunity to preach a crusade sermon. Armed with a letter from Pope Innocent, he spoke to the meeting and recruited the abbots of Cernanceaux, Perseigne and Vaux-Cernay. As the English Cistercian, Ralph of Coggeshall, reported: 'Truly, an exigency of great magnitude demanded that many men of proven religion accompany the army of the Lord on such a laborious pilgrimage – men who could comfort the faint of heart, instruct the ignorant, and urge on the upright to the Lord's battle, assisting them in all matters that endanger the souls.'[25] Perhaps carried away by the occasion, Fulk is said to have broken into tears as he told the General Chapter that over the last three years he had personally recruited 200,000 people 'who had all relinquished for the time being parents, homeland and the joy of life in order to serve Christ'.[26] It is true that Fulk had travelled through the Low Countries and France, but this number was clearly an exaggeration, particularly given the subsequent shortfall in the numbers of crusaders who reached Venice. There is evidence of Fulk gathering some support for the crusade, but it seems that he preached mainly to the poor. One writer suggested that he exhorted only the poor because 'he believed the rich were not worthy of such a benefit'. In reality, therefore, Fulk was not the great success that he claimed to be and his contribution to the crusade was ultimately very limited.[27]

Before the assembly at Cîteaux, it had principally been the people of Champagne and Flanders who had committed themselves to the crusade, but Boniface's involvement generated a new momentum. Now a number of Burgundian nobles – including Odo of Champlitte and his brother

William; Richard of Dampierre and his brother Odo; and Guy of Pesmes and his brother Aimery – took the cross. This trio of fraternal crusaders again shows how certain families, often with crusade traditions, whole-heartedly embraced the cause of the Holy Land. In addition, Count Hugh of Berzé and his son (also called Hugh) joined the expedition, along with important churchmen such as Bishop Walter of Autun. And the crusade gained some recruits further south, such as the Provençal nobleman Peter of Bromont.[28]

As the French crusaders set about making their preparations, Boniface (as befitted the leader of the expedition) engaged in a round of diplo-macy to smooth the way for the campaign and to gather extra support. From Cîteaux he rode more than 200 miles north-eastwards to Hagenau in the Rhine valley in the German Empire (today, however, in France, just north of Strasbourg) where he visited his overlord and cousin, Philip of Swabia, king of Germany. At the beginning of the thirteenth century the German Empire was split between two rival claimants to the impe-rial throne: Philip himself and Otto of Brunswick. Boniface, naturally, favoured the former, but Pope Innocent III supported Otto – a conflict of interest that would be a source of some tension during the crusade.

Boniface remained at Hagenau over Christmas 1201. During this time he had encountered an individual who would play a pivotal role in the destiny of the Fourth Crusade. Prince Alexius Angelos (b. 1182 or 1183) was an ambitious but immature young man with a claim to the imperial title of Byzantium.[29] He was touring the courts of Europe in an attempt to secure backing to recover what he regarded as his rightful inheritance. Almost all contemporary figures and writers condemn some aspect of his personality, although the lack of a source putting his side of the story may account for some imbalance. The doge came to see Alexius as 'a wretched boy.'[30] The Byzantine writer, Niketas Choniates, regarded him as 'womanish and witless' and scorned his later drinking and dicing with the crusaders.[31] The author concluded that he was 'deemed an abomina-tion by sensible people'.

In the autumn of 1201, however, these judgements were yet to emerge. Because Prince Alexius's sister Irene was married to Philip of Swabia, the young Byzantine was the German's brother-in-law, hence his visit to Hagenau. Some historians regard the meeting between Boniface and Prince Alexius as a sinister precursor to the sack of Constantinople.[32] They view the encounter as calculated to turn the crusade towards Byzantium, thereby giving Boniface the chance for revenge over the death of his brother Renier and an opportunity for Philip of Swabia to gain power and prestige in his attempt to become German emperor. This outcome might have fitted the more outlandish daydreams of the parties concerned, but to claim that Baldwin, Prince Alexius and Philip could have steered the Fourth Crusade through the sinuous twists of fortune that dragged the expedition through 1203 and 1204 is not credible.[33]

Nevertheless Prince Alexius's claim to the Byzantine throne was a crucial influence on the Fourth Crusade. His father, Isaac II Angelos, had ruled the Byzantine Empire between 1185 and 1195 when he was deposed by his own elder brother, also called Alexius (III). When Isaac took over the imperial throne after the collapse of the Comnenian line, he was the first member of the Angeloi dynasty to rule in Constantinople and he had to cope with the aftermath of a period of violent upheaval.

A generally amiable man, much given to luxury, Isaac was ill equipped for the task. Niketas Choniates described him thus:

Daily he fared sumptuously . . . tasting the most delectable sauces, feasting on a lair of wild beasts, a sea of fish and an ocean of red wine. On alternate days, when he took pleasure in the baths he smelled of sweet unguents and was sprinkled with oils of myrrh . . . The dandy strutted around like a peacock and never wore the same garment twice . . . As he delighted in ribaldries and lewd songs and consorted with laughter-stirring dwarves, he did not close the palace to knaves, mimes and minstrels. But arm in arm with these must come drunken revel, followed by sexual wantonness and all else that corrupts the healthy and sound state of the empire. Above all, he had a mad passion for raising massive buildings and . . . he built the most splendid baths and apartments, extravagant buildings . . . he razed ancient churches and made a desolation of the outstanding dwellings of the queen of cities; there are those who pass by to this day and shed tears at the spectacle of the exposed foundations.[34]

In spite of his love of luxury, Isaac stirred himself sufficiently to see off an invasion from the Normans of Sicily in late 1185 and to resist an internal revolt in 1187, helped, as we saw above, by Conrad of Montferrat. He was less successful, however, against two other enemies. First, he faced a series of revolts from the Bulgarian and Vlach lands in the Balkans. Second, he chose to form a positive relationship with Saladin to protect himself against their mutual enemy, the Seljuk Turks of Asia Minor. This, of course, brought him into conflict with the army of Emperor Frederick Barbarossa when the Germans marched to the Holy Land on the Third Crusade. There had been decades of rivalry between the Byzantine and German Empires and on this occasion, with the two sides in close proximity, tensions erupted into open warfare. The westerners swept the Greek armies aside in northern Thrace in late 1189. Then, because Frederick's army posed a direct threat to Constantinople, Isaac was compelled to provide shipping across the Bosphorus, food at fair prices and to waive any claim for losses already incurred against the Germans.[35] In the longer run this episode was damaging to both sides. So far as western Europe was concerned, it showed the Byzantines as enemies of the crusaders; again, for the Greeks it illustrated the danger that such campaigns posed to their territories.

Isaac tried to develop a power base in Constantinople through the patronage of a clique of bureaucrats, but the enmity of rival noble families, jealous that they had not managed to secure more favours for themselves, coupled with continued military failures against the Bulgarians and the Vlachs, meant that the emperor's days were numbered. Conspirators plotted to replace Isaac with his brother, Alexius Angelos, whom they hoped would be more sympathetic to their wishes. Alexius himself was dissatisfied with the honours and position accorded to him and the idea of a coup gathered momentum.[36]

A hunting expedition to Thrace offered the perfect opportunity: on 8 April 1195, as the imperial party left the main camp and rode off to hunt, Alexius and his men made their move. Feigning ill-health, the challenger remained in the camp. Once Isaac was fully engaged in the chase the conspirators led their man to the imperial tent and acclaimed him emperor. The army favoured Alexius and the imperial bureaucrats who were present prudently followed suit. Isaac became aware of the uproar and learned exactly what had happened. He thought to charge back into the camp, but his men were too few to fight effectively and so he fled. Alexius followed in pursuit, knowing that he had to capture his brother before he returned to Constantinople and reasserted his imperial authority in public. Isaac was soon caught and taken to the monastery of Vera, near Makre, in southern Thrace. There, as Niketas tells us, he endured an excruciating torture: 'he looked upon the sun for the last time, and his eyes were soon gouged out'. The Byzantines judged that blinding rendered an individual unfit to rule; Isaac was then cast into prison.[37] Once enthroned, Alexius III (as he became) kept Isaac under a relaxed house arrest and extracted a promise from him and his son, Prince Alexius, that they would not conspire against him. Unsurprisingly the promise was not kept: father and son hatched a plot in which the young man would be sent to Germany to seek the help of his brother-in-law and sister: Philip and Irene of Swabia.

In 1201 the captives engaged two Pisan merchants based in Constantinople to engineer the prince's freedom. When he joined Alexius III on a campaign in Thrace, the Pisans arranged for their boat to follow the expedition and lie offshore. The moment Prince Alexius saw a chance to flee, he bolted to an agreed rendezvous with the Pisans at the port of Athyras on the nearby Sea of Marmara. A waiting rowing boat quickly took him out to the Italians' trading ship, although his safety was still far from assured. Once Alexius III discovered the daring escape he commanded that all ships in the vicinity should be searched.

There are different explanations of how his quarry escaped detection: Niketas Choniates wrote that Prince Alexius cut off his long hair, put on western-style clothing and, by mingling with the crew, evaded the emperor's men.[38] The *Chronicle of Novgorod*, a thirteenth-century account composed in Russia and based on information provided by a German source from the time of the Fourth Crusade, gives an alternative version. It states that the young Alexius hid in a false-bottomed water barrel and when the emperor's agents checked the container by opening the plug they saw water flow out and, believing it to be full, moved on.[39] Whichever story is true, the Pisans' plan worked and their ship sailed off, docking at Ancona, from where Irene's escorts brought the escapee to Hagenau and eventually to his meeting with Philip and Boniface of Montferrat. Irene pleaded her brother's case, but to little effect. Boniface was determined to take the crusade to Egypt and Jerusalem. Philip was embroiled in the German civil war with Otto of Brunswick. Neither would be distracted.

Prince Alexius was no less determined to raise help. He left for Rome in early 1202, but he was never likely to elicit much sympathy from the papacy and his appeal was rejected. Innocent was not prepared to divert his crusade to assist an individual related to Philip of Swabia, who by this time had been excommunicated in the course of his struggle with the pope's preferred candidate. Furthermore, relations between Alexius III and the papacy, if rather chilly, were not so bad as to cause the pontiff to try to unseat the Byzantine ruler. In the early years of Innocent's pontificate, the atmosphere between Rome and Constantinople had seen several changes of direction.

At first, Innocent hoped to work in conjunction with Alexius III to support the crusade and to bring the Orthodox and Catholic Churches closer together.[40] In November 1199, however, the pope had, at length, castigated the Greek ruler for failing to relieve the plight of the Holy Sepulchre and the Christians in the East, and for the continuation of the schism between the two churches. If the emperor did not help the cause of the crusade, Innocent suggested that his 'negligence would incur divine displeasure' – an unerringly accurate prediction.[41]

Alexius III's reply reminded the pope of the injuries inflicted by Barbarossa's crusade and offered to discuss the union of the churches at a great council. In turn, Innocent attempted to persuade Alexius III of his Christian duty to assist the new crusade and hoped that he would bring the Greek Orthodox Church to recognise papal authority.[42]

In the event, Alexius III did little to follow the papal directives and argued that the Byzantine emperor was above papal power. Such a notion was utterly unacceptable to Innocent, who believed the Bible provided ample authority for the subordination of all secular rulers to the priesthood. Nonetheless, in late 1200 or early 1201, Innocent moderated his tone to the Greek ruler in order to smooth the way for the imminent crusade:

Your Highness knows whether or not we have been able to lead your Imperial Excellency to welcoming the good and the useful through our letter and whether we have advised you of proper and honourable courses of actions because we remember that we invited you to nothing other than the unity of the Church and aid for the land of Jerusalem. May He, who holds the hearts of princes in His hand, so inspire your mind that you acquiesce to our advice and counsel and do that which should deservedly produce honour for the Divine Name, profit for the Christian religion, and the salvation of your soul.[43]

The open hostility between the Greeks and the Third Crusade – an unnecessary drain on the westerners' energies – together with a mutual dislike of Philip of Swabia were strong reasons for the pope to ensure that Alexius III behaved well towards the new crusade. Perhaps he had also recognised that the Byzantine emperor was not going to be bullied into line and, with the crusade poised to set out, Innocent decided to adopt a more emollient tone.

After the pope had rebuffed Prince Alexius, it was the turn of Boniface to have a papal audience. As the leader of the crusade, it was logical that the marquis should meet the spiritual guardian of the Catholic Church. They may well have discussed Alexius's case, but Innocent would have been swift to dissuade Boniface from showing an interest in any diversion to Constantinople.

In April the marquis turned north towards home, pausing en route to try to establish peace between the warring cities of Pisa and Genoa. His idea was to create greater stability in the West before the crusade set out and to open up the possibility of other sources of naval help for the expedition. Boniface must have arrived back in his homelands in early May 1202; he had been away for around nine months since the first summons to lead the crusade and now, as a matter of urgency, he had to prepare himself for a much longer absence in the East.

Over the winter of 1201 and into the New Year of 1202 whole communities across Europe were gripped by preparations for the expedition. The leaders had set a date of Easter for the northern French armies to assemble and to begin the march south. The crusaders needed to work hard to gather the money and equipment for their journey. Some nobles had access to considerable wealth and could afford to sell assets to raise further revenue. The less well off often had to mortgage lands or rights to raise money. Some of these arrangements were made with other nobles, or with the commercial classes of the growing urban elite, but the vast majority of surviving documents record dealings with religious institutions whose deeply rooted traditions of literacy and record-keeping have resulted in the preservation of thousands of such agreements. Knights and nobles negotiated loans and gifts with local churchmen. Charters enshrined these agreements in writing and were witnessed by clergy, nobles, their families or household members.

Given the Church's strictures against usury, nothing like the explicit lending of money for interest is found, but contracts that allowed the lender the free use of, or profits from, the land during the owner's absence seem dangerously close to the spirit – if not the exact letter – of the practice.

Some charters were executed to make good a dispute and for a departing crusader to clear his moral as well as his practical obligations. A contemporary charter from the abbey of Floreffe, in the county of Namur (near Flanders), shows how Thomas, a knight, wanted to repent for his earlier behaviour and to put his soul at peace, as well as to end a long-standing argument:

> Because what is not retained in writing slips easily from the memory, I, Wéric, by God's grace abbot of Floreffe, and the community, make known to those present and future, that Thomas, a knight of Leez, a free man, was struck by the goad of covetousness and took back the eight *bonuaria* of land which he had legitimately bestowed in compensation for the damages often inflicted upon us, and he made accusation against us. Finally, because he was ready to go on crusade and recognised that he was guilty, he completely gave up, renounced and abandoned the aforesaid land and its fruits before many suitable witnesses . . . Lest there be a possibility for someone to weaken the contents of this agreement and trouble our church in this matter, to verify its authenticity we append the seal of prudent men to this document, namely, the abbots of Gembloux, Corneux and Leffe.[44]

Other charters simply record charitable bequests to assist the donor's soul, although it is possible that unrecorded gifts were given in exchange. The following extract from a charter shows a knight of the Fourth Crusade making such a donation:

> I, Geoffrey of Beaumont make it known to all in the present and the future that, setting out on the road to Jerusalem, with the agree-

ment and wishes of my wife Margaret and my daughters Dionysie, Margaret, Aales and Heloise, I give and I concede to the poor monks of St Josaphat, for the love of God and the salvation of my soul, 5 solidi a year from my income at Beaumont. [It will be given] on the festival of Saint Remigius [13 January] to the hands of those of the brothers who bring forward these present documents. In order that this may be fixed and preserved I strengthen the confirmation of this present charter with my seal. Enacted in the year 1202 in the month of May.[45]

For some men, a clause in Pope Innocent's crusade bull of December 1198, *Graves orientalie terrae*, provided a source of income. The pope had imposed a tax of one-fortieth on the annual income of the Church and decreed that: 'If the crusaders cannot afford the journey you should make suitable grants to them from this cash, after receiving sufficient assurance from them that they will remain to defend the eastern land for a year or more, according to the amount of the grant.'[46] We do not know the sum of money raised by this measure – much may never have been collected at all, or may have failed to reach the intended recipients – but a number of men probably had their crusades financed in this way.

In addition to money, the crusaders needed to gather all the equipment needed for a military expedition several thousand miles from home. Hundreds of horses had to be obtained, from the finest chargers to the heavy pack-animals required to pull cartloads of equipment down to Venice. The forges of northern France pounded out thousands of spare horseshoes, and leather workers laboured over extra saddles and bridles. Arms and armour were manufactured and purchased, shields freshly painted; tradesmen ensured that each noble was fitted out in the finest equipment that he could afford and lords chose splendid cloaks and banners to adorn their contingents.

Some personalised their equipment. During the Third Crusade, Sancho Martin, a Spanish nobleman, wore a green tunic and decorated his helmet with the antlers of a stag. Sancho's conspicuous display certainly attracted attention because, when he appeared on the battlefield, 'the Saracens all rushed up, more to see his fine bearing than anything else'.[47] The men themselves trained for war, practising their swordsmanship and fighting skills. The ban on tournaments was restated and this time it was observed in case the contests injured or killed valuable crusader warriors. The army also had to be fed. Some provisions could be carried: smoked pig carcasses were often conveyed in their thousands; dozens of carts arrived, piled high with preserved foodstuffs, sacks of wheat and barrels of wine. Other edibles would have to be bought along the way and this meant that the crusaders had to take cash or valuables with them. To us, accustomed to using credit cards and taking foreign currency overseas, the notion of transporting bulky gold and silver objects abroad as a means of payment seems wildly inconvenient. However, given the sudden huge demand for coins created by thousands of men wanting cash – at a level well beyond anything most institutions could supply – the practicalities of taking thousands of small-denomination coins, and the mechanics of money-changing at the time, there was really no option. Crusaders had to carry with them great ornaments from churches, precious jewels or cloth, or household items such as plates and cutlery, to exchange for food and drink when it was needed.

As the moment of departure grew near, a mixture of excitement and dread must have affected all the crusaders, from the greatest of lords to the lowliest of servants. Similar emotions would have permeated the thoughts of the households and communities they were about to leave. What adventures awaited the crusaders? Fame and wealth? Or suffering, pain and death? Nobles often marked this time with a magnificent feast where they gathered together friends and family. This was also the moment to set any outstanding affairs in order, to resolve any existing disputes and to pray for a safe homecoming. For the clergy, a similar process took place; churchmen had to take leave of their brethren – their 'family' – and, as clerics, armed only with their prayers and faith, they too must have wondered what God's judgement would bring them.

Finally, on the day of leaving, everyone had to brace themselves for their farewells: final promises, last words and last embraces. Fulcher of Chartres described the anguish of a crusader parting from his wife:

Then husband told wife the time he expected to return, assuring her that if by God's grace he survived he would come back home to her. He commended her to the Lord, kissed her lingeringly, and promised her as she wept that he would return. She though, fearing that she would never see him again, could not stand, but swooned to the ground, mourning her loved one whom she was losing in this life as if he were already dead. He, however, like one who had no pity – although he had – and as if he were not moved by the tears of his wife nor the grief of any of his friends – yet secretly moved in his heart – departed with firm resolution.[48]

As Robert of Clari wrote: 'many were there of fathers and mothers, sisters and brothers, wives and children, who made great lamenting over their loved ones'.[49] The troubadour knight Conon of Béthune sang of his fears and pain at leaving his wife and, even though this verse has a strongly chivalric aspect, Conon's true feelings also emerge:

> Alas, Love, what a hard parting I
> Shall have to make from the best
> Lady ever to be loved and served.
> May God in his goodness bring me
> Back to her as surely as it is true
> That I leave her with great pain.
> Alas! What have I said? I am not
> Leaving her: even if my body goes
> To serve our Lord, my heart remains
> Entirely at her service.[50]

Villehardouin related that 'many a tear, as you may imagine, was shed for sorrow at parting from their lands, their own people and their friends'.[51] A later crusader captured the pain of the moment exquisitely, balancing feelings of both loss and anxiety: 'I never once let my eyes turn back . . . for fear my heart might be filled with longing at the thought of my lovely castle and the two children that I had left behind.'[52]

Many of the northern French crusaders began their journey to Venice in the late spring and early summer of 1202. Villehardouin did not set out until Pentecost (2 June). which made the planned sailing date of 29 June wholly unrealistic and meant that those who arrived in northern Italy on time would have to tolerate a long wait for their colleagues.[53]

The crusaders marched along some of the major trade routes of the time. Coincidentally, the Champagne region was at the heart of the European economy and enthusiastic comital patronage had led to the development of a series of four annual international fairs (held at Provins, Troyes, Lagny and Bar-sur-Aube) that together constituted the most important commercial events in the medieval West. These fairs were a meeting place for merchants from England, Flanders, Germany and northern Italy, as well as France itself. The needs of those attending them created an enhanced network of roads for the crusaders to use. For those marching from Flanders, a road ran from Bruges to Reims, to Châlons and from there to the scene of the biggest of the fairs, the city of Troyes. Just south of Troyes they followed a section of the River Seine and then joined the routes to Italy. For the crusaders this journey possessed the advantages of following well-established roads (in winter, still little more than atrociously muddy tracks) with all the associated facilities for buying food and for prayer and rest. By far the easiest way to transport bulky items was by river and the crusaders may have moved some of their equipment in this way, although the majority of the army would have remained on horse, foot or cart, and marched alongside the boats carrying their possessions. Down beyond Châtillon-sur-Seine the road passed through a deeply forested area where merchants were often attacked by robbers, although in the crusaders' case sheer weight of numbers protected the main contingents. As the Seine became unnavigable, any riverborne equipment was moved back onto land. The road went south across a limestone plateau and then over a series of hills and valleys before reaching Dijon and continuing alongside another arterial river, the Saône, to move deep into Burgundy.

This road passed within 12 miles of the enormous abbey of Cluny, which, together with Cîteaux, was one of the most powerful and prestigious religious institutions in medieval Europe. Some northern French knights held lands with priories affiliated to Cluny and they would have taken the opportunity to visit the great mother abbey itself. The church of Cluny was founded in 909, rebuilt in 1088 and finally consecrated in 1130. A magnificent 161 yards in length, it stood as the biggest building in the Christian West for centuries, and in sheer size and splendour was a paradigm for all religious houses. The Cluniacs believed in celebrating the glory of God through lavish decoration and rich, ornate frescos and sculptures. The great choir at Cluny was lit by a web of candelabra and the altar surmounted by a golden pyx studded with precious stones. In contrast to the austere Cistercian abbeys, the Cluniacs flaunted their wealth and were famous for their lengthy liturgical rituals and fine food and wine. As patrons of the abbey and as holy warriors, those who made the detour must have been received with particular good favour and the prayers of the black monks (the colour of their monastic habits) would have followed the crusaders southwards.

The road carried on past Lyon and Vienne before it turned towards the Alps. In normal times, merchants and travellers had to pay customs tolls to the local lords to secure a passage over the Alps, but the crusaders, as knights of Christ, were exempt from these charges. Villehardouin crossed the Alps using the Mount Cenis pass, which today is closed to wheeled traffic from November to April; but, incredibly, in medieval times a steady flow of traders and travellers braved its steep and precipitous paths throughout the year. In the summer, conditions were relatively good and the journey of 1202 is recorded as uneventful. A vertiginous descent towards Susa completed the passage into northern Italy; a couple of days later, a gentle march down the valley of Susa brought the army to Turin and the edge of Boniface of Montferrat's lands. Here, it is likely that Baldwin and the other northern French crusaders again met the marquis to discuss the expedition's progress. To reach this point would have taken about a month from Troyes, a distance of around 340 miles. From here it was a relatively easy route through Asti, Tortona, Piacenza, along the River Po and, finally, northwards again to Venice itself.[54]

CHAPTER SIX

'It seemed as if the sea were all a-tremble and all on
fire with the ships'

The Crusade at Venice and the Siege of Zara,
summer and autumn 1202

O N THEIR ARRIVAL in Venice, the crusaders were warmly
welcomed by their hosts. The Venetians had thought carefully
about where to accommodate the Frenchmen and had prepared
land on the island of St Nicholas, known today as the Lido. This long
(8 miles), flat sandbar lies to the east of the city, around 7½ miles away
from St Mark's Square, but only around 1,300 feet from the nearest point
of the main Rialto Island. The Lido protects the central islands from
the open sea and today is famous as a beach resort. Back in the thirteenth century it was almost entirely undeveloped except for the eleventh-
century monastery of St Nicholas. The decision to house the crusaders
on the Lido represented a careful mix of diplomatic pragmatism and
simple practicality. The unique topography of Venice precluded the
majority of the Frenchmen from setting up camp in, or just outside, the
city itself, and the Lido was the closest open space that could take such
a large force. Equally, if the crusaders proved to be ill disciplined – as
so many had been in the past – then they were away from the heart of
Venice and reliant on Venetian shipping to get off the island in large
numbers. In other words, they might find it difficult to threaten their
hosts directly, even if they wished to.

As the summer wore on and more of the crusaders gathered in the
city, disturbing rumours began to reach the camp: some of those who
had promised to meet in Venice were said to be choosing other routes
to reach the Holy Land. Villehardouin, as one of those responsible for

negotiating the original deal with the Venetians, was highly alarmed at this development because it meant the crusaders might fail to fulfil their side of the contract. They had sworn to pay the Venetians 85,000 marks in the expectation that 33,500 men and 4,500 horses would come to Venice and make up this sum at a particular rate per man and per horse. The total figure was fixed and, even if fewer crusaders appeared, the full amount was still owed. With fewer men, therefore, the cost to each individual would rise dramatically – probably beyond the means of many – which, in turn, meant that the leadership would need to find substantial extra funds to make up the shortfall.

The marshal was especially scathing of those who, as he saw it, let down their comrades by not coming to Venice and his narrative pointedly named the individuals whom he felt especially culpable. As one of the men who had negotiated the Treaty of Venice in 1201, this was also a way of distracting attention from his own overestimation of the numbers of crusaders who would gather at Venice and of trying to convince posterity that he was not at fault for this error. Privately, however, in the late summer of 1202 the marshal must have felt a real apprehension that he and his fellow-envoys had made a terrible mistake and that the crusaders would not be able to meet their agreement with the Venetians.

Those who resolved to travel to the Holy Land by some other route often had entirely sound reasons for doing so. One group of Flemings, led by John of Nesles, the governor of Bruges, was to sail from Flanders, down the English Channel and around the Iberian peninsula – a quite logical decision given that several earlier expeditions from the Low Countries to the Holy Land had followed the same route. John's ships carried soldiers, clothing, food and other supplies for Count Baldwin and the main Flemish contingent and promised to join him 'at whatever place they might hear that he had gone'.[1] Rather disingenuously Villehardouin claimed that this group broke their oath and abandoned their colleagues because 'they were afraid to undertake the many perils that the army in Venice had undertaken'.[2] In fact, when John of Nesles's men later heard of the diversion, they chose not to fight at Constantinople and elected to sail directly to the Levant.

Crusaders from Burgundy and the Île-de-France also avoided Venice and chose instead to sail from Marseille or from Genoa. Here, more starkly, another fundamental flaw in Villehardouin's reasoning is revealed:

aside from overestimating the total number of crusaders, he had failed to allow for the fact that those who did take part were under no compulsion to sail from Venice. Blinded, perhaps, by the prospect of the wonderful Venetian navy, and believing (not unwisely) that in pure military terms this *was* the best way for the crusaders to reach Egypt, he had assumed that all the holy warriors would wish to join the same fleet. Crucially, the only signatories to the treaty with Venice were the representatives of Champagne, Flanders, Blois and Saint-Pol. Beyond these contingents there was no obligation for any of the crusaders to travel with the Venetians. Likewise, there was no papal directive ordering such a course of action and none of the expedition's nobles had sufficient authority to compel everyone to gather at the head of the Adriatic.[3] The main leaders, Boniface, Baldwin and Louis, could encourage their own men to do this if they thought it sensible – but they could not realistically force people of independent standing such as the Burgundians, Bishop Walter of Autun and Count Guigue of Forez to meet on the Adriatic. It was much easier for these crusaders to sail down the River Rhône and take ship from Marseille than to travel across to northern Italy; it was also possible that the people of Marseille offered a cheaper crossing than the Venetians.[4] Most previous crusading expeditions had travelled in a fragmented and *ad hoc* manner, each major contingent taking its own route to the Levant and making its own arrangements. Sometimes these groups gathered for convenience or, once in Asia Minor, joined together for safety, but to ask such a polyglot force as the Fourth Crusade to meet in Europe was unprecedented. As the summer of 1202 wore on, the plan for the expedition to travel in one enormous fleet looked increasingly implausible.

The crusaders' plight was becoming apparent to all. Baldwin of Flanders had arrived in Venice, but Louis of Blois and many more nobles had yet to appear. It was confirmed that others were taking ship from alternative ports and, as this news began to drift into the camp, the prospect of a shortfall of men and money became ever more real. Those at Venice took council and decided that Louis, at least, had to be won over. A delegation led by Villehardouin and Count Hugh of Saint-Pol rode from Venice to Pavia (about 150 miles as the crow flies) to meet the Blesevin. For one of the primary signatories of the original contract to attempt to evade the agreement was a calamity: it was profoundly disloyal to his comrades and deeply discouraging to all. Geoffrey and Hugh chided

Louis and his colleagues for their lack of courage, reminded them of the plight of the Holy Land and argued that the best way to help the faithful was by joining the main army at Venice. This direct appeal worked and Louis and his men agreed to march to the head of the Adriatic. For others, however, this form of personal intervention was not a feasible approach and Villehardouin lamented that many, such as Villain of Neuilly, whom he described as 'one of the finest knights in the world' – a reputation probably gained on the tournament circuit – chose to march south from Piacenza and take ship in Apulia, thereby avoiding Venice.[5]

By the mid-summer of 1202 those Frenchmen who had crossed the Alps and reached Montferrat and Lombardy would have learned of the potential troubles brewing for their colleagues to the east. Some may have calculated that there was no possibility that the crusaders at Venice could fulfil their contract with the doge, and travelling there to become ensnared in such an impossibly awkward situation must have seemed undesirable. Given the lack of any formal requirement to go to Venice, there was no reason why they could not march down to southern Italy and sail on to the Eastern Mediterranean free of the contractual restrictions and financial disputes that would inevitably attend their colleagues at the head of the Adriatic. These men remained holy warriors, dedicated to fulfilling their vows and fighting in the Holy Land – simply because they failed to sail from Venice did not, as Villehardouin would prefer us to believe, render them traitors to their cause.

In spite of this unhappy state of affairs, the arrival of Count Louis and his knights brought delight to those already in Venice. The newcomers were met with feasting and celebrations as they took up their quarters on the shell-strewn shores of the Lido. At first, all was well, and the Venetians provided a market to provision the men and horses. The crusade leaders went across to the city, where they were shown the Arsenal and the numerous private shipyards on the islands. The Frenchmen saw how the doge's men had accomplished their side of the contract and they marvelled at the superb fleet constructed on their behalf. The *Gesta Innocenti* records that 'the Venetians prepared a magnificent fleet, the like of which had not been seen since long ago'.[6] Villehardouin wrote: 'The fleet that they had got ready was so fine and well equipped that no man in the whole of Christendom has ever seen one to surpass it.'[7] Even allowing for the medieval propensity for exaggeration, this was undoubtedly one of the biggest, and certainly the most splendid, fleets yet assembled in the Christian West. The *Devastatio Constantinopolitana* stated that there were 40 ships, 62 galleys and 100 transports. Robert of Clari wrote that the doge himself had 50 galleys of his own.[8] The contemporary letter of Count Hugh of Saint-Pol recorded that 200 vessels reached Constantinople in the summer of 1203, and the Byzantine writer Niketas Choniates counted more than 70 transports, 110 horse transports and 60 galleys at the same stage of the expedition.[9] Drawing on a diverse range of sources, it seems likely that a fleet of some 200 ships had been mustered. It is true that earlier crusader fleets had approached a similar size, most notably the northern European force of around 160 vessels that captured Lisbon in 1147, although the form of these vessels was far smaller than those used in the Fourth Crusade. We know of no horse transports at Lisbon, for example, and there is no possibility that this group of maritime crusaders had the financial resources or expertise to construct anything like the extraordinary fleet gathered at Venice in 1202.

As the summer drifted along, further crusaders arrived. On 22 July, the papal legate, Cardinal Peter Capuano, reached Venice. He spent time on the Lido preaching to the troops and is said to have done much to bolster morale. In late July, Gunther of Pairis and the Upper Rhineland crusaders completed their journey. On 15 August, Boniface of Montferrat appeared and, as nominal head of the crusade, his presence must have given good heart to the men already there. It was also the first occasion that all three elements of the crusade leadership – the marquis, the northern French and the Venetians – were present together and it would have afforded an important opportunity to discuss strategy and planning. Around the same time, the German contingent led by Bishop Conrad of Halberstadt (in northern Germany) and Count Berthold of Katzenellenbogen (from the central Rhineland) marched down to the shores of the Adriatic. This offered further cheer to those on the Lido.[10]

Notwithstanding these moments of optimism, the harsh reality of the situation began to set in. Much of the intense labour and massive resources expended on the Venetian armada was in vain: by the autumn it was abundantly clear that far too few crusaders had assembled. The envoys' estimate had been wildly inaccurate and only around 12,000 of the promised 33,500 had gathered. Villehardouin wrote: '[The fleet] comprised so great a number of warships, galleys, and transports that it could easily have accommodated three times as many men as were in the whole army.'[11]

Lines of ships lay drawn up in dockyards, while others sat bobbing and bumping at anchor, ready to sail. Yet the shortfall of holy warriors condemned dozens of these vessels to ghostly inactivity. For both the crusaders and the Venetians this was a catastrophic state of affairs: the crusaders faced the humiliation of failing to keep to the contract and the need to find huge amounts of cash; the Venetians contemplated financial ruin and the waste of at least a whole year's labour. Dandolo had to act: he summoned the leaders of the crusade and bluntly demanded the money due to him. Robert of Clari suggests that this was coupled with a threat. The doge exclaimed:

> Lords, you have used us ill, for as soon as your messengers made the bargain with me I commanded through all my land that no trader should go trading, but that all should help prepare this navy. So they have waited ever since and have not made any money for a year and a half past. Instead, they have lost a great deal, and therefore, we wish, my men and I, that you should pay us the money you owe us. And if you do not do so, then know that you shall not depart from this island before we are paid, nor shall you find anyone to bring you anything to eat or to drink.[12]

The *Devastatio Constantinopolitana*, an anonymous eye-witness account of the expedition written by a Rhineland crusader, paints a grim picture of conditions on the barren Lido: trapped, for day after day on the dull, flat sandbar; bored, hungry and condemned to wait on the decisions of their commanders. The author emphasised the suffering of the poor and their sense of being exploited by the crusade leadership – regardless of whether they were French or Venetian.[13] He wrote of hugely inflated food prices, and grumbled that 'as often as it pleased the Venetians, they decreed that no one release any of the pilgrims . . . consequently the pilgrims, almost like captives, were dominated by them in all respects'. These feelings of tedium and powerlessness, as well as the difficulties of survival, are representative of the lot of the average crusader and reveal how arduous such expeditions were. The *Devastatio* also mentions that many crusaders deserted and either travelled home or went south to Apulia. Of those who remained, 'an unusual mortality rate arose. The result was that the dead could barely be buried by the living.'[14] Although this latter claim might be tenuous, the outbreak of some form of disease on the Lido during the hot summer months seems more than likely. For these disaffected individuals, a resentment of the Venetians' apparently hostile behaviour nurtured ill-feeling that would boil over into open conflict after the siege of Zara a few weeks later. Other writers record that some crusaders managed to make the short journey over to Venice and acquire food; and Robert of Clari maintained that the doge continued to provide food and drink because he was such a worthy man.[15] The variety of viewpoints reflects the different experiences of the eye-witnesses and makes plain that members of the nobility were better able to secure supplies than the impoverished foot-soldiers.

Dandolo's request for payment can hardly have been a surprise. The crusade leaders' first response was to ask everyone to contribute the cost of their passage. However – and as an illustration of the difficulties in raising money for such expeditions – many were unable to do so. Perhaps they had hoped that a wealthy lord would take them under his patronage (as quite often happened on crusade), or else they believed that the general fund, including the sums raised by the papal taxes, would contribute towards their expenses.

For some men, the initial attraction of the crusade had paled and the enthusiasm to recover the Holy Land was becoming an increasingly distant and ephemeral dream when set against the day-to-day needs of survival. Cardinal Peter Capuano tried, unsuccessfully, to intervene with the Venetians and to persuade them to be patient with the crusaders. He also attempted to streamline the expedition. Prudently, he granted letters releasing the sick, the destitute, women and 'all feeble persons' from their vows, which allowed them to return home without the penalty of excommunication.[16] From those who remained, the nobles collected all that they could but, even so, more than half the overall fee was still missing. Further discussion was clearly needed.

The French acknowledged that the Venetians had fulfilled their side of the bargain in good faith, and that the problem lay with the crusaders. Once again Villehardouin blamed the breach of the contract on those who had failed to come to Venice: 'This is the fault of those who have gone to the other ports.'[17] He made no mention of the gross overestimation of the crusaders' numbers and the fact that there was a free choice as to which port the crusaders could embark from. Again, Villehardouin was refusing to acknowledge his own responsibility in the original estimate of the numbers and was trying to deflect blame for this increasingly grotesque mistake.

With insufficient money to pay the Venetians, the nobles faced the grim prospect of the expedition collapsing before it had even begun. They fretted over the injury to their honour and lamented the continuing danger to the Holy Land. Some men were ready to abandon the arrangement with Venice entirely and argued that they, as individuals, had paid the agreed sum for their passage and, if the Venetians were unwilling to take them to the Levant, then they would sail from elsewhere or, as Villehardouin suspected, simply return home. The more determined majority resolved to persist: 'We'd much rather give up all we have and go as poor men with the army than see it broken up and our enterprise a failure. For God will doubtless repay us in His own good time.'[18] The ominous tone underlying this last remark again betrays the knowledge of the outcome of the crusade in Villehardouin's account. As he saw it, the sack of Constantinople was God's way of recognising the willingness of his men to sacrifice all their worldly goods in His cause and to hold firm to their crusade vows.

The leadership dug deep into their personal resources to try to bridge the gap between the sum raised and that owed to the doge. Gold and silver vessels, jugs, plates and cutlery were all handed over and transported to Dandolo's palace to help pay the debt. In spite of some nobles borrowing money, the crusaders were still, according to Villehardouin, 34,000 (or 36,000 by Robert of Clari's reckoning) marks short of the 85,000 required – and there appeared no way out of this impasse.[19]

The crusaders had not, however, counted on Doge Dandolo's ingenuity. He had, as Robert of Clari reported, already spent much of the anticipated payment in the construction and equipping of the fleet and he had also required the Venetians to cease trading for more than a year – with obvious financial consequences. As the man who had led his people in the original negotiations, Dandolo had a duty to ensure that Venice did not lose out. He was clearly under enormous pressure to keep the city's finances in proper order and to realise the huge investment made in the crusader fleet. Furthermore, the doge was a proud man and by leaving a legacy of bankruptcy to his mother city his reputation would be fatally compromised. He was also a canny politician with an appreciation of the wider diplomatic picture. Dandolo argued that if, as they were legally entitled, the Venetians kept what had been paid, but did not take the crusade to the Holy Land because of the overall shortfall, they would provoke widespread ill-feeling across the Christian West. More pertinently, he would enrage the crusading army on his doorstep. As these were equally unacceptable options, the crusade had to go on and he had to find a way for the crusaders to relieve the debt in full. The doge made an offer: a pragmatic proposal and one that was certainly of advantage to Venice, yet it was an idea that would strike at the very core of the crusaders' motivation and provoke deep unease amongst many of those committed to the cause of Christ. Dandolo suggested that the crisis could be alleviated by the Venetians and the crusaders attacking the city of Zara on the Dalmatian coast, around 165 miles south-east of Venice.

Control of Zara had long been an aim of the Venetians and here was an excellent opportunity for them to assert their authority. The doge decided that payment of the debt should be suspended and subsequently, God permitting, the crusaders would be able to win the money they owed by right of conquest.[20] In any case, it was now September, almost too late to journey to Egypt in safety. A diversion to Zara would at least start the campaign and move the men away from the environs of Venice itself.

Although Dandolo's proposal seemed, in some respects, simple enough, there was a sinister catch: Zara was a Christian city and at the same time it was under the jurisdiction of King Emico of Hungary (1196–1204). Even worse, Emico was marked with the cross and nominally committed to the same cause as themselves. Dandolo was, therefore, asking the crusaders to direct their energies against a Christian city and, crucially, against a man whose lands – as a crusader – were under papal protection. Was this Venetian empire-building or just an ingenious way to keep the crusade going? The answer is probably both, yet as the campaign unfolded, it was a combination that increasing numbers of crusaders found themselves unable to stomach.

The crusade leaders discussed the offer and, according to Robert of Clari, chose not to reveal the plan to go to Zara to the rank and file of the army for fear of an adverse reaction. They simply announced that payment of the debt to the Venetians was to be deferred, to be paid 'out of the first gains you shall make for yourselves', and that the expedition was finally to set out.[21] The masses were delighted and they celebrated by lighting great torches and carrying them around the camp on the tips of their lances, parading their happiness to all.

As Villehardouin relates the decision to go to Zara, there was some initial dissent from those amongst the leadership who wanted the army to disband anyway, but this was soon overcome and the agreement to besiege the city was quickly concluded.[22] In fact, as the plan to invest Zara leaked out, it would begin to open up a serious rift amongst the crusaders and to provoke open disobedience to the papacy.

The city of Zara was a wealthy, independent mercantile power compelled to live under the economic shadow of the Venetians. The contemporary author of the *Deeds of the Bishop of Halberstadt* described it thus: 'Zara is surely an exceedingly rich city . . . it is situated on the sea. It is properly fortified with a first-class wall and extremely high towers.'[23]

On many occasions during the twelfth century it had tried to break free from the supervision of its powerful northern neighbour. At the times when they operated under Venetian overlordship, Zaran merchants were given the same privileges in Venice as the native merchants themselves. Patrolling galleys ensured that the Zarans directed their goods through Venice, rather than trading freely to other ports, so that all the taxes flowed into the doge's treasury. Zara was also important in providing much of the wood so essential in the construction of the Venetian fleet; the forests of Dalmatia supplied excellent oak – in contrast to the paucity of such material in the Veneto by this time. In 1181, however, the Zarans had thrown off Venetian authority and six years later they forged a deal with King Bela III of Hungary (1173–96) to move under his protection. Three Venetian attacks on the city failed, but in 1202 the opportunity for the doge to crush his rebellious neighbour and to quell a possible source of disorder during his absence on the crusade was extremely tempting.

Around the same time as he advanced this proposal, the doge bound himself ever closer to the crusading cause – ironically, of course, just as he was about to attack a Christian city. He called together the most important citizens of Venice, along with the leading crusaders, to the church of St Mark's. There, before mass began, he climbed the steps of the lectern and, with the great central dome arching above him, addressed the congregation. Up to this point Dandolo had simply been a commercial contractor, arranging for the transportation of the crusade and acting solely in a business capacity. But in terms of status and spiritual standing he desired to move forward. Dandolo's father, grandfather and uncle had taken part in the crusade of 1122–4 and now he, like the French nobles with crusading traditions, wished to join the line of holy warriors. He acknowledged his physical infirmities, barriers to almost everyone else of his age and condition – 'I am an old man, weak and in need of rest, and my health is failing' – but he pleaded to be allowed to take the cross and 'protect and guide' the Venetians.[24] The congregation cried out their approval: 'We beg you in God's name to take the cross.' There was also a practical political angle here: Enrico ensured that the citizens approved the choice of his son, Renier, to act as his regent, effectively confirming the Dandolo dynasty in power for a second generation. After securing a continuity of government – and, of course, the position of his own family – the old man was led down from the lectern towards the high altar under the easternmost dome of the church. There he knelt sobbing, before handing over his cotton cap to the churchmen standing there. Perhaps in recognition of his status, they departed from convention and sewed a cross onto his headgear rather than his shoulder. Dandolo wanted everyone to see him as a crusader and this in turn inspired many of his citizens to come forward to take the cross. This spiritual commitment drew the Italians and the Frenchmen into a closer bond than before and helped to intensify a shared aim that would sustain the crusade over the next few years. Villehardouin noted that: 'Our [men] watched the doge's taking of the cross with joy and deep emotion, greatly moved by the courage and wisdom shown by this good old man.'[25] For those crusaders who had doubted the Venetian's true intentions this was a persuasive public sign of a religious dimension to his endeavours. Some of the crusaders, meanwhile, had yet to come to terms with the prospect of a campaign at Zara and, the longer they considered it, the more unpopular an idea it became.

The notion of a crusade attacking Christian lands was not new. In 1107–8, Bohemond of Antioch had led an expedition against the Greeks with the endorsement of Pope Paschal II.[26] More recently (1191) Richard the Lionheart had seized Cyprus from Isaac Ducas Comnenus, a renegade member of the Byzantine family, and this had provoked little disquiet in the West. The basic differences between these cases and the Venetian plan was that Zara was a Catholic city. Besieging a city subject to the overlordship of a crusader (in this case, King Emico of Hungary) would mean conflicting with the papal promise to protect the property of all who took the cross. It would, therefore, open up the prospect of excommunication for the attackers. It seems that news of the target began to reach the ordinary troops and there were increasing murmurs of dissent. At this point, however, the level of ill-feeling simmered just below the surface and did not prevent the final preparations for setting sail. The crusaders' horses were led into their stalls below decks and the doors caulked over. Villehardouin mentions that more than 300 siege machines were loaded aboard, including equipment and material for constructing towers and ladders – more evidence of how thoroughly the Venetians had prepared the fleet for the invasion of Egypt and an assault on Alexandria.

Finally, in early October 1202, the Venetians' great fleet took to the seas – at last, the crusade was truly on the move. After the long, morale-sapping months on the Lido, real activity gave renewed energy and vigour to the holy warriors. The eye-witness accounts make plain what a magnificent and stirring sight this made – a kaleidoscope of patterns and movement. Dandolo's own vermilion galley led the way, with the doge himself sheltering under a samite canopy. Before him stood four trumpeters, while above him flew the banner of St Mark depicting a winged lion; on other ships, drummers set up a relentless, driving beat. Each of the crusading nobles had his own vessel: Baldwin, Louis, Hugh, Geoffrey, Martin of Pairis, Conrad of Halberstadt were all accompanied by their own men. Everyone bore the crusaders' cross – traditionally red for the French and green for the Flemings. The knights hung their shields, brightly decorated with their own family colours, from the front of their ship and hoisted their banners aloft to top the masts. A dazzling array of flags and pennons fluttered and shimmered in the autumn breeze. Robert of Clari reported that a hundred pairs of trumpets, of silver and of brass, all sounded at the departure, and he marvelled at the pounding of so many drums and tabors and other instruments. The tumultuous noise generated huge excitement in the crusaders and the explosive array of colour and military strength thrilled everyone and inspired powerful feelings of confidence and anticipation. Yet this conspicuous display of worldly honour and pride did not exclude the spiritual element of the crusade. The pilgrims (as Robert described them) had their priests and clerics mount the towers at the front of each ship and chant the hymn

Veni creator spiritus, a song traditionally associated with crusading that begins with the lines: 'Come Holy Ghost, our souls inspire and lighten with celestial fire.'[27] Everyone wept with emotion as they realised that the great adventure was under way; they slid slowly out from the island city that had been home for the past few months and headed into the Adriatic – the holy war had begun.

As the fleet edged out to sea, the ships began to unfurl their sails like a mass of pupating caterpillars, shedding their cocoons and extending their wings. Robert described the spectacle as 'the finest thing to see that has ever been since the beginning of the world'.[28] He wrote that 'it seemed as if the sea were all a-tremble and all on fire with the ships'. Again, the sense of shared power, of an almost uncontrollable force, seeps out from his writing and conveys the thrill felt by the Christian army.

All did not go smoothly for everyone, however. The *Viola*, one of the largest transport ships, sank. Several French nobles were unable to embark because of ill-health, and one group, led by Stephen of Perche, chose instead to travel to Apulia from where they sailed to the Levant in the spring of 1203. More significantly, Boniface of Montferrat claimed that he needed to attend to urgent matters in his homelands and would rejoin the army as soon as he could. This neatly removed him from participation in the attack on Zara and ensured that the marquis stayed in good standing with the pope.

Sailing east from Venice, the crusade passed by the cities of Trieste and Muglia and secured their submission.[29] In essence, the fleet toured the coast of the north-eastern Adriatic and used the muscle of the crusade to assert Venetian authority over the region. It compelled Istria, Dalmatia and Slavonia to pay tribute and stopped at Pula, where the crusaders landed briefly to gather food and water before carrying on towards Zara, where they arrived on St Martin's Day, 11 November 1202.

By this time, the Zarans had learned of the Venetians' intentions. Spies were ubiquitous in the medieval world and, once the plan became known amongst the crusaders, it was inevitable that the Zarans would discover it soon enough. They prepared to defend themselves.

In Rome, meanwhile, Pope Innocent was well aware of this disturbing development from his representative with the crusade, Cardinal Peter Capuano, who had travelled from Venice to the papal court in the late autumn. Peter had tried to convince the doge to take the crusaders to

Alexandria as originally intended, but he could not persuade Dandolo to excuse payment of the crusaders' debts. The cardinal had some sympathy with the crusaders and appreciated the dreadful dilemma in which they found themselves. For him at least, the greatest priority was to see the crusade carry on. Bishop Conrad of Halberstadt sought Peter's thoughts on the matter; his reply was unequivocal: 'The lord pope would prefer to overlook whatever was unbefitting of them rather than have this pilgrimage campaign disintegrate.'[30] Peter had, in essence, endorsed the move on Zara.

The pope, however, had a different view and one may imagine a particularly frosty reception for the legate as he broke the news of the diversion to Zara and its purpose. Innocent was deeply troubled by this turn of events. He wrote a letter – now lost – in which he utterly forbade the attack on the city under pain of excommunication. In later correspondence he made reference to having taken 'care to prohibit you [the crusaders] strictly from attempting to invade or violate the lands of Christians unless either they wickedly impede your journey or another just or necessary cause should, perhaps, arise that would allow you to act otherwise in accordance with the guidance offered by our legate, [this] should have deterred you from such a very wicked plan'.[31] The *Gesta Innocenti* repeats a similar message. The pope had not envisaged that his legate would sanction such an act. By the threat of excommunication he was deploying the strongest possible weapon in a pope's spiritual armoury. Excommunication meant complete exclusion from the Christian community and an excommunicate was, therefore, denied access to the sacraments and services of the Church, thereby exposing him or her to certain damnation – a matter of the gravest possible concern to all medieval people. For Innocent to consider such a move clearly indicated the depth of his horror at the situation. Abbot Peter of Lucedio conveyed the pope's letter to Zara, where it arrived just as the crusaders encamped outside the city walls.

As the fleet had reached Zara, its citizens had closed their gates and armed themselves as fully as possible, but they were intensely aware that they had virtually no chance of holding out against the crusaders. On 12 November they sent an embassy of leading men to the doge's pavilion and offered to surrender the city and all their possessions if their lives were spared. Dandolo, prudently, said that he could not agree to such terms without first discussing the matter with the crusading nobles – an indication of the doge's unwillingness to be seen by his colleagues as acting independently. Even though the siege of Zara was most obviously a Venetian project, Dandolo was very careful to carry the crusaders with him. Now, however, a damaging rift began to open within the French army.

A group of nobles, headed by Simon of Montfort, were hostile to the campaign and attempted to subvert the entire siege. With many of the senior crusaders closeted with Dandolo, Simon's faction acted boldly. They approached the Zaran envoys and claimed to speak for the French crusaders as a whole. They asked why the Zarans wanted to surrender as they only had to fight the Venetians, and not the Frenchmen who, they promised, would not join in the attack. 'You have nothing to fear from them [the French],' said the negotiators, according to Villehardouin. The Zarans asked for the offer to be repeated publicly and Robert of Boves was chosen to go up to the walls, where he spoke again. On this basis, believing all the crusaders to be at odds with the Venetians, the Zarans chose to break off discussions with their oppressors. Simultaneously, however, the doge had spoken to the majority of the crusading nobles, who had urged him to accept the Zarans' offer. Fortified by this mandate, Dandolo and his advisers returned to his pavilion to inform the envoys of this decision, only to find them departed. The Zarans had no way of knowing that they had dealt with only a splinter of the French nobility and that Robert of Boves was not a spokesman for all his countrymen.

Dandolo was furious at this breach of the crusaders' unity; he had, after all, been at pains to preserve a consensual approach to decision-making. Yet the situation was about to worsen: the intervention of Guy, the Cistercian abbot of Vaux-Cernay (a monastery about 22 miles south-west of Paris), did much to inflame the matter even further. Guy was a close supporter of Simon of Montfort and he had managed to obtain the letter sent by the pope explicitly forbidding the attack on Zara and threatening excommunication on those who disobeyed.

This was, of course, political and emotional dynamite. The abbot read to the assembled nobles from Pope Innocent's letter; he said: 'My lords, in the name of the pope of Rome, I forbid you to attack this city; for the people in it are Christians, and you wear the sign of the cross.'[32] There was no ambiguity in this message – the army was wrong to besiege a crusader's city. For the doge, however, this order took second place to the solemn contractual agreement made between his people and the Frenchmen. When the papal letter was proclaimed, Dandolo reacted angrily: quite apart from the financial question, the Zarans had, in the past, done great harm to his people and deserved to be besieged. Robert of Clari quoted him as saying: 'Lords, know you well that I will not in any degree give over . . . not even for the apostolic [the pope].'[33] He appealed to the crusade leaders to support him: 'You have given your promise to assist me in conquering it [Zara], and now I summon you to keep your word.'[34] The French were faced with a dreadful quandary: disobey the pope and face excommunication, or refuse Dandolo's request and risk the immediate collapse of the crusade.

A furious argument broke out between the doge and Simon of Montfort. Peter of Vaux-Cernay, the nephew of Abbot Guy, wrote that the Venetians threatened his uncle and that Count Simon had to leap up to intervene and prevent the doge's men from murdering Guy.[35] Simon had already shown his displeasure by distancing his force from the siege and now he said: 'I have not come here to destroy Christians.' He spoke of doing no wrong to the Zarans and promised that they 'would suffer no harm from his men'. His mind was made up and he withdrew from the camp.

The crusade was fragmenting ever more seriously. The first fracture had occurred when various contingents chose to embark from ports other than Venice; this episode at Zara represented a second and deeper crack in the cause of the holy war. Earlier crusading campaigns, such as the First Crusade or the siege of Lisbon in 1147 (during the Second Crusade), had succeeded, in large part, because of a unity of minds and military strength; in 1202 these precious and vital attributes were already slipping away fast. The departure of Simon affected both the spiritual and practical aspects of the crusade: their unease over the legitimacy of an attack on a Christian city and the loss of a powerful contingent of knights. The remaining crusaders were even more open to offers of military support from outside parties who might also seek to influence the direction of the expedition.

The actions of Robert of Boves and Simon of Montfort did not only enrage and alienate the Venetians; they also embarrassed their fellow-Frenchmen, who, having given the doge their word that they would besiege the city, felt that their honour would be compromised if they now failed to join the assault. In a remarkable piece of manipulation the leaders of the crusade deliberately chose to conceal the papal letter from the bulk of the army (only the nobles were aware of its contents) and so began the attack on the city. Clearly expediency had triumphed over strict ecclesiastical theory.

The siege of Zara began on 13 November 1202. The defenders hung crosses from the walls in the vain hope of pricking the collective conscience of the remaining crusaders, but to no avail. The holy warriors closed their grip on the city. The navy had already disgorged many of the men and the engines of war so carefully assembled in Venice. The crusaders deployed their formidable array of siege weapons, including petraries and mangonels that set up a steady bombardment of stones and other missiles at, and over, Zara's walls and towers. Unfortunately there is much inconsistency amongst medieval writers concerning the nomenclature and description of these machines. In Roman times a *mangana* was a torsion-driven device that used a single beam whose lower end was embedded into a great horizontal winding of sinew. The arm was pulled back against the tension of the sinew and released to thud against a cross-frame and hurl a stone from a cup at the top end of the beam. Yet it is generally believed that, by the late twelfth century, lever-arm artillery was the main form of siege machine. These devices originated in China and came to Europe via the Arab world in the ninth century. They took the form of a beam pivoted between two uprights. A team of men pulled on one end of it and the other flew up, releasing a missile from a cup or a sling. They could probably throw a 33-pound stone about 400 feet – a capability that would have had little effect against strong castle walls, though it might damage the more vulnerable walkways and overhanging wooden structures known as machicolations. They could also harass soldiers and cause serious casualties, which meant that defending troops employed them as well. The petrary was probably a bigger version of these machines and was designed for use against city walls, while the mangonel was more appropriate as an anti-personnel device.[36]

On their arrival at Zara the crusading fleet had smashed through a chain that stretched across the harbour entrance (and acted as a gate to the port). This allowed them to draw up their ships close to the walls and set scaling ladders from them to mount the defences. The *Devastatio*

Constantinopolitana records: 'They besieged Zara from every side, both on land and water. They erected more than 150 machines, mangonels, as well as ladders, wooden towers and numerous instruments of war.'[37]

For five days the crusaders tried to batter or climb their way into the city, but to little avail. They decided, therefore, to employ probably the most effective of all medieval siege weapons: the mine. The creation of a mine was a dangerous and complex affair that usually involved the construction of a series of underground galleries running towards the walls of the besieged city or stronghold. The type of ground determined how easy or difficult it was to dig such a structure. Marshy land or extensive water defences afforded some protection against the mine. In firmer conditions the passage was dug out and supported with wooden posts. When the mine was judged to be under the walls, the end of the shaft was filled with brushwood and other inflammable material and ignited. This explosion and the burning of the supports was intended to bring down both the tunnel and the wall above it, leaving a gaping chasm for the attackers to pour through. Muslims and Christians alike had used these techniques to deadly effect throughout the medieval age: at the siege of Lisbon in 1147 the crusaders constructed a huge series of mines. The eye-witness *Conquest of Lisbon* states:

> The [crusaders] began to dig a mine beneath the wall of the strong-
> hold – a mine which, marvellous to relate, had five entrances and
> extended inside to a depth of forty cubits from the front; and they
> completed it within a month . . . When the wall had been under-
> mined and inflammable material had been placed in the mine and
> lighted, the same night at cockcrow about thirty cubits of the wall
> crumbled to the ground. Then the Muslims who were guarding the
> wall were heard to cry out in their anguish that they might now
> make an end of their long labours and that this very day would be
> their last.[38]

Three years earlier, Zengi, the Muslim ruler of Aleppo, had mined his way into the Christian city of Edessa in northern Syria. In 1202 the Zarans recognised the lethal nature of a mining campaign and immediately offered to surrender on the original terms they had proposed.

On 24 November the city opened its gates and, as with almost all medieval sieges, the victors divided the spoils. The crusaders had promised to spare the lives of those within, but this did not prevent the city being ransacked. One church held the body of St Chrysogonus; ironically, 24 November was his feast-day, but unfortunately for the Zarans he afforded them no divine protection.[39] Gunther of Pairis claimed that Zara fell without slaughter or bloodshed. Pope Innocent, on the other hand, accused the crusaders of taking lives in the course of the siege, rather than in the later occupation of the city.[40]

Once Zara fell, the expedition was obliged to pause. Dandolo pointed out the practicalities of the sailing season – winter was upon the crusading host and it was impossible to continue any further. In any case, Zara was a wealthy city that could provide the supplies the expedition needed. The doge's men took the half of the city nearest the harbour and the French the other part, each group commandeering the finest houses for its leading men.

As 1202 drew to a close Dandolo could reflect with some satisfaction on having quelled his rebellious neighbour. His crusading associates must have had more mixed feelings; their great enterprise had made a number of faltering steps: the loss of Thibaut of Champagne; the near-disaster of the shortfall of men at Venice; and then the limited progress of the campaign, still high up in the Adriatic. On the other hand, Thibaut's replacement was a highly prestigious man, the expedition was still moving, it was superbly equipped and had already revealed lethal military effectiveness. Overarching all of this, however, the crusaders' immediate anxiety was the reaction of Pope Innocent when he heard of the fall of Zara.

The leaders' concern was soon apparent because they sent a mission to the pope in the hope of securing absolution from their excommunication. In part, this seems questionable because they had already taken Zara and were not likely to surrender it, whatever Innocent decreed. Yet an embassy to Rome was also a way to mollify the mass of crusaders who would almost certainly react with anger and violence when the news of the excommunication was publicly announced. The sack of Zara did not mean that the senior nobility had entirely abandoned the spiritual dimension of their work. The very fact that these men were on crusade in the first instance was a clear demonstration of their religious sincerity, yet trying to reconcile that piety with the demands of leading a crusade so deeply in debt was a challenge that seemed almost beyond the experience and the abilities of any of them.

An embassy of four men – Bishop Nivelo of Soissons; John of Noyen, a cleric who was Count Baldwin's chancellor; Robert of Boves; and John of Friaise – set out for Rome in December 1202 to seek absolution for the crusaders' actions. The Venetians did not send a representative, feeling that they had done nothing wrong and had no case to answer: an apparently confrontational approach, although one that Dandolo explained in a later letter to the pope. So far as he was concerned, the Zarans had deserved to be attacked because they had broken their feudal oaths to the Venetians. More contentiously, Dandolo asserted that he could not believe that the pope would offer protection to a man such as Emico who bore the cross for false reasons. He wrote that the king assumed the cross 'only in order to wear it, not even to complete the journey for which pilgrims normally assume the cross but to acquire the possessions of another and to criminally hold them'.[41] The doge knew that Emico had taken the cross in 1200 mainly to use as a shield in a civil war with his brother Andrew, and that he had little intention of ever journeying to the Holy Land. Hindsight would bear this view out but, in the short term, it was not an argument well received in Rome.

Gunther of Pairis records that Abbot Martin joined the mission as an unofficial delegate to represent the German crusaders. Gunther has left an account of his abbot's thoughts about this episode. In part, this may be an attempt to distance Martin from the events at Zara, but it also demonstrates the abbot's profound spiritual unease at the direction of the crusade: 'When Martin saw not only the entire business of the Cross tied up in delays but also our entire army being forced to shed Christian blood, he did not know where to turn or what to do. He was totally terror-stricken, and from many choices, all of which displeased him, he opted for the one which, in that particular situation, seemed best.'[42] A sense of being boxed into a corner, of being powerless to follow his own wishes, ensnared the abbot. Just 19 months earlier he had been sobbing with religious zeal, exhorting the people of Basel to help save the Holy Land. For a man who had inspired hundreds of individuals to take the cross to be so drained of motivation shows how the cruel realities of the Fourth Crusade contrasted with the high hopes with which the expedition had started. So distraught was Martin that he had tried to remove himself from the crusade: he went to Cardinal Peter Capuano and asked to be dispensed from his vow in order to return to the cloister. The cardinal rebuked him for his weakness and utterly forbade Martin to go home before completing his pilgrimage.

Some crusaders had already left Venice and gone to Rome to obtain a similar dispensation where, unwillingly, Innocent had granted such permission on the condition that their vow was deferred for a few years. Most of these individuals were poorer men whose absence would have only a limited effect on the expedition, although, as Gunther of Pairis observed, 'their defection . . . dampened the deep fervour' of others planning to join the crusade and affected the morale of those who remained.[43] The idea of allowing so important a figure as Abbot Martin to leave could not be countenanced and, by way of tying him to the crusade even more closely, Capuano confirmed him in the role of spiritual guardian of the Germans on the expedition and charged the abbot to remain alongside the soldiers at all times to try to restrain them from shedding Christian blood. Martin was saddened that his request was turned down, yet as Gunther relates, he steeled himself to carry on, to fulfil his vow and to bear his new responsibilities:

> How Martin groaned, when leave was denied him.
> Who could imagine it, who would believe it if I tried to relate it?
> He stands wavering; a man of devout mind, he stands with
>   breaking heart.
> Pained in his breast, he has no wish for such things, and,
>   like one constrained,
> He fears for himself and his comrades. He fears even more
> For himself and his people lest he be party to wicked slaughter.
> Yet he submits and suffers to yield to his vows;
> He pledges to go on; barely the better course, but his heart is
>   not in it.[44]

Back in Zara, trouble soon erupted amongst the crusading forces as they settled down for winter. In the event of a successful siege, conflict between the victorious contingents was a frequent occurrence. Sometimes this reflected long-standing tensions between groups from different areas, rather like modern-day football fans reliving old grudges and running riot through the streets of a foreign city. The problem in Zara had a different cause: only three days after the conquest a furious affray broke out between the Venetians and what Robert of Clari described as 'the lesser people' from France. This was not the product of some old enmity, but more likely a squabble over the division of booty: a legacy of the controversy over the payment for the sea passage and the relative poverty of the Frenchmen.

The cost of the sea passage would have made a substantial impact on the resources of most of the rank-and-file crusaders. Furthermore, as we saw earlier, the nobles had tried to extract from them even more cash to cover the financial shortfall caused by the lack of men arriving at Venice. For the ordinary soldiers, the sack of a city was a rare opportunity to acquire money and to cover the large sums already spent. The fact that Zara was a Christian city was a matter of real concern to some of these men, but, by late November, it had been captured, whether morally right or wrong. If another party (in this case, the Venetians) tried to appropriate desperately needed booty – and if that group was already perceived as being wealthy and greedy anyway – then men would fight to hold on to their winnings.

In the early evening of 27 November an argument broke out between groups of Frenchmen and Venetians. Conflict soon ripped through the city. What began as a localised brawl became all-out war with men rushing to arms, the streets ringing with the clash of swords, the whirring of crossbow bolts and the cries of the angry, the wounded and the dying. Faced with this breakdown of proper order, the crusade leaders had to intervene. Baldwin and Louis donned their full armour and charged into the affray to try to break it up, but so ferocious was the disturbance that, like a wild forest fire, as soon as it was quelled in one area, it sprang alight in another. All through the night the riot carried on until the combatants wore themselves out and finally calm prevailed. It was fortunate that the city itself was not burned to the ground, because the likelihood of fire during a riot was always high. Both the Venetians and the French suffered losses; a Flemish noble, Gilles of Landast, was struck in the eye and later died of his wound, and many lesser men were lost. The *Devastatio Constantinopolitana* gives a figure of almost 100 dead.[45] In the days afterwards, both the doge and the French nobles laboured steadily to bring peace to the two groups and to heal whatever the source of the conflict was. Villehardouin felt that the whole episode had been so serious that the army had a 'narrow escape from being completely wiped out'.[46] Yet Baldwin, Louis and the doge evidently soothed the situation to good effect because Robert of Clari was able to write that 'they made so good a peace that never afterwards was there ill-will between them'.[47]

Before the crusaders' envoys could reach Rome, a letter from the papacy arrived at Zara. Innocent had heard of the capture of the city and was plainly both furious and saddened at this turn of events. His message made the depth of his feelings abundantly plain, and to anyone reading the letter his sense of anger and distaste rings out loud and clear. He believed that the sense of moral right that a successful crusade army should naturally possess had been compromised and corrupted: 'Behold, your gold has turned into base metal and your silver has almost completely rusted since, departing from the purity of your plan and turning aside from the path onto the impassable road, you have, so to speak, withdrawn your hand from the plough . . . for when . . . you should have hastened to the land flowing with milk and honey, you turned away, going astray in the direction of the desert.'[48]

Innocent blamed the Devil – envious of the sacrifice the crusaders were making – for causing them to make war on their fellow-Christians, 'so that you might pay him [the Devil] the first fruits of your pilgrimage and pour out for demons your own and your brothers' blood'. Aside from Satan, others were at fault, too: Innocent did not hide his view as to who the real culprits were and noted that the crusaders had fallen in 'with thieves' – by which he undoubtedly meant the Venetians. 'Although they stripped you of the mantle of virtues laid upon you . . . so far they have not wished to depart or to leave you half alive.' Innocent criticised the taking of supplies from Trieste and Muglia, before turning to the sack of Zara. More seriously, he accused the crusaders of showing no mercy to a people whose city walls were decorated with the cross: 'but you attacked the city and the citizens to the not insubstantial injury of the Crucified One, and what is more, by violent skill, you compelled them to surrender'.[49]

The pope also railed against the fact that King Emico of Hungary and his brother, Duke Andrew, were signed with the cross. Innocent reminded the crusading army of his earlier prohibitions against turning against Christian territories.[50] Clearly he had disapproved of Peter

Capuano's advice to the crusaders that the greater good of sustaining the crusade took precedence over the necessary evil of attacking Zara. It is noticeable that Peter did not rejoin the crusade until 1204, a delay that may be explained by Innocent's anger.

The pope could not let this flagrant disregard for his authority pass and he concluded his missive with a punishment. He reminded his audience that, had they listened to his earlier letters, they would remember that those who contravened his orders were to be excommunicated and – crucially for a crusader – denied the benefit of the indulgence (the remission of all sins), one of the principal reasons for taking the cross in the first instance. Such a sentence would have enormously perturbed many of the crusaders. Innocent also mentioned that the Venetians had knocked down walls and buildings and robbed churches in Zara and he ordered, in the strongest possible terms, that this should stop. The letter closed with another reminder that the granting of the remission of sins was withdrawn from the excommunicate army.

Here, for the first time during the crusade, the limitations of papal authority are clearly revealed. Innocent had the power to call a crusade and to direct its preaching and aspects of its fundraising. In spite of having legates to represent him, however, he could not exert direct control over them especially if, as in Peter Capuano's case, they exercised their own judgement. While he could threaten excommunication and expressly forbid certain actions, Innocent's power, to a large extent, relied on the consent of the other parties involved. At Zara the crusade leaders faced the terrible dilemma of attacking a Christian city or seeing their great enterprise fold. In the circumstances they chose to suppress Innocent's letter in order to pursue their own ends and to prevent widespread disquiet amongst the crusader host. In acting thus, they ignored papal authority and Innocent could do little to undo what had already happened.

The Venetians, of course, had a different agenda from the papacy. Their basic religiosity should not be underestimated, but it was a faith coupled with an intensely practical edge. As we have seen, they had (in common with the Pisans and the Genoese) engaged in commercial relations with the Muslims. With the failure of the crusaders to deliver the promised men and payment, the doge felt that his city's survival was threatened; in such a case the interests of Venice were placed first and those of the papacy had either to fall in line with those needs or be turned aside.

After the capture of Zara, Innocent must have been painfully aware of his restricted ability to direct the crusade. The disobedience to papal commands, the Venetians' insouciance and the sacking of a crusader city were not forgotten as he tried to steer the expedition in a way pleasing to God. Innocent was not, of course, powerless – the mission seeking papal absolution for the conquest of Zara was proof of that – but recent events had given him much to be concerned about.

CHAPTER SEVEN

'It is your duty to restore their possessions to those who
have been wrongfully dispossessed'

The Offer from Prince Alexius,
December 1202–May 1203

IN LATE DECEMBER 1202, with the army settled down to winter at
Zara, ambassadors arrived seeking an audience with the doge and the
crusade leaders. The envoys represented Philip of Swabia and Prince
Alexius and they put forward an intriguing proposition, artfully phrased
and carefully calculated to fulfil the wishes of the Byzantine prince, the
crusaders and, by association, Pope Innocent III. Also present was Boniface
of Montferrat who had now joined his fellow-crusaders at Zara. The
envoys' message began:

> Since you are on the march in the service of God, and for right and
> justice, it is your duty to restore their possessions to those who have
> been wrongfully dispossessed. The Prince Alexius will make the best
> terms with you ever offered to any people and give you the most
> powerful support in conquering the land overseas . . . Firstly, if God
> permits you to restore his inheritance to him, he will place his whole
> empire under the authority of Rome, from which it has long been
> estranged. Secondly, since he is aware that you have spent all your
> money and now have nothing, he will give you 200,000 silver marks,
> and provisions for every man in your army, officers and men alike.
> Moreover, he himself will go in your company to Egypt with 10,000
> men, or, if you prefer it, send the same number of men with you;
> and furthermore, so long as he lives, he will maintain, at his own
> expense, 500 knights to keep guard in the land overseas.[1]

Clearly the young Alexius was not deterred by his earlier rebuttals from Boniface and Pope Innocent and now continued in his efforts to convince the westerners to help him. The prince's approach was based on a combination of moral justification – linking the purpose of the crusade in restoring Christian lands to the recovery of his own claim to the Byzantine inheritance – and the prospect of material and political advantages.

Undeniably, on the surface, these were hugely attractive inducements that seemed to answer the needs and aspirations of almost all the parties involved in the expedition. The first part of the offer concerning the recognition of the primacy of Rome was primarily aimed at the pope. Prince Alexius and his advisers knew of Innocent's profound hostility to deploying the army against the Christians of Zara; they were also aware of his earlier rejection of the idea of removing Emperor Alexius III. To overcome this opposition would require something of singular allure. The prince had just such an idea: if the usurper were deposed, he indicated that the long-desired acknowledgement of papal authority over the Orthodox Church would follow. Perhaps Prince Alexius had already made this suggestion to Innocent at their meeting in early 1202. At Zara, however, he was hoping to persuade the crusader churchmen to agree to the plan, counting on the fact that the material advantages for the expedition could help to win them over. The prince might have calculated that the need to keep the crusade going, coupled with the submission of the Orthodox Church to Rome, formed an irresistible combination. If the churchmen at Zara could be convinced, might not Innocent too be persuaded? Or, more cynically, if the agreement was already a *fait accompli*, Innocent could have little hope of preventing the deal going through – in the same way that his pronouncements on Zara had been ignored.

Gunther of Pairis pointed to a more aggressive undercurrent to the envoys' offer to the crusaders: 'It helped that they knew that this very city [Constantinople] was rebellious and offensive to the Holy Roman Church, and they did not think its conquest by our people would displease very much either the supreme pontiff or even God.'[2] While this was not Innocent's position thus far stated, it is interesting that he was perceived as having such a viewpoint and it might help to explain the envoys' chosen line of approach.

For the French crusaders, Prince Alexius held out a tantalising prospect: relief from the debts that had crippled their expedition for so long. The capture of Zara had not alleviated their financial position – it had only been intended as a means to defer payment – and, as the envoys so candidly pointed out, the crusaders had nothing. Thus the sum of 200,000 silver marks, plus provisions for the entire army, would remove these worries in one sweep. Coupled with this financial bonanza, the addition of 10,000 men to the crusader army would do much to make up for the initial shortfall at Venice and would help replace those who had slipped away from the army en route. The terms of Prince Alexius's offer had an eye to the future as well: the notion of a fully financed garrison of 500 knights to help sustain the Christian hold on the Holy Land was also highly desirable. Experience had shown that after completing their vows most crusaders returned home, leaving only the limited resources of the Frankish settlers in the Levant to face the inevitable Muslim counter-attack. An extra 500 knights would massively strengthen the army of the Holy Land and do much to secure the Christian presence in the eastern Mediterranean.

In return for all of this, however, there was the need to restore the prince to power, an enterprise that required the crusade to divert to, and possibly attack, the Christian city of Constantinople. For a second time therefore the expedition would have to turn its weapons against people of its own faith, rather than the infidel. The envoys assured their audience that they had full power to conclude such an agreement and closed their address by pointing out that 'such favourable conditions have never been offered to anyone, and the man who could refuse to accept them can have little wish to conquer anything at all'.[3] The doge and the crusade leaders could not be rushed into a decision of this importance. They realised that a wider assembly of the nobles and leading churchmen had to debate the matter and a meeting was called for the following day.

The Fourth Crusade had already endured a series of crises: the death of Thibaut of Champagne, the lack of men arriving at Venice, the decision to attack Zara and the papal bull of excommunication. This new proposal was, however, potentially the most inflammatory and destructive of all. The deficit in men and money at Venice continued to exert a terrible grip on the crusade and the continuing requirement to redress these issues was the prime reason why the expedition found itself in such an invidious position.

'There was a great divergence of opinion in the assembly.'[4] With masterly understatement, Villehardouin opened his account of the meeting: the lines of argument were familiar and the manner in which each side expressed its case as unbending and forceful as ever. The events at Zara had shown that there were already sharp divisions amongst the crusaders and, here again, it was Abbot Guy of Vaux-Cernay who opened the debate by emphasising the most basic reason for his opposition to any agreement with the prince – that 'it would mean marching against Christians. They [the crusaders] had not left their homes to do any such thing and for their part they wished to go to Syria [as the Holy Land is sometimes called].'[5] 'We must insist,' came the fairly predictable response 'that only by way of Egypt and Greece [in other words, Constantinople] can we hope to recover the land overseas.'[6]

So deep were the differences amongst the crusaders that even the Cistercian abbots on the crusade disagreed with one another. Guy of Vaux-Cernay found a bitter opponent in his fellow white monk, Abbot Simon of Loos. Simon was a close associate of Count Baldwin of Flanders and represented those who wished to keep the expedition going. He preached to the crusaders and exhorted them to accept the agreement because 'it offered the best chance of winning back the lands overseas'. Guy of Vaux-Cernay was unmoved – this plan was flawed and the expedition should go to Syria to achieve something of worth.

Those in favour of the campaign could claim that the crusade was not, in a formal sense, being directed against the Greeks but, according to Prince Alexius's reasoning, was a morally justifiable war to reinstate the rightful ruler of Byzantium. To their opponents, the distinction was not so plain and the image of men bearing the cross of Christ fighting their way into another Christian city – particularly one of the five great patriarchal seats of the faith (the others were Jerusalem, Rome, Antioch and Alexandria) – was utterly repugnant and abhorrent.

Some may have raised questions about the validity of Prince Alexius's claim. He was born before his father's reign began and not, therefore, 'in the purple' (a reference to the colour of the purple chamber in the Bucoleon palace where the consorts of reigning emperors gave birth to their children) and so by custom had no legitimate right to the throne. Innocent himself demonstrated his awareness of the issue in a letter of November 1202 and knowledge of this point was probably widespread.[7]

The prince's emphasis on the wrongful deposition of his father was, however, a stronger basis to claim redress. Some opponents of the diversion, however, might have remembered that Alexius's father, the blinded Isaac Angelos, had been supportive of Saladin at the time of the Third Crusade. Why should the army of Christ assist Isaac and his son now? Alexius would argue, of course, that he was not party to that agreement and now desired to help the crusaders.

Underlying this high-level debate were the opinions of the lesser men, illuminated for us by Robert of Clari. Unlike Villehardouin, Robert's first concerns during the winter in Zara were not matters of high politics, but of an immediate and practical nature. Their stay in the city was cutting into the crusaders' supplies and, for all the descriptions of Zara's apparent prosperity, it seems that the conquest had yielded little real profit to those in the lower ranks. Robert describes the crusaders talking anxiously with one another and fretting because they had insufficient money to get to Egypt or Syria, or indeed to accomplish anything of value anywhere. All these needs might be answered, however, if they accepted Prince Alexius's offer. On the other hand, there still remained the moral dimension to the debate. These men had taken the cross out of a fervent desire to help recover the Holy Land for the Christian faith. The balance between what was necessary to keep the crusade going and the outright distortion of that vow was proving extraordinarily difficult to achieve and required the men to make some very uncomfortable choices. The other source from around the camp-fire, the *Devastatio Constantinopolitana*, shows that for some the two issues could not be reconciled and a section of 'the rank and file . . . swore that they would never go [to Constantinople]'.

For those less dogmatic there was still a need to justify the diversion to Byzantium. Robert of Clari gives his own account of this, although his chronology is confused because he places the main debate about the diversion on Corfu, the crusaders' next destination after Zara. Nonetheless, he provides some interesting views of what he — as a lesser knight — perceived as the ideas of several key players. For example, he credits the doge and Marquis Boniface with encouraging Alexius's offer. Dandolo acknowledged the crusaders' poverty and made the point that Greece [Byzantium] was a wealthy land and that if 'we could have a reasonable excuse for going there and taking the provisions and other things . . . then we should well be able to go overseas'.[8] The need for a 'reasonable excuse' echoed Pope Innocent's earlier prohibition on attacking Christian lands unless 'a just or necessary cause should arise'. By an uncanny coincidence, Boniface was on hand to provide this and he described meeting Prince Alexius at Hagenau and how Emperor Isaac had lost the throne by treason. He argued that it would be right to reinstate him and that this in turn would release the much-needed supplies.

Robert represents Boniface of Montferrat as a particularly passionate advocate of the deal with the prince. He explains the marquis's motivation thus: 'he wanted to avenge himself for an injury which the emperor of Constantinople . . . had done to him'. Boniface was said to 'hate' Emperor Alexius III.[9] The episode at issue dated from 1187 when, as we saw earlier, Boniface's brother Conrad had married Theodora of Constantinople and had helped the emperor to fight off a rebellion, only to be poorly rewarded and hounded into leaving the city for the Holy Land. In fact, Robert was seriously mistaken because the emperor at the time was Prince Alexius's father, Isaac Angelos. Some of the lesser crusaders clearly saw Boniface as motivated by personal revenge in wanting to direct the crusade to Constantinople: a proportion of the French crusaders at least seemed rather suspicious of their north Italian leader.

The doge, too, was suspected by some (often with the benefit of hindsight) of advocating the move to Constantinople for purely financial reasons. Gunther of Pairis felt that the Venetian interest view was based 'partly in the hope of the promised money (for which that race is extremely greedy), and partly because their city, supported by a large navy, was, in fact, arrogating to itself sovereign mastery over that entire sea'.[10]

Venetian involvement in Constantinople dated back centuries and encompassed close political, economic and cultural ties.[11] The period leading up to the Fourth Crusade had witnessed several turbulent episodes in the relationship between the two cities and this formed a difficult background to the campaign. As far back as 1082 the Venetians had been granted generous privileges across most of the Byzantine Empire and this had resulted in a flourishing community based in Constantinople, exporting oil and pepper. Under Emperor John Comnenus (1118–43) the concession of rights on Crete and Cyprus boosted trade with North Africa and the Holy Land and led to a substantially increased investment in the Byzantine Empire. Theban silk came to be an important part of Venetian trade. It is difficult to ascertain why, on 12 March 1171, Emperor Manuel Comnenus ordered the arrest of all Venetians in his empire and the seizure of their property. A dispute between Venetians and their Genoese rivals in Constantinople was the immediate reason for tension, but there were other causes lying beneath the surface. The Greek sources hint at friction over the status of Venetians settled and intermarried in Byzantine lands. This gave them even greater privileges and created a powerful, but effectively independent, group of people within Manuel's territory. The wider politics of the complex relationship between Manuel, the German Empire, the papacy and the Italian trading cities was also a contributory factor in the violence between Genoese and Venetians in Constantinople.

The Venetian response was to send a fleet led by Doge Vitale Michiel to ravage the Byzantine island of Euboea and then to spend the winter of 1171 on Chios. There the Italians were struck with plague, which ruined their military strength and led them to make several attempts to find a diplomatic solution to the problem. In the end, Vitale Michiel was compelled to return home where an angry mob murdered him on account of his failure to avenge the damage to Venetian interests in Constantinople. A treaty was eventually settled upon, which assessed compensation at 1,500 pounds of gold (or 108,000 coins) for the Italians' losses in Constantinople. The post-Comneni regime endorsed these arrangements and in 1187 and 1189 Isaac confirmed and enlarged the Venetians' old privileges, although he also offered good terms to the Pisans and Genoese.[12] In 1195 the pro-Pisan Emperor Alexius III raised tensions with the Venetians and another round of embassies agreed to pay the 400 pounds of gold still owed. Yet in reality, by the turn of the twelfth century, the relationship between the Greeks and the Venetians, which by treaty had seemed to restore much of the latter's good standing, was probably damaged beyond repair. This background, unsurprisingly, led men such as Gunther of Pairis to look upon Dandolo's actions as motivated by the prospect of commercial advantage.

Whatever the masses thought, and regardless of the discord that would inevitably follow, a core of the crusader elite was determined to accept Prince Alexius's offer and to push ahead with the expedition to Constantinople. Gunther of Pairis astutely grasped the reality of the situation, recognising the cumulative effect of these different interests: 'Through the union of all of these factors and, perhaps, of others, it happened that all unanimously found in favour of the young man and promised him their aid.'[13] Doge Dandolo expressed his support for the proposal; Boniface, Baldwin of Flanders, Louis of Blois and Hugh of Saint-Pol concurred and summoned the envoys to the doge's quarters in Zara, where they swore to the agreement and signed and sealed charters confirming the covenant.[14] The crusade was headed for Constantinople.

The unswerving resolve of these men was plain. Baldwin, Louis and Hugh had been the driving force of the crusade since the tournament at Écry in November 1199. They had been bound together by the fateful agreement of April 1201 (with Venice), through which Dandolo and Boniface became tied in with them. For these crusaders, a sense of honour and obligation required them to continue the expedition at all costs, to try to bring succour to the Holy Land and to preserve their vow to assist the Christian cause. The allure of Prince Alexius's wealth was such that his offer could not be resisted, but his position as a wrongfully deposed heir also struck a deep chord with the ruling families of Europe. A usurpation was an upset to the natural order of things and it was for this very reason that the prince's envoys laid such emphasis on the matter. A number of the crusading bishops ruled that to help the prince would be 'a righteous deed', which doubtless helped to smooth over the concerns of some about the morality of their actions.[15]

The leadership needed every morsel of justification because, outside the inner group of nobles, very few supported the decision to go to Constantinople. Once again, the unity so crucial to a successful crusade was being eroded. Villehardouin offers this candid comment: 'I must tell you that only twelve persons in all took the oaths on behalf of the French; no more could be persuaded to come forward.' This was a desperately small number from those available and was a blunt demonstration of the limited enthusiasm for this plan.[16] The tensions amongst the senior nobles themselves, and the strain of a part of the leadership trying to impose its will on a divided and disconcerted army, created enormous pressures in the crusader camp. The marshal noted: 'I can assure you that the hearts of our people were not at peace, for one party was continually working to break up the army and the other to keep it together.'[17] In addition to these anxieties, there was a constant fear of attack by King Emico of Hungary, who was understandably angered at the loss of Zara.

The corrosive effects of the decision to assist Prince Alexius soon touched every part of the camp. Villehardouin wrote that many of the lower ranks took ship and, when one sank, 500 men were lost. Others tried to march north through Slovenia, but were attacked by locals and the survivors were compelled to return to Zara. The Bavarian noble, Werner of Boland, stole away on a merchant ship, much to the contempt of those who remained. Even more seriously, a contingent of several senior French knights, led by Reynald of Montmirail (a cousin of Count Louis of Blois, no less), begged leave to go on a mission to Syria, apparently to inform those in the Levant of what was happening and to visit the holy sites as pilgrims. These men swore on the Bible that they would remain in the Holy Land for no longer than two weeks and that they would then return to the main host. They duly departed, but in spite of their oaths, they did not reappear at the siege of Constantinople, although Reynald rejoined his colleagues after the capture of the Byzantine Empire and fought and died in its defence in April 1205.[18] Villehardouin summarised the position at Zara: 'Thus, our forces dwindled seriously from day to day.'[19] In one sense these desertions had a positive effect on those who remained because they banded together even more closely – a kinship born of adversity. While the crusader force shrank, its resolve to continue grew ever stronger. According to Villehardouin, only divine favour allowed the remains of the army to stay firm in the face of its trials.

One ray of hope appeared to lie in the news that the Flemish fleet under John of Nesles had reached Marseille and, after wintering there, awaited orders as to where to meet the main force. The French nobles and the doge counted greatly on the manpower and logistical support that this contingent would provide. They ordered John to leave Marseille in late March 1202 and to rendezvous with the Venetian fleet at the port of Methoni on the westernmost finger of the Peloponnese peninsula. Evidently, however, John and his fellow-crusaders cared little for the plan to attack Constantinople and they sailed directly to Syria to join the growing number of men who preferred to fight in the Holy Land.[20] Without the immediate pressure of debt to the Venetians, the persuasive presence of Alexius's envoys or the iron determination of the leadership, these Flemings plainly disapproved of the new direction of the crusade.

In parallel to the disturbing events at Zara was the ongoing mission to Rome. The envoys begged Innocent for absolution from his ban of excommunication and the removal of the crusaders' spiritual rewards. The embassy argued that the men had no choice in the matter and that the fault lay with those who had not arrived in Venice. Those who did assemble and went on to fight at Zara had acted out of the need to keep the army together.

In February 1203 Innocent sent a letter back to the crusader force. The envoys seem to have done much to mollify him. He still expressed anger that 'although you bore the Cross of Christ, you later turned your arms against Him. And you, who should have attacked the land of the Saracens, occupied Christian Zara.' The pope noted the crusaders' explanation that they were compelled to act out of necessity, although he said that this did not excuse their cruelty. Nevertheless, he acknowledged their wish to perform penance and told them (meaning particularly the Venetians) to return all the spoils gained at Zara. He ruled that the absolution granted by the bishops on the crusade was invalid and ordered Peter Capuano or his representative to perform this properly. Innocent also demanded oaths – in by now familiar terms – that required the crusaders to guarantee that in future they would 'neither invade nor violate the lands of Christians in any manner, unless, perchance, they wickedly impede your journey or another just or necessary cause should, perhaps, arise, on account of which you would be empowered to act otherwise according to the guidance offered by the Apostolic See'.[21]

This latter clause is intriguingly ambiguous; what constituted 'just and necessary cause'? Although the requirement of papal approval was some attempt to guard against a self-interested interpretation of this, there was, perhaps, room for a generous understanding of the papal mandate to suit a variety of situations.

Innocent himself faced a difficult time as the city of Rome underwent one of its frequent periods of civil unrest. He was forced to flee to nearby Ferentino where he reflected on the progress of the crusade. The pope recognised the problems created by the limited size of the armies that had assembled at Venice. He recalled his original conception of the campaign as being led by the rulers of England (now King John) and France, and in letters sent to these men he expressed his frustration that their continuing conflict was making a major crusading expedition impossible. He linked the Anglo-French struggle directly to problems in the Levant, where the Muslims rejoiced in Christian discord because it allowed them to grow ever stronger. He also connected the enemy's optimism to the crusaders' diversion to Zara and hinted that they 'have planned to try worse things' – a possible reference to the proposed diversion to

Constantinople. Once again, the pope's mention of the content of these rumours (as they were at the time) shows his problems in exercising genuine influence over the expedition.[22]

A little later the crusade leaders sent a letter to Innocent reporting that Cardinal Peter's nuncio had visited them and absolved them of their sins, although the Venetians refused to repent and had been formally placed under a bull of anathema. The letter also pleaded with the pope to view leniently Boniface of Montferrat's suppression of this bull, which was done to keep the fleet together and so help the cause of the Holy Land.[23]

Boniface himself wrote a letter in the same vein, again arguing for the need to conceal the bull in order to hold the army together. While this was true, it is also plain that the publication of a bull excommunicating the Venetians would give considerable ammunition to those who argued against the diversion to Constantinople.[24]

As spring drew on the crusaders began to prepare to leave Zara and they refettled their ships, packed their equipment and loaded up their horses. The Venetians, however, had neither forgiven nor forgotten the Zarans' repeated efforts to escape their overlordship. As a gesture of their strength and a dire warning to the Zarans not to forget their new oaths of fealty, they razed the city to the ground, including all its walls and towers; only the churches were spared.

Before the fleet embarked there was one final, if predictable, twist of events. Simon of Montfort and his associates, including Abbot Guy of Vaux-Cernay, declined to join their colleagues and went over to King Emico of Hungary's lands. Simon was a senior figure and this represented a serious desertion, but it did at least remove the most vocal critics from the crusader force.

Just before the doge and Marquis Boniface departed from Zara, Prince Alexius himself arrived. The prince's appearance was well timed – possibly deliberately – to coincide with St Mark's Day (25 April); a moment likely to find the Venetians in particularly good spirits. The young man was given a warm reception and the Venetians provided him with galleys and crew.[25]

The main crusader fleet planned to sail south and reassemble at Corfu. As the prince and the Venetians followed the bulk of the force, they passed the city of Durazzo, located on the north-western edge of the Byzantine Empire. Here, encouragingly, the citizens immediately gave their town over to Prince Alexius and swore allegiance to him. Whether this was simple prudence, particularly given the crusaders' recent actions at Zara, or a genuine enthusiasm for the pretender is unclear. The young man must have been cheered by this development and it probably heartened the crusade's leaders that Alexius's people seemed to welcome his appearance — perhaps Constantinople would embrace the prince equally quickly.

Ultimately, such hopes would prove to be without foundation, although at first all seemed to be progressing to plan. Because Prince Alexius reached Zara after the majority of the French crusaders had sailed southwards, his first encounter with most of them took place on Corfu. The crusaders had already pitched their tents and pavilions and were giving their horses much-needed exercise when the news of his arrival began to spread. Knights, nobles and ordinary crusaders hurried to the port, curious to see the man in whom their leaders had vested so much and who promised to answer so many of their needs. Initial impressions were positive: the prince was greeted with great ceremony and honour and his tent was erected in the centre of the crusader army, right next to that of Boniface of Montferrat in whose charge Philip of Swabia had placed his young brother-in-law.

Because the deal struck between the nobles and the Byzantine envoys had not commanded full support, the controversy had rumbled on. The presence of Prince Alexius inevitably reopened the festering issue of advancing on Constantinople. Now yet another section of the army threatened to fracture away. Alexius would soon be left in the company of such a small force that his hope of forcing his way back into Constantinople would be extinguished.

A letter written by Hugh of Saint-Pol to various acquaintances in the West in the summer of 1203 described Alexius as making a personal plea to the crusaders that they should not be swayed from his cause. Again, the prince emphasised the unjust usurpation of his father and his offer of generous assistance. Notwithstanding the welcome given to Alexius when he first reached Corfu, it seems that the battle for the support of the rank and file needed to be won as well. Hugh wrote of the disquiet: 'a good deal of disagreement was engendered in our army and there was an enormous uproar and grumbling. For everyone was shouting that we should make haste for Acre, and there were not more than ten who spoke in favour of Constantinople.'[26] These men again included Hugh himself, Baldwin of Flanders, Villehardouin and Bishop Conrad of Halberstadt. As Hugh argued: 'we all clearly demonstrated to the entire army that the journey to Jerusalem was fruitless and injurious for everyone insofar as they were destitute and low on provisions, and no one amongst them could retain the services of knights and pay the men-at-arms or could provide for the employment of petraries or the introduction of other weapons of war. Well, at last, they barely gave in to us . . .'[27] Alexius probably repeated the offer he had made to the leadership back at Zara and the terms were again agreed by the named individuals, although as events were about to reveal, they represented only a fraction of the entire army.

A group of senior French crusaders, including Odo of Champlitte, Jacques of Avesnes, and Peter of Amiens (Robert of Clari's patron) – all influential men of high rank – decided that they would prefer to remain on Corfu when the Venetian fleet sailed. They planned to send messengers across to Brindisi in southern Italy, where Walter of Brienne, another important crusader, was known to be based and to ask him to dispatch shipping for them so that, presumably, they could continue on to the Holy Land. Villehardouin hinted that these men feared the likely duration, as well as the danger, of an attack on Constantinople. He allowed that while some hid their true feelings, 'more than half the army were of the same mind'.[28] A division of this magnitude would obviously mean the end of the crusade. Boniface, Baldwin, Louis and Hugh were aghast at this development and realised that they had to take immediate and decisive action. Villehardouin reports an unattributed speech from amongst this group: 'My lords, we're in a pretty desperate position. If these men leave us, as so many have already done on different occasions, the army's doomed, and we'll never conquer anything. So why don't we go and beg them, for God's sake, to show some consideration for themselves and for us, and not disgrace themselves, nor deprive us of the chance of delivering the land overseas.'[29] The marshal chose to portray the issue as one of chivalric honour, combined with the need to assist the Holy Land – a plain demonstration of the necessity to keep one's word and not lose face. The crusade leaders acted immediately and rushed off to meet the other group who were assembled in conference in a nearby valley.

What followed was one of the most dramatic incidents of the entire crusade. Boniface, Prince Alexius and the bishops and abbots sympathetic to them mounted their horses and rode away at a gallop. When they saw their comrades gathered in discussion, they halted and approached them on foot, perhaps as a sign of humility, perhaps to convey no sense of threat. On seeing the frenzied approach of the leadership, Odo, Jacques and Peter had saddled up, fearing an attack, but when the others dismounted, they followed suit. The two parties drew close and then, in what could only have been a last-ditch effort to sway the hearts and minds of their fellow-crusaders, Boniface, Baldwin, Louis and Hugh threw themselves at the feet of their friends. They cried out for help, they wept and sobbed that they would not move until the others promised to stay and fight alongside them.[30]

Modern diplomacy rarely extends to such graphic and emotional displays but, as with the scene in Basel cathedral, such a lachrymose performance was not at all unfamiliar in the medieval period. This episode on Corfu was a volatile mixture of genuine feeling, utter desperation and emotional blackmail. With friends, relatives and lords lined up opposite one another, a direct appeal of this nature was almost certain to hit home. The would-be deserters duly burst into tears as well and everyone was overcome with emotion. They were not so carried away as to agree to help the prince on the spot, however, and once everyone had regained their composure they asked for some privacy to discuss the matter.

Withdrawing from the others, they debated the terms of their continued participation in the expedition to Constantinople. They undertook to stay with the army until Christmas 1203, but demanded that any time thereafter the leaders had to provide them with ships to go to Syria within two weeks of making such a request. The agreement was confirmed by oath. A sense of relief flooded through the army; for the immediate future at least, the direction of the campaign was confirmed.

Even then, the crusaders' stay on Corfu was not trouble-free. The island was part of the Byzantine Empire and while the inhabitants of Durazzo had dutifully acknowledged Alexius's authority, the prince's reception from others of the islanders was much more hostile. The city of Corfu refused to open its gates and the inhabitants declared their opposition to Alexius by using catapults and petraries to compel the crusader fleet to withdraw from the harbour. It seems unlikely that there was a formal siege of the citadel, largely because the crusaders realised that it was too strong to take quickly and that their priorities lay elsewhere, but this antipathy towards the young pretender made clear that he could not count on a friendly welcome throughout the empire and that loyalty to the existing regime was not as brittle as he would have liked.

A second episode on this island revealed another of the potential flaws in Alexius's promises to the crusaders. As the army camped outside the city of Corfu, the local archbishop invited over some of the Catholic churchmen for lunch. While the opposing armies fought using swords and missiles, their churchmen warred with words and ideas. This was no relaxing, drawn-out affair to demonstrate local hospitality, but an intense and passionate debate about important theological issues, particularly the Catholic Church's endless claims for the primacy of Rome over the Greek Orthodox Church. With delicious irony, the Orthodox archbishop observed that 'he knew of no basis for the Roman See's primacy other than the fact that Roman soldiers had crucified Christ' – a perfect response to the ambitions of the crusader churchmen.[31] Underlying this observation was the more serious point that, in this instance at least, a senior member of the Orthodox clergy was not prepared to submit to the papacy – an ominous hint (for those who chose to heed it) that Prince Alexius might struggle to deliver this particular strand of his offer to the crusaders.

As the expedition prepared to leave Corfu, the prince encouraged the crusaders to ravage the island as a signal that his wishes should be respected: a gesture to those ahead that he was determined to reclaim the throne.

CHAPTER EIGHT

'That city which reigns supreme over all others'

The Crusade Arrives at Constantinople, June 1203

THE ARMY SET sail for Constantinople on the eve of Pentecost, 24 May 1203. With the full fleet assembled, the crusading force must have looked impressive. Villehardouin testified that 'so fine a sight has never been seen before'. Again, as at the moment of departure from Venice, the marshal expressed pride in the Christian army and, with a touch of hindsight, wrote: 'It seemed, indeed, that here was a fleet that might well conquer lands, for as far as the eye could reach there was nothing to be seen but sails outspread on all that vast array of ships, so that every man's heart was filled with joy at the sight.'[1] The galleys, transports and warships were now accompanied by many merchant vessels, which took advantage of the protection offered by the main body of ships to supply the crusaders with food and other goods. They may also have hoped to profit from the new regime in Constantinople, although the Venetians were in the prime position to secure any large-scale trading privileges.

The voyage from Corfu was fairly uneventful. The fleet sailed past the islands of Cephalonia and Zakynthos before beginning to round the Peloponnese peninsula, passing by the port of Methoni near the south-westerly tip (today Methoni boasts the splendid remains of a huge fortified town constructed largely by the Venetians later in the thirteenth century), and thence to the eastern Peloponnese at Cape Malea. As the expedition sailed onwards it encountered two ships full of crusaders returning home from Syria. These men had embarked at Marseille, presumably in the summer of 1202 when the main army was still at Venice, and had spent the autumn and winter season campaigning in the Levant. Baldwin of Flanders sent a boat over to learn of their experiences. Villehardouin characterised the men on board the ships as feeling ashamed that they were not part of the main expedition, but this is manifestly unfair. They had, after all, fought in the Holy Land and accomplished their crusade vows without compromising them in the way the main army had already done. One man, however, saw a chance for further glory and he jumped down into the count of Flanders's boat. He called back: 'I'm going with these people, for it certainly seems to me they'll win some land for themselves.'[2] Not the most piously motivated thought for a crusader, but a reflection of some of the hopes and aspirations engendered by the new campaign to Constantinople. Villehardouin reported that the man was given a hearty welcome by the troops and commented in a self-satisfied way that 'no matter how a man may have gone astray he can still come round to the right way in the end'.[3]

From Cape Malea the ships turned northwards, past the Athenian peninsula to the large island of Euboea. The leaders conferred and decided to divide the fleet. Boniface and Baldwin were to sail southwards to the island of Andros, while the remainder of the ships headed north-east across the Aegean towards the coastline of Asia Minor, where they passed the ancient city of Troy before entering the Dardanelles (known then as the Hellespont). The reason for this move probably lay in the search for supplies. Andros was a wealthy island and, as the crusaders overran it, the inhabitants appealed to Prince Alexius for mercy and offered him money and goods if he would spare them. The only moment to mar the crusaders' diversion was the death of Guy of Coucy, a powerful northern French nobleman, who was buried at sea.[4]

The majority of the fleet passed into the Dardanelles, where they stopped at the ancient city of Abydos on the coast of Asia Minor. They were now striking deep into the heart of the Byzantine Empire. About 150 miles away, down at the end of the Sea of Marmara and into the Bosphorus, lay Constantinople itself, determined to fight and repulse the intruders.

The citizens of Abydos prudently surrendered to the crusader army. Mindful, as they neared Constantinople, that they needed to make as positive an impression as possible, the leaders set up a secure guard on the city and prevented any ill-disciplined looting by the army. This did not mean that the crusaders took nothing: the winter corn crop was due to be harvested and the westerners commandeered everything that was available because their own supplies were beginning to run low. Good weather allowed Baldwin and Boniface to join their colleagues at Abydos within a week. Reunited, the fleet prepared for the final approach to Constantinople.

Passage of the Bosphorus was far from easy, largely because of the prevailing north-easterly winds and adverse currents that headed down from the Black Sea, running at up to six or seven knots.[5] The skill of the Venetian sailors saw them safely through, however, and as they sailed up towards Constantinople, 'the full array of warships, galleys and transports seemed as if it were in flower. It was indeed, a marvellous experience to see so lovely a sight,' as Villehardouin expressed it.[6] For the Byzantines, of course, the crusaders' ships, for all their colour, embodied a terrible threat. On 23 June, the eve of St John the Baptist's Day, the fleet arrived at the abbey of St Stephen, about five miles south-west of its target. Soon the crusaders had their first real sight of the city they had come to attack, and as their ships cast anchor they began to absorb what lay before them.

Constantinople was indisputably the greatest metropolis in the Christian world. Its huge population – estimated at 375–400,000 – dwarfed every city in the West. In comparison, Paris and Venice probably had about 60,000 inhabitants each. Girded by its formidable walls, Constantinople excited awe, admiration and not a little trepidation amongst the crusaders.[7] What had they taken on? Villehardouin provides a vivid insight into their feelings:

> I can assure you that all those who had never seen Constantinople before gazed very intently upon the city, having never imagined there could be so fine a place in all the world. They noted the high walls and lofty towers encircling it, and its rich palaces and tall churches, of which there were so many that no one would have believed it to be true if he had not seen it with his own eyes, and viewed the length and breadth of that city which reigns supreme over all others. There was indeed no man so brave and daring that his flesh did not shudder at the sight. Nor was this to be wondered at, for never had so grand an enterprise been carried out by any people since the creation of the world.[8]

Robert of Clari echoed the sense of awe: 'the fleet regarded the great size of the city, which was so long and so wide, and they marvelled at it exceedingly'.[9]

Constantinople lay at the heart of an empire that encompassed parts of the modern countries of Turkey, Greece, Macedonia, Albania, Serbia and Bulgaria, up to the northern frontier along the River Danube. It also included the western half of Asia Minor and much of its northern and southern coastlines, as well as the Greek islands, Crete and Cyprus. It was a huge, heterogeneous and culturally complex entity. The inhabitants of Constantinople took great pride in their city – they called it 'New Rome', or 'the Queen of Cities' – descriptions based on its powerful history and sustained by its continued splendour. The Emperor Justinian wrote of 'the imperial city guarded by God'.[10] Rome, of course, could boast an imperial past and many great buildings, but the ravages of barbarian invasions and the instability of the early medieval papacy had done little to preserve its heritage. Of all cities known to Christians at this time, only Baghdad was greater in size, although by reason of faith and physical distance only the most intrepid merchants and travellers had seen it. The inhabitants of Constantinople had adopted the Virgin Mary as their special protector and the discovery of relics associated with her in the eleventh century further enhanced this sense of their city having been divinely blessed.[11]

Constantinople was founded in the fourth century when the Emperor Constantine established his control over both the eastern and western parts of the Roman Empire. To commemorate this victory (in the year 324) he ordered the Greek settlement of Byzantium to be renamed Constantinople in his honour and took measures to make the city the heart of his empire. Four years later, on foot and with spear in hand, he paced out the limits of his capital, although later emperors enlarged this first city. It was no coincidence that the new Rome was built on seven hills, the same number as its illustrious predecessor. Constantine had chosen the site carefully, poised between Asia and the West, at the gateway to the Black Sea and provided, for the most part, with strong natural defences. The Bosphorus and the Hellespont offered entrances to the Sea of Marmara, described by one historian as 'a natural moat'.[12] The city has a triangular shape, with the Sea of Marmara to the south and the inlet of the Golden Horn to the north, creating two of the sides.

The Golden Horn is just over six miles long and forms a perfect harbour. The weakest side of the triangle is the landward: few natural obstacles stand between this and the great plains rolling north-west towards the Danube – the frontier with the barbarian world – and the need for a massive system of fortifications here was to concern many future emperors.

On 11 May 330 Constantinople was formally rededicated and became the effective capital of the Roman Empire. Eighteen years previously Constantine had been the first emperor to convert to Christianity and to publicly endorse the faith. Constantinople emerged, therefore, from a synthesis of Roman imperialism, the Hellenic tradition and the emerging power of Christianity.[13] The impact of these three forces can be seen in the physical, intellectual and spiritual development of the Byzantine Empire as its fortunes ebbed and flowed over the next few centuries. The reign of Justinian (527–65) was a particular high point as he did much to recover parts of the empire lost to the Goths in previous decades, while in Constantinople itself he initiated a remarkable building programme, centred upon the church of Hagia Sophia.

Over the centuries Byzantium had to face threats from all points of the compass. The period 600–800 was particularly difficult, with the emergence of Islam as a dynamic and aggressive new force to the east and the rise of a powerful empire to the west under Charlemagne (d. 814). In the late ninth and early tenth centuries the Christianisation and takeover of the kingdom of Bulgaria represented an advance for the Byzantines, but their crushing defeat at the Battle of Manzikert in 1071 saw the loss of most of their lands in Asia Minor and the humiliating capture of their emperor. The advent of the crusades led to greater engagement with western Europe. At some levels this was positive: with the help of the First Crusade, Alexius I Comnenus recovered the western regions of Asia Minor, although the Greeks' efforts to impose their overlordship on the principality of Antioch proved a struggle. Furthermore, the Normans of Sicily emerged as a violent and expansionist power in the central Mediterranean and the ambitions of both the papacy and the German Empire also needed to be kept in check. Under Manuel Comnenus (1143–80) the empire had established a position of genuine strength, although after his death the subsequent decades of political turmoil in Byzantium did much to create the conditions in which the Fourth Crusade found itself outside this magnificent city. A serious degeneration of political order had taken place in

Constantinople prior to the crusade. The period from 1101 to 1180 witnessed very few problems, yet between 1180 and 1204 there were 58 rebellions and conspiracies. This demonstrates the build-up of tensions under Manuel and how the different elements within the imperial family were dissatisfied with their position. There is a further conjunction between this situation and the growing number of provincial uprisings, such as the establishment of the Bulgarian Empire and the losses of Cyprus and Thessalonica.[14]

Many of the buildings of late antiquity survived to dominate the skyline and topography of medieval Constantinople. Together they told the story of its history and formed the essence of its identity and appearance at the time of the Fourth Crusade. The crusaders saw before them a true marvel – a mixture of formidable defences, splendid churches and sumptuous palaces, as well as the essential everyday workings of any city, although in almost all cases on a scale unknown to most of them. The city itself, broken up by small hills, encloses an area of approximately 11½ square miles, although even in medieval times suburbs extended outside the walls to the north and on to the other side of the Golden Horn at Galata.

One of the most impressive and intimidating features of Constantinople were the land walls. As the city expanded back in the fifth century, the Emperor Theodosius II (408–50) took measures to accommodate the extra citizens and to provide adequate defence against the ravaging Huns.[15] These fortifications, more than 3½ miles long, formed a mighty impediment to any potential aggressor. Even today they are, for the most part, complete. Some sections are restored and others still ruined, yet as the walls rise and fall along the contours of the land, the sheer length of this barrier seems endless, at times stretching from horizon to horizon in front and behind.

The walls consist of a multi-faceted series of obstacles (see plate section). The inner wall has 96 towers, 58 feet high and 175 feet apart, which punctuate a wall 30 feet high and 15 feet thick at its base. Then between the inner and outer walls runs a terrace 55 feet wide to allow movement of the troops manning the outer wall. This is 27 feet high from the outside and up to 6½ feet thick. Its towers are 32 feet high and they alternate between the bigger towers of the inner wall to provide the best protection. Next, to maximise the distance between the attackers and the defenders, there is another terrace, 60 feet wide; and then a moat of similar width, now much filled in, but which was 22 feet deep, although it is not certain whether this was ever full of water.

Ten gates pierced Theodosius's walls. Important visitors who arrived by land entered through the Golden Gate at the southernmost end of the walls, in the south-west of the city. This was the way in which returning emperors processed into their capital: across the deep moat and thence through the powerful defensive complex. Two great marble towers flanked the Golden Gate. Originally this had been a triumphal arch constructed by Theodosius I in 391 and then incorporated into the main walls in the next century. Its name derived from the fact that the three gates across the entrance were inlaid with gold.[16] Two huge copper elephants also stood guard over the gate at the time of the crusades.[17] The entry towers still remain, absorbed into a later defensive complex, although their decoration is inevitably long gone. All around, decorating the gateway and towers, were statues of classical scenes, such as the labours of Hercules.

From the Golden Gate to the imperial centre of Constantinople was a distance of about three miles, a journey along avenues decorated with statues and punctuated by a series of *fora* (public squares) dating from the fourth, fifth and sixth centuries. In the Forum of the Bull stood a huge bronze equestrian statue, while the oval Forum of Constantine contained many wonders, such as a great bronze statue of the goddess Hera, whose head was so large it is said that four yokes of oxen were needed to transport it. At the forum's centre was the column of Constantine. The original had fallen in a storm in 1106, but Manuel Comnenus had it rebuilt. Bereft of its statue today, six of the seven porphyry drums still stand – defiant but rather badly battered – on top of a rough stone casement.[18] Alongside these fairly conventional monuments were some that were more idiosyncratic. For example, the Forum of Constantine also boasted a massive wind-vane, the *Anemodoulion* or Wind-Servant: a towering, four-sided bronze mechanical device decorated with birds, shepherds and fish. At its apex it terminated in a point like a pyramid, above which was suspended a female figure who turned in the wind.[19]

Around 500 yards past the Forum of Constantine was the mighty complex of buildings that lay at the very heart of Constantinople: namely the Hippodrome, the Imperial Palace and the awesome church of the

Hagia Sophia. Here the sacred and the secular met and overlapped in dazzling displays of imperial power and piety, grounded in the city's classical past, yet utterly essential to the maintenance of the medieval emperors' authority. The fundamentals of government – finance and justice – lay here: treasuries, barracks, prisons; religion and spectacle thrived too in the mighty spaces inside the Hagia Sophia and the Hippodrome.

The Great Palace, often known to westerners as the Bucoleon on account of its sculpture of a lion in a death struggle with a bull, was an enormous complex of buildings on the south-eastern corner of the city, bounded by the Hippodrome, the square of the Hagia Sophia and, on the other two sides, the Sea of Marmara. Based upon Constantine's original palace, this had been developed and expanded many times over the centuries.[20] William, archbishop of Tyre and chancellor of the kingdom of Jerusalem, described a visit to Emperor Manuel Comnenus by King Amalric in 1171. As a special honour the Franks were allowed to dock at the sea gate, from where they followed 'a marvellous pavement of magnificent marble'. The palace possessed countless corridors and hallways and the emperor greeted Amalric in an audience chamber screened by curtains of precious fabrics with, at its centre, two golden thrones, one lower than the other to demonstrate to the king his lesser rank.[21] Robert of Clari struggled to convey the true scale of the palace where, he claimed, 'there were 500 halls, all connected with one another and all made with gold mosaic'. According to Robert, there were more than 30 chapels alone in the Great Palace, including the most dramatic of all, the church of the Blessed Virgin of the Pharos (lighthouse), which 'was so rich and noble that there was not a hinge nor a band nor any other part such as is usually made of iron that was not all of silver, and there was no column that was not of jasper or porphyry or some other rich precious stone. And the pavement of this chapel was of a white marble so smooth and clear that it seemed to be of crystal, and this chapel was so rich and so noble that no one could ever tell you of its beauty or nobility.' The list of relics it held was remarkable, including two large pieces of the True Cross, some of the nails driven through Christ's hands and feet, a phial of His blood, the Crown of Thorns, a part of the robe of the Virgin Mary and the head of John the Baptist.[22]

The Great Palace also contained a massive gilded hall, constructed by

Manuel Comnenus and decorated with mosaics depicting his victories. He, or Isaac Angelos, also built the marvellous *Mouchroutas* (from the Arabic word for cone), described here by the contemporary Byzantine author Nicholas Mesarites:

> The steps leading up to it are made of baked brick, lime and marble; the staircase, which is serrated on either side and turns in a circle, is coloured blue, deep red, green and purple by means of a medley of cut, painted tiles of a cruciform shape. This building is the work of . . . a Persian hand. The canopy of the roof, consisting of hemispheres joined to the heaven-like ceiling, offers a variegated spectacle; closely packed angles project inward and outward; the beauty of the carving is extraordinary, and wonderful is the appearance of the cavities which, overlaid with gold, produce the effect of a rainbow more colourful than the one hidden in the clouds. There is insatiable enjoyment here – not hidden, but on the surface.[23]

Sadly, the Great Palace has been almost completely destroyed over the centuries. One small section of the outer wall survives overlooking the Sea of Marmara. At ground level, however, one remarkable archaeological discovery (from the 1950s) has yielded a stunning impression of the opulence of the palace. The huge area of sixth-century mosaics showing hunting scenes is open to the public and this, taken in conjunction with literary texts, gives some sense of the magnificent marble pavements that decorated the medieval palace.[24]

From one of the buildings in the Great Palace a passage ran directly into the imperial box at the great sporting arena of the Hippodrome. Constructed by Emperor Septimus Severus in the early third century, enlarged by Constantine and still in use in the twelfth century, the stadium, at over 350 yards in length, may have held as many as 100,000 people. Races must have created an incredible scene of noise, dust and drama as the horses sped around the oval track. Benjamin of Tudela described entertainments involving jugglers, or contests with wild animals fighting each other; we also know of gymnastic displays, tightrope walkers and, of course, horse races, still held between teams of Reds, Blues, Greens and Whites, as in classical times.[25] Today the Hippodrome has largely disappeared, although

Twelfth-century sculpture from the priory of Belval in Lorraine,
showing Count Hugh of Vaudémont and his wife Aigeline of Burgundy.

Pope Innocent III (1198–1216), from the church of San Speco, Subiaco.

A devil pours molten metal down the throat of a false moneyer, from the twelfth-century tympanum, Conques.

Spectators watching an early tournament.

Thirteenth-century silver grosso of the doge of Venice showing (*left*) Christ and (*right*) the doge and St Mark.

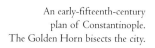

A Venetian ship depicted in the
Venetian Maritime Code of 1255.

An early-fifteenth-century
plan of Constantinople.
The Golden Horn bisects the city.

A knight receives communion from a priest, Rheims Cathedral, early thirteenth century.

The land walls of
Constantinople.

The crusaders attack
Constantinople by land and sea,
from a later manuscript of
Geoffrey of Villehardouin.

The interior of Hagia Sophia. The disc displaying a Koranic inscription dates from the building's use as a mosque.

A late-eleventh or early-twelfth-century icon of St Michael, taken from Constantinople after the Fourth Crusade.

a park partially tracing the shape of the track and the remains of three columns, formerly in the centre of the arena, give some impression of the scale of the place.

Outside the Hippodrome was the Forum of the *Augusteion*, dominated by a huge column, topped by a statue of Justinian, and vividly described by Robert of Clari:

> There was a great column which was fully three times the reach of a man's arm in thickness . . . It was made of marble and of copper over marble and was bound about with strong bands of iron. And on top of the column lay a flat slab of stone which was [14½ feet x 14½ feet] and on this stone there was an emperor made of copper on a great copper horse, and he was holding his hand towards heathen lands, and there were letters written on the statue which said that he swore that the Saracens should never have a truce from him. And in the other he held a golden globe with a cross on it . . . On the croup of the horse and on the head and round about there were fully ten nests of herons, who nested there every year.[26]

Across the square from the Hippodrome stands the Hagia Sophia (meaning Holy Wisdom), which, together with the abbey of Cluny (with its immense church, 531 feet long), was one of the great buildings of medieval Christendom. While many riches of the Byzantine Empire have been destroyed over time, the basic format and stupendous scale of the Hagia Sophia are still apparent today – a breathtaking testimony to the grandeur of the imperial age.[27]

In 532 a fire destroyed an existing structure on the site and Emperor Justinian took the opportunity to construct a new building on a previously unimagined scale. Massive in concept, with its huge supporting piers, high vaults and cavernous dome, the church was first dedicated in 537. From the top of the dome, based on a square 100 feet high and carried on arches 176 feet wide (designed to compare with the vault of heaven), the 230-foot-long nave gives off to a series of semidomes that, from the outside, cascade down to give an impression of enormous solidity, completely belying the soaring space inside the church. The contemporary historian Procopius gives this description:

The Emperor, disregarding all considerations of expense, hastened to begin construction and raised craftsmen from the whole world . . . So the church has been made a spectacle of great beauty, stupendous to those who see it and altogether incredible to those who hear of it . . .

It boasts of an ineffable beauty, for it subtly combines mass with the harmony of its proportions . . . it abounds exceedingly in gleaming sunlight. You might say that the [interior] space is not illuminated by the sun from the outside but that the radiance is generated within, so great an abundance of light bathes this shrine all around . . .

Rising above this circle is an enormous spherical dome that makes the building exceptionally beautiful. It seems not to be founded on solid masonry, but to be suspended from heaven by that golden chain and so cover the space. All of these elements, marvellously fitted together in mid-air, suspended from one another and reposing only on the parts adjacent to them, produce a unified and most remarkable harmony in the work, yet do not allow the spectators to rest their gaze upon any one of them for a length of time, but each detail readily draws and attracts the eye to itself.[28]

The huge dome was decorated with mosaics of Christ Pantocrator (Christ the All-Ruler) and, in the apse, mosaics of the Virgin Mary. Christ's earthly ministries were represented on the side galleries, but not all the imagery was biblical. Few of these beautiful creations survive, but in the end bay of the south gallery remains a superb mosaic of Emperor John Comnenus and his wife, the red-haired Empress Irene, along with their son, Alexius. The sheer size and dazzling mosaics made the Hagia Sophia a source of wonder to all who saw it. Robert of Clari, probably used to the rectangular plan of most northern European churches (although some, such as Nivelles, were rounded), was captivated by its shape. He wrote that the church was 'entirely round and within the church there were domes, round all about, which were borne by great and very rich columns . . . of jasper or porphyry or some other precious stone'.[29]

Today's visitor to the Hagia Sophia can experience some of the same assault on the senses that the crusaders felt. While much of the gold and silver ornamentation has been lost, the remarkable marble walls survive.

At least 10 different sorts of marble were used in the church, all carefully arranged to maximum visual effect. In some cases, huge sheets have been split open and placed back-to-back like gigantic butterfly wings to best display their beautiful patterns. The architects of the Hagia Sophia searched far and wide to assemble the astonishing array of colours and patterns that adorn the building. For example: the white marble came from Laconia (in the Peloponnese), the pale green from the island of Euboea, the pink and white from Phyrigia (in western Asia Minor), the imperial purple porphyry from Egypt, the green porphyry from Laconia, the yellow from Numidia (Algeria), the green from Thessaly and the white on black from the Pyrenees.

A partial collapse in 558 and reconstruction over the next five years led to the building taking the basic form in which we see it today. Later structural supports proved essential and, when the Ottomans ruled Constantinople (after 1453) and the building gained its third religious custodians (following Orthodox Christians and Catholics), the addition of four prominent minarets signalled its conversion to a mosque. Under Atatürk, however, the building was secularised in 1934 and survives as a museum.

Its treasury housed untold riches: relics of Christ's Passion – pieces of the Holy Lance which pierced His side, a section of the True Cross upon which He was crucified, the Crown of Thorns, a Nail of the Crucifixion, the Shroud, the Stone from the Tomb, and so on.

The Hagia Sophia, however, was far from being the only magnificent church in Constantinople. In fact, there were hundreds of ecclesiastical institutions in the city; churches and monasteries abounded within its walls. Alberic of Trois-Fontaines, a thirteenth-century Cistercian writer from Champagne, wrote of 'around 500 abbeys or conventual churches'.[30] Many contained wonderful relics and western pilgrims eagerly sought the chance to venerate such objects. Odo of Deuil, a French monk who visited Constantinople during the Second Crusade in 1147, wrote of 'the many churches unequal to [Hagia] Sophia in size but equal in beauty, which are to be marvelled at for their beauty and their many saintly relics. Those who had the opportunity entered these places, some to see the sights and others to worship faithfully.'[31]

Two are worth particular mention. First, the church of the Holy Apostles, said by Robert of Clari to be even richer and nobler than the

Hagia Sophia.[32] This building was constructed by Justinian and contained the tombs of many emperors, as well as relics of St Andrew, St Luke and St Timothy. It was also, as we saw earlier, the model for St Mark's in Venice.

Another church of note, and one that (unlike the church of the Holy Apostles) survives today, is the monastery of Christ Pantocrator, now known as Zeyrek Camii. This lay at the centre of a complex founded by Emperor John Comnenus around 1118–36.[33] It was, like many other Byzantine institutions, a multi-purpose site containing a monastic community, a large body of clergy to minister to the laity and a hospital for 50 people, staffed by 76 medical and 27 service personnel.[34] By comparison with western practices, the twelfth-century Hospital of St John in Jerusalem could house more than 1,000 patients, but had only four doctors.[35] Today the monastery of the Pantocrator is a working mosque, though somewhat ravaged by time. However, the colossal rust-brown marble doorways still stand proud and, high up in what was formerly the main church (now the prayer hall), small crosses are still visible on vaults just below the roofline. The complex became the family mausoleum for the Comneni dynasty, but the tombs of John and Manuel Comnenus are long gone, although they were still extant around 1750 and on display in the Topkapi palace.[36]

The other important building in Constantinople – and one familiar to earlier western visitors – was the second major imperial palace of Blachernae, a well-fortified site up at the northern end of the land walls. This had been developed by Emperor Alexius I (1081–1118), and was often utilised in conjunction with the Great Palace (the Bucoleon) as a centre of imperial authority and as a place to entertain visitors. Its position meant that emperors such as Manuel Comnenus, a man devoted to the hunt, made frequent use of it because he could ride straight out into the countryside. The Blachernae was important because it was next to the principal sanctuary of the Virgin Mary, the guardian of Constantinople, and it was a safer location during times of civil unrest because it was comparatively remote from the restive city mob.[37]

Odo of Deuil saw the palace in 1147: 'Its exterior is of almost match-less beauty, but its interior surpasses anything that I can say about it. Throughout it is decorated elaborately with gold and a great variety of colours, and the floor is marble, paved with cunning workmanship . . .'[38]

Alexius I had built a sumptuous throne-room at the palace and this was probably the area used to receive envoys. William of Tyre visited it just over 20 years later and saw valuable draperies, numerous servants, vestments and royal robes adorned with a profusion of precious stones and pearls, as well as 'the vast amount of massive gold and silver furniture in the palace, of untold value'.[39]

The city that the crusaders gazed upon in June 1203 was not simply made up of fine buildings and manifestations of imperial power. Trade (and hence taxes) was one source of wealth for the Byzantines and along the side of the city facing onto the Golden Horn were based many communities of merchants. Constantinople was a focal point for trade from the Byzantine Empire itself, but also from the Black Sea, the Mediterranean and western Europe. The Italian cities of Venice, Amalfi, Pisa and Genoa all had their little communities, staffed by their own people and served by warehouses and landing stages that brought their goods in and out of Constantinople. On the other side of the Golden Horn, reached by ferry-boat, the suburb of Galata housed elements of society that the other citizens preferred to keep at a distance. In 1171 Benjamin of Tudela reported a Jewish community of about 2,500, many of whom were skilled in working silk. They had also become very wealthy, although he wrote that the Greeks oppressed and reviled his people.[40] Alongside the Jews were the tanners, pushed away from the main city because of their malodorous trade, and also, out of fear of contagion, a colony of lepers.

Given the enormous size of Constantinople there were large districts of crowded, impoverished communities, relying on charity or finding work in the great institutions of the city. Odo of Deuil wrote that it 'is squalid and fetid and in many places harmed by permanent darkness, for the wealthy overshadow the streets with buildings and leave these dark, dirty places to the poor and to travellers'.[41] A near-contemporary of the Fourth Crusade, John Tzetses, described life in his own apartment, trapped between the children and pigs of the priest who lived upstairs and the hay stored by a farmer on the ground floor.[42] These people often lived in crowded wooden tenements; only the wealthy could occupy the many fine buildings and smaller private palaces. Practicality dictated that schools, public baths and orphanages also existed. Because Constantinople lacked sufficient natural springs, the supply of water was another crucial matter which earlier rulers had attended to with the construction of huge aqueducts and cisterns.

The Byzantines continued to employ these utilities left over from the late Roman age, most visibly the great aqueduct of Valens (364–78), half a mile of which still stands in the centre-north of the city. Several immense underground reservoirs survive today and the most accessible, known as the Basilica Cistern, dates from the reign of Justinian. It is located just outside the Hagia Sophia and demonstrates the phenomenal scale of just one civil engineering project. This huge cavern is 224 feet wide, 450 feet long and has 336 columns. It was capable of holding 2,800,000 cubic feet of water, brought from the Black Sea more than 12½ miles away.

The bulk of Constantinople's population constituted what Niketas Choniates termed 'the mob', a seething mass of the underclass, entertained and placated by the Hippodrome games, but otherwise largely restless and self-serving in their support of the changing regimes of the 1180s.[43] The sheer size of the populace made it essential for the emperor to take note of their moods and wishes. Such was their number that Ralph of Coggeshall, a monk writing in Essex in the early thirteenth century, claimed: 'People who know the ins and outs of this city say with confidence that it has more inhabitants than those who live in the area from the city of York all the way to the River Thames [about 195 miles].'[44]

As they stared across the Sea of Marmara, the crusaders must have fully realised the scale of the commitment that they had made to Prince Alexius. The vast and powerful Queen of Cities lay before them, solidly supported by centuries of imperial rule and secure in the knowledge of never having fallen to a conqueror. Some of the crusader army had been inside the city before and were aware of the spiritual and secular treasures within its walls, the opulence of its churches and palaces and the wealth of its rulers. Others would be told of this and might have had the great sights identified to them on the skyline. All must have fervently hoped that Prince Alexius would indeed be welcomed back to the city and that they could fulfil their side of the bargain with minimal force. In spite of the scale of the task they might face, there were some encouraging signs. Most pertinently, the violence, disorder and usurpations over the previous 20 years demonstrated a volatility that might work to the crusaders' advantage.

These decades had, in part, sapped some of the military strength of

Constantinople; the walls were not kept in perfect repair and the once formidable Byzantine navy had practically disappeared. In addition, Alexius III had declined to make adequate preparations for the crusaders' attack. Niketas Choniates provides a splendidly caustic description of the emperor's efforts to organise the defence of Constantinople. Apparently Alexius III had been aware of the crusaders' movements for a long time; however:

> his excessive slothfulness was equal to his stupidity in neglecting what was necessary for the common welfare. When it was proposed that he make provisions for an abundance of weapons, undertake the preparation of suitable war engines, and, above all, to begin the construction of warships, it was as though his advisers were talking to a corpse. He indulged in after-dinner repartee and in wilful neglect of the reports on the Latins [the crusaders]; he busied himself with building lavish bathhouses, levelling hills to plant vineyards . . . wasting his time in these and other activities. Those who wanted to cut timber for ships were threatened with the gravest danger by the eunuchs who guarded the thickly wooded imperial mountains, that were reserved for the imperial hunts, as if they were sacred groves . . .[45]

Only when the emperor learned that his nephew and the crusaders had reached Durazzo on the Adriatic (May 1203) was he roused into action, although the measures he introduced hardly constituted a comprehensive and rigorous level of preparation: 'Accordingly he began to repair the rotting and worm-eaten small skiffs, barely twenty in number, and making the rounds of the city's walls, he ordered the dwellings outside to be pulled down.'[46]

Perhaps Niketas is being a touch too harsh here, given that there was no certainty of an attack on Byzantium until the agreement between Prince Alexius and the crusaders was completed at Zara in late April. Certainly the emperor was aware of his challenger's attempts to raise support in the West, but given the prince's failures at Rome and Hagenau there was little indication that he would be any better received by Dandolo, Boniface and Baldwin. Given the usual tensions between crusading armies and the Greeks it might, however, have been prudent to make some preparations, but

Alexius III had evidently chosen not to. In any case, Niketas's real complaint here is of a more long-term nature and concerns the lamentable decline of the Byzantine navy. The emperor may also have placed some reliance upon a letter from the pope in late 1202. This had reassured the Greek ruler that Innocent had rejected any suggestion of turning the crusade towards Constantinople to help Prince Alexius.[47]

Back in the reign of Manuel Comnenus the Greeks had been able to send out mighty fleets to participate in, for example, invasions of Egypt with the rulers of Jerusalem. William of Tyre recorded that in 1169 Manuel dispatched 150 'ships of war equipped with beaks and double tiers of oars . . . there were, in addition, sixty larger boats, well-armoured, which were built to carry horses . . . also ten or twenty vessels of a huge size . . . carrying arms and . . . engines and machines of war'.[48] Yet, such was the decline of the navy after Manuel's death, the Greeks came to rely on hiring pirates to fight for them and by 1203, as Niketas revealed, only 20 half-rotten ships could be raised to resist the crusade. Prince Alexius would have known this and the Venetian merchants in Constantinople would have informed Dandolo of the situation over previous years. There is little doubt that the knowledge of Byzantine naval weakness must have contributed significantly to the crusaders' assessment of whether they could offer military support to Prince Alexius if it was needed. The thought of having to face a fleet of the size that Manuel had sent to Egypt might well have deterred them from any such commitment. Fortunately for the crusaders, the prospect of a massive naval battle against more or less equal forces, or even the idea of being harassed by a remotely seaworthy squadron of ships, was something they would not have to contend with. In Dandolo and his Venetians, the westerners had the most astute and experienced fleet in the Mediterranean. If used properly, control of the seas could give the crusaders a vital initiative for the forthcoming assault.[49]

The Byzantine land forces were not so feeble, however. While they had declined in strength since Manuel's death in 1180, they still constituted a formidable enemy.[50] Emperor Alexius's army consisted of a mixture of native Byzantine troops, mercenaries (hired from Bulgaria, Asia Minor, western Europe and the Slavic lands) and, most dangerous of all, the legendary Varangian guard, an elite body of men sworn to remain loyal to the emperor. Over the centuries the Greeks had acquired a reputation for being unwarlike and effeminate. Benjamin of Tudela assessed their military capabilities thus: 'They hire from amongst all nations warriors called barbarians to fight with . . . the Turks, for the natives [the Greeks] are not warlike, but are as women who have no strength to fight.'[51] If the employment of outsiders to form the central element in their army did nothing to dispel such an impression, the Greeks had at least been wise in the choice of warriors. The Varangians were heavily armed soldiers famous for using mighty single-edged battle-axes, which they carried on their shoulders. The size of this force numbered just over 5,000 men and it represented the core of the imperial army. It was formed mainly from Scandinavians lured to Constantinople by high levels of pay. Many of the English warriors defeated at the Battle of Hastings in 1066 or displaced in the subsequent Norman Conquest also travelled east to join the guard. Other recruits came from forces such as that which accompanied King Sigurd of Norway on his expedition to the Holy Land in 1110, and who stopped off en route home to join the guard or to temporarily serve the emperor.[52]

Two other contingents who helped to defend Constantinople in 1203 were made up of Pisans and Genoese. These representatives of the merchant communities transferred their bitter commercial rivalry with the Venetians to the arena of the crusades and the Bosphorus. The crusade leaders later claimed that they faced a Byzantine force of 60,000 knights, plus infantrymen.[53] Modern historians estimate a figure of in excess of 30,000 for the imperial army; plus, of course, the citizenry of Constantinople who could support and fight alongside this force, if so motivated.[54] If either of these figures is at all accurate, then the Greeks had an overwhelming numerical advantage, as well as the benefit of the substantial defences of Constantinople itself.

The doge and the nobles had now to decide on their next move. Dandolo, practical as ever, counselled caution. Based on his previous visits to Constantinople (1171 and 1183) and the detailed knowledge derived from the Venetian presence in the city over many decades, he emphasised the need for the crusaders to gather adequate supplies and proceed with due care. He argued: 'You are now engaged on the greatest and most dangerous enterprise that any people up to this day have ever undertaken; it is therefore important for us to act wisely and prudently.'[55] Dandolo claimed that the crusaders' lack of food and money could cause them to range too widely over the surrounding lands. They would scatter too much and lose some men: something that the army could ill afford, given the scale of the task they faced.

Nearby lay the Isles of the Monks (today called the Princes' Isles, located around 5½ miles south of the main city), known by the doge to produce corn and meat. He advised that the fleet should moor there, gather supplies and then make ready to assault the city. Dandolo put forward a thirteenth-century version of one of the most famous military aphorisms of all time: 'for the man who has something to eat fights with a better chance of winning than the one with nothing in his stomach'.[56]

On 24 June, St John the Baptist's Day, the men readied their ships. During the long voyage much of their equipment had been stowed away, or covered up, to protect it from the elements. Now, as they drew closer to Constantinople, banners and pennants were hoisted onto the ships' castles and the knights' shields were hung from the bulwarks. The fleet transformed itself into the same colourful spectacle that had left Venice almost nine months earlier. This time war was imminent: not against the infidel, but against the schismatic Greeks and their usurping emperor. The ships made their initial pass of the walls of Constantinople. First to appear were the transport ships, then the warships. As their vessels moved closer to the city, the scale of its defences and the density and majesty of its skyline, packed with palaces, churches and monuments, must have chilled the crusaders' hearts. They glided past the sea walls, the great bulk of the Hippodrome, the glory of the Bucoleon palace. Then came the Hagia Sophia, squatting indestructibly on the hilltop nearest the easternmost point of the city. Some men were so excited at the chance to engage the enemy that they loosed off arrows and missiles at the Byzantine ships lying before the walls, although they inflicted little damage.

For their part, the Greeks packed the walls of the city, curious to see their enemy; they too must have been filled with trepidation. The last major crusading army to pass through the Byzantine Empire, that of Frederick Barbarossa in 1189–90, had brushed aside their challenge and marched through their lands. Warlike westerners had been viewed as a danger to Constantinople since the time of the First Crusade and many Greeks had long felt that the crusades were just a pretext for an attack on their city.[57] Thus far, this had never actually happened, but with the presence of a claimant to the imperial title in the westerners' midst, the danger in 1203 was perhaps greater than ever before. In military terms there was a difference, too. The force coming by sea presented a new challenge compared to the earlier, landbound armies. The combination of the presence of Prince Alexius and the crusader fleet created a unique threat.

A brisk following wind took the fleet past their planned stop on the Isles of the Monks and the sailors steered as best they could towards the mainland of Asia Minor, where they made harbour at the imperial palace of Chalcedon, opposite the main city, which lay almost two miles away across the Bosphorus. The nobles, naturally, took their quarters in the palace, 'one of the most beautiful and enchanting that ever an eye could see', according to Villehardouin.[58] They also pitched their tents, and the knights and foot-soldiers set up camp while the horses were brought ashore and carefully reacquainted with *terra firma* after the weeks at sea. The crusaders were fortunate because the corn harvest had just been reaped and lay piled up, ready for them to gather as much as they wanted. This, surely, was an indication of Alexius III's lack of serious preparations: to leave an enemy readily available food supplies within easy reach of a city they were about to besiege was woefully inept.

Two days later the crusaders transferred their entire force a further three miles up the eastern side of the Bosphorus to another imperial palace at Scutari. They continued to collect all the foodstuffs possible in preparation for the siege. Alexius III, meanwhile, had begun to react to the danger by moving his army out of Constantinople and establishing a position on the European shore, opposite the crusaders, in order to resist a landing. In late June 1203 the two armies faced each other across the Bosphorus, poised for war.

CHAPTER NINE

'Never, in any city, have so many been besieged by so few'

The First Siege of Constantinople, July 1203

THERE REMAINED TWO ways in which conflict could be averted. First, the crusaders might be persuaded to leave; second, with or without Emperor Alexius III's agreement, the Greeks could open their gates to the prince and allow him to reassume control of the city. The emperor was the first to move. On 1 July, a crusader raiding party had routed a large force of Greek knights about nine miles to the east of the invaders' camp. They had captured many valuable war-horses and mules and the Byzantines had fled in terror at the enemy charge. The menace of the western forces was made plain, as was the damage to Greek morale. Perhaps it was time for the emperor to engage in diplomacy. The following day, Alexius III dispatched a Lombard, Nicolo Rosso, to hear at first hand why the crusaders had come to Byzantium and to ask them to justify their actions. Doubtless he was also told to gather as much information as possible about the crusader forces – a usual part of a diplomatic envoy's function. Nicolo duly delivered the emperor's message to the leader of the expedition, Marquis Boniface. Some feared the effect of this approach, and Hugh of Saint-Pol reflected the age-old suspicion of Greek duplicity: 'we did not want the Greeks to solicit or soften us with their gifts'.[1] Once he was certain that Nicolo's credentials were in order, Boniface invited him to address the nobles. The envoy posed the obvious question: why, as crusaders sworn to deliver the Holy Land and the Holy Sepulchre, were they threatening Constantinople? As Alexius must have known for months, they were short of food and money and, if this was all they needed, then Nicolo was pleased to assure them that the emperor would provide as much as possible if they would leave.

Beneath this veneer of diplomatic politesse, however, lay a threat: 'If you refuse to leave, he [Emperor Alexius III] would be reluctant to do you harm, yet it is in his power to do so. For were you twenty times as many as you are, you would not, supposing he chose to harm you, be able to leave this country without losing many of your men and suffering defeat.'[2] These words indicate imperial confidence in the sheer weight of numbers in the Byzantine capital, although, as events of the previous day had shown, their military effectiveness was not entirely assured.

The crusaders chose Conon of Béthune to present their reply. Conon was a senior figure amongst the nobles present and he was known for his skill as a writer of *chansons de geste* and as an eloquent public speaker. Conon elegantly turned Nicolo's question back against him: 'My good sir, you have told us that your lord wonders very much why our lord and nobles have entered his dominions. Our answer is that we have not entered *his* dominions, since he has wrongfully taken possession of this land, in defiance of God, and of right of justice. It belongs to his nephew, seated here on a throne amongst us.' Conon thus presented the crusaders' justification for their actions – to redress the wrong committed by Emperor Alexius III against his brother, Isaac Angelos, and his nephew, Prince Alexius. Like the Byzantine envoy, Conon ended his speech with a threat: if the emperor were to agree to submit to the prince, they would give him sufficient money to live in luxury, 'but unless you return to give us such a message, pray do not venture here again'.[3] The crusaders' position was, on the surface, therefore, similarly uncompromising. In reality, however, they too wished to avert a war; aside from simple self-preservation, it would avoid the loss of valuable men and resources as they tried to keep alive their ultimate aim of a successful campaign in the Holy Land.

The doge conceived of one last strategem to avoid a fight: he planned to parade Prince Alexius to the people of Constantinople in the hope that popular acclaim would see the usurper dethroned and his nephew welcomed back into the city. The nobles approved the idea.[4] A letter written by them in the late summer of 1203 and circulated widely in western Europe makes it clear that the crusaders firmly believed that there was a groundswell of popular support for the young prince amongst the people of Constantinople: 'persuaded by believable rumours and arguments that the stronger city faction (and the bulk of the Empire) longed for the arrival at the royal [imperial] court of . . . [Prince] Alexius . . .', they had proceeded to Byzantium.[5] Such rumours were evidently a basic reason why the crusaders struck the deal with the prince in the first place. Already, however, there were disquieting signs that this support was, to say the least, hard to find. Hugh of Saint-Pol's letter to the West mentioned that when the crusaders first arrived at Constantinople, they were 'stunned [indeed] very much astonished that none of the friends or family of the young man who was with us, or any messengers of theirs, came to him who might tell him about the situation in the city'.[6] Perhaps, they felt, the prince needed to make a more public display of his presence.

The doge and Marquis Boniface, together with Prince Alexius, boarded an armed galley with the other nobles following in nine further ships. Under the flag of truce, the young prince and his companions rowed close to the walls of Constantinople and the crusaders called out: 'Here is your natural lord.' They asserted that Emperor Alexius III had no right to the imperial throne because of his blinding of Isaac and his wrongful seizure of power. They urged the populace to do right and support the prince, although again they added a threat: 'if you hold back, we will do to you the very worst we can'.[7] Robert of Clari claimed that no one knew who the prince was or, indeed, anything about him.[8] Perhaps there was resentment at the crusaders' coercive approach, or, as Villehardouin argued, fear of reprisals from Alexius III: 'not a single man of that land or in the city dared show himself on the young prince's side'.[9]

The overt links between Prince Alexius and an outside party comprising French crusaders and Venetians, neither of whom had a happy record of relations with Constantinople, was another likely explanation for the cool reception. Emperor Alexius III had exploited this with a propaganda offensive. The crusaders wrote that he had 'infected both the aristocrats and the plebs with venomous harangues to the effect that . . . they [the westerners] had come to destroy their ancient liberty, and they were hastening to return the place and its people to the [papacy] and to subjugate the empire . . . Certainly this story moved and, in equal measure, mobilised everyone against us.'[10] Furthermore, by this point Alexius III had ruled Byzantium for eight years. Prince Alexius, on the other hand, had no experience of government and had been away from the city for several years.

To the crusade leaders – and, indeed, to the prince himself – the complete absence of explicit support must have been devastating. One imagines the short voyage back across from Constantinople to the camp at Scutari as a sombre, silent affair. Without a shadow of doubt the crusaders now knew that they had placed far too much faith in the young man's assurances and, more pertinently, that they needed to fight to secure the supplies that he had promised. Plainly, the hostility shown to Prince Alexius by the people of Corfu had been an accurate portent of the reception that awaited him at Constantinople.

On 4 July 1203, the expedition's leaders attended mass, determined to fortify themselves and to secure spiritual guidance. There was little option but to go to war and the nobles began to draw up a battle plan. They broke the army into seven divisions, led by Count Baldwin of Flanders. He was given the prime role of taking forward the advanced guard, because he had the biggest contingent of experienced men (notwithstanding the loss of the Flemings who sailed to the Holy Land via Marseille) and the greatest number of archers and crossbowmen. The latter forces would be crucial in gaining a bridgehead when the crusading army came ashore, because their firepower could fend off the Greeks and allow time for the bulk of the attacking knights to disembark safely. The second division was led by Baldwin's brother, Henry, and also consisted of Flemish nobles and their men. Hugh of Saint-Pol led the third group and with him was Peter of Amiens, in whose company fought the chronicler Robert of Clari. Count Louis of Blois led the fourth division; Matthew of Montmorency, Geoffrey of Villehardouin and the knights of Champagne formed the fifth; Odo of Champlitte commanded the Burgundians in the sixth; and, finally, there was the rearguard of Lombards, Tuscans, Germans and Provençals, all under the leadership of Boniface of Montferrat. The Venetians were to look after the fleet. These detailed arrangements make clear the importance of preserving different regional identities in forming an order of battle. For reasons of discipline and familiarity, it was essential to keep these groups intact if possible; sometimes this might cause rivalry between particular contingents, but in the heat of conflict every possible precaution to preserve cohesion had to be a priority.[11] The conflict was set for the following day; the crusaders were to sail across the Bosphorus and open their campaign to take Constantinople.

Villehardouin expressed the situation concisely: 'the troops were to embark upon their ships and go forward to take the land by force and either live or die. It was, I assure you, one of the most formidable enterprises ever to be undertaken.'[12] For all the crusaders, whether a great noble or a lowly foot-soldier, the night of 4 July was one of reflection and anticipation. Robert of Clari related how all the men were 'very fearful of landing'.[13] For some veterans of the Third Crusade, the prospect of a great battle would have been familiar, but for many others a military engagement on this scale would have been a new and terrifying ordeal. As a crusade, spiritual issues had to be addressed because no one knew whether they would live to see the following evening; it was essential for everyone to give a full confession of their sins and to make a testament. Bishops and clergy exhorted everyone to cleanse their souls before the battle; they preached to the troops and then moved through the camp, listening to the crusaders make their peace with the Lord, administering communion and asking for His protection.[14] As Hugh of Saint-Pol wrote, 'yet we trusted in God's help and might'.[15] This was also the time to make final organisational and logistical preparations. Weapons and equipment were polished, sharpened and fettled one last time; horses were girded for their knights; and ammunition was gathered.

The crusaders planned to take Constantinople in two stages. They shied away from a direct assault on the walls and instead proposed to take the suburb of Galata that lay over the Golden Horn to the north of the main city. A great chain hung across the water, protecting the Byzantine fleet in the Golden Horn and guarding that side of the metropolis. The crusaders' first priority was to break the chain and to expose this flank of Constantinople. Because of their inferior numbers they had to exploit the one area in which they did hold a clear advantage – the sea. If they had access to the inlet it would allow them to use their land and sea forces together, which probably gave them their best chance of success.

The morning of 5 July dawned fine and clear. The crusaders prepared for the largest amphibious invasion yet attempted in medieval Europe. On board the horse-transports the crusader knights saddled their warhorses and dressed their steeds in brightly coloured caparisons. A hundred silver trumpets sounded the attack, the drums and tabors were beaten and with a tidal wave of noise the siege of Constantinople began. To try to ensure a safe passage each galley pulled a transport ship the short distance across the Bosphorus. This would guard against the vagaries of wind and current and, keeping the fleet together, would maximise the impact of the invasion force. Opposing them, Emperor Alexius had drawn up his army in full battle order.

Hugh of Saint-Pol wrote of more than 200 ships, transports and galleys in the crusader fleet.[16] To land a force of this size in the face of sizable enemy forces was an incredibly bold move, requiring complex co-ordination, good fortune with the weather and the right balance of warriors. William the Conqueror's invasion of England in 1066 was on a substantial scale, yet his landing at Pevensey was, fortunately for him, unopposed. Many sieges in the course of the crusades – such as the capture of Tyre in 1124 – had involved combined attacks (rather than landings) by land and sea forces. The westerners sought to make use of this experience, although the forced landing planned for Constantinople was somewhat different from a conventional siege.

The crusaders were faced with a mass of armed Byzantines lining the shores of the Bosphorus. Robert of Clari reported that the doge himself took charge of this seaborne part of the operation and led the host across. Archers and crossbowmen were put at the front of the ships in the hope that they might drive the Greeks away.[17] As the horse-transports reached the shore, the doors opened, a bridge was thrust out and, fully armed, knights already mounted on their chargers splashed ashore – a truly terrifying sight.[18] Archers, foot-soldiers and crossbowmen jumped down as soon as their vessels came to anchor. The first knights drew up in formation and lowered their lances to charge, but the Greeks, seeing that the crusaders' most fearsome tactic was about to be unleashed upon them, simply turned and ran. As Hugh of Saint-Pol wrote: 'all the Greeks, who had assembled for the purpose of preventing our crossing, by the grace of God, withdrew to such a distance, that we could barely reach them even with a shot arrow'.[19]

Familiar as modern readers are with stories of the intense fighting on some of the Normandy beaches during the Second World War, it seems surprising that the Byzantines did not make more of a stand against the crusaders' landing. Logically, at the moment of arrival and disembarkation the attackers would be at their most vulnerable. While the crusaders' archers and crossbowmen did much to disperse the Greeks, it still seems odd that they allowed the cavalry to form up relatively unhindered. Perhaps the daring and the novelty of the crusader tactics caught Alexius III by surprise (few would have encountered an amphibious landing before) or maybe his troops simply lacked the stomach for a fight – scarcely a good omen for the emperor.

More crusader troops poured from the ships and the men gathered into their pre-arranged regional contingents. Count Baldwin led the advance guard towards the abandoned imperial camp where they found rich pickings. Alexius III had retreated so quickly that he had left his tents and pavilions standing and the crusaders happily took possession of these and much other booty.

The next obstacle faced by the army was the Tower of Galata: a solid defensive complex that held one side of the great iron chain that stretched across the Golden Horn to the main city.[20] All medieval ports had such chains because they were the simplest and most effective method of controlling entry to and exit from a harbour. They were for defence, but also existed as a taxation point: in normal trading conditions a ship wishing to sail into or to leave a port had to pay a fee to have the chain raised or lowered. At Constantinople it was crucial that the crusaders should break through the chain and gain access to the Golden Horn. From the Venetians' point of view, it would be much easier for their ships to assault the walls facing the Golden Horn, because the inlet offered calmer waters than those on the Bosphorus or the Sea of Marmara.

The crusaders had to confront more than the strength of the Tower of Galata and the iron chain. Lurking behind the metal barrier was a line of Greek ships: not just the galleys of the navy, but all of Constantinople's merchant vessels – the barges and the ferries – as well.[21] While these were not in themselves a dangerous threat, they formed yet another obstacle to the western fleet.

The army camped outside the Tower on the night of 5 July, but around nine o'clock the following morning the Greeks made a surprise attack. The emperor sent a contingent of soldiers across the Golden Horn by barge and, joining up with the garrison of the Tower, they poured out towards the crusader camp. So swift was their advance that the westerners did not even have time to mount their horses. Caught unawares, the knights had to start the fight on foot and the Flemish noble, Jacques of Avesnes, son of a famous warrior of the Third Crusade, led the resistance. The shock impact of the Byzantine raid cut into the crusader forces and Jacques himself took a searing lance-wound to the face. He seemed doomed – wounded and isolated from his colleagues. Spotting the danger, one of his knights, Nicholas of Jenlain, managed to commandeer a horse and charged towards his lord. The arrival of a mounted soldier, at speed and with all the impetus of a fully armed knight, was enough to burst through the Greeks who surrounded Jacques. Faced with such a formidable opponent, the Byzantines were forced to abandon their prize and Nicholas rescued his lord, to wide praise for his gallant conduct.[22]

While this intense small-scale drama unfolded the crusaders were called to arms and they began a concerted counter-attack. The Greeks had stirred up a hornet's nest and soon they were driven back in disarray. Some ran to take shelter in the Tower, others tried to escape back onto their barges. Many were caught as they attempted to board the vessels and others drowned as they struggled to save themselves, although a few did manage to break free and return to the safety of Constantinople itself. The crusaders chased hard after those who fled towards the Tower, grimly closing down upon their enemy. The first Greeks began to pour back through the entrance gate, propelled by the sensation of having to run for their lives. They thought they had won at least a temporary respite, but this was not to be. The fastest of the pursuers had caught the slowest of the Greek soldiers and managed to stop them from closing the gate. Fierce fighting erupted as the crusaders scented the chance of a vital breakthrough. To capture the Tower by siege might take days, or even weeks: it would expose the attackers to the risk of raids from the main city and it would mean the consumption of valuable supplies. If, however, they forced the gate, then a clear advantage – if not total victory – would be within their grasp.

Soon the defenders of the Tower realised their position was hopeless and they surrendered – to the intense delight of the crusaders. Shortly afterwards the *Eagle*, one of the biggest ships in the fleet, crashed through the chain: the harbour and the Byzantine vessels lay at the Venetians' mercy.[23] The attack galleys hunted down the sorry remnants of the Greek fleet, sinking some and capturing others, while a few Greeks chose to scuttle their ships rather than be taken. Breaking the chain was a tremendous blow to the Byzantines: tearing through this vital protective barrier meant the westerners could now push into the inner waters of the Golden Horn. This in turn allowed them to bring their fleet close up to the walls of the Queen of Cities, dramatically increasing their pressure on the Greeks. All of the crusaders took great heart from their success and thanked the Lord for His divine approval. Alberic of Trois-Fontaines reported that the chain was later sent to the port of Acre (in the kingdom of Jerusalem) as a symbol of this triumph.[24]

The following day the full crusader fleet sailed around from its mooring on the Bosphorus and up into the safety of the Golden Horn. This prudent, practical move by the Venetians must have increased anxiety within Constantinople a further notch; the westerners were making too much progress for comfort. To see the enemy ships enter the city's harbour and then to watch them pass by in their dozens must have brought home the grave and imminent danger. On the other hand, the walls of the New Rome had successfully withstood many invasions over the centuries — surely this latest threat would be resisted, too.

The army's leadership had to decide on its next move. The Venetians wanted to mount the whole assault from scaling ladders on their ships; the French protested, feeling uncomfortable with this unfamiliar form of warfare. They preferred to deploy themselves on land where they believed that their fighting skills, practised on the tournament fields of Europe, could be of greatest use. Logic prevailed and both parties agreed to operate in tandem, each engaging the enemy in their customary manner: the French on land, the Venetians by sea.

Over the next four days the crusaders rested and set their weapons and equipment in good order. Then on 11 July, again in proper forma-tion, they marched two miles along the shore to the Blachernae bridge over the Golden Horn.[25] The Greeks had destroyed the stone bridge after their earlier retreat to the city, but the crusaders set to rebuilding it as fast as they could. There was another bridge several miles up the Golden Horn, but the westerners did not wish to divide their forces or expend the energy in an unnecessary march. Again, it seems strange that the emperor had not demolished the bridge more thoroughly (the crusaders rebuilt it in a day) and that he did not harass the reconstruction work. He might also have opposed the crossing of the bridge: a contingent of the fearsome Varangian Guard would have been hard to dislodge from such a narrow place. Simply by keeping the crusaders away from the land walls of the city or, at least, by forcing them on a detour and thereby splitting the land and sea forces, he would have gained an advantage. As

Hugh of Saint-Pol wrote: 'separated significantly from our fleet, we would have, perhaps, run a great risk and incurred casualties'.[26] Given the attackers' failing supplies, the longer the emperor drew out the siege, the better chance he would have, because with the small size of the western army a complete blockade of Constantinople was not possible. In the event, Alexius III took none of these courses; Robert of Clari noted minimal resistance before the crusaders drove the Greeks away and crossed the Golden Horn.[27]

They took up a position outside the Blachernae palace in the northernmost corner of the city – posing a direct threat to the imperial residence. Although its walls lay close to the foot of a slope, the palace was well defended by impressively thick fortifications that rose about 50 feet high. The crusaders made their main camp on the hill across from the Blachernae palace. Here stood a building known to the crusaders as the castle of Bohemond (the Norman prince of that name had stayed there during the First Crusade), but which was in fact the abbey of Sts Cosmas and Damian. The Venetian fleet stationed itself opposite the waterbound side of the palace and so the crusader forces formed a hinge around the north-eastern edge of the city. From here, on top of the hill, the French had their first real view of the land defences of Constantinople: stretching up and down over the rolling hills to the west was the 3½-mile-long obstacle of the Theodosian walls. No comparable defensive structure existed in western Europe and, given the relatively small size of the crusader force, an attack on the whole length of the walls was utterly impractical. Nevertheless, Villehardouin felt a sense of satisfaction that the crusaders were prepared to bring the Greeks to battle – a challenge of this scale would be a true test of their bravery and daring. He was also level-headed enough to appreciate that the task would be by no means easy, writing: 'It was a sight to fill the heart with pride and apprehension.'[28]

The two parts of the crusader army readied themselves to begin the siege. Robert of Clari provides a wonderfully detailed description of the 'marvellous engines' constructed by the doge's crews on top of their ships. The Venetians took the cross-spars (or yard-arms), the diagonal beams from which the sails were hung, and lashed enough of them high up on the masts to form a makeshift bridge. These bridges, measuring about 110 feet long, were then covered in planks to form a walkway wide enough for three or four knights. Handrails and coverings of hides and canvas were added to help protect the attackers against arrows and crossbow bolts. In effect, they had suspended huge leather and wooden tubes high above their ships, from which bodies of heavily armed knights might be disgorged onto the battlements of Constantinople.[29] The Venetians also set up mangonels and catapults on their transport ships. Thus the fleet bristled with menace and carried a lethal cargo of men and weapons, poised to unleash its firepower against the Greeks.

While the French forces also set up their engines of war and prepared to attack by land, they were relentlessly harried by the Byzantines. Six or seven times a day they sallied out of the various gates along the city walls of Constantinople and caused a call to arms around the camp. Thus the besiegers were themselves pinned down: the close attention of the Greeks meant that no one dared venture further than four bowshots from the camp in search of food. Supplies were running extremely low and, except for flour and bacon, there was nothing to eat apart from the flesh taken from horses killed in battle. Villehardouin stated that there was only enough food to last the crusader forces three weeks: 'Our army was thus in an extremely desperate situation for never, in any city, have so many been besieged by so few.'[30] Given the westerners' inability to blockade so huge a site as Constantinople, there was little likelihood of the Byzantines running short of food, in spite of their recent military setbacks. The crusaders understood that they had to bring the siege to a head immediately. There was no question of a long, drawn-out investment of the city – such as the siege of Lisbon in 1147, which had lasted 17 weeks, or that at Acre, which had run from August 1189 to July 1191.

In response to the Greek raids the crusaders fortified their camp. This was common practice amongst besieging armies and signalled (whether true or not) a determination to dig in. They excavated trenches and constructed a strong palisade of planks and crossbeams to increase security. Even so, the Byzantine forces continued their sallies. Villehardouin reports that the crusaders usually repulsed these vigorously and managed to inflict heavy losses on the enemy. The western contingents rotated guard duty to share the burden of this task. One day, on the Burgundian watch, there was a lightning thrust by the Varangian guard. The crusaders responded fiercely and their opponents fell back towards the gate, but this may have been a ruse because, when the pursuers followed too closely, they were suddenly subjected to a barrage of heavy missiles thrown from the walls. The Byzantines hurled great stones onto their attackers and one broke the arm of William of Champlitte. The engagement was not without some profit, however, because Walter of Neuilly managed to capture a member of one of the most important families of Constantinople, Constantine Lascaris. He was taken prisoner and held by the crusaders – such bargaining counters could always be useful in any future negotiations, as well as fetching a substantial ransom.

For 10 days there was a succession of sallies, counter-attacks, bombardments and cameos of individual bravery or tragedy. Men such as Peter of Bracieux and Matthew of Wallincourt won renown for themselves, while others such as William of Gi perished. Meanwhile the crusaders were carefully constructing scaling ladders to be used in a full assault on the city. Both sides fired wave upon wave of arrows and missiles at each other: on the one hand, falling amongst the westerners' tents; on the other, sometimes passing through the palace windows or hitting its walls. Niketas Choniates described encounters between horsemen and knights in which the deeds of the Greeks 'were not ignoble', suggesting a stalemate at this point of the struggle.[31]

On Thursday 17 July the onslaught began. The crusaders feared an assault on their camp while their forces were occupied trying to take the walls of the city. They therefore divided their troops to leave three divisions, led by Boniface of Montferrat, to stand guard, while another four, headed as ever by Baldwin of Flanders, were to give battle. The Venetians were to begin an attack from the water, thereby subjecting the defenders of the Blachernae quarter to pressure from two sides simultaneously. The trumpets of war sounded and the French forces made a determined advance towards the walls. The carrying of scaling ladders made their intent plain to all inside, and Alexius III had taken care to deploy his crack troops, the Varangian guard, at this crucial location. A hail of enemy missiles greeted the crusaders' approach, but a group of four men managed to duck and weave through the deadly storm to place two ladders against a barbican close to the sea. They struggled up the ladder and made enough of a bridgehead for another eleven men to join them. The Varangians wielded their heavy battle-axes and the crusaders defended themselves with their swords. In the cut and thrust of the fight the sheer power of the Byzantine army's elite won the day and the crusaders were driven back down the ladders, except for two unfortunate individuals who were captured and paraded before a delighted Emperor Alexius. For the first time his soldiers had succeeded in resisting the enemy and many of the Frenchmen had been wounded or suffered broken limbs from missiles or by falling from the scaling ladders. Hugh of Saint-Pol mentioned that the crusaders had even managed to tunnel under the walls and collapse a tower, but such was the scale of the city's fortifications and the ferocity of the defenders' resistance that they could not exploit this breakthrough. Perhaps the emperor's policy of relying on his city's formidable walls and the savage determination of his personal bodyguard would be enough to save Constantinople. It seemed that the French forces might be contained, although the Venetian fleet posed another, and very different, threat.

Dandolo had drawn up his ships in a huge line facing the northern walls of the city. These particular defences were only a single layer thick and, at around 35 feet high, relied upon their proximity to the Golden Horn as much as on their own innate strength to repel the enemy. The Golden Horn is only about 250 yards wide at this point, which created a narrow, funnelled arena for this stage of the conflict. A triple barrage of weaponry flew from the Venetian vessels. From the castles at the top of each ship crossbowmen sent their stubby, lethal bolts fizzing across the water; archers shot their slender arrows soaring higher; while down on deck the crew released the mangonels that hurled stones towards the crowded walls of Constantinople. Once again there was stern resistance from the battlements, where a group of Pisans, determined to protect the commercial interests of their home city, stood shoulder-to-shoulder with a few Varangians. In some areas the walls came almost to the sea and the Venetians' ship-mounted scaling ladders lurched close enough to allow an exchange of blows with the enemy. Villehardouin wrote of the tremendous noise of this struggle: the creaking of the timber ships, the slap of oars as rowers held their boats steady, the shouts and screams of war and the sharp ring of metal on metal. In one area a group of heavily armed knights managed to land and bring a battering-ram to bear against the wall. The dull, rhythmic thud of the machine announced its presence and soon smashed through the stonework. Yet the Pisans, Varangians and Greeks resisted sternly and the attackers were forced out.[32] Niketas Choniates lamented that 'the horrendous battle that followed was fought with groanings on all sides'.[33]

Standing at the prow of his vermilion galley, Doge Dandolo sensed that his men were making too little progress; he needed to inspire them. With the winged lion on the banner of St Mark flying in front of him, he threatened dire punishment for any shirkers and demanded that the sailors land him on the shore. The crew immediately obeyed and propelled the galley forwards with a series of vigorous pulls on the oars. The Venetians saw the doge's ship move ahead and their banner land. As Dandolo had calculated, they were shamed by the old man's bravery; they could not abandon their venerable leader and rushed to join him. As soon as the first vessels reached the shallows the men did not wait to touch the shoreline, but jumped down and waded to land. The bigger ships with their deeper draught could not risk disaster by getting so close, but their crews let down smaller boats and raced for the shore. Dandolo's charismatic leadership paid off. At this sudden onslaught the Byzantine defenders lost heart and fled, leaving the Venetians free to stream in through the gates and take control of a section of wall containing 25 towers.[34] It seems that Alexius III had made a calamitous mistake. He had concentrated most of the Varangian guard opposite the French forces at the Blachernae palace, believing that this was where the main threat to his city lay. He had underestimated the ability of the Venetians to deliver a serious attack against the sea walls and to land their troops. While the defenders on the walls of the Golden Horn had been content to bombard the Venetians from the comparative safety of the battlements, the prospect of hand-to-hand fighting was enough to make most of them flee. Given the strength and determination of the Varangians up at Blachernae, had a larger contingent of the guard been deployed with the Pisans and the local forces along the Golden Horn, the Venetians would have encountered far more serious resistance.

Villehardouin described this success as 'an event so marvellous it might be called a miracle'.[35] The doge understood the value of this news to the French forces and dispatched messengers to tell them of the breakthrough. He also showed an acute awareness of their needs when he immediately ferried as many as 200 captured horses or palfreys up to the main camp to replace those that had been lost in battle. Without war-horses the knights clearly lacked the speed, weight and manoeuvrability so crucial to their military role.[36]

Alexius soon realised the gravity of the incursion and ordered a contingent of Varangians to try to force the Venetians out. The arrival of these men dramatically changed the balance of the struggle and the Venetians began to fall back. As they did so they tried to slow the Byzantines' advance by setting fire to the buildings between the two forces. Whether by chance or calculation, the wind blew from behind the Venetians and into the faces of their adversaries. As the flames were fanned ever higher the Venetians disappeared behind a dense cloud of smoke that created an impenetrable protective screen. The breeze continued to take the fire towards the Greeks, allowing the attackers to consolidate their hold on the walls and towers. The blaze grew stronger still and swallowed homes and businesses inside the wall. The hill of Blachernae stopped the conflagration from heading north-west towards the palace, but the gentler slopes to the south were a less serious barrier and only the open cistern of Aetius halted the inferno. Historians have calculated that just over 120 acres of the city were destroyed by the blaze, leaving 20,000 Byzantines homeless and without their possessions. Niketas Choniates grimly recounted the damage: 'It was a piteous spectacle to behold that day, one that required rivers of tears to counterbalance the fire's extensive damage . . .'[37]

At this moment it appears that Alexius III appreciated, as if for the first time, that if he was to win the battle and save his throne he had to seize the initiative. As Niketas wearily wrote: 'he at last took up arms'. The emperor's relative inactivity had started to provoke discontent amongst the citizenry; some accused him of cowardice, staying safely inside his palace, rather than taking on the enemy face-to-face. 'It was as though he had not realised that forethought is superior to afterthought, that it is better to anticipate the enemy than to be anticipated by him' was the Byzantine chronicler's exasperated assessment of Alexius III's performance.[38] There were, however, some grounds for optimism amongst the Greeks. Notwithstanding losses of life and property, they had successfully fended off one French assault and next they sought to drive them from the field of battle. It was hoped that such a victory would compel the Venetians to give up their slim hold on the sea walls, at which point the crusade might effectively disintegrate.

As if the city walls and the Blachernae palace did not provide a dramatic enough skyline, the billowing clouds of smoke from the burning metropolis behind added a distracting, doom-laden atmosphere to the situation. Against this sombre backdrop the emperor assembled a large body of men and marched them out of the St Romanus Gate about a mile south-west of the crusader camp.[39]

As line after line of Greek troops strode out of the city, the sheer size of the Byzantine army daunted Villehardouin: 'you would have thought that the whole world was there assembled'.[40] Niketas stated that 'when the opponents' land forces suddenly beheld this huge array they shuddered'.[41] Robert of Clari believed that the Greeks had 17 divisions, compared with the seven mustered by the crusaders. Alexius III planned to trap his enemies in a pincer movement: as the main army drew up to face the westerners on the plain outside Constantinople, he had another contingent of men ready to surge out of the three gates nearest to the camp.

The crusaders acted quickly to deal with this terrible threat. They divided their forces, leaving Henry of Flanders's division to guard the siege machines while the bulk of the men formed into six divisions in front of the palisade. The westerners took up their positions with care. To compensate for their lack of numbers they tried to present one formidable target to the vastly bigger Byzantine army. In the first line the archers and crossbowmen stood ready to unleash a lethal rain of metal against any who dared come close. Behind them were at least 200 knights who had to fight on foot because they had lost their horses. Even so, the training and armour of these troops would make them difficult adversaries. The remainder of the crusader army consisted of the mounted knights – numbered at only around 650 by Robert of Clari; or 500 knights, 500 other mounted men and 2,000 foot-soldiers, according to Hugh of Saint-Pol.[42] Villehardouin believed that so great was the size of the Greek army that, had the crusaders advanced from this position, 'they would, so to speak, have been drowned amongst them'.[43] The Byzantine force seemed to cover the plain. This terrifying sight, flanked to the crusaders' left by the walls of Constantinople, once again crammed with enemy troops, made clear to the westerners the stark fact that they were a small, isolated army, thousands of miles from home and trying to conquer one of the greatest cities in the world. In fact, the crusaders were so desperate that they armed the stable-lads and cooks by covering them with horse-blankets and quilts to protect their bodies and giving them copper cooking pots for helmets. For weapons they carried kitchen implements. This motley collection of individuals was turned to face the walls of the city and Robert of Clari claimed that 'when the emperor's foot-soldiers saw our common people so hideously arrayed they had so great fear and so great terror of them that they never dared move or come towards them'.[44]

Slowly the Greek army advanced towards the French knights, gradually increasing the pressure on them, inexorably closing the space between the forces. The crusaders were not daunted, and they too began to move forwards. Like boxers sizing each other up, the two sides shadowed and feinted, yet neither was willing to deliver the first blow. The leaders of the French army had laid down the strictest, most explicit instructions for the knights to maintain order and not to charge before any formal command. Countless times in the past, small groups of crusading knights, fired by the chance to perform heroic deeds, had hurtled into the enemy and fatally fragmented their own forces, often losing their lives as well. This was such a problem in western armies that the Rule of the Knights Hospitaller (the regulations governing the order) threatened the loss of his horse to any man who broke ranks before a general instruction to charge. The idea of maintaining good order sounds so simple, but in the heat of a battle, with communications almost impossible and adrenaline coursing through the warriors' veins, it was incredibly difficult to achieve.

The crusaders decided to choose two of the bravest warriors from each contingent to take command of each section of the army. They were to order the men to 'trot' to move forwards and to 'spur' if they wanted to attack. Count Baldwin of Flanders led his men forwards at a trot, followed by the count of Saint-Pol and Peter of Amiens, and then Henry of Flanders in the third group. In contrast to their bizarrely clothed camp followers, the main body of knights was a splendid sight. Set in close formation with all their horses brightly covered in silk or cloth caparisons, their banners bearing the different coats of arms fluttering above them, their shields gleamed and their helmets and chain mail shone brightly. This undulating array of colour moved gently along, accompanied by the clicking of their horses' hooves and the clinking of weapons and equipment. The foot-soldiers marched behind them, again keeping close order.

By this time, news of the impending battle had reached the doge over on the Golden Horn. Dandolo again showed how fiercely loyal he was to his crusading comrades and declared that he would live or die in the company of the pilgrims. Quickly he led as many of his men as possible towards the crusader camp at the Blachernae.

When Baldwin had moved two full bowshots from the camp, the senior warriors in his contingent advised him to halt. 'Lord, you do not well to fight the emperor so far away from the camp, for if you fight him there and have need of help, those who are guarding the camp will not be able to help you.'[45] They recommended that he return to the palisades where the crusaders could engage in combat more effectively. Baldwin agreed and he, along with his brother Henry, began to turn back. The matter of preserving good, coherent order in a medieval army was not simply a question of discipline, however. One central concern to the whole knightly ethos was the issue of honour. When Hugh of Saint-Pol and Peter of Amiens saw Baldwin turn back, they were shocked and felt that he brought shame upon the crusading army for doing so. Disregarding the earlier instructions to hold together, they resolved to take over the vanguard themselves in order to preserve the honour of the French forces. Baldwin was appalled and sent urgent messages that they should drop back, but three times Hugh and Peter refused. On the contrary, they started to move towards the Greeks. The crusaders' carefully constructed unity looked perilously compromised. Peter of Amiens, along with Eustace of Canteleux, one of the senior knights in the Saint-Pol contingent, gave the order: 'Lords, ride forward now, in God's name, all at the trot.'[46] Far from being cowed by the size of the imperial army, it seems that some of the crusaders were prepared to take an emphatically aggressive approach. The rest of the army saw what was happening and cried out for God to protect these brave men. Robert of Clari described the windows of the Blachernae palace and the walls of the city as being filled with ladies and maidens watching the battle, who said that 'our men seemed like angels because they were so beautiful, so finely armed and with their horses so finely accoutred'.[47] Here, Robert appears to be drawing rather too heavily on the conventions of a tournament and one doubts that the crusaders were viewed by their adversaries as being remotely angelic.

The actions of Hugh and Peter threatened chaos in the crusader ranks. Those knights with Count Baldwin became agitated: they could not bear to abandon their colleagues, nor could they lightly pass up the chance of glory. So corrosive was this mood that they threatened revolt: 'Lord, you are doing great shame not to advance, and know that if you do not now ride forward, we will no longer hold ourselves to you.'[48] When he heard this, Baldwin had little choice but to comply. He spurred his horse and, joined by Henry's men, he caught up with the vanguard. Quickly the crusaders rearranged themselves into one long battle line, now within crossbow range of the emperor's men but back in proper formation. Robert of Clari, our humble knight, is the source for this fascinating insight into the machinations of the crusading nobility. Intriguingly, when Hugh of Saint-Pol, one of the main protagonists of the entire episode, wrote a report of the battle in late July, his account was much simpler: 'we advanced in an orderly and co-ordinated fashion against the battle-line opposing us'.[49] He made no mention of the awkward disagreements between himself and Count Baldwin and the fact that he had, in effect, challenged the count's integrity and position as commander of the vanguard. In the afterglow of victory it seemed unnecessary to tarnish the day's outcome by describing these difficult and divisive moments.

The crusaders' indecision offered a fleeting opportunity for the Greeks to act. A more alert commander than Alexius III might have noticed this temporary weakness, assessed the situation and chosen to strike a swift, sharp blow against the isolated contingent under Hugh and Peter as they marched alone at the front of the army. But with the arrival of the other divisions, the moment – which may have been very brief – had passed.

Between the two armies lay a small rise and, towards the emperor's side, the River Lycus. When the crusaders reached the top of the hill, both sides paused. The Byzantine troops were joined by those soldiers who had surrounded the camp and so they became an even stronger force. Once again the westerners conferred and this time Baldwin's arguments were heeded. The Frenchmen were now out of sight of their reinforcements back at the camp and to engage with the Byzantine army would necessitate crossing the Lycus river. Even though this was only a small waterway, it would inevitably slow their advance and taking it might well lead to heavy losses. The crusaders resolved to halt and were probably on the point of retreating when they noticed activity in the enemy lines.

This, surely, was the moment for Alexius III to exploit his massive numerical superiority and order an overwhelming charge to drive the barbarians from his city. He held the banks of the Lycus and could cross it with ease. Like heavy, humid thunderclouds, the Greek forces stood poised to break over the crusaders. Yet the onslaught never came. Incredibly, the emperor gave no instruction to charge and, as time wore on, he gave the order to withdraw his troops, turning them around and heading back towards the city. Whatever tactical reasons lay behind this move, psychologically it appeared to all as a devastating admission of defeat.

Niketas believed that Emperor Alexius's heart had never been in the fight and that he had always planned to flee. The Byzantine writer felt that had the imperial army moved with real conviction, victory would have been possible. He sensed that Alexius's own unwillingness to engage in battle transmitted itself to his commanders and prevented the Greeks from striking the lethal blow.[50]

The crusaders could hardly believe what they saw. A letter sent by the leading nobles back to the West conveyed their understanding of what had taken place: 'Astounded at our steadfastness (given our small number), he [the emperor] ignominiously turns his reins and retreats into the burning city.'[51] Hugh of Saint-Pol commented: 'When they saw that we were brave and steadfast and that we moved forward one after the other in formation and that we could not be overrun or broken they rightly became terrified and confused. Retreating before us they dared not fight by day.'[52] When the emperor did not dare to commit his troops to the fray, the westerners' belief in the cowardice and effeminacy of the Greeks seemed justified. The crusaders must have experienced overwhelming relief and a feeling of renewed hope and resolve. To capitalise on the moment, Baldwin ordered the army to advance slowly after the Greeks, in order to emphasise further the Byzantines' humiliating withdrawal from the field. Crucially, the westerners now retained their discipline. On the brink of victory it was all too easy to be carried away with success, to break ranks and charge after the enemy.

Villehardouin eloquently conveys the crusaders' almost uncomprehending relief: 'I can assure you that God never delivered any people from greater peril than that from which He saved our troops that day. There was not a man in the army, however bold and courageous, whose heart was not filled with joy.' Even so, living through days anticipating battle and hours facing the Byzantine forces outside the walls took an intense physical and emotional toll. In addition, there was a marked lack of food. Thus, in spite of the day's triumph, the crusaders were unable to drop their guard. The Byzantines were still, numerically at least, the superior force, and it was vital for the westerners to preserve their confidence and not to compromise their military strength.

Why had Emperor Alexius failed to attack, given the Greeks' apparent superiority in numbers, at least? In part, it seems that the emperor was a man of little innate aggression or military experience. He had hoped that the Byzantines' display of strength would be enough to break crusader morale, causing them to concede and retreat. Yet he had not grasped just how determined and desperate the westerners actually were. They had made great progress in their advance across the Bosphorus and then the Golden Horn; furthermore, the Venetians had taken a section of the walls. These were surely indications enough that the crusaders were a dangerous force. The presence of the westerners' heavy cavalry also caused the Greeks serious concern. While some of the knights' horses had been lost, enough remained to form a potent attacking unit. The lethal strength of the crusader cavalry charge was well known in Byzantium. Back in the 1140s Anna Comnena had memorably written that a western knight on horseback 'would make a hole through the walls of Babylon'.[53] The plains outside Constantinople offered the ideal conditions for the Frankish charge – relatively flat land and a fixed target. The Greeks may have had some cavalry themselves, but their horsemen were almost certainly less well practised than the French knights, who had spent years honing their skills on the tournament fields of northern Europe.

Inside Constantinople there was disbelief and anger. It was the emperor's responsibility to protect the city. He had so great an army and the crusaders were so few, yet he had not fought them. As Niketas commented: 'he returned [to the city] in utter disgrace, having only made the enemy more haughty and insolent'.[54] The damage caused by the Venetians' fire further weakened Alexius III's standing in the eyes of his people. They clamoured for action. A group came to the emperor and told him that if he continued to act so feebly, then they would seek out his nephew amongst the crusaders and offer him the imperial throne. Reluctantly, Alexius III promised to fight the following day. In reality, however, he had already decided on a different course of action.

The emperor no longer had the stomach for battle. Niketas depicts a gentle, mild man, accessible to the people and deeply troubled by his blinding of Isaac Angelos. Today we might say that he was not tough enough for the job.[55] He was unwilling to risk his own life and he sensed that the people of Constantinople were not prepared to engage in a protracted campaign – which, given the westerners' lack of supplies, may

well have been the Greeks' best chance of victory. The emperor was sufficiently versed in the politics of Constantinople to realise that he had lost
the confidence of the people – and he was experienced enough to recall
the grisly and excruciating fate of earlier rulers who had been removed
by the mob. Equally, he could hardly expect much mercy from his brother
or his nephew, were he turned over to them. Wisely, therefore, he decided
to flee.

During the evening of 17 July he conferred with his daughter Irene
and his most trusted advisers. Hurriedly they collected 1,000 pounds of
gold and as many precious ornaments and objects as could be carried.
Near midnight the emperor and his closest associates stole away from
the city heading for Develton, a fortified town more than 90 miles away
on the Black Sea. Niketas Choniates was both scathing and despairing
of Alexius III's motives and actions. He gives us a vivid and haunting
image of the Byzantines' view of their emperor: 'it was as though he had
laboured hard to make a miserable corpse of the city, to bring her utter
ruin in defiance of her destiny, and he hastened along her destruction'.[56]
Niketas scorned Alexius III's lack of care for his precious city and decried
his eagerness to save his own skin.

As dawn broke on the morning of 18 July, the news began to spread:
Constantinople, the Queen of Cities, the New Rome, had been abandoned by its emperor – a devastating and unheard-of blow to the pride
and self-esteem of the great metropolis. So deep was this wound that the
Greeks could not face prolonging the struggle against the crusaders. Rather
than using the moment to try to turn their fortunes around, they despaired.
The westerners' seemingly relentless progress and their refusal to back
down outside the city walls, plus the Venetian foothold on the Golden
Horn – made apparent to all by the continuing palls of smoke rising
above it – made them fear the utter destruction of their city. In terror,
they sought the one person who could save them. Imperial officials went
to the rooms in the Blachernae palace where the blinded Isaac was held.
In him they saw 'their last hope'.[57] The minister of the imperial treasuries, a eunuch named Philoxenites, took charge. He assembled the
Varangian guard and secured their support for the idea of making Isaac
emperor again. Even though blinding was usually taken to bar a man from
holding such an office, the situation demanded that precedent be set aside.
Alexius III had abandoned his wife Euphrosyne (with whom he had had

a stormy relationship), but she was now seized – in case she sought to create a rival faction – and her relatives imprisoned. The senior figures in the city went to Isaac and explained the situation to him. His reaction is unknown. Did he gloat at his brother's humiliation? Was he intimidated at the prospect of becoming emperor again, handicapped as he was? Or was he delighted at the thought of exercising ultimate authority again? Servants brought him the imperial robes and insignia. He dressed and left the Blachernae palace as a free man. Poignantly, his blindness meant that Isaac had to be led up to the imperial throne, but he was, after all, proclaimed emperor.[58]

He wished to make immediate contact with Prince Alexius in the crusader camp. The news of Alexius III's escape and the recrowning of Isaac could not be concealed for long. The leading men of Byzantium needed to hold on to whatever initiative these developments afforded them. Messengers were sent to tell the prince that his father was emperor again and that the usurper had fled. As soon as the information reached the young Alexius he told Marquis Boniface, who in turn called together all the nobles.

The men assembled in the prince's tent where he announced the wonderful news. A huge cheer burst from the pavilion. As Villehardouin wrote, 'their joy on hearing it was such as cannot be described, for no greater joy was ever felt by anyone in this world'.[59] The crusaders thanked God for delivering them from the depths of despair to such a great height. They had no doubt that divine favour had blessed their actions: 'The man whom God desires to help no other man can harm.' Their decision to go to Constantinople had been correct – God had approved of their actions – how else could they have succeeded?[60]

CHAPTER TEN

'I should like you to know that a number of my people
do not love me'

Triumph and Tensions at Constantinople,
July–August 1203

IN SPITE OF the crusaders' successes, they needed to keep a very firm
check on their emotions. While the news of Emperor Alexius's flight
and Isaac's return to power seemed to guarantee the status of the
young prince, the standing of the westerners was far less clear. They had,
after all, just been bombarding the very city that was now poised to open
its gates to them – how would its inhabitants react to the prince's allies,
particularly in light of Alexius III's intensive anti-western propaganda
over recent months? The overwhelming feeling throughout the camp was
one of caution. Suspicion of Byzantine duplicity dated back to the First
Crusade when Emperor Alexius I had failed to bring support to the
crusaders at the siege of Antioch in 1098. Greek treachery was widely
trumpeted as the reason for the crushing defeats suffered by the kings of
France and Germany during the Second Crusade. The massacre of westerners in 1182 and the later alliance with Saladin served to consolidate a
deeply held scepticism concerning Byzantine reliability. With firm news
yet to emerge, the crusaders donned their armour and wearily prepared
their weapons just in case Isaac, or his advisers, continued to resist the
holy warriors.

Throughout the morning of 18 July a steady trickle of information
and messengers came out from Constantinople, but all repeated the same
story. The emperor was gone and his blind brother was back on the imperial throne. The doge and the nobles determined to clarify their own position. They selected four envoys: two (unnamed) Venetians and two

Frenchmen, Matthew of Montmorency and Geoffrey of Villehardouin. They were instructed to ask Isaac to confirm the agreements made by the prince – covenants that, without a shadow of doubt, the future of the crusade rested upon. Prince Alexius was an asset of paramount importance to the westerners. They were counting on his father feeling sufficient paternal devotion and a moral obligation to ratify the promises made by the young man.

Thanks to Villehardouin's presence on the embassy we have an eye-witness account of the events inside Constantinople on 18 July 1203. The four envoys rode out of the crusader camp and headed the few hundred yards towards the city walls. Escorts met them and they proceeded to the Blachernae palace. The presence of the Varangian guard at the gates showed that the new regime had the support of this vital faction. Shouldering their heavy battle-axes, the guard formed a menacing corridor right up to the main door of the palace itself. As he had in St Mark's 15 months earlier, Villehardouin found himself amongst a small group of crusaders entering a magnificent but unfamiliar building, not knowing how he would be received. In Venice he was, at the very least, assured of the support of the city's ruler, the doge, but in Constantinople he had no such guarantees. After several days of trying to batter their way into the Blachernae palace, four of the crusaders now found themselves freely entering the magnificent building.

They were taken into one of the ceremonial halls and there, waiting for them, was the Byzantine court in all its splendour. The room was crammed with the noble families of Constantinople, so tightly packed that there was hardly room to move. All wore their most splendid apparel: shining silks, dazzling jewels and long, flowing robes. As Villehardouin and his three companions moved into the room filled with the buzz of an alien language, they fell under the gaze of hundreds of eyes. Some expressions conveyed fear towards the men who threatened calamity on their city; some transmitted anger at the death and destruction already inflicted on Constantinople; others still may have viewed the westerners with disdain – the barbarians of popular Byzantine imagination. Yet more may have tried to appear welcoming, to reassure the aggressors that the struggle was over.

At the end of the hall, seated on their imperial thrones, were Isaac and his wife, Margaret, the sister of King Emico of Hungary.

Villehardouin described the emperor as being dressed in the most costly robes imaginable; he was also quite taken by the empress whom he described as 'a very beautiful woman'. Villehardouin appreciated the irony in seeing the couple seated there in such splendour when, only the previous day, they had been held as prisoners by the very same people who now fawned around them. If these people could change allegiance to one of their own so quickly, what of their loyalty to outsiders?

The Byzantine nobles paid their respects to the envoys and the four men walked down the hall to the imperial thrones. Isaac acknowledged them with due honour and, through an interpreter, asked them to speak. The crusaders replied that they wished to converse with the emperor in private, on behalf of Prince Alexius and their companions in the western army. This was a carefully calculated move: the promises made by the young man included many highly sensitive issues, such as the submission of the Orthodox Church to Rome and the payment of huge sums of money to the crusaders. If these matters were raised in front of the full Byzantine court they were likely to provoke outrage. At worst the physical safety of the envoys might be threatened; more likely, Isaac would face such an immediate and spontaneous demonstration of anger that he would be unable to agree any of the proposals put to him.

The emperor accepted the suggestion and stood up. Maria took him by the hand and led him into another chamber, accompanied only by a man identified by Villehardouin as his chancellor (probably a senior Byzantine noble), an interpreter and the four envoys. Thus far the whole tenor of the meeting had revealed a remarkable compliance on the part of the Greeks, dictated by the perilous and turbulent circumstances of the moment. Foreign rulers who visited Constantinople were usually treated to displays designed to show off the power and wealth of the Byzantine Empire and an integral part of this procedure was to demonstrate the manifest superiority of the Greeks. For example, while a visiting ruler was allowed to sit next to the emperor, his throne would be lower, making clear to all the proper order of affairs. King Louis VII of France had been obliged to submit to this gentle humiliation when he met Manuel Comnenus in 1147. The contemporary Greek writer, John Kinnamos, reported: 'When he came inside the palace, the emperor was seated on high, and a lowly seat, which people who speak Latin call a chair, was offered to him.'[1] In 1203, however, Villehardouin and his colleagues were in an unprecedentedly strong position for visitors to the imperial court – made evident by the rapid acceptance of their request for a private audience.

Once sequestered with the emperor, Villehardouin acted as the crusaders' spokesman. He respectfully pointed out the great service they had rendered to Prince Alexius and how they had kept the terms of their agreement with him. Then he played the crusaders' best card: 'We cannot, however, allow him to come here until he has given us a guarantee for the covenant that he has made with us. He therefore, as your son, asks you to ratify this covenant in the same terms and the same manner as he himself has done.'² With some apprehension, Isaac enquired as to the details of the agreement and Villehardouin duly spelled them out.

Isaac's scarred and sightless eyes could betray nothing, but his shocked silence revealed that he was deeply taken aback by the terms of the covenant. The scale of these demands was quite horrifying and he knew it might well be impossible for him to deliver everything required, particularly given the weakness of his own political power base. On the other hand, he longed to embrace his own son again, the young man whom he had not held, or spoken to, for over three years. Moreover, although he was still determined to rule, Isaac recognised that his authority was compromised by his blindness. It was therefore necessary to have a successor and co-ruler from the Angeloi dynasty firmly in place. The fact that the Byzantines' inner circle had chosen to restore him to the throne showed how much they feared the crusaders and how badly the flight of Alexius III had damaged morale. Isaac had to hope that this fear extended to accepting the loss of their religious independence and fulfilling a huge financial commitment to the papacy's holy warriors.

Isaac's reply to Villehardouin displayed the tensions between the political reality and his personal emotions: 'These are very hard conditions and I do not really see how we can put them into effect. All the same you have rendered both my son and me such outstanding services that if we were to give you the whole of our empire, it would be no more than you deserve.'³ Villehardouin may be finessing the moral worth of the crusaders' actions here, as well as casting an uncannily accurate prophecy into Isaac's mouth, but the general sentiment expressed by the emperor is just about credible. More revealing is Villehardouin's aside that various opinions were expressed in the course of the interview, which is probably intended to convey that there was an intense and heated discussion. Yet the crusaders were unbending: Prince Alexius had made a deal, guaranteed by Isaac's son-in-law, Philip of Swabia; the westerners had completed their part of the bargain and, if the emperor wished to meet his son again, he had to consent to the agreement in full. Finally, Isaac relented and swore to fulfil the covenant. A charter was drawn up by way of confirmation and the golden imperial seal was affixed. One copy remained with Isaac, the other was given to the envoys. With the formalities now completed, they bade the emperor farewell and, doubtless highly satisfied with their work, returned to the camp bearing the imperial charter.

For Prince Alexius this must have been a huge relief. The turmoil and uncertainty in Constantinople could have meant disaster for his father and brought about a final rejection of his own claim to the throne. Yet at this particular time everything seemed to have fallen his way. The nobles told the prince to prepare himself to re-enter Constantinople. The Greeks threw open the gates of the city and received him enthusiastically. For the young Alexius this was the end of a remarkable journey. From the dark years between 1195 and 1201 when he had spent months as a prisoner inside the city, to his bold escape in Thrace, to the rejections at Hagenau and Rome; the success of his approach to the crusade leaders; the near-implosion of the expedition on Corfu; and then the weeks of besieging his home city – this moment marked the close of his quest. He was fêted and welcomed by the people of Constantinople and was reunited with his father at last.

A splendid ceremonial feast celebrated these momentous events. Hugh of Saint-Pol reported a joyous and dignified occasion; Niketas Choniates, as a Byzantine eye-witness, expressed a rather more jaundiced view of the proceedings. The leading crusader nobles came to the Great Palace, doubtless dressed in their finest cloaks and robes, where they sat at tables in one of the halls. At the head of the room, Isaac and Prince Alexius presided over the event. At a victory dinner there were speeches and both Isaac and his son delivered glowing eulogies to the men who had restored them to power. Niketas, who rarely missed an opportunity to express his dismal view of the young man, scorned the 'power-loving' and 'childish' prince. He also deplored the lavishness of the occasion. Jesters, entertainers and musicians performed; the servants produced fine, dainty foods, all in the opulent and ornate surroundings at the heart of imperial

Constantinople. Niketas could not stomach this sycophantic behaviour towards the western barbarians, the men who had just humiliated his beloved city. The fact that Isaac and Prince Alexius could barely afford such luxuries only exacerbated his feelings of dark displeasure.[4]

With the end of the siege, the crusaders had achieved their primary short-term goal and the immediate, sapping tension of war slackened. They had succeeded in defeating the Byzantine emperor and had done so without incurring terrible casualties. Their worries concerning food and security seemed over; with these practical matters assured they could look to the future and, fortified by the honour and the victory granted to them by God, they could turn to the Holy Land.

For the people of Constantinople, in the short term, the mortal threat to their city appeared to be at an end. Isaac's return to power quelled the fear of the fires, the bombardment and the slaughter that the barbarian warriors outside their walls might wreak. Yet, as Isaac had doubtless indicated during his discussions with the envoys, in spite of appearances, many of the Greeks viewed the westerners with the deepest suspicion and those aware of the agreement between the emperor and the crusaders were profoundly unhappy at the tenor of the terms. Conscious of this awkward atmosphere, Isaac acted prudently and quickly to alleviate the situation. The crusader army camped just outside the walls was too obvious a reminder of the westerners' military might. Thousands of his people had lost their homes and possessions and they had no reason to rejoice at the crusaders' all-too-visible presence. Isaac begged them to move back across the Golden Horn to the districts of Galata and Estanor where there was slightly less risk of dispute with the citizens of Constantinople. The nobles recognised the good sense in this proposal and immediately agreed to it. The emperor further smoothed the move by arranging for a good supply of food. The crusaders took over houses and settled in while the Venetians drew up their fleet along the shore of the Golden Horn to protect their boats from harm over the winter months and to repair any that had been damaged during the siege operations.

As the new regime took over, it had to respond – as new rulers always must – to petitions for clemency or favour. One individual released was Alexius Ducas, a leading Byzantine nobleman who had been imprisoned for the last seven years. Ducas, known universally as Murtzuphlus on account of the heavy eyebrows that grew together over his nose, was duly freed and soon took over the post of *protovestarius*, or chamberlain, a high court official. Within twelve months this formidable operator would give the crusaders grave cause to regret his liberation.

Another request came from a Muslim, Kaykhusraw, the brother of the sultan of Iconium. Like Isaac, he had been dispossessed by his younger brother and he too wanted the crusaders' help in regaining what he regarded as rightfully his. Their success at Constantinople encouraged him to ask them to serve him in the same way. As Prince Alexius had done, Kaykhusraw proposed huge financial incentives and, in another similarity, even offered to be baptised a Christian and to lead his people into the Catholic fold as well. Robert of Clari reports that the French nobles and the doge assembled to discuss the matter at length. Many of the ruling houses in the medieval world had claimants and counter-claimants. Were the crusaders to be cast as the perpetual forces of right, forever intervening to re-establish proper order? And did their remit now extend to the Muslim world as well? While Kaykhusraw may have had a just cause, and the introduction of the Seljuk empire into the Christian orbit would be an astonishing achievement, the meeting decided to reject his plea. Their whole enterprise was beginning to rely on too many, as yet unfulfilled, promises of money and religious submission. How might those in the West — already hostile to their enterprise — react when they heard of an alliance with a Muslim emir, however positive his intentions purported to be? In truth, Kaykhusraw's idea may not have been quite as far-fetched as it first appears because in later decades the papacy made serious attempts to persuade the Seljuks to convert to Christianity and there was a genuine dialogue between the two parties.[5] In the circumstances of 1203, however, this was not a realistic idea and Kaykhusraw was told as much. He asked the crusaders why they could not help and was informed that the frailty of the regime in Constantinople — and the fact that the westerners were still waiting for the money promised to them — meant that they could not leave the city. Kaykhusraw was furious at this rejection and stormed back to Asia Minor to try to retake his lands without the crusaders' help.[6]

Elsewhere in Constantinople, Count Louis of Blois was particularly interested in tracking down one prominent member of the former imperial entourage. His aunt, Agnes, had married Theodore Branas, a member of an important Byzantine family.[7] Several French nobles went to see

Agnes; they showed her due respect and offered to serve her, but were met with complete hostility. Agnes's husband had been part of Alexius III's regime and, with his demise, her own standing was dramatically reduced; thanks to the crusaders she could no longer expect to be part of the ruling elite. She refused to talk to her visitors and then pretended that she was unable to speak French. Her nephew then introduced himself, although Robert of Clari does not reveal whether this promoted any amiability from the count's aunt.[8]

During the crusaders' stay in Constantinople they came across peoples from lands they had never previously known. One day when the nobles were visiting the emperor, the king of Nubia arrived at the palace. Robert of Clari reported some curiosity about his black skin – as a northern Frenchmen, he was unlikely to have met individuals from the lands below Egypt – and, more remarkably to the knight, the presence of a cross branded onto the royal forehead. Prince Alexius gave the king a full and formal welcome, as befitted a royal visitor, and introduced him to the crusader nobles. Through interpreters they learned that the king had come to Constantinople as a pilgrim. He claimed that his own lands were 100 days' journey beyond Jerusalem and that when he started out he had 60 companions; 50 of them had perished on the way to the holy city and now only one remained alive. After visiting Constantinople this intrepid man wanted to go to Rome, then on to Santiago di Compostela in northern Spain before returning to Jerusalem to die: a suitable resting place for such a pious and devoted pilgrim. The nobles learned that all Nubians were Christians and that when a child was baptised, he or she was branded with the sign of the cross. In all respects they were impressed with this visitor and, as Robert of Clari commented, 'they gazed at this king with great wonder'.[9]

As the crusaders began to relax over the following days, they started to behave as tourists and pilgrims, crossing over by bridge or barge into the great city to marvel at the palaces and churches. Constantinople was a true spiritual treasure chest. Villehardouin could hardly believe the number of relics contained in the city: 'as many as in the rest of the world', as he admiringly wrote.[10] For these tough, pious men, the sight of so many relics intimately connected with Christ's life, such as parts of the True Cross and the Crown of Thorns, displayed in such stunning and opulent locations, would have stirred feelings of great devotion. They could venerate these objects and give the deepest thanks to God for delivering them safely thus far on their journey. The relics might also serve to remind them of the ultimate object of their campaign, the liberation of Christ's patrimony. Alongside these spiritual matters, the practicalities of trade and exchange also took place and the Venetians doubtless assessed the commercial possibilities of their new-found ascendancy in the city.

For all their relief at the end of the siege, the westerners still regarded the Greeks with some suspicion. In an attempt to create greater security for the crusaders, the French and Venetians demanded that a long section of the city wall (perhaps about 320 feet, according to Robert of Clari) be demolished. This stark exposure of the innards of Constantinople was yet another blatant reminder of the crusaders' uninvited presence.[11]

The crusaders also had the opportunity to reflect on their achievement and to inform relatives and various interested parties in the West of their success. How would their conduct be received by the pope? Innocent had written to the crusaders in late June, making it plain that he did not want them to attack Constantinople except in particular circumstances and only with his, or his legate's, permission. He restated his hostile attitude towards the doge and his people and reminded the Venetians of their continued status as excommunicates. The pope expressed hope that the crusaders would behave well, or else they would not be like 'a penitent, but a trickster, and a penitent returning to his sin is regarded as a dog returning to its vomit'.[12]

Despite his mistrust of the Venetians, another letter from this time demonstrates Innocent's recognition of a need to show flexibility if the crusade was to be kept on the move. He ruled that the French crusaders could sail on Venetian ships to the Levant, even though this would mean travelling on boats manned by excommunicates. However, if the doge's men were not absolved by the time of war in the Levant, he ordered that the other crusaders should not fight alongside them or else they risked defeat. God would not look kindly on the battles of excommunicates and the other crusaders would suffer by association. Such was Innocent's antipathy towards the doge that he even gave the crusaders leave to attack the Venetians if they impeded the expedition. He also gave them permission to take necessary food from Byzantine lands whenever it was needed and as long as it was done 'without hurting people'.[13]

In spite of Innocent's efforts to steer the crusade, the limitations of medieval communications were such that his instructions were often out of date by the time they reached the holy warriors. His letter of 10 August, written almost a month after Constantinople actually surrendered, was of a rather resigned tone. He knew that the expedition had gone to the Byzantine capital and lamented that the crusaders 'seem to have neglected the relics of the Holy Land'.[14]

These letters give us some insight into Innocent's mind at the time and show his mistrust of the Venetians, his concern for the Crusader States and his worries about the direction of the expedition. The crusaders, therefore, had to attempt to reassure the pope in all of these matters. The missive of Hugh of Saint-Pol is the most detailed of the existing letters sent by the crusaders to the West after July 1203 and it shows the conquerors' view of their recent achievements. At least four copies of his letter survive; others (since lost) were almost certainly sent, too.

As one of the crusade leaders, Hugh had much to tell. The news of the expedition's diversion had spread through the courts of western Europe and, depending upon how the information had been relayed, it might well have portrayed the crusaders in a very negative light. In August 1203, in the immediate afterglow of victory when they were basking in God's approval for their decision to go to Constantinople, Hugh had the perfect opportunity to put his side of the story. Aside from providing a splendid eye-witness account of the siege, the Frenchman vigorously asserted the spiritual merit of the crusaders' actions and roundly criticised those who had left the army in the course of the campaign. His perspective is a compelling mixture of the devoted holy warrior and a man steeped in chivalric values. Most significantly, it shows the thoughts of an individual who still maintained one clear goal for the expedition: Jerusalem. There is no sense that Hugh had set out originally intending to capture Constantinople; rather, that he and his fellows had been obliged to follow that particular path in order to achieve their objective: the liberation of Christ's patrimony.

After his description of the fall of Constantinople he rounded on those who had abandoned the crusade: 'I especially want you to know this: Stephen of Perche, Reynald of Montmirail, Enguerrand of Boves . . . Simon of Montfort . . . and the abbot of Vaux[-Cernay] are creating great discord in the fleet. They are proceeding to Jerusalem . . . and they have left our army and us in mortal danger.'[15] As well as the need to counter hostile propaganda, one can sense in Hugh's words genuine anger at the decision of these men to strike off on their own.

Perhaps more of a diplomatic agenda lay behind his glowing endorsement of Doge Dandolo: 'We truly have much to say in praise of the doge of Venice, a man, so to speak, who is prudent, discreet, and skilled in hard decision-making.' Some people in the West, such as Pope Innocent III and, indeed, some on the crusade, such as Gunther of Pairis, saw the Venetians as greedy and solely motivated by money. From Hugh of Saint-Pol's perspective, however, Dandolo's excellent leadership skills and his often perceptive advice were worthy of fulsome praise and this testimony was an attempt to redress the simplistic and hostile picture some had of the doge.

Hugh also presented the core of his case as to why the diversion to Constantinople was justified. He had already mentioned the reasons for placing Prince Alexius on the throne and the financial inducements offered by the young man, but he had saved what he regarded as his best and most 'glorious' reason until the conclusion of the letter:

> We carried on the business of Jesus Christ with His help, to the point that the Eastern Church (whose head is Constantinople), along with the emperor and his entire empire, reunited with its head, the Roman Pontiff . . . acknowledges itself to be the daughter of the Roman Church. It also wishes, with humbled head, to obey the same more devoutly in the future – in accordance with normal custom. The patriarch himself, who desires and applauds this step, petitions all the way to the Roman See to receive the pallium of his office and on this issue, he along with the emperor swore a sacred oath to us.

In other words, Hugh was able to demonstrate that the holy warriors had acted properly because through their actions an enormous spiritual benefit had come to the Catholic Church. In theory, the schism of 149 years was over – surely this was a cause for celebration and congratulation? In fact, Hugh was running ahead of himself: later events would show him to be wildly overoptimistic in his assessment of the Byzantines' enthusiasm for their promised subjection.

Another reason to emphasise the scale of the crusaders' achievements

was that Hugh had to announce that the expedition would not be travelling on to the Holy Land until the following spring; again, a revelation
that might open the crusaders to criticism. He explained that delay was
unavoidable if they were to benefit from the young Alexius's military
support for the campaign in Egypt and argued that the scale of this
backing was well worth waiting for. The crusaders and the emperor had
already written threateningly to Sultan al-Adil (Saladin's brother, known
as Saphadin in the West) of Egypt, 'the impious invader and occupier of
the Holy Land', informing him that the combined Christian forces would
soon be attacking him. Hugh also expressed the hope that those in the
Levant might take heart at this news and wait for help with renewed
confidence.

One copy of Hugh's letter – that sent to Count Henry of Louvain
(who had taken part in the 1197–8 German Crusade) – contained an
additional paragraph in which he urged men to join the expedition. This
forthcoming Egyptian campaign is couched in highly chivalric terms: 'You
should also know that we have accepted a tournament against the Sultan
of Babylon [Cairo] in front of Alexandria. If, therefore, anyone wishes
to serve God (to serve him is to rule), and wishes to bear the distinguished and shining title of "knight", let him take up the cross and follow
the Lord, and let him come to the Lord's tournament, to which he is
invited by the Lord himself.'[16]

This remarkable imagery fully integrates the knightly obsession with
tournaments with the idea of the crusade. The invasion of Egypt is characterised as a tournament, called by God, and is presented as a magnificent opportunity for knightly deeds. Yet unlike normal tournaments
fought for selfish motives, these deeds will be for the Lord's sake. As a
layman trying to convince others to take the cross, Hugh clearly believed
that this emphasis on a more secular aspect of holy war was most likely
to achieve the desired results. Perhaps this fusion of the tournament and
the holy war provides some insight into the way in which the crusaders
themselves, rather than the churchmen, viewed their activities.[17]

Doge Dandolo also wrote a letter (now lost) in which he tried to
explain the reasons for the attack on Zara – described by Innocent as 'an
outrage that is already notorious throughout almost the entire world' –
and to stress that the action at Constantinople was of certain benefit to
the Catholic Church and the recovery of the Holy Land.[18]

As the crusaders and the Byzantines grew accustomed to their new relationship, preparations got under way for the formal coronation of Prince Alexius. In recognition of the effort to move the Orthodox Church closer to Rome, the ceremony was set for 1 August, St Peter's Day, when, amidst great pomp, the young man, now aged about 21, joined his father as ruler of the Byzantine Empire. Both Villehardouin and the letter written by the crusade leaders chose to omit the fact that Isaac reigned as co-emperor in Constantinople. This may have been because Isaac's earlier alliance with Saladin meant that he would be viewed in a poor light in the West and the crusaders did not want the stigma of this old associa-tion to tarnish their present success. By focusing on Alexius IV – towards whom the crusaders always claimed to have acted properly – Villehardouin could more easily demonise him when he subsequently acted traitorously.

Soon after his coronation Alexius IV wrote to the pope with his own account of events and to add his own praise and thanks for the crusaders' actions. We must remember that the two men had met in early 1202 when Innocent had turned down the young prince's request for help. Alexius also wanted to add his positive gloss to the letters of Hugh of Saint-Pol and the doge to counter the derogatory comments made by those crusaders who had left the expedition at Zara and Corfu. Like Hugh, Alexius was desperately anxious to swing papal and western European opinion behind an expedition that many saw as utterly misguided and driven by avarice. This was a profoundly serious task and the crusaders and their ally worked tirelessly to redress their obvious disobedience to the pope at Zara, to stress their subsequent successes and to make clear how their work had indeed brought benefits to the Catholic Church.

The twin emphases of the new emperor's letter were, first, the moral justification of his cause – namely to reinstate his unjustly deposed father – and, second, the glorious news that the Orthodox Church accepted papal supremacy. Naturally he acknowledged God's hand in his own and Isaac's deliverance. He also took pains to explain why the crusaders had needed to besiege Constantinople, although he provided no details of the military engagements. In line with Hugh of Saint-Pol's report, he argued that it was 'a totally unforeseen task' that caused force to be needed to establish his power in the city. He blamed the wicked propaganda spread by the usurper Alexius III: 'He had so polluted with poisonous speeches the royal city, which sighed for us, that he declared the Latins [the crusaders] came to subvert ancient public freedom.' In fact, of course, Alexius III had, quite naturally, been playing on negative perceptions of westerners to help his cause. The essence of these ideas was certainly attractive to the Byzantines and undoubtedly remained a potent factor under the new regime, too.

Alexius IV then addressed the issue of greatest interest to Pope Innocent, the standing of the Orthodox Church. He stressed how much this had motivated the crusaders to help him: 'One factor, I confess, especially disposed the hearts of the pilgrims to our aid.' In other words, the crusaders were not driven by the earthly desires of greed or glory, but by higher motives. He continued:

> . . . we devoutly promised that we would humbly recognise the ecclesiastical head of all Christendom, namely, the Roman pontiff . . . and we would, with all our might, lead the Eastern Church to him if Divine Mercy should restore the throne due to us, knowing full well that tremendous honour and advantage should accrue to the empire and eternal glory to our name if the Lord's seamless tunic should regain its unity in our time and through our efforts.

Alexius also stressed his own determination and desire to recognise papal supremacy.

After all these good tidings, however, a complication emerged that revealed Alexius's weakness as an emperor and the potentially porous nature of his promises. He wrote: 'we will prudently and with all our might influence the Eastern Church toward the same end'. Pope Innocent might have smiled wryly at this line. Alexius was, in effect, saying that he would try to persuade the Orthodox churchmen to follow his lead, but such was his restricted power that he could not – as emperors in times past had done – simply order his ecclesiastics to take a particular course of action, certain in the knowledge that they would agree. Even if the Orthodox patriarch consented to this, such was the fragmented nature of imperial authority at this time that churchmen in the provinces might continue to act differently, if they so wished. To the cynic, therefore, Alexius's promises had a hollow ring: only his own restoration to power was the one certain accomplishment of the crusaders.

Once Alexius was crowned, the crusade leaders *en masse* sent copies of a letter to the West parading their achievements.[19] To their advantage, of course, was their success and, self-evidently, God's favour, although as Alexius IV's own letter revealed, a few issues were not as clear-cut as might have been hoped. The nobles' letter survives in similar copies addressed to King Otto IV of Germany, to all western Christians and to the pope himself. Several other copies of this message may have been sent, but are not extant.

The letter covers the main points of the story: the Treaty of Zara, the journey to Constantinople, the surprise at the poor reception accorded to Prince Alexius, the conflict with the usurping Alexius III, the crusaders' steadfastness against superior forces, the emperor's ignominious flight and the coronation of Alexius IV. All of this was made possible because they were divinely blessed. The opening line makes this clear: 'How much the Lord has done for us – on the contrary not for us, but for His name – how much glory he has bestowed in these days we will briefly narrate . . .' Later on, similarly: 'if anyone of us wishes to be glorified, he be glorified in the Lord and not in himself or in another'. That the crusaders acted with absolute propriety is made resoundingly clear. The scale of their achievement lends the letter a predictably upbeat tone and their decision to remain at Constantinople over the winter of 1203 is portrayed in the most positive manner. Furthermore, Alexius IV's financial and military support for the crusaders also seemed assured.

The copy of the letter addressed to the Christian faithful tried to capitalise on this encouraging presentation of events by urging churchmen to rouse volunteers to complete the Lord's work. In other words, more crusaders were needed. Strong, virile men were required and, perhaps overoptimistically, they were assured that the easier section of the campaign was to come: 'Certainly, the vexing and almost unbearable great mass of hardships that stretched across our backs does not await them, for the power that descends from Heaven has mercifully relieved us of it.' The crusade leaders argued that 'a modicum of tribulation and labour will not only make for them a momentary name, but it will also bestow upon them an eternal hundredweight of glory'. Thus, the usual allurements of honour and divine approval were enhanced by the thought that the campaign would succeed quite quickly.[20] It was hoped that these new recruits would not only ensure a greater chance of success in the Holy Land, but would help to make good the losses of men at Zara and Corfu.

Alexius was quick to begin to honour his undertaking to pay over a large sum of money to the crusaders. He presented 50,000 marks directly to the Venetians and a further 36,000 were given to the doge as the outstanding balance owed by the crusaders from the original contract of April 1201. The remainder went to the crusade leaders and allowed those who had borrowed money for their passage on the ships to pay it back.[21] At last it seemed as though the burden under which the expedition had been labouring was beginning to lift. Yet underneath, all was not well.

While the crusaders' financial situation improved, that of Isaac and Alexius was becoming critical. The huge sums of money needed to keep their promises to the westerners were far beyond their means. Alexius III had managed to take considerable wealth with him into exile, and this, plus the cost of fighting the crusaders and the general degeneration of imperial authority over recent months, meant that the treasuries were almost bare. Yet the new emperors knew that they had to satisfy the demands of their warlike guests.

One option remained, a route that opened them up to divine punishment: to provide the necessary gold and silver, they started to melt down some of the precious ecclesiastical ornaments that made Constantinople a spiritual powerhouse. This decision shows just how desperate the Greeks had become; to commit such an act of sacrilege was surely to provoke God's wrath. There are occasional examples of churches in western Europe melting down precious vessels to generate cash for departing crusaders, but at least this could be excused as helping God's work. Here, it was the rapacious demands of the crusaders – 'thirsting after libations as copious as the Tyrrhenian Sea', as Niketas Choniates vividly described it – that led to this outrageous behaviour. Words could barely express the mixture of fury, exasperation and shock that Niketas felt. He saw this as a turning point for Byzantium, a moment at which Alexius IV so shattered the proper order of things that he destroyed the integrity of the empire. Niketas wrote: 'In utter violation of the law, he touched the untouchable, whence, I think, the Roman state was totally subverted and disappeared.' The emperor's men went to their work with vigour: 'It was a sight to behold: the holy icons of Christ consigned to the flames after being hacked to pieces with axes and cast down, their adornments carelessly and unsparingly removed by force, and the revered and all-hallowed vessels seized from the churches with utter indifference and melted down and given over to the enemy troops as common silver and gold.' For Niketas this heresy was compounded by the apparent indifference of both the emperors and the general population. As he concluded: 'In our silence, not to say callousness, we differed in no way from those madmen, and because we were responsible, we both suffered and beheld the most calamitous of evils.'[22]

As the summer wore on, the emperor often came to see the crusader nobles. He had grown close to some of them, particularly Boniface of Montferrat. While his dealings with the westerners were cordial enough, he was finding the imposition of his authority on the people of Byzantium a much more challenging task. Just as the crusaders had viewed the Greeks with suspicion for decades, so the reverse was true: the Byzantines were always sceptical about the motives of western armies passing by Constantinople and feared their possible aggression. It should also be remembered that the anti-Latin riots of the early 1180s had attracted massive popular support. The role of the crusaders as the men who had delivered Prince Alexius to the imperial title raised potentially enormous anxieties and animosities. As we have seen, the young man had no experience of power, or any base of loyal supporters to call upon. In effect, Alexius had only become emperor because of the danger that his western allies posed to Constantinople and the cowardice of Alexius III. In the weeks since his return the new ruler had become painfully aware of the antipathy that many of his people bore him and his allies. He also needed to impose his control on those parts of the Byzantine Empire outside Constantinople. In the days before television broadcasts could transmit images of authority to the provinces, a medieval ruler – and particularly one who had come to the throne in such complicated circumstances – had to get in the saddle and go out to show his face. The emperor needed to process around his territories and receive the submission of his subjects or, if they resisted, bring them to heel by force. A progress of this sort would also raise more of the funds he so urgently needed, but to undertake this Alexius would require help and inevitably it was to the crusaders that he turned.

He came to the camp and summoned a meeting of the leading nobles. This was no social visit; all assembled in Baldwin of Flanders's tent. Alexius paid tribute to his allies' help – 'you have done me the greatest service that any people have yet rendered to any Christian man' – but he had to state what must have been increasingly apparent to all: 'I should like you to know that a number of my people do not love me, though they make a fair pretence of doing so. Moreover, the Greeks as a whole are full of resentment because it is by your help that I have regained my empire.'[23]

Alexius knew that the crusaders' contract with the Venetians was due to expire in late September and that they would, therefore, be leaving Constantinople very soon. He acknowledged that he had little chance of fulfilling his promises to the westerners by then: he needed time to gather the money, the shipping and the military forces that he was obliged to provide. More pertinently, he had his own fate to think of. Villehardouin's report of the emperor's speech has an authentic whiff of desperation: 'The Greeks, I must tell you, hate me because of you; if you leave me, I shall lose my empire, and they will put me to death.'[24]

The new emperor simply had not had the time to cement his position. He pleaded with the crusaders to help him and, again, he offered hugely attractive financial incentives. Alexius asked them to stay with him until March 1204, the time of the next-but-one sea passage. If they remained he vowed to pay for the cost of the fleet until September 1204, one year after the expiry of the deal with the Venetians, and to provide foodstuffs for the Frenchmen and Italians until their departure in the spring. By then, he estimated, he would have established genuine order in his lands and there would be no danger of his predecessor regaining them. With Alexius holding real power, taxes and tributes would be available to pay the crusaders and to provide the fleet to transport the Byzantine forces. If these proposals were adopted, the crusaders would have the entire summer of 1204 to fight the Muslims – properly supplied and with their army enhanced by the support of the Greeks.

The nobles absorbed what the emperor had just told them. To many, Alexius's present weakness was all too plain and the advantages of the deal he suggested were obviously mutually beneficial. They were painfully aware, however, of just how excruciatingly difficult it had been to persuade the army to accept the young man's first offer at Corfu. The fact that much of it had not yet been fulfilled, coupled with the need for an even greater delay before sailing to the Holy Land, would be a truly awkward proposition to sell. The leadership told Alexius that they needed to consult their men, and the emperor returned to his city.

The following day Baldwin, Boniface and Dandolo summoned the nobles and the knights to a meeting. Inevitably there was uproar when these new ideas were presented and the same fault-lines as on Corfu opened up afresh. The bulk of the leadership, having committed themselves to the attack on Zara and to the support of Alexius, wanted to accept the plan and winter in Constantinople. To the faction that had threatened to go to Brindisi, this was merely another delay: the whole affair seemed to them to be dragging on interminably. The dissenters reminded Baldwin and Boniface that they had agreed to come to Constantinople on the condition that they could leave the city when they so requested.

The senior crusaders' argument played upon the lateness of the sailing season. If they allowed a couple of weeks to gather everything together and to fettle the fleet, and then were a month at sea, the crusade would not arrive in Syria until the early winter. Rain and cold meant that the Holy Land would be unsuited to warfare. Instead the army would be penned up in one of the coastal cities, probably creating tension with the locals and certainly consuming valuable supplies. Waiting in Constantinople until March meant free provisions, and would ensure that Alexius was safely established in power, thereby enabling him to give his full support to the expedition. The Venetians would remain in the city as well and a rested, properly equipped, force would be very much better placed to conquer the land overseas.

In the end this last argument won the day. If, as a majority of the leaders seemed to believe, it was possible to accept that Alexius would and could keep his promises, then the logic in delaying until the spring was overwhelming. The Venetians swore to remain in the service of the army until Christmas 1204 and, according to Villehardouin, Alexius 'paid them enough to make it worth their while'.[25] The crusaders in turn took an oath to remain in association with the Venetians over the same length of time and the matter was settled.

With this important decision made, the emperor and the crusaders began to ready themselves to tour the provinces. The seniority of the men who accompanied Alexius on this campaign makes it clear just how serious a matter this was. Boniface of Montferrat, Hugh of Saint-Pol and Henry of Flanders, to name but a few, chose to take part in the expedition where their presence as powerful knights and skilled military men would be greatly valued. There was also, of course, the possibility of financial reward and an opportunity to accomplish feats of bravery. The *Devastatio Constantinopolitana* described Alexius proposing 'substantial bonuses and money to our army's knights and infantrymen for coming with him'.[26] Niketas Choniates suggests that the emperor offered Boniface of Montferrat 16 hundredweight in gold – an irresistible incentive.[27] It would not be prudent for the entire crusading army to leave Constantinople, however, because this might expose Isaac to danger. His son and the French nobles must have been well aware of the need to provide some protection to the ageing co-emperor. Thus Count Baldwin and Count Louis of Blois remained at Constantinople, along with the Venetians whose naval expertise was not required on this particular occasion.

The crusaders' preparations were marred by the death of Matthew of Montmorency, one of the most senior knights on the whole campaign and a veteran of the Third Crusade. Matthew had strongly supported the diversion to Constantinople and headed one of the seven contingents of the army outside the city. He fell ill in August 1203 and died the same month, deeply mourned by all. Villehardouin paid glowing tribute to 'one of the best knights in the whole kingdom of France, one of the most deeply loved and respected'.[28] Interestingly, Matthew was buried in Constantinople in the church of the Knights Hospitaller of Jerusalem, a most appropriate choice for a man who had died in the service of Christ and was striving to reach the earthly Jerusalem at the time of his death.

In mid-August Alexius and his crusader allies moved out of Constantinople to begin their task. Another object of their campaign was to capture Alexius III, who harboured hopes of a return to power. Given his present weakness, however, the renegade was unlikely to stray too close to such a formidable force. The ignominious departure of Alexius III and the presence of his successor and the western soldiers meant that most of the local tributaries to Constantinople came to pay homage to the new ruler as was required.

Alexius IV and the crusaders did not, however, travel especially widely. It seems that they chose not to visit western regions of the empire, such as Thessalonica and the Peloponnese, probably out of fear of being away from Constantinople for too long.

One important figure who chose not to acknowledge Alexius was someone who would come to haunt the crusaders when they took control of Byzantium for themselves – Johanitza, the king of Bulgaria (1197–1207).

The Bulgarians, the neighbouring Vlachs and the pagan Cumans had been a thorn in the side of the Byzantines for more than 20 years and Johanitza had established independent rule over a sizeable territory. Bulgaria was formerly subject to Greek overlordship, but its rulers had cast this aside in the 1180s. The advent of a new emperor, whether he had western allies or not, gave Johanitza no reason to sacrifice his autonomy and so he declined to acknowledge the young man's authority.[29]

The emperor travelled north-west to the city of Adrianople in Thrace, where his rival Alexius III had briefly tried to establish himself – although he had prudently departed before his enemies arrived. Niketas reports that the joint crusader and Byzantine force subjugated the Thracian cities and then extracted as much money as possible from them.[30] Dissent broke out between the crusaders and the emperor because Henry of Flanders claimed that he had not been paid a sum of money promised to him. Without this incentive, the count and his troops departed for Constantinople, showing just how fragile the relationship between Alexius and at least some of the crusaders was. It also suggests – in spite of his successful campaign – the scale of the emperor's struggle to find the cash to keep his lavish promises to the westerners. Boniface and the others remained with Alexius and completed their journey without further mishap.

CHAPTER ELEVEN

'The incendiary angel of evil'

The Great Fire of August 1203

THOSE CRUSADERS WHO remained in Constantinople settled down for the autumn and winter, waiting for their colleagues to return and preparing for new adventures in the spring. In theory, this should have been a relatively uneventful time, but the westerners were soon to witness a most terrible event – and one largely triggered by their presence. In spite of incidents such as the anti-western purge of the 1180s and other occasional attacks on outside groups over the previous decades, a sizeable number of Europeans still lived and worked in Constantinople. Some, like the Pisans, had shown loyalty to the imperial regime during the siege, but in the aftermath of Alexius III's demise they prudently changed policy and came to terms with Isaac and his son. Clearly this opportunism upset many Byzantines, and Niketas reports that Greek hostility towards the Pisans and a colony of Amalfitans led a Constantinople mob to burn the westerners' dwellings, which in turn prompted most of them to move over the Golden Horn to 'share a table and a tent' with their fellow-Catholics.[1]

The crusaders' overt responsibility for imposing a change of regime on the Greeks and their continued presence as a blunt instrument of the young emperor fuelled resentment towards all aliens. On 19 August 1203 a brawl started between a group of Greeks and a party of indigenous westerners, in the aftermath of which someone started a fire – 'out of malice', according to Villehardouin. Other sources indicate that the conflict was between crusaders and the Greeks and that the former, lacking any other way to defend themselves, set fire to a building. Niketas Choniates, who was present in the city at this time, gives a different and more detailed version. He makes plain that the crusaders initiated what became a catastrophic series of events and that their voracious desire for money lay at the root of the incident. Intriguingly, their initial target was not the Byzantines, but the occupants of a mosque located just outside the city walls, across the Golden Horn from the crusader camp. This building was not the only mosque in the city (there had been such buildings in Constantinople for centuries), but the others lay comfortably behind the walls. Its construction probably dated from the period of Isaac's rapprochement with Saladin. Almost certainly as a response to the recent anti-western activity in Constantinople, a group of Flemish crusaders, along with a few Pisans and Venetians, commandeered a group of local fishing boats and ferried themselves over to the mosque.

They fell upon the building and started to seize its possessions. Taken completely by surprise, the Muslims defended themselves as best they could and used whatever came to hand to resist the drawn swords of the crusaders. They called for help from the Greeks, who came running, eager to fight back against the hated invaders. The combined efforts of the Muslims and the locals put the crusaders on the back foot, but as the Venetians did during the first siege, they resorted to arson to protect their withdrawal and as a way of inflicting retribution upon their opponents.

Not content with destroying the infidels' place of worship, the westerners spread out to several other locations and set them ablaze, too. What Niketas describes to us, therefore, is a serious effort to avenge the earlier anti-western riots. It is doubtful whether this was sanctioned by the crusade leadership because they would not have wanted to damage the already fragile relationship with the Greeks any further, and certainly not in such a dramatic and destructive manner. The presence of Pisans, as recent victims of the mob, and the use of local rather than crusader shipping also indicate an unofficial and unauthorised raid. Notwithstanding his aversion to the westerners, Niketas provides sufficiently compelling detail for us to regard his account as the most accurate account of the incident.

In any event, the consequences were appalling. While the fire of 17 July had caused quite a lot of damage, this new conflagration was very much worse. In the dry summer heat the blaze quickly gripped the densely packed wooden houses that lay inland from the Golden Horn, about one-third of a mile from the easternmost tip of the city. No one could control the flames, let alone quell them. To Niketas it was 'a novel sight, defying the power of description'. There had been fires in the city before, but this one 'proved all the others to be but sparks'.[2] The first two days and nights witnessed the worst damage as the north wind carried the blaze across the city towards the Forum of Constantine. At times the breeze must have turned and the fire twisted and meandered like a starving beast gorging itself on everything in its path. It was not just the wooden buildings that fell prey to the inferno. The great Agora (market place) was consumed and its elegant porticoes toppled to the ground, while mighty columns were ensnared and licked to destruction by the flames.

The crusaders, based on the opposite shore of the Golden Horn, could only watch as the fire devoured great churches, huge private houses and wide streets, packed with merchants' shops. Smoke billowed into the sky as the flames leaped from building to building. Screams of the trapped and dying pierced the air. The crackle of burning wood, the abrasive rattle of disintegrating stonework, the percussive thud of falling masonry pierced by the sharper, staccato crack of shattering roof tiles, all generated a truly hellish noise.

For day after day the blaze rolled onwards, its front now hundreds of yards long and swallowing huge areas of the most densely populated parts of the city. The fire reached down towards the harbour and even clawed towards the great Hagia Sophia itself. Niketas reports that the nearby Arch of the *Milion* (this was the point in Constantinople from which all roads were measured) was burned, as was the ecclesiastical court complex known as the Synods, whose baked brick walls and deep foundations failed to resist the heat – 'everything within was consumed like candlesticks'.[3]

· The fire had torn a huge strip across the city, stretching from the Golden Horn to the Sea of Marmara. Constantinople was rent by 'a great chasm or river of fire flowing through her midst', and people with relatives at the opposite end of the city had to sail around the flames to reach them.[4] While the Great Palace escaped unscathed, the Hippodrome and the Forum of Constantine were slightly damaged. A westerly wind pushed the blaze towards the Port of Theodosius, where it leaped over the walls and the sparks even ignited a ship passing close by.

Finally, after three days the fire satiated itself and began to subside. Water from the cisterns and aqueducts helped to quell what remained, leaving no fewer than 440 acres of land a charred and smoking ruin. Niketas – a man with a deeply engrained love of, and pride in, his city – lamented the pitiful scene that confronted him: 'Woe is me! How great was the loss of those magnificent, most beautiful palaces filled with every kind of delight, abounding in riches and envied by all.'[5]

The locals firmly believed that the westerners were responsible for the conflagration. From that time on, Villehardouin informs us, it was not safe for any to remain in Constantinople and, he estimated, 15,000 men, women and children fled, carrying all that they had managed to save, across to the crusader camp. In one sense, with more mouths to feed, these people caused a short-term problem. However, they were also a potential source of fighting strength and skilled labour: 'one army was fashioned from all', as the *Devastatio Constantinopolitana* summarised.[6] In any event, aside from the loss of life and property, the fire created a suppurating rift between the Byzantines and the crusaders, something that would do much to create further tensions in an already difficult relationship.

Ignoring the crusaders' likely culpability for the fire and the huge financial hardships that many thousands of the citizens now faced, Isaac continued to gather up sacred treasures in order to make the financial payments required by the westerners. Niketas fulminated at the emperor's apparent failure to respond to the fire and his continued defilement of religious artefacts. He condemned Isaac as 'the incendiary angel of evil', a play on the old emperor's family name of Angelos that clearly indicated the writer's anger.[7] In spite of the continued plundering, the losses caused by the fire meant that the flow of money to the crusaders now began to dry up, which inevitably caused ill-feeling.

Soon, with or without imperial direction, the Greeks rebuilt the section of wall that had been demolished at the crusaders' request. The absence of around half of the western army, and the anger they felt after the fire, gave the Byzantines the incentive to execute such a confrontational move and showed how the popular mood was growing ever more militant. Frustrated by these developments, Baldwin sent messengers to the army with Emperor Alexius to inform his colleagues of the cessation of payments and urging them to return to Constantinople as soon as possible. On 11 November 1203 the expedition arrived back at the city, in part satisfied with the way in which the new emperor had been received, but also grimly worried at the deteriorating relations with their nominal allies.

For Alexius this was a rare moment of triumph – he had imposed his authority on at least one section of his lands. As befitted a returning emperor, the people of Constantinople received their ruler in style and it was essential for the senior families of the city to pay him the appropriate respect. The leading lords and ladies donned their finest robes and rode out to meet the emperor and escort him back into the city. The crusaders also came out to meet their friends, doubtless relieved to be able to greet their colleagues and to see that all had returned safely.

As they drew close to Constantinople, Alexius and the crusaders would have seen the tremendous devastation wrought by the great fire. While the westerners stopped at their camp on the northern side of the Golden Horn and the emperor carried on across the inlet to the Blachernae palace, the terrible black scar left by the blaze would have been evident to all. News of the conflagration had reached Alexius and his allies as they moved around Thrace, but the huge scale of the damage was stunning. The emperor must have been chastened by the loss of so many fine buildings, and to see his people living as squatters amongst their ruined houses. To realise that his western allies were held responsible for this atrocity probably took much of the satisfaction away from his achievements in the empire. The crusaders would have appreciated this too and must have recognised that a long, tense winter lay ahead before the expedition could leave for the Levant.

Once settled back in Constantinople, Emperor Alexius was a changed man: the acclamation of the provinces and his welcome back into the city acted as a massive boost to his self-confidence. Before, he had been in the shadow of his father, but now, as an anointed emperor with a successful campaign under his belt, he sought to stand free and assert his own independence.

On returning from campaign one of his first acts was to order the hanging of all those who had been involved in the deposition and blinding of his father in 1195. The removal of these potential plotters was a sensible move given the unpredictable situation in Constantinople. But of much greater impact on the stability of the Byzantine Empire was a calamitous deterioration in the relationship between Alexius and his father. Put simply, their familial bond was not strong enough to overcome the desire of each man to exercise ultimate power. Alexius had, with his allies, managed to remove the usurper from Constantinople and now he had just toured the nearby imperial territories and been recognised as emperor. These were the actions of a young and successful ruler. While it was prudent that Isaac had stayed in Constantinople, his blindness, the fact that he had already been deposed, and the presence of his son as a co-emperor meant that he was experiencing a very different form of imperial authority to that which he had enjoyed in 1195.

Niketas Choniates reports that people looked increasingly towards Alexius as the senior figure in the imperial partnership. The young man's name began to appear first in public pronouncements, while Isaac's followed 'like an echo'.[8] With his blindness a constant reminder of his limitations, the older emperor felt the reins of power slipping from his hands and he grew bitter and resentful. He began to murmur of Alexius's lack of self-control and started to spread rumours about the younger man's sexual preferences, suggesting that 'he kept company with depraved men whom he smote on the buttocks and was struck by them in return'.[9]

During the first few weeks after his return from Thrace, Alexius stayed in close contact with the crusaders. They had worked together now for more than a year and had built up a reasonable affinity. The emperor enjoyed socialising with the westerners – he had, after all, spent several months at the courts of Europe, too – and he frequently went to the crusader camp where he passed the day drinking heavily and playing at dice. So relaxed was the atmosphere that Alexius was happy for his companions to remove the golden and jewelled diadem from his head and replace it with a shaggy woollen headdress. To Niketas Choniates such behaviour was disgraceful and brought shame to the imperial name and sullied the glory of the Byzantine Empire.[10]

The Greek chronicler also notes a sharp decline in Isaac's political skills. Earlier he had been characterised as a mild and unwarlike man, but now, perhaps worn down by his suffering and feeling pressured by his weakening authority, he sought respite in the company of seers and astrologers. To Niketas, these men were simply scroungers who exploited the situation and only looked to gorge themselves on imperial hospitality. The blind emperor had always been attracted to divination and fortune-telling, but now he turned to such practices even more; it was, perhaps, a way of shielding himself from the realities of his own incapacity and the rise of his son.

Under the influence of the fortune-tellers, Isaac began to imagine himself as the sole ruler of Byzantium and then, incredibly, his ambitions stretched even further to encompass uniting the Eastern Empire (Byzantium) with the Western (the German imperial title) in his own person. While Manuel Comnenus, for example, had sought to assert his pre-eminence over Frederick Barbarossa, he had never seriously entertained the notion of taking over and joining the two empires together to form one mighty unit. For an ageing, blind man, penned in a city with a determined and desperate foreign army outside its walls, the conception of such an idea revealed an abject failure to grasp reality. Isaac also believed that he would rub his eyes and his blindness would go, the gout that so plagued him would abate and he would be 'transformed into a godlike man'.[11] Certain monks with beards grown 'full like a deep cornfield' spurred Isaac on in his delusions while they indulged in the finest food and wine the imperial palace could offer. The credulous emperor was hugely receptive to the prophecies of these men and delighted in their alluring predictions.

In one of his more eccentric decisions, Isaac ordered the removal of the famous Boar of Kalydon, a creature from Greek mythology, from its pedestal in the Hippodrome.[12] This fearsome beast – complete with hair bristling up its back – was now placed in front of the Great Palace in order to protect the emperor from the rabble of the city. While this constituted some recognition of the dangers posed by the mob, it was hardly a serious way to protect his hold on the throne. To a modern reader these seem like the actions of a feeble figure, far distant from reality and heading inexorably towards calamity. Isaac's physical sightlessness was matched by a blindness to any sense of political awareness and, like his son, he was soon despised by the people of Constantinople.

A more astute political operator could have exploited the overt links between Alexius and the crusaders to his own advantage. Given Isaac's desire for power and his growing dislike of his son, there was an opportunity to harness the genuine groundswell of opposition to the outsiders. Although the westerners undoubtedly posed a serious military threat, had the older Greek leader taken the battle to the crusaders in the way that Alexius III had failed to, or had he taken advantage of the crusaders' total reliance on the Byzantines for food, then Isaac might have been able to seize the supremacy that he so desired. In reality, both father and son

were so wrapped up in their personal obsessions and the political machinations of the palace that they marginalised themselves from the fundamental wishes of the people of Constantinople. The imperial name was
being damaged and sullied in every way: the cowardice of Alexius III,
followed by the remoteness and unpopularity of his two replacements.
The aura and dignity of the Byzantine throne – built up over the centuries
and an essential element in the self-image of the people of Constantinople
– was in grievous decline. The monolith of power had been severely
eroded and this in turn meant that loyalty to the individuals who held
the title was fragile and, at times, barely existent. Isaac and Alexius needed
to wake up and act to bring their own interests in line with those of
Constantinople. The alternative was a predictable, and probably painful,
political exit.

The patent lack of leadership encouraged unrest amongst the citizenry.
The people of Constantinople, angered at the desertion of Alexius III,
humiliated by the crusaders' strength and enraged by the destruction
wrought by the great fires, sought answers to their predicament. One
victim of the 'wine-bibbing portion of the vulgar masses' (as Niketas
Choniates so elegantly described them) was a statue of the goddess Athena
that stood on a pedestal in the Forum of Constantine. Niketas rhapsodised over the beauty of this 10-foot-high bronze creation and his
description lingeringly traced the statue's body from foot to head. He
lovingly recalled the deep folds in the robe that covered her body, the
tight girdle around her waist and the goatskin cape, decorated with the
Gorgon's head, that covered her prominent breasts and shoulders. He
delighted in the sensuality of her long bare neck and suggested that her
lips were so fair that, if one stopped to listen, a voice would be heard.
So lifelike was this creation that Athena's veins seemed dilated as if filled
with blood and the body seemed infused with the bloom of life. The
eyes were said to be full of yearning, her helmet topped by a horsehair
crest, while her own hair was braided tightly into tresses at the back of
her head and fell in braids around her face. Athena's left hand was folded
into her dress, but it was the bearing of her right hand that sealed her
fate from the mob. According to Niketas, her head and right hand were
directed southwards, but the masses (ignorant of the points of the
compass) believed the goddess to be looking to the west and, therefore,
beckoning the crusader army to the city. For this perceived act of treachery

the statue was dragged from its pedestal and broken into pieces. To Niketas this was akin to an act of self-mutilation and to turn against a patroness of war and wisdom was a foolish mistake. He was careful, of course, not to grant her divine status and referred to her only as a symbol of these virtues.[13]

Alongside such open manifestations of unrest, the emperors continued their remorseless extraction of money to satisfy the demands of their allies; naturally an unenthusiastic populace resisted all demands to pay. Faced with a potentially explosive situation, the imperial administrators turned to softer targets, namely the Church and the wealthy. Some of the treasures that could be moved from the Hagia Sophia were taken away and melted down – the dozens of silver lamps that hung from the ceiling of the great church were gathered together and cast into the flames. Citizens of means (probably including Niketas himself) were required to contribute. The author contemptuously dismissed this as throwing meat to dogs and wrote of 'an unholy mingling of the profane with the sacred'.[14]

The money-gatherers used informers to lead them to sources of wealth and ceaselessly sought out new objects of value. The crusaders also began to apply pressure to gather resources and paid visits to the prosperous estates and religious institutions that lay near Constantinople to take the money they needed.

By the winter of 1203 the situation in Constantinople had reached crisis point. Niketas Choniates paints a vivid and compelling picture of a great civilisation rotting from within. The sense of internal decline and disintegration in Constantinople was palpable. The Queen of Cities, with all its great buildings and symbols of power, was being brought to its knees by incompetent rulers, its own febrile citizenry and its uncompromising enemies.

Of the Byzantines, Alexius was, of course, the key figure. With each passing day the young ruler became boxed into an ever-tighter corner. He owed his position entirely to the crusaders and had promised them large sums of money. His political survival depended on their military strength and he had evidently formed a close friendship with several of their number. He also recognised as early as August – when he asked the crusaders to move their camp to Galata – that his allies were acutely unpopular. The great fire and the continued exactions of money salted the wound further. Put simply, the people of Constantinople wanted the westerners gone. The young emperor therefore had to achieve a balancing act: he had to remain in power until their departure and, meanwhile, he had to use the crusaders' presence to try to build up his own position so as to stand a chance of surviving once they did leave in March 1204.

He had to placate his people while taking their gold; at the same time, he could not risk alienating his allies by failing to pay them or by appearing to sanction any military aggression towards them. A contemporary oration in favour of Alexius praised the emperor, as convention dictated; more interestingly it omitted any reference to Isaac (suggesting that his son held practically full power) and displayed an overt hostility towards the westerners: 'Just because they conveyed you, emperor, who have come hither by God's will, let them not grow wanton, but because they, restoring the lord emperor, have fulfilled servants' roles, let them be bent to servile laws.' The speech warned against the greed of the 'old' Rome trying to renew its youth at the expense of the 'new' Rome.[15]

Alexius Ducas, the nobleman known as Murtzuphlus, was prominent in the anti-crusader party in Constantinople and castigated the emperor for paying so much money to them, for mortgaging so many lands. He urged Alexius to 'make them go away'.[16]

The crusaders, of course, relied on Alexius for food and wanted his financial and military support in the spring. Yet, as the ferocious arguments on Corfu had shown, a large proportion of the army was lukewarm in their support of the emperor and had little patience with broken promises. The longer Alexius failed to pay over the money he owed, the greater the sense of dissatisfaction that stirred in the crusader army. Mistrust of the Greeks grew like a canker.

Boniface of Montferrat tried to use his close personal relationship with Alexius to persuade him to restore the proper flow of cash. He visited the emperor to point out the moral debt he owed the crusaders for restoring him to the throne and urged him to keep his promises. Given the pressures Alexius faced in Constantinople, he had little choice but to continue his policy of appeasement, staving off Boniface with requests for patience and giving assurances that he would indeed honour his commitments.[17] Yet soon the delivery of funds dried to a trickle and then stopped altogether. By this time of year, late November, the emperor knew that the crusader fleet could not set sail onto the winter seas and he may have believed that this enforced immobility, along with their vulnerability over food, would have been enough to dissuade the westerners from war. In addition, he hoped that by ending payment to them he would earn himself a breathing space in Constantinople.

On 1 December the antipathy between the westerners and the Byzantines spilled over into open violence. The mob set upon any outsiders and brutally murdered them and burned their corpses. The Greeks tried to attack the crusaders' ships, but were quickly beaten off and lost many of their own vessels.

The smouldering tensions between the two sides now seemed poised to burst into outright war. The crusader leadership had to decide upon its next move and resolved to establish with absolute clarity the emperor's intentions towards his allies. They chose to send Alexius a formal delegation to remind him once again of his contractual obligations to them and to demand that he fulfil them. If he refused, then the crusaders would tell him that they would 'do everything in their power to recover the money due'.[18]

Inevitably, given their diplomatic experience and oratorical skills, Conon of Béthune and Geoffrey of Villehardouin were chosen as two of the six envoys. The Frenchman Milo of Provins and three senior Venetians formed the remainder of the party. They girded their swords and rode along the Golden Horn, across the Blachernae bridge, to the nearby palace.[19] They dismounted at the gate, as envoys were required to do, and went into one of the great halls. There, enthroned at the head of the room sat the two emperors, bedecked in their magnificent robes. Also present was Margaret, Isaac's wife and Alexius's stepmother, who again attracted Villehardouin's approving eye as a 'good and beautiful lady'.[20] To emphasise the importance of the occasion the hall was filled with senior Byzantine nobles. Both sides knew that this was not one of the crusaders' social calls, but a decisive face-to-face meeting that would either result in conflict or would succeed in calming a dangerously volatile situation.

Conon presented the westerners' familiar case: the crusaders had done a great service to the two emperors, and in return Alexius and Isaac had promised to fulfil their covenant, but had failed to do so. The crusaders displayed the sealed documents that embodied the original agreement. Then came an ultimatum: if the Byzantines fulfilled their obligations, the crusaders would be content; if they did not, 'they will no longer regard you [Alexius] as their lord and friend, but will use every means in their power to obtain their due. They ask us to tell you that they will not do anything to injure either yourself or any other person without fair warning of their intention to commence hostilities.'[21] Conon's closing comments carried an undercurrent of venom towards his hosts, for after his assurances of due warnings before a war, he said: 'For they [the crusaders] have never acted treacherously – that is not the custom of their country.'[22] This barbed aspersion against the Greek character reflected the westerners' long-held prejudices and signified their growing mistrust of Alexius. It was also, of course, calculated to give extreme offence.

Uproar greeted the end of Conon's speech. His words outraged the gathered Byzantine nobles. All their resentment against the western barbarians swelled up; Villehardouin reported that they declared that no one had ever had the temerity to come into the imperial palace and dictate terms to the emperor in such a way. The hall was filled with shouts and cries; men gestured violently towards the small group of westerners. Even if Alexius had wanted to offer a more conciliatory response to the envoys, the mood inside the hall meant that this would have been suicidal. Provoked and cornered, the young emperor scowled fiercely at the envoys.

To Villehardouin and his colleagues the message was plain. No amount of diplomacy was going to change the mood in the palace. In spite of their nominal security as envoys, such was the sense of rage within the room that the crusaders feared for their lives. To an experienced man such as Villehardouin who, as we have seen, was accustomed to acting in such a capacity, this was a new and obviously terrifying ordeal. The westerners must have felt extraordinarily isolated and threatened. Hastily they turned to leave and hurried back along the corridors to the courtyard outside and their waiting horses. 'There was not a man amongst them who was not extremely glad to find himself outside.'[23] Hugely relieved to have survived, they rode at high speed back over the Golden Horn. As they entered the crusader camp the tension on their faces must have made plain to all the reception they had received. The nobles were summoned and informed of the events in the palace. 'Thus the war began' was Villehardouin's succinct and emotionless comment.[24]

Robert of Clari records one further interesting episode from this period, although it proved to have little effect on the overall outcome of events. He reports that on hearing of Alexius's reaction to the crusader envoys, Doge Dandolo decided to make a last-ditch personal appeal to the emperor. He sent a messenger asking that they meet at the harbour. The Venetians sent four heavily armed galleys to convey their leader to the rendezvous. Alexius rode down to the shore and the two men exchanged words. Dandolo must have had a reasonably cordial relationship with Alexius to believe that such an approach might be worthwhile. Perhaps the doge hoped that, away from the pressured environment of the Byzantine court, the young emperor might recognise his responsibilities to the crusaders more clearly.

'Alexius, what do you mean by this?' he asked. 'Take thought how we rescued you from great wretchedness and how we have made you a lord and have had you crowned emperor. Will you not keep your covenant with us?'[25] The emperor's response was uncompromising: 'I will not do any more than I have done.' Dandolo was furious that the man upon whom the crusaders had expended so much time and energy now appeared to be abandoning them. The old man lost his temper: 'Wretched boy, we dragged you out of the filth and into the filth we will cast you again. And I defy you, and I give you warning that I will do you all the harm in my power from this moment forwards.'[26]

From early December onwards there was desultory fighting between the two forces. Neither side launched a major offensive: on the one hand, the crusaders were unwilling to provoke the outright enmity of the Greeks and, on the other, Alexius was reluctant to mount an open assault on the powerful western armies. The imperial entourage seems to have become ever more remote. Isaac urged his son to ignore the talk of the vulgar masses, while courtiers refused to fight against the crusaders – 'being quicker to avoid battle with [them] than an army of deer with a roaring lion', in Niketas's contemptuous words.[27]

The most serious threat to the western forces came on 1 January 1204. In the months since the crusader army had set up camp at Galata, normal trading and fishing had taken place, with Greek, Venetian and other vessels mingling in the waters of the Golden Horn. The Byzantines could see that the crusaders' most precious lifeline was their fleet. Without it the westerners would be trapped and would have to surrender – or march away, across the hostile territories of Bulgaria, or be ferried over the Bosphorus to face the winter in the inhospitable mountains of Asia Minor. If the crusader fleet were destroyed the hated westerners would be at their mercy. The Greeks took 17 vessels and filled them with logs, wood shavings, pitch, discarded hemp and wooden barrels. Fire-boats had been used in naval warfare in the eastern Mediterranean for centuries; the famous Battle of Salamis in 480 BC had featured burning ships, and the details of this legendary fight were doubtless remembered and repeated by many in the medieval world. One evening, at midnight, when the wind blew from the south-west, the Greeks unfurled the sails of the ships, ignited the boats and set them loose towards the crusader fleet. They had prepared the vessels well; the cargo rapidly ignited and the flames soared up to the sky as these ghostly, crewless incendiaries glided inexorably towards the Venetians' ships.

The tension between the two sides meant that the crusaders had posted sentries and guards and, as the enemy ships came across the Golden Horn, bugles sounded the alert and everyone rushed to arm themselves. The Venetians ran to their ships and did whatever they could to row, tow or sail them to safety. Villehardouin himself witnessed the attack and vouched that 'no men ever defended themselves more valiantly on the sea than the Venetians ever did that night'.[28] Some of their sailing boats could not be readied quickly enough to be moved and so a more direct strategy was needed. The most manoeuvrable of their vessels were the oar-powered galleys and longboats. Quickly crewed, they were rowed out towards the enemy and grappling irons were slung over the lethal vessels, which were then heaved into the Bosphorus, where the current carried them away to burn and disintegrate harmlessly at sea. The Greeks did not just abandon their fire-ships and commit them to the vagaries of battle, however. Thousands gathered on the shore of the Golden Horn to howl and yell their hostility against the westerners, while others boarded any available boats to shadow and bombard those trying to tow the burning vessels away.[29] Many crusaders were wounded in this struggle and the men laboured on through the night to repel this threat to their precious navy.

In the main camp the call to arms went out. Some feared the seaborne attack was a prelude to a land assault and the crusaders rushed to don their armour and saddle their horses. The noise from the Golden Horn and the dark of night gave them little opportunity to form up in their usual good order and a rather ramiform crusader force poured out onto the plain in front of the camp to meet any impending Greek advance. By first light, however, only one Pisan merchant ship had been lost – an incredible achievement on the part of the Venetian mariners and yet another demonstration of their superb skill as seafarers. They were well aware of just how crucial their endeavours were; Villehardouin noted: 'we had all been in deadly peril that night, for if our fleet had been burned we should have lost everything, and could not have got away either by sea or by land'.[30]

It is unclear who amongst the Greeks was responsible for the fire-fleet. In spite of his cold response to the recent diplomatic missions, it was perhaps unlikely that Alexius would have initiated such an overtly hostile move. More likely, the attack was the work of a party bent upon the destruction of the crusaders – in which case it showed how the young emperor's authority had weakened. Such political nuances were irrelevant to the crusaders, however; so far as they were concerned, the blame lay firmly with Alexius himself. As Villehardouin sarcastically observed: 'Such was the return Alexius had wanted to make for the services we had rendered him.'[31] Thus the westerners' estimation of the emperor was damaged still further, and such was the antipathy towards the Greeks as a whole that any previous warmth between the two parties was almost entirely a thing of the past.

CHAPTER TWELVE

'Our excessive disagreement allowed for no humane
feeling between us'

The Murder of Alexius IV and the
Descent into War, early 1204

IN EARLY 1204 Murtzuphlus took the fight directly to the crusaders. The *Devastatio Constantinopolitana* recorded that on 7 January a body of Greek horsemen came out of the city to confront the western forces. They were met by the marquis of Montferrat who routed his opponents, killing or capturing a number of wealthy Byzantine nobles at the cost of two knights and a squire. Niketas Choniates described the same incident, but from his perspective it was important to show Murtzuphlus as the lone Byzantine noble prepared to ignore Alexius's ban on such actions. Unsurprisingly, his bravery won favour with the general populace, although at one point in the struggle Murtzuphlus's horse slipped and collapsed to its knees. The Greek may well have been trapped under his mount and, had the crusaders managed to capture or kill him, then the Byzantine contingent would have been routed entirely. Fortunately for Murtzuphlus, a group of young archers appreciated the danger and quickly rallied to defend their leader, which allowed him to escape.[1] As the horsemen fought up near the Blachernae palace, the Venetians launched their ships and menacingly prowled up and down the Golden Horn and along the sea walls that faced the Sea of Marmara. They harassed the shoreline and snatched any booty they could lay their hands on. Once again the crusaders' land and sea forces worked in close co-ordination and their combined strength was more than the Greeks could cope with.

By way of reprisal for this incident, once the Byzantine land forces were beaten back, the crusaders mounted a large raid up to two days' journey from their camp. Ravaging expeditions, known as *chevauchées*, were very common in western Europe and involved inflicting maximum damage on enemy lands and seizing all possible booty, whether it was prisoners, herds of cattle or sheep, or valuables. There was no attempt to engage in full-scale fighting – the process was simply designed to break the economy and the morale of an opponent and to demonstrate to the hapless victims that their lord was incapable of offering proper protection. The *Devastatio* suggests that this episode was the final straw for those who detested Alexius's former allies: it was this incident that created a powerful desire to break the man who had brought the barbarians to the walls of Constantinople.[2]

In fact the crusader *chevauchée* did not provoke the actual murder of Alexius, but probably led to a terminal dissatisfaction with his rule. Niketas Choniates related that on 25 January 1204, 'like a boiling kettle, to blow off [a] steam of abuse against the emperors', the mob took over the Hagia Sophia and compelled the senate, the assembly of bishops and the senior clergy to gather to elect a new ruler. They had had enough of the western-loving Alexius and, with Isaac in chronic physical decline and no longer a significant figure, they wanted an emperor of their own choosing. As a senior court official and renowned orator, Niketas was present at the meeting and described the crowd urging an attack on Alexius and demanding that a name be put forward to replace him. Niketas and his colleagues took a longer view, however. They recognised that such an action would simply push Alexius and the crusaders back together again and they feared that the westerners would use their military strength to defend their protégé. The senate and the churchmen continued to stonewall in the hope that the energy of the crowd might dissipate, but they were to be disappointed. Niketas wept as he foresaw that disaster would follow. Name after name was put forward from the ranks of the Byzantine nobility, but no one was prepared to accept. Even senior administrators were suggested: 'Thou hast raiment, be our ruler', as Niketas cuttingly dismissed such a prospect. Finally, after three days of debate the senate and the mob settled upon Nicholas Kannavos, a hapless young noble, and, against his will, he was anointed emperor on 27 January.[3]

Alexius was appalled at the emergence of a rival emperor. Now that the opposition had an overt figurehead, he feared a military coup and – as Niketas Choniates anticipated – he again looked to the crusaders for help. Regardless of the poor relations between the Greek masses and the crusaders, both the emperor and the westerners could still find common ground in their opposition to the vast, seething mob of Constantinople that was so bent on destroying them both. Alexius asked the crusaders to drive out Kannavos, in return for which he offered, according to a letter of Baldwin of Flanders written in May 1204, the Blachernae palace itself as a security until he fulfilled his other promises. The surrender of an imperial residence was a remarkable gesture and showed how desperate Alexius had become. In an attempt to conciliate another of his enemies he chose Murtzuphlus as his envoy, and the noble conveyed the proposition to the crusader camp. Although the vast majority of the westerners despised Alexius, they were aware that while he still needed them, he would provide food for their army. Furthermore, he was more likely to discharge the Byzantines' moral and financial debts to the crusaders than any other emperor. For these reasons, along with the near-certainty that an aggressively anti-western regime would take over from him, he had to be given help.

On 27 January, Boniface of Montferrat went into the city to see Alexius and discuss the plan. According to Baldwin of Flanders, the emperor mocked the marquis and scorned to fulfil his own promises. This seems incredible, given that Alexius had been the one to initiate this proposal and the emperor must have realised that keeping his oaths was central to winning the crusaders' goodwill. Baldwin was probably just sniping at Alexius's character, and it is Niketas Choniates who offers a more realistic account of a relatively amenable meeting in which it was agreed that crusaders had to enter the imperial palace to expel Kannavos and the mob who had elected him.[4]

This was the decision that really precipitated Alexius's fall. The demands of the crusaders and the political pressures within Constantinople were so contradictory that eventually it was inevitable that the emperor would run out of alternatives and one or other of his conflicting tormentors would try to remove him. It was from the Byzantine court that this threat ultimately emerged. Many there had no wish to restore relations with the crusaders and, indeed, wanted to expel them. The election of Nicholas Kannavos was one manifestation of this, but it was Murtzuphlus – the man originally freed at the crusaders' request and recently trusted as an envoy by Alexius – who now stepped forward as leader of the anti-western faction from his position high in the Byzantine hierarchy.

Both Niketas Choniates and Baldwin of Flanders recorded that it was Alexius's offer to install the crusaders in the Blachernae palace that provoked Murtzuphlus to denounce the emperor and to call for his overthrow.[5] Robert of Clari places Murtzuphlus in a more proactive role in which he offered to rid his people of the crusaders within a week if they made him emperor. The Greek hierarchy agreed to the idea and the conspirators stepped into action. Murtzuphlus had calculated that the presence of westerners inside the walls of Constantinople would bring the full imperial machinery behind him in a way that the popularly elected Nicholas Kannavos lacked. So Murtzuphlus acted quickly. First he secured the treasury by offering the eunuch in charge whichever titles the man wished. Then he called the Varangian Guard together and told them of Alexius's plan to bring crusaders back into the city. He pointed out how unpopular this was with all the Greeks – surely the guards should support the wishes of the people. The logic was inescapable: Alexius had to be removed.

On the night of 27–8 January, as the young man slept in his chambers, Murtzuphlus and the palace guards crept into his room, surrounded his bed, snatched him away and hurled him into a dungeon. Niketas gives a detailed account of the betrayal, glossing Murtzuphlus's treachery with one final act of duplicity. The writer describes Murtzuphlus rushing into the imperial bedchamber and telling Alexius of a terrible uprising. Members of the Angeloi family, the mob and, most seriously, the Varangian guard were said to be pounding the doors of the palace, set upon tearing the emperor limb from limb because of his close friendship with the crusaders. Half asleep, Alexius struggled to comprehend the extent of the danger. He turned for salvation to Murtzuphlus, the one man who still seemed loyal to him. His visitor threw a robe over the young man and together they slipped out of the chamber towards a pavilion in the palace complex, the emperor offering profuse thanks to his saviour. Perhaps this was the moment when Murtzuphlus revealed his true intentions; his lie had meant that Alexius had left the bedchamber quickly and without fuss. Now, in the palace grounds, he was at the mercy of his challenger. As the emperor reeled under the revelation of Murtzuphlus's treachery, the guards bundled him down to a prison cell where his legs were cast into irons.

The pretender assumed the imperial insignia, donning the scarlet buskins (calf-length boots) that symbolised his office, and proclaimed himself ruler. Within hours he was crowned in the Hagia Sophia – the fourth emperor present in Constantinople and certainly the one with the strongest power base. (Murtzuphlus should really be known as Emperor Alexius V – his proper name was Alexius Ducas – but most contemporary authors use his nickname and we should be thankful that yet another 'Alexius' does not appear in the narrative.) A position at the pinnacle of political and secular life gains much of its aura of power from its exclusivity. There were many kingdoms in the Christian world, but only two imperial regimes: those of Germany and Byzantium. When more than one person claimed one of those titles it was devalued: for four men to assert a right to the same honour was absurd and showed the almost complete disintegration of the imperial dignity.

The quartet would not last long, however. Men from the new regime rushed to the apartments of Emperor Isaac and told him the dramatic news. Certain sources report that the old man was so overcome by fear for his own safety and that of his son that he became ill and very soon died. In real political terms Isaac had become such a feeble figure that he was no longer a credible ruler. There is some suggestion that he may already have been dead, but if this was not the case, it was undeniably convenient that he passed away so quickly. It is also possible that he received more direct assistance in his death. Robert of Clari wrote of strangulation, although this may have been just one of many rumours in the crusader camp.

The removal of Alexius and the emergence of Murtzuphlus polarised opinion in Constantinople. The palace officials and the Varangian Guard stood by the latest holder of the imperial title, while the masses continued to acclaim their own favourite, Nicholas Kannavos, a man whom Niketas Choniates described as gentle and intelligent and an experienced warrior. The tone of Niketas's comments indicates that he felt Kannavos to be a superior man to Murtzuphlus, but soon the mood of the mob swung in favour of the latter: 'Inasmuch as the worst elements prevail among the Constantinopolitans, Ducas [Murtzuphlus] grew stronger . . . while Kannavos's splendour grew dim like a waning moon.'[6]

In spite of his positive qualities, Nicholas quickly slipped from grace: it seems that Murtzuphlus's control over the key elements of the hierarchy gave him a political base that his rival could not match. The *Chronicle of Novgorod* relates that Murtzuphlus tried unsuccessfully to win Nicholas over to his side by promising him a prominent role in his administration if he were to step down. Perhaps Nicholas did not trust the other imperial claimant, or else he hoped that his own popularity with the people was sufficient to preserve his position. Faced with this rejection, Murtzuphlus soon acted to displace Nicholas. He offered rewards and honours to those who would endorse his claim and in the first week of February, as the fickle citizenry of Constantinople began to sense where the real power lay, he ordered the Guard to arrest his rival. Nicholas had remained in the Hagia Sophia, symbolically the heart of his authority. Murtzuphlus's troops forced their way into the building, and the masses, who had so recently forced the imperial title on Nicholas, dissipated; no one defended him and a second emperor was cast into prison. The *Devastatio Constantinopolitana* reports that Nicholas was later decapitated. He had paid a heavy price for being a pawn of the capricious mob and had ruled for less than a week.

Murtzuphlus immediately signalled his aggressive stance towards the westerners by issuing a threat that they should depart within seven days or risk death. This was, in part, posturing to satisfy his own people and was unlikely to intimidate the crusaders unduly. Their hostile reply accused Murtzuphlus of treacherously murdering his lord (such rumours had evidently begun to circulate already) and warned him that they would not abandon the siege until Alexius was avenged and the full payment due to them was delivered.[7]

Murtzuphlus started his reign by reorganising the imperial administration: he swept away many of the officials who had worked under the Angeloi and rewarded his own supporters. One of those dismissed was Niketas Choniates himself, and this, together with the subsequent fall of Constantinople, does much to explain the writer's largely hostile portrayal of the latest ruler of Byzantium. Niketas characterises Murtzuphlus as highly intelligent, but arrogant, deceitful and someone who worked in a way 'that nothing that needed to be done escaped him and that he had in hand all issues'; in today's language, he was, therefore, a control-freak.[8] Niketas was especially critical of Philokales, Murtzuphlus's father-in-law and the man who took over his own post of *logothete* of the *sekreta*, essentially the head of the Byzantine civil service. The author scathingly observed that his replacement did not sit with men of high rank and, by pretending to be afflicted with gout, he thoroughly neglected his duties – a performance that evidently horrified such a devoted and status-conscious bureaucrat as Niketas.

The new regime also inflicted financial hardship on Niketas. Because the imperial treasury was completely empty, Murtzuphlus turned to the leading families and officials of the Angeloi dynasty to provide cash. These people lost huge sums of money, simply confiscated by the emperor and applied to the defence of the city.

The Greeks feared that the crusaders would mount a second attack on Constantinople in the spring and Murtzuphlus therefore ordered that the fortifications be considerably strengthened. The Greeks also assembled forty petraries, stone-throwing machines, and placed them in the areas where they believed the assault was most likely to come from.

While Niketas had an intense dislike of Murtzuphlus, he was sufficiently conscientious as an historian to acknowledge the man's personal bravery. On several occasions, armed with a sword in one hand and a bronze mace in the other, the emperor sallied forth to confront his enemies. There is little doubt that Murtzuphlus led from the front and did much to reinvigorate the imperial army.[9] On one such occasion he captured three of the doge's knights. Alberic of Trois-Fontaines, our only source for this episode, relates how these men met a particularly gruesome fate. By way of trying to intimidate the crusaders, Murtzuphlus ordered the Venetians to be suspended from iron hooks on the walls. Psychological tactics were an important part of medieval warfare, and the firing of decapitated heads over the battlements of an enemy city was a familiar practice. The First Crusaders even catapulted captured spies over the walls of Jerusalem in 1099.[10] Outside Constantinople comrades of the Venetians tried to win their freedom through offers of ransom and prayers for mercy, but to no avail. To demonstrate his abhorrence and contempt for the westerners, the emperor himself set them on fire – an act of shocking barbarity. The screams of the dying men and the stench of burning flesh pervaded the air and such a hideous spectacle must have stoked an implacable desire for revenge.[11]

In the short term, however, the basic struggle for survival became the crusaders' most pressing priority. Murtzuphlus withdrew all the markets upon which the westerners had relied and it was impossible to enter Constantinople itself to buy food there. Robert of Clari, as a lesser knight, was more immediately affected by such hardships than the likes of Villehardouin and the other leaders. Robert provides figures for the cost of various basic commodities: a *sestier* of wine sold for 12 or even 15 sous, an egg for two pennies and a hen for 20 sous. On the other hand, Robert noted a surfeit of biscuit, enough to supply the army for some time.[12] Robert's figures mean relatively little to us without a context, but Alberic of Trois-Fontaines gives an indication of the level of inflation. He reported that three-day-old bread worth two Parisian dinars now cost 26 dinars! Some men were even forced to devour their horses, the very basis of a knight's standing and military strength; truly this was 'a time of great scarcity'.[13]

Soon the crusaders were compelled to roam far and wide in their efforts to gather food. Henry of Flanders led a body of men (30 knights and many mounted sergeants according to Robert of Clari), including James of Avesnes and the Burgundian knights Eudes and William of Champlitte, in an attempt to secure supplies. They left in the dark of an early evening to avoid detection and rode all night and the following morning to the town of Philia on the Black Sea. They succeeded in capturing the castle and plundered enough food to last the army almost a fortnight. The crusaders seized cattle and clothing, the latter a less obvious form of booty, but nonetheless invaluable when it came to surviving the winter months. As the westerners spent a couple of days enjoying the spoils of victory, some defenders escaped and fled to Constantinople where they told Murtzuphlus of these events. With his ascendancy to the imperial throne based upon an aggressive attitude towards the westerners, the new emperor was bound to strike hard at the enemy as soon as possible and he set out to intercept them.

He took with him the icon of the Virgin Mary. Alberic of Trois-Fontaines gives the only detailed description of the object: 'On this icon the Majesty of the Lord was wonderfully fashioned, as well as an image of Blessed Mary and the apostles. And relics were set in it: Therein is a tooth that Jesus lost in childhood, and therein is contained a piece of the lance by which He was wounded on the Cross, a portion of the Shroud, and relics from thirty martyrs.'[14] The presence of this enormously revered icon must have given Murtzuphlus great confidence; Niketas Choniates wrote that the Byzantines regarded the relic as 'a fellow general'.[15]

It was common for Christian armies to carry relics into battle: the crusaders in the Holy Land had taken the True Cross into all their battles between 1099 and its loss at the Horns of Hattin in 1187. Murtzuphlus was aligning himself with one of the greatest icons of the Orthodox Church and claiming her protection. He was also making plain his defence of that institution and showing that he had the support of its hierarchy in his war against the Catholic aggressors. Patriarch John X Camaterus, the senior figure in the Orthodox Church, accompanied the army to emphasise this point.

Murtzuphlus gathered a substantial force of several thousand warriors (4,000, according to Robert of Clari) and set out to track down the crusaders, who were moving slowly, in part hampered by the need to drive the cattle back to their camp. Murtzuphlus soon found and briefly shadowed them. He decided to attack the rearguard first. He watched the main force pass by escorting their prisoners and the captured animals and then, just as the crusaders, led by Henry of Flanders, were about to enter a wood, he sprang into action and rushed towards his enemy.

At first, the westerners feared the worst: seriously outnumbered, they called on God and the Virgin Mary to deliver them. But they quickly pulled themselves together and turned to face their opponents. A group of eight crossbowmen were set at the front of their troops in order to take the initial sting from the Greek onslaught. This must have had some effect, but the charge was not stopped and the two forces were soon engaged in fierce hand-to-hand combat. The crusaders threw away their lances and drew their swords and daggers to better fight at close range.

A Spanish mercenary, Peter of Navarre, headed the Greek advance guard. Alberic of Trois-Fontaines gleefully records that Peter was so confident of success that he entered the fray bareheaded except for a golden crown. As the two sides locked into combat, Peter came up against Henry of Flanders, an experienced warrior and a skilled swordsman. The Fleming engaged his opponent and immediately aimed for his weak spot: with one accelerating, arcing blow, doubtless practised countless times in the courtyards of the comital castles of Flanders, he brought his sword down upon Peter's head. The golden crown snapped and the sword buried itself to a depth of two fingers into the skull of the Navarrese. The power and discipline of the crusader cavalry again showed its superiority and soon the front ranks of the Greeks crumbled. By this time the western forces had been working together for more than a year: at Zara, Corfu, outside

Constantinople, and on Alexius's campaign in Thrace. They were polished and co-ordinated in a way that only direct battlefield experience could provide. By contrast, the Byzantine forces, a mixture of Greek nobles and mercenaries, lacked the cohesion and power to match their enemy.

As the battle intensified, the crusaders quickly penetrated to the senior men amongst the enemy. Theodore Branas was struck with a huge blow that dented his helmet and severely bruised him. Peter of Bracieux, who had already distinguished himself in the exchange outside the Galata fortress in July 1203, was again to the fore and here he decided to seek even greater glory by trying to capture the icon. Whether he saw Patriarch John from a distance and spurred towards him, or whether he simply found himself close by the Byzantine in the heat of the battle, is unknown. In either event, Peter's heart leaped at the prospect of taking such a magnificent and important relic. The patriarch was said to be wearing a helmet and armour as well as his robes, although because Byzantine clergy were known not to bear arms this element of the story may well be untrue.[16] In any case, as Peter closed in on him, he probably chose deliberately not to kill a man of such high standing. Nonetheless he dealt a fierce crack across the front of the patriarch's helmet that caused him to fall from his horse and drop the sacred object. As it lay shining in the dust, Peter leaped from his horse to seize it and, while John knelt stunned on the ground, the crusader gathered the icon into his arms. When the other Greeks saw what had happened they howled in rage and turned all their efforts on Peter. They surged towards the Frenchman, but the crusaders reacted sharply enough, closed ranks around their comrade and then mounted a brutal counter-attack. Murtzuphlus was hit so hard that he fell over his horse's neck; his men were thrown into disarray, and the Byzantine army broke and fled. So desperate was Murtzuphlus to escape that he threw away his shield, dropped his arms and spurred his horse into a gallop. He also abandoned the imperial standard – another humiliation for the emperor. While the Greeks had lost around 20 men, not a single crusader knight was killed in this engagement. Proudly bearing their great trophies, the westerners headed back to the camp.

News of the battle had reached the main army and a contingent of men prepared themselves to go to the help of their friends. As they hurried in the direction of the fray they were overjoyed to meet their comrades already coming victoriously towards them. Unsurprisingly the foraging party was welcomed with huge delight. When they approached the camp the bishops and clerics processed out to meet them and to receive the holy icon. Showing the deepest reverence they took it into their midst and entrusted it to Bishop Garnier of Troyes, a man who had already been to the Holy Land as a pilgrim. Garnier carried the icon back into a church in the camp and the clergy sang a divine service to celebrate its capture. In thanks for their victory, the crusaders donated the icon to the Cistercian order, whose abbots of Lucedio and Loos had provided such sterling spiritual and emotional guidance to the expedition. Alberic of Trois-Fontaines was himself a Cistercian monk writing in the county of Champagne where the abbey of Cîteaux was located. He chose to record this story because he may possibly have seen or heard a detailed, or garbled, description of the object.

Not only had the foraging party secured a substantial amount of food, but it had dealt a terrible blow to the standing of the new regime. This was the crusaders' first significant military success in months and it provided a massive and much-needed morale boost.

For Murtzuphlus, on the other hand, this was a crushing disappointment. Having looked to the Virgin for divine support and trusting in her power to defeat the crusaders, the loss of the icon was devastating. The westerners knew of its importance to the Greeks and naturally drew their own conclusions as to why Murtzuphlus had lost it. Robert of Clari commented: 'They have so great faith in this icon that they fully believe that no one who carries it in battle can be defeated, and we believe that it was because Murtzuphlus had no right to carry it that he was defeated.'[7] The emperor was painfully aware of this same possibility. The Virgin was felt to have a special affinity with Constantinople and the episode appeared to be a divine judgement on his rule.

To avoid this uncomfortable truth from being broadcast, he resorted to a desperate stratagem. In an outrageous misrepresentation of reality he asserted that he had been victorious in the battle. When asked the whereabouts of the icon and the imperial standard, he replied that they had been put away for safekeeping. After a little while it seems that this travesty gained some currency, but the purported outcome of the battle could not remain inside the walls of Constantinople for ever. Stories concerning the emperor's claims of success and his denial of losing the icon and standard soon reached the crusader camp. The information must have provoked amazement at such bravado, and then a realisation that something had to be done to set the record straight.

The westerners had a rare opportunity to exert complete control over the situation. They decided to publicly humiliate Murtzuphlus by making plain the truth. The Venetians prepared a galley and placed the imperial standard and the icon prominently at the prow. Then, blowing trumpets to attract attention, they slowly rowed the ship up and down, alongside the city walls, displaying the objects to the astounded populace. The citizens recognised the icon and the banner: Murtzuphlus's deception was exposed and many mocked him for his defeat and were angered by his lies. The emperor lamely attempted to explain away the episode and to rally support by promising that he would wreak vengeance on his enemies.[18]

Almost immediately Murtzuphlus tried to launch another attack with fire-ships, but this too failed. Recognising that his military efforts were proving bad for morale as well as inflicting little damage on the crusaders, he tried a less bellicose approach. On 7 February he sent envoys to the crusader camp seeking a meeting with the doge. Murtzuphlus evidently regarded Dandolo as less closely bound to Alexius than, for example, Boniface of Montferrat. The doge was also widely respected for his wisdom and prudence.

Dandolo boarded a galley and was rowed up the Golden Horn to a point outside the monastery of St Cosmos and St Damian, just outside the city walls to the north. A squadron of crusader cavalry also crossed over the inlet and shadowed the negotiations. Murtzuphlus rode out from the Blachernae palace and came down to the shore where the two men exchanged views. Niketas Choniates and Baldwin of Flanders provide the two accounts of the meeting and, while both display predictably divergent viewpoints, the information they supply is fundamentally similar. Baldwin wrote that Dandolo was aware of the dangers in trusting a man who had already disregarded his oaths to his lord and cast him into prison, and who now disregarded the covenant with the crusaders. Nonetheless the doge sounded a conciliatory, if somewhat unrealistic, note by asking Murtzuphlus to free Alexius and to request his forgiveness. Dandolo also promised that the crusaders would be lenient on Alexius, attributing his foolishness to a youthful one-off lapse of judgement. Beneath this veneer of politeness lay a sense of threat, however. It was the crusaders who now seemed to be dictating the terms; it was

Dandolo talking about being lenient and maintaining the peace. The westerners' recent military successes and the extraordinary disarray within Constantinople gave them an ascendancy that a few weeks earlier would have seemed unthinkable. The real message behind the doge's emollient tone was the crusaders' demand that the Greeks hold firm to the agreement made by Alexius and provide the promised military support for the expedition to the Holy Land and the submission of the Orthodox Church to Rome. Baldwin of Flanders stated that Murtzuphlus had no reasonable response to the doge's propositions and that, in rejecting them, he 'chose the loss of his life and the overthrow of Greece'.[19]

To Niketas Choniates, as a Byzantine, there was little that was reasonable about the offer. The repetition of these detested conditions, compounded by the demand of an immediate payment of 5,000 pounds of gold, was completely unacceptable. Niketas tersely characterised the crusaders' terms as 'galling and unacceptable to those who have tasted freedom and are accustomed to give, not take, commands'.[20] In effect, the usurping emperor was being asked to stand down, to get his people to bow to the crusaders' force, his city to strip itself of even more gold and his clergy to surrender their authority. It was inconceivable that Murtzuphlus could consider such concessions. If he agreed to the crusaders' demands, his own power would probably flow back to Alexius, and the citizens of Constantinople, who had supported him on the basis of his resistance to the westerners, would simply turn against him and almost certainly kill him.

The usurper's reluctance to give ground was communicated to the doge's land escort, and the crusader knights suddenly charged at the emperor to try to capture him – not in itself an act of temperate high diplomacy. Murtzuphlus managed to wheel his horse around and escape back into the city, although a number of his companions were less fortunate and fell prisoner.

The situation had, therefore, reached an impasse. Mistrust and mutual antipathy brought war ever closer. Niketas assessed the relationship between the Greeks and the crusaders thus: 'Their inordinate hatred for us and our excessive disagreement with them allowed for no humane feeling between us.'[21]

The breakdown of this attempt to find a peaceful solution to the struggle meant a slow, but inevitable, descent into a new and horrifying vortex of violence. The crusaders' continued insistence on the reinstatement of Alexius illuminated Murtzuphlus's most telling source of vulnerability. Even in prison, Alexius still posed a potential threat to his rival emperor. In these circumstances the young man had to be eliminated: three times he was offered poison, three times he refused. Perhaps an innate sense of self-preservation prevented him from taking the hemlock, or perhaps he nursed a vain hope that his supporters might persuade the crusaders to rescue him. Nothing of the sort happened and, in the end, Alexius was slain. Murtzuphlus himself was said to have gone on 8 February to the dark prison cell in which Alexius lay and to have squeezed the life out of his rival, either with a cord or with his own bare hands.[22] Baldwin of Flanders's letter adds the gruesome details that, as the emperor was expiring, Murtzuphlus took an iron hook and ripped open the sides and ribcage of the dying man. This particularly colourful version of events may have been a rumour circulating in the crusader army – perhaps in an attempt to further blacken the name of the usurping emperor (or Judas, as Baldwin called him).[23]

Thus ended a brief but complex life. Alexius IV had been the cata- lyst for the most seismic changes in the Byzantine political system for centuries, but the forces that he had unleashed were impossible to control and now he had forfeited his life against his imperial ambitions.

Alexius's death had to be explained to the people at large. Murtzuphlus spread word that the emperor had succumbed to an accident, and to try to bolster this impression he organised a state funeral in accordance with Alexius's proper standing. Murtzuphlus performed splendidly at this event, as he mourned and showed the sorrow of a man regretting the passing of his former leader. It was, of course, all an act and once the ceremony was over he could get on with the business of planning how to deal with the crusaders.

To some the news of Alexius's death was an immediate cause of suspi- cion, and Robert of Clari reported that a letter attached to an arrow was fired into the crusader camp informing them that it was murder. Some of the nobles professed indifference to Alexius's fate because he no longer wanted to keep faith with them; others, more sympathetically, expressed regret that he had died in such a fashion. For Murtzuphlus, the price of killing his most important rival was to make himself even more detested by the westerners and provide an irrefutable justification for his removal.

CHAPTER THIRTEEN

'Break in! Rout menaces; crush cowards; press on more bravely!'

The Conquest of Constantinople, April 1204

T HE MURDER OF Alexius marked an irrevocable break between the Byzantines and the crusaders. Despite the problems between the young emperor and the westerners, while Alexius remained alive there was always a possibility that his need for support and his moral and contractual obligations towards the crusaders might prevent open war. The two sides had teetered on the brink of conflict since November 1203. Episodes such as the attack of the fire-ships constituted short and savage escalations of violence, but they had been followed by efforts to make peace. Now there was no further room for manoeuvre: Murtzuphlus was known to have killed the emperor and he refused to fulfil his victim's promises to the crusaders. Both sides realised that war was a certainty and they began to prepare for battle.

The crusaders' position had become desperate. They had tied themselves ineluctably to Alexius and his death left them completely exposed, thousands of miles from home and camped outside a hostile city. His failure to deliver the anticipated financial backing meant that the Venetians remained substantially underpaid for continuing to provide the fleet, and the crusaders themselves lacked the money to mount an effective campaign in the Holy Land. More pressing still was the shortage of food. Anonymous of Soissons wrote: 'Perceiving that they were neither able to enter the sea without danger of immediate death nor delay longer on land because of their impending exhaustion of food and supplies, our men reached a decision.'[1]

A series of grim choices confronted the leaders. None of the alternatives open to them offered an easy way forward. Even if they did manage to scavenge enough food to start out for home, they would face enormous criticism for failing to help the Holy Land, particularly after their protestations justifying the diversion to Constantinople in the first instance. For men so steeped in notions of honour such a retreat would be intolerable. On the other hand, the often antagonistic relationship between Byzantium and the West, coupled with the treachery of Murtzuphlus and their hopeless situation on the shores of the Bosphorus, meant that the crusaders could more readily construct a case to explain an attack on the Greeks.

Through Lent 1204 the citizens of Constantinople and the western armies made ready to fight. Both sides looked to learn from their experiences in 1203 and sought to capitalise on any perceived advantages of their own and to exploit particular weaknesses of their enemy. The westerners' greatest success had come through the Venetian troops scaling the walls on the Golden Horn. Once again, therefore, they chose to concentrate their efforts on that section of the city.

The Venetians prepared their petraries and mangonels; frames were checked, ropes readied and hundreds of missiles gathered and stored. Many of these machines were placed on board the ships where they would provide covering fire for the intrepid men perched on the great flying bridges, once again hoisted high upon the masts. The engineering on the Venetian ships was almost identical to that described by Hugh of Saint-Pol and Robert of Clari in July 1203, although this time the Venetians hung grapevines over and across the protective boards to absorb the impact of missiles and limit the damage to the men and the ships.[2] They also covered the vessels with vinegar-soaked hides in an attempt to lessen the effect of incendiary devices.

The French soldiers readied their own missile-firing engines and organised mining equipment. Back in July 1203 they had achieved little against the high walls at the north-west of the city. Now they planned to work more closely with the Venetians and to devote their attention to the section of the Blachernae palace that lay in front of a narrow strip of land looking onto the Golden Horn. The French believed strongly in the idea of mining under, and battering through, the walls and they made machines known as 'cats', 'carts' and 'sows' to wheel up to the battlements and protect those working underneath.[3] These squat constructions consisted of a shelter covered in hides and doused in vinegar. Under this canopy was slung a metal-tipped log that swung backwards and forwards in order to break into the city. The mobile shelter also provided cover for miners trying to hack through the walls with pickaxes and shovels.

The Greeks anticipated that the crusaders' attack was most likely to come from along the Golden Horn. Here were the weakest sections of the wall because they were built primarily to line the harbour rather than as fortifications *per se*. In theory the chain across the Golden Horn should have prevented enemies from gaining access to the inlet and to this part of the defences. In other words, the designers of Constantinople's walls had not foreseen the present situation. Now, in order to combat the Venetians' mast-top ladders, the Byzantines had topped their fortifications with a nightmarish confection of wooden towers. Huge beams were used to form structures that raised the height of the walls between the stone towers and also sat on top of the existing turrets. As these strange, ramshackle constructions took shape, the profile of the walls must have changed dramatically. Normally the towers, gates and battlements had a regular, regimented outline, broken up only by the demands of topography or the intrusion of occasional modifications. Several sources attest to the fact that these creations were up to six or seven storeys high.[4] Like the Venetian ships, they too were covered in hides soaked in vinegar to protect them from burning and to reduce the impact of the crusaders' bombardment. The fortifications of Constantinople had assumed a ponderous top-heavy appearance because these vast constructions projected out from the stonework beneath them. This was deliberate because anyone working at the foot of the walls would have to contend with a constant threat from above. The overhang allowed the wooden towers to have openings in their underside to enable defenders to deposit stones, hot oil or tar onto the heads or machines of the attackers below. As well as fortifying the walls on the Golden Horn, Murtzuphlus did not neglect the landward side of Constantinople and ordered all the gates there to be bricked up for extra security.

The two sides could see and hear each other organising for war. On both shores of the Golden Horn the pounding of hammers rang out day and night as carpenters and engineers sought to assemble the war machines they hoped would carry them to victory.

As the crusaders made the practical preparations to enter Constantinople, they also turned their attention to the division of spoils in the event of successfully capturing the city. Anticipatory agreements of this sort were standard practice in medieval warfare because they helped to prevent bitter arguments in the often-confused aftermath of a siege. Many victorious campaigns had degenerated into vicious and divisive squabbles as to who had rights to the booty gained when a city fell. In 1153, for example, at Ascalon, the Knights Templar had attempted to prevent other crusader knights from entering a breach in the walls as a way of trying to stop anyone else taking plunder.[5] Their selfishness was punished when their men became isolated and were killed. Given the protracted campaign of 1203–4, and the contrast between the poverty of the crusaders and the riches known to be inside Constantinople, it was even more essential to make some binding arrangements to constrain the lesser soldiers. An uncontrolled looting session might open a besieging army to a counter-attack, or could stir even greater resentment from a soon-to-be-subject population towards their new rulers.

Plunder was not the only issue under discussion, because the possible seizure of Constantinople presented the French and the Venetians with a larger and, in medieval terms, unprecedented issue. They were not, of course, just conquering a city or a castle, but stood to gain control over an entire empire. They would be required to choose a new emperor and to raise one of their number to an unsurpassed level of power. As an independent force, free from the control of, for example, the king of France, there was no question of taking the land on behalf of another. By the laws of conquest, Constantinople was theirs and its new ruler would come from within the ranks of the crusaders. The senior leadership such as Dandolo, Baldwin of Flanders and Boniface of Montferrat were certainly amongst the most influential men in Europe, but none was a crowned monarch, let alone one with the history and standing of the Byzantine emperor.

In March 1204 Dandolo, Boniface, Baldwin, Louis of Blois and Hugh of Saint-Pol drew up a formal covenant 'to secure unity and lasting concord between us'. The full text of the arrangement still survives and Villehardouin and Robert of Clari provide an abbreviated summary of the document, known to historians as 'The March Pact'.[6]

Together the crusaders pledged themselves to conquer the city and if, through divine assistance, they succeeded, all the booty was to be collected together in one place and then shared out equitably. Robert of Clari defined loot as gold, silver and new cloth to the value of five sous or more, recognising that the smallest of items were not worth worrying about. Food and tools were formally excluded from this part of the contract.[7] The largest sum of money remaining from Alexius's agreements was that owed to the Venetians. Some of this dated from the Treaty of Zara and some from the one-year extension of the Treaty of Venice – that is, payment for the upkeep of the fleet from March 1203 to March 1204. To settle this debt required the Venetians to take three-quarters of all the spoils of conquest against one-quarter for the crusaders until the sum of money required (200,000 silver marks) was covered. Once this amount was reached, all booty beyond that figure would be divided equally between the Venetians and the crusaders. The only goods excluded from these regulations were foodstuffs, which, logically, were fairly split between everyone in order to sustain the campaign.

The covenant then addressed the future of Constantinople itself. In the event of gaining full control of the city, six Frenchmen and six Venetians would be selected to choose the man whom they, having sworn true faith on the Bible, felt would make the most suitable ruler. This parity between French and Venetian electors reflected the shared labour between the two forces outside the city. The person elected emperor was to receive one-quarter of the conquered lands and would be given both the Blachernae and the Bucoleon palaces. The group who did not have their representative elected as emperor was entitled to choose one of their members to become patriarch and to hold the Hagia Sophia. Thus, in the case of a French emperor, there would be a Venetian patriarch; with a Venetian emperor there would be a French (or conceivably German or northern Italian) patriarch.

There remained the allocation of the lands, titles and possessions of the Byzantine Empire itself. Another committee, this time of 12 Venetians and 12 Frenchmen, would dispense the fiefs and offices and decide the levels of service owed to the emperor by particular fief-holders. The crusaders had a chance to divide out a whole political entity here: something akin to the situation faced by William the Conqueror when he took over the kingdom of England in 1066. Although it was William himself, rather than any group of Norman nobles, who made the decisions concerning rewards, he – like the crusaders and the Venetians – had also acquired a wealthy and well-established state. By contrast, 30 years after Duke William's success, the First Crusaders took almost a decade to take over the complex and heterogeneous political entities that existed in the Levant and this, in turn, led to the creation of four distinct Crusader States.

The French and the Venetians were well aware that the fall of Constantinople was unlikely to signal the automatic submission of the entire Byzantine Empire. The citizens of Constantinople and its environs would probably be hostile to the westerners and, further afield, Alexius III remained at large to act as a possible focus for Greek opposition. The crusaders agreed, therefore, to stay in the area until March 1205 to consolidate their new acquisitions. This meant that the expedition to the Holy Land was, if not quite abandoned, deferred yet again. Everyone recognised that if they conquered Constantinople and left the same summer, then the chances of this new Latin Empire surviving were remote. Any who chose to remain after March 1205 would come under the jurisdiction of the new emperor and had to serve him as required.

Inevitably, and prudently, the Venetians acted to enshrine their commercial dominance within the document. It was agreed that the new emperor would not engage in business with any state at war with the Italians, thereby shutting out hostile economic rivals from this enormously wealthy trading region.

Finally, some attempt was made to regulate the behaviour of the crusaders when they entered the city. Robert of Clari relates that the crusader host was obliged to swear on relics that women should not be sexually assaulted and that they should not be forcibly despoiled of any fine garments. Furthermore, the crusaders were not to lay hands on a monk or a priest, except in self-defence, and they should not break into churches or monasteries.[8] The release of pent-up sexual tensions was a horrifying, if familiar, component of medieval warfare, and similarly the seizure of church vestments was always another easy target for conquering forces. The penalty for breaking these regulations was death. Given the overt antipathy between the Byzantines and the crusaders, some effort to rein in the more predictable excesses of war was a prudent if, as we shall see, largely unsuccessful initiative. Just to remind everyone that the campaign was still being fought under the banner of a holy war, the crusading churchmen included a threat of excommunication to those who broke the terms of the agreement.

By early April the crusaders were poised for battle. The months sitting outside Constantinople had witnessed many changes in their position: first, as invited allies of the man who claimed to be the rightful emperor; then as the people who delivered him to the throne; next as disappointed and deserted outsiders, shunned by their former ally and reviled by his successor; and finally, as a small but determined besieging army with little food and few other choices but to take on the most mighty city in the Christian world.

On the evening of 8 April the fleet was loaded up and made ready to sail at dawn. Horses were embarked onto their special ships and everyone planned to set out at first light. A sense of anticipation gathered intensity. Prior to all medieval battles, particularly crusading conflicts, spiritual preparations were essential, too — prayer and confession being the necessary prerequisites to secure the heavenly rewards of a martyred crusader. The men were granted absolution and received the Body of Christ in the sacrament. The crusaders must have implored divine aid: how else might an army of around only 20,000 men take Constantinople?

All of these men, from the senior nobles to the most humble foot-soldiers, knew that the coming days were the most crucial of the whole campaign. The first siege of Constantinople had seen them take on incredible odds and succeed. By April 1204 the murder of Alexius meant that the crusaders had lost the man who legitimised their presence outside the city and who could give them huge material support. Now they confronted a far more hostile citizenry and their own position was ever more precarious. Alexius had provided foodstuffs for the westerners and, having survived through the winter with his help, they were now reduced to foraging ever further afield. The conquest of Constantinople would release food and money to offer the crusaders their only realistic way forward. They felt morally justified in their actions and, it cannot be denied, they had an impressively strong military record against the Greeks. Even so, the walls of Constantinople now loomed higher than ever before and this time the Byzantines had a cruel and determined ruler at their head.

What would the following day bring? Swift death from an unseen arrow? A slow, excruciating end with limbs crushed and shattered by boulders or a fall from a ladder? A shrieking immolation in burning tar? Or perhaps, with God's favour, glory and riches. The men who had chosen to lead the assault across the flying bridges were the most vulnerable. Niketas reports the offer of huge rewards to those who would climb aloft and fight from the masts. To these men a desire for fame and fortune must have outweighed the terrible risk they were taking.[9] Throughout the camp, as men talked over their lives, spoke of their loved ones and confided messages to friends to pass on should they not survive, they had to conquer their fears, prepare their weapons and pray for victory.

In the early morning of 9 April the crusader fleet approached the section of walls running from the monastery of Evergetes to the Blachernae palace. With characteristic pride Villehardouin recalled what a splendid sight this made as the alternating warships, galleys and transport ships stretched out over a mile long.[10] Each of the familiar divisions formed up on groups of boats, their banners fluttering in the breeze. Filled with fighting men, laden with catapults, ladders and battering rams, the crusader ships moved up close to the battlements and began the assault.

The walls of the Blachernae palace did not come down to the shore and the crusaders disembarked from their ships and concentrated their attack on the narrow strip of land between the fortifications and the water. Both sides launched a deadly bombardment of rocks and missiles. The first men ashore unloaded the ladders and other fighting equipment under heavy enemy fire. As the crusaders heaved their wooden burden towards the walls, the first arrows thudded into shields and armour. They rarely pierced the chain mail and its protective padding right through to the flesh (or if they did, caused only a light wound), yet the arrows stayed fixed to their prey and the soldiers began to resemble giant porcupines covered with feathered quills. As they started to mount the walls, the two forces meshed together and the exchange of missiles was supplemented by the thrust of lances and the swing of axes and swords. Some of those on the scaling ladders were pushed away from the walls to fall backwards in a deadly, graceful arc; others were prised from their ladders and plummeted to the ground to die or to sustain crippling injuries; still more were killed by sword blows as they climbed. The cries of the injured and dying, of orders bellowed in Greek, Danish, Italian, German and French, the occasional blast from the imperial trumpeters, and the crashing and splintering of missiles exploding into fragments against the city walls comprised a truly hellish cacophony.

The crusaders repeatedly attempted to set up their battering rams at the foot of the walls. The feeling of claustrophobia in one of these machines must have been intense. As they moved up to the walls, defenders gathered above bearing huge vats of boiling oil or fat to pour down onto the attackers. The noise, smell and heat generated as this scorching rain cascaded down upon those inside can barely be conceived – sometimes the 'cats' caught fire and the occupants were terribly burned. Screaming, they would run from under the canopies looking for water or open ground to roll on – yet in their search for relief they exposed themselves to the arrows and missiles from the battlements. In addition to fire, the defenders might also drop huge boulders onto their enemies and many of the crusaders' machines, as well as the men operating them, were crushed. The westerners tried to protect their troops by launching a bombardment of their own. The ships' catapults concentrated on the defenders above a 'cat', while archers and knights with scaling ladders might also turn their attention on the same section of wall.

On this day, however, the Greeks resisted strongly. Murtzuphlus, foreseeing the attack, had directed his men well and his visible leadership did much to encourage his troops. He set up his own vermilion tents on the hill of the monastery of the Pantepoptes behind the section of walls under fire. Thus he could see over his own fortifications and follow the movements of his enemy – a rare luxury for the medieval general lacking the high-technology surveillance equipment available today. Equally, however, the westerners could watch Murtzuphlus ('the traitor', as Robert of Clari called him), and his presence acted as a goad to their efforts.

The Byzantines had prepared carefully for the land assault and had gathered hundreds of huge boulders to use against the crusaders. The destruction wrought by the fires of 1203 had left large piles of debris lying around the city – ideal material for using in this way. The Greeks in the towers pushed and dropped these enormous projectiles onto the crusaders' siege engines, shattering many of them. So great was the damage that the westerners were forced to abandon their machines and run for safety.[11]

But it was the weather conditions that proved the most serious hindrance to the crusaders. Soon after the attack began, the wind started to blow from the shore, which prevented most of the ships from drawing close enough to the walls to launch an assault that would give vital extra impetus to their comrades further along. Only five of Constantinople's towers were actually engaged and none of these could be secured; by mid-afternoon it was evident to all that the attack had failed. The signal was given to withdraw. A huge cheer went up from the walls of Constantinople – the city had survived its first test in the new struggle. The defenders jeered at their opponents and Robert of Clari reports that many dropped their trousers and displayed their buttocks to the crusaders. Murtzuphlus was keen to capitalise on the moment of victory and ordered his trumpets to sound a triumphal blast. He lavished praise upon his men and chose to view the victory as proof of his own prowess and of his worth as their ruler. 'See, lords, am I not a good emperor? Never did you have so good an emperor! Have I not done well? We need fear them no longer. I will have them all hanged and dishonoured.'[12]

The crusaders were deeply discouraged. Many good men had been killed and much of their equipment had been lost or destroyed; they interpreted the outcome as God's judgement and felt that their sins had caused them to fail. Baldwin of Flanders was forced to acknowledge that his troops had 'retreated in shame from our enemies, a portion of whom on that day proved superior in all matters. On that day so it seemed we were fatigued to the point of impotence.'[13] The campaign was in serious trouble. The leadership assembled: they needed to make immediate and substantial progress or else they were doomed. Some argued for a change in approach and advocated pressing the siege in a different area, prefer-ably along the walls facing the Bosphorus where the crusaders could again co-ordinate their land and sea forces. This was quickly rejected when the Venetians pointed out that the current there was far too swift and would carry their ships away.

The senior French nobles, together with Marquis Boniface and the doge, considered their position. They recalled their success along the Golden Horn in 1203 and reasoned that the treacherous winds were the main cause of their present difficulties. They resolved to make another attack against the same section of the city, but first they would pause to repair and modify their ships and wait for better wind and sea conditions.

While these were prudent practical measures, there was also a need to rebuild morale – a task that initially fell to the churchmen. Success would only follow if the main army believed that its work was still divinely endorsed. Many amongst the rank and file had had enough fighting, and so bad were the day's casualties that large numbers of the lesser men were reluctant to press the siege any longer and wanted to leave. They pleaded to be allowed to sail on to the Holy Land where they might complete their vows and regain God's approval. As Villehardouin reported: 'certain people in the company would have been only too pleased if the current had borne them down the straits [and away from Constantinople] . . . and they did not care where they went so long as they left that land behind'.[14]

The clergy discussed the situation amongst themselves and settled upon the message they wished to spread through the demoralised army. They had to convince the men that the events of 9 April were not God's judgement on a sinful enterprise: the campaign, they argued, *was* righteous and with proper belief it *would* succeed. The concept of God testing the determination of the crusaders through temporary setbacks was a familiar means for the clergy to explain failure in the course of a campaign.[15] Such an interpretation still permitted divine approval for the expedition, but was a way in which God could discern the true resolve of His army. It was announced that sermons would be preached on the morning of Sunday 11 April and each senior churchman accordingly gathered his flock together. The bishops of Soissons and Troyes from northern France, the bishop of Halberstadt from the German Empire, Abbot Simon of Loos from the Low Countries and Master John of Noyen from Flanders all addressed the troops; even the Venetians, who were technically still excommunicate, were included.

The clergy's message was designed to reassure and encourage the crusaders. Their argument that the attack on Constantinople was spiritually just revolved around two themes. First, the Greeks were traitors and murderers since they had killed their rightful lord, Alexius IV. To a society bound by obligations to the feudal lord and where the killing of an anointed ruler was a genuine rarity, this breach of normal boundaries was a matter of serious disquiet and it was easy to justify vengeance for such a crime. The churchmen used highly inflammatory language and claimed that the Greeks were 'worse than the Jews', and they invoked the authority of God and the pope to take action. To introduce the Jews as a point of comparison indicates how strongly the clergy wished to convince their audience of Murtzuphlus's evil. As the killers of Christ, the Jews were the target of huge obloquy in western Europe and to connect Murtzuphlus to them was to tap into a powerful and violent set of feelings. All the men were commanded to confess again, to take communion and to have strength. The Greeks were the enemies of God and deserved to be destroyed.

The second element of the bishops' justification emphasised the schism between the Greek Orthodox Church and Rome. The Greeks' disobedience to the see of Rome and their contempt for the papacy and Catholics in general were worthy of punishment. It was asserted that the Greeks believed that 'all those who followed [the law of Rome] were dogs'. The use of canine imagery was to employ the sort of language usually reserved for Muslims. The clergy were at pains to distinguish the Byzantines from other Christians and they described their opponents as 'the enemies of God'. For this reason the westerners should have no fear of incurring divine disapproval when attacking the Greeks.

Finally, the churchmen ordered all the prostitutes to be cast out of the camp: a familiar move intended to ensure the apparent purity of the crusading army's motives. The First Crusaders had done the same before the successful Battle of Antioch in June 1098 and prior to the final assault on Jerusalem in July 1099. Down to this time, however, the Fourth Crusade had not resorted to such painful self-sacrifice; now, however, the prostitutes were taken on board and sent away from the camp.

The clergy fulfilled their role perfectly: the crusaders were spiritually refortified and convinced that their fight was morally just. The bishops ordered everyone to confess and take communion and then to prepare for battle. Huge lines formed as the men poured out their sins to the priests and received consolation and forgiveness.

Alongside these vital psychological preparations, the weekend was also spent refettling the ships and equipment. The crusaders had seen that, even with a flying bridge, single vessels lacked the fighting power to take a tower alone. In order to overcome this they bound the boats together in pairs to double the strength that could be deployed against a particular point. This construction enabled the ladders from the two assault towers to extend out like arms on either side of the Byzantine fortifications. This lethal embrace was designed to allow the attackers a secure foothold on the walls and to permit a more concentrated weight of firepower and men to be directed on the enemy. On Saturday and Sunday the French and Venetians dedicated themselves to the creation of the new double-towered ships.

Inside Constantinople the Greeks were hugely cheered by their victory.

They were far more confident than hitherto: having repulsed the crusaders once, they were less afraid of their enemy. Revelling in the events of 9 April, Murtzuphlus marched his men over the Golden Horn and symbolically pitched his scarlet tent opposite the crusaders before returning to the safety of his walls. Buoyed by the defeat of the westerners, more of the inhabitants of Constantinople were encouraged to participate in another triumph for the Queen of Cities.

On the morning of Monday 12 April the assault began again and the crusaders boarded their vessels and sailed across the Golden Horn towards the same northern corner of the city. The great transport ships and galleys drew as close to the walls as they could and dropped anchor. From there they could unleash their siege artillery. Catapults launched a hail of stones towards the towers and wooden structures opposite. Huge cauldrons bubbled with Greek fire, as it was called, a weapon first used in Byzantium during the seventh century. The Turks employed it against the early crusaders, but the westerners soon adopted it for their own armies. A contemporary Arab source records a recipe that combined naphtha, olive oil and lime, distilled several times. Other possible ingredients included tar, resin, sulphur and dolphin fat.[16] Whatever combination the crusaders settled upon, the deadly cocktail was poured into ceramic vessels and fired against the Byzantine fortifications. Horsetails of smoke marked the trajectory of these lethal containers as they hurtled across the narrow gap between the ships and the walls, before shattering and exploding against their targets. The Greeks had prepared well, however, because the hides hanging over their battlements were so heavily soaked in anti-inflammatory liquids that the incendiaries could not take hold.

From the Byzantine side, more than 60 petraries cast rocks and stones down onto the crusaders' ships, but the westerners were carefully protected too and the vine nets ensured that damage to the vessels was minimal. Robert of Clari claimed that stones 'so large that a man could not lift them from the ground' had little impact.[17]

As morning moved towards midday the battle intensified. Villehardouin commented that 'the shouts that rose from the battle created such a din that it seemed as if the whole world were crumbling to pieces'. Yet in spite of the ferocity of the struggle there was stalemate; both sides had armoured themselves so effectively that neither the Greeks' catapults nor the Franks' fire-bombs could harm their targets.

Murtzuphlus again directed his people from the Pantepoptes hill, urging his men on and steering them to where he saw the crusaders' onslaught was most fierce. Baldwin of Flanders wrote of 'tremendous Greek resistance' and how 'the fortunes of war were uncertain for a short while'.[18] By midday the westerners were beginning to tire and it appeared that the Greeks again held the upper hand. Niketas Choniates, who was present in the city, felt that at this point in the battle the Byzantines prevailed. The assault appeared to have stalled.[19]

Just as the fortunes of war seemed set against the crusaders, nature intervened to hand them the decisive stroke of good fortune they needed to take them to victory. The winds on the Monday morning had been light and provided little real impetus to their efforts. But, in the early afternoon, the breeze shifted to blow strongly from the north. The sharp snap of a sail swollen by the breeze signalled the change: this, at last, gave the assault a genuine punch that had thus far been lacking.

Robert of Clari wrote: 'by a miracle of God, the ship of the bishop of Soissons struck against one of the towers, as the sea, which is never still there, carried it forward'. In other words, the wind drove one of the massive double-ships closer than before to the enemy fortifications. Appropriately enough the two vessels were called the *Paradise* and the *Lady Pilgrim* (the latter contained the bishop of Troyes) and they touched against the battlements near the Petrion Gate. As Baldwin of Flanders observed: 'with an auspicious omen, they [the boats] carried pilgrims fighting for Paradise'.[20] Murtzuphlus had arranged his defences so well that the makeshift extra storeys to his fortifications made them higher than almost every besieging ship. As a consequence, his men had an advantage over the vast majority of the western vessels: for the most part, the crusader troops could not set their ladders on top of the battlements and were thus unable to create a bridgehead. Only four or five of the mighty double-ships had the height needed to top the Greek turrets, but until this point they had been unable to get close enough to the walls to bring them into play.

Now, with conditions in their favour, the crusaders had to exploit their opportunity. In a display of precision seamanship the ladders of the *Paradise* and the *Lady Pilgrim* were steered either side of one part of the fortification and for the first time a crusader ship hugged one of Constantinople's towers. At last the westerners had a chance to break into the city.

Three men stood at the front of the flying bridges preparing to set foot on enemy territory: surely they expected to die – or perhaps they had complete faith in God's mercy. Death or glory would each provide untold riches, either the spiritual reward of a martyr in heaven, or ever-lasting fame as the hero who first entered Constantinople. There was also the prospect of immediate financial reward. Gunther of Pairis noted an offer of 100 silver marks to the first man onto the walls, with 50 for the second.[21] Whatever combination of motives impelled these men to act, the conditions in which they worked were incredibly difficult. Dressed in full armour, balanced high on the ladders, at least 95 feet above the *Lady Pilgrim's* deck, swaying backwards and forwards on the swell, they had to line themselves up with a gap in the battlements or the top of a tower. At this moment there was no way to secure the vessel to the fortifica-tions; the knights had to judge the movement of the waves and then time their jump to perfection or plummet to their death below. As if this were not enough, they also had to face the heavily armed warriors who defended the city.

The first man across was an unnamed Venetian who grasped the tower and pulled himself over. Almost immediately, the defenders – identified as members of the Varangian Guard – rushed at him with axes and swords and cut him to pieces. The martyr's companions were not deterred. On the next forward surge of the sea, one of the Frenchmen, Andrew of Dureboise, managed to scramble across, only to fall to his knees. Before he could rise, his enemies rushed at him and struck him many times, but Andrew was much better armoured than his Venetian companion and he was hardly hurt. The defenders paused and, to their horror, the crusader stood up and drew his sword. In terror, the garrison fled down to the next level of the tower. Andrew's faith began to reap rewards. As Robert of Clari wrote: 'by God's mercy they did not wound him – as if God were protecting him, because He was not willing that they should hold out longer, or that this man should die'.[22]

Jean of Choisy was the next man to enter the tower and many others followed. Quickly the crusaders raised their flag to signify the break-through. They tied the boat to the tower and started to cross in larger numbers, but their momentum was soon to be slowed. The wind that had been so vital in pushing the vessels against the wall now created such a swell in the sea that the boats threatened to pull the tower down. The crusaders decided to release the ships – leaving their comrades isolated in the tower and with no immediate escape route.

In the short term, however, the flight of the Greeks and the Varangians obviated this. Baldwin of Flanders later wrote that 'the banners of the bishops are the first to gain the walls and the first victory is granted by Heaven to ministers of the heavenly mysteries'.[23] Plainly, the crusaders gained considerable encouragement from this and took even greater heart from the fact that God had directed those particular ships to the battlements. But even though the crusaders could see the first of their flags on top of the walls, there was little the men in the tower could do to push further into the city.

From his hilltop view Murtzuphlus tried to rally his troops and direct them to the threatened tower, but the crusader assault was gathering an inexorable momentum. Further along the walls the sea had taken the ships of Peter of Bracieux up and against another tower and soon this also fell; the crusaders now held two locations. Their men could look down on a mass of enemy troops below them and to their sides - in other towers, and strung out along the walls nearby. For the westerners to make further progress they needed to get more men inside. Peter, the lord of Amiens, took the initiative. He realised the importance of creating a hole in the wall at sea level and, when he caught sight of a small bricked-up postern gate, resolved to breach it.

Peter went down from his ship with his contingent of ten knights and sixty sergeants and set to work. Robert of Clari had a special interest in describing this episode because its hero was his own brother, Aleaumes, a most warlike cleric who had already distinguished himself in the conflict at the Galata tower in July 1203.[24] As some of the men crouched down to break through the wall, their colleagues hunched over them using shields for protection against the missiles that rained down upon them. When the Greeks saw the crusaders' intentions they rushed to defend the gate and mounted a fearsome onslaught against the attackers. A deluge of crossbow bolts and stones thundered onto the crusaders' screen of shields. The Byzantines brought up vats of boiling pitch and Greek fire and poured them down onto the westerners, but 'by a miracle of God' the crusaders seem not to have been seriously burned or crushed. The determination of these men was remarkable, but on such acts of courage entire wars can turn. Axes, swords, bars and picks were used to shatter the brickwork and finally they created a ragged hole through which to enter the city.

What awaited them on the other side? For once, a medieval chronicler's sense of exaggeration seems warranted. Robert wrote: 'they looked through the hole and saw so many people, both high and low, that it seemed as if half the world were there, and they did not dare risk entering in'.[25] Whoever crawled through the gap first would be assured of a very warm welcome indeed.

For a moment the crusaders faltered. Then Aleaumes came forward and prepared to enter. Robert panicked – he was faced with the prospect of his brother committing himself to the most incredible danger and almost certain death. As a churchman, Aleaumes obviously had complete faith in divine protection - a faith that, in spite of canon law prohibiting clerics from using violence, he buttressed with a sword. Robert pleaded that he should not go forward, but Aleaumes shrugged him aside and crouched down to struggle through the hole. Robert's description indicates that it must have been like squeezing through a small fireplace. As Aleaumes started to inch forwards, his brother grabbed his feet in desperation and tried to pull him back, but the cleric kicked him away. He squeezed on forwards, pushing past the grainy grasp of the dry stone. Once he was through, the Greeks started towards him and a rain of stones descended from the walls above, although none hit their target. Aleaumes drew his sword and rushed at the enemy, who were so shocked by his aggression that they turned and were said to have 'fled before him like cattle'. The bravery and belief of a single man created the crucial breakthrough. Aleaumes called to his friends: 'Lords, enter hardily! I see them drawing back dismayed and beginning to run away.' When Peter of Amiens and Robert heard this they followed quickly in, accompanied by the other knights and sergeants in their contingent. Now seventy crusaders were in the city: not a massive force, but sufficient to break the morale of those Greeks nearby.

The defenders started to flee, but Murtzuphlus himself was close enough to see the danger and spurred his charger towards the crusaders. Peter of Amiens rallied his men: 'Now lords, now to acquit yourselves well! We shall have battle - here is the emperor coming. See to it that no one dares to give way, but think only to acquit yourselves well.'[26] When he saw the determination of the westerners, Murtzuphlus hesitated, then halted and turned back to his tents. He had lacked the support to engage the enemy and, as word of their presence in the city spread, resistance began to haemorrhage. With the immediate danger gone, Peter ordered a group of men to break down the nearest gate from the inside and, using axes and swords, the crusaders fractured the great iron bolts and bars that held the entrance shut. They threw open the doors and the horse-transports glided up to the shore and disgorged their cargo.

Peter of Amiens's prominence was acknowledged by Niketas Choniates who described the knight in typically florid language:

> He was deemed the most capable of driving in rout all the battal-
> ions, for he was nearly nine fathoms tall [a classical allusion taken
> from the *Odyssey*] and wore on his head a helmet fashioned in the
> shape of a towered city. The noblemen about the emperor and the
> rest of the troops were unable to gaze upon the front of the helm
> of a single knight so terrible in form and spectacular in size and took
> to their customary flight as the efficacious medicine of salvation.[27]

Regardless of Niketas's style, we can appreciate that Peter's martial qualities terrified the Byzantines and it was the breakthrough made by his men that really precipitated the Greek collapse. More transport ships drew up to land their horses, additional gates were broken down and the mounted knights poured into – and rapidly spread through – the city.

The horsemen headed for Murtzuphlus's camp on the Pantepoptes monastery hill. The emperor's own men were drawn up to face the crusader charge, but once they caught sight of the western warriors pounding towards them they panicked and scattered. Niketas Choniates was furious at their spinelessness: 'Thus, by uniting and fusing into one craven soul, the cowardly thousands who had the advantage of a high hill, were chased by one man [Peter of Amiens] from the fortifications that they were meant to defend.'[28] Murtzuphlus had little option but to escape himself and he abandoned his tents and his treasure to head back into the heart of the capital and the castle of the Bucoleon palace. Meanwhile, Peter took control of the emperor's former headquarters and immediately secured the treasures stored there. All around them the Greeks were fleeing. The sight of the crusaders streaming into the city, and the flight of their emperor, put the Byzantines into headlong retreat; as Robert of Clari observed concisely: 'thus the city was taken'.[29] Many Greeks rushed to the Golden Gate on the far side of the city and, tearing down the stonework that blocked the exit, they ran out 'deservedly taking the road to perdition', as Niketas Choniates angrily related.[30]

As the crusaders swept into Constantinople, the next stage of the battle began. The frustration of the months spent waiting across the Golden Horn, coupled with the perceived treachery of the Byzantines, unleashed a terrible wave of violence. Villehardouin wrote: 'There followed a scene of massacre and pillage: on every hand the Greeks were cut down . . . So great was the number of killed and wounded no man could count them.'[31] Valuable horses, palfreys and mules were seized as booty and as replacements for the thousands of animals lost during the campaign to date. Baldwin of Flanders described the crusaders as being 'occupied with killing' and sending 'many Greeks' to their deaths.[32] The *Devastatio Constantinopolitana* wrote of 'a tremendous slaughter of Greeks'.[33] These three eye-witnesses provide indubitable testimony of just how brutal this phase of the campaign was.

Gunther of Pairis imagined Christ leading the holy warriors to victory and his text lauded their achievement and portrayed it as a manifestation of divine will. He also added an unrealistic call for mercy, something that the other eye-witness sources suggest was not a priority at the time:

> You [the crusaders] fight Christ's battles. You execute Christ's
>   vengeance,
> By Christ's judgement. His will precedes your onslaught.
> Break in! Rout menaces; crush cowards; press on more bravely;
> Shout in thundering voice; brandish iron, but spare the blood.
> Instill terror, yet remember they are brothers
> Whom you overwhelm, who by their guilt have merited it for
>   some time.
> Christ wished to enrich you with the wrongdoers' spoils,
> Lest some other conquering people despoil them.
> Behold, homes lie open, filled with enemy riches,
> And an ancient hoard will have new masters.[34]

Many Byzantine nobles fled to the safety of the Blachernae palace and then out and away though its gates. After their exertions throughout the day, the crusaders decided not to pursue them further. The leaders were worried that their men might become diffused across the sprawling metropolis and they feared either a Greek counter-attack or the use of fire to separate off one part of the army from the other. Given the massive size of Constantinople, they could not hope to take over the entire city in one afternoon and needed to consolidate their gains. The bulk of the western forces crossed the Golden Horn and camped outside the gates and battlements that faced the water. Baldwin of Flanders took over the magnificent imperial tent (a significant portent, given future events) and his brother Henry set up his troops in front of the Blachernae palace. Marquis Boniface and his men based themselves just to the south-east of Baldwin in one of the more densely populated regions of the city.

Only one leading crusader failed to take part in the siege. Count Louis of Blois had been afflicted with a debilitating fever since the winter and he was so weak that he could not fight. Determined not to miss the action, however, he had ordered himself to be carried onto one of the transport ships from where he could at least view the deeds of his friends and comrades.[35]

Exhausted and elated, the crusaders settled down to try to rest and recover some strength. It must have been at the front of their minds that in July 1203 the Venetians had gained a foothold around the same district, only to be driven out by a fierce Byzantine counter-offensive. On that occasion, the crusader forces had been divided between a contingent outside the land walls and a group within the city; on 12 April 1204 they had a much firmer hold in Constantinople and their armies were all in the same general area.

The senior nobles resolved that early the following morning they would move the bulk of their troops to an open region further to the south-east and there they would face the Greeks. The crusaders knew that a slow campaign fighting their way through the streets of Constantinople would likely favour the inhabitants. They were therefore determined that if a battle was to be fought, they should fight it on their own terms. A large, relatively flat area would enable the westerners to use their heavy cavalry to best advantage and, given the Byzantines' profound reluctance to engage with the knights in July 1203, this tactic offered the best hope of a swift resolution to the conflict. Well aware that Murtzuphlus might choose neither to fight nor surrender, the crusade leaders agreed that if the wind was behind them, they would deliberately start a fire and try to compel the Greeks to yield by that means. It was possible, of course, that the wind might change direction, in which case the crusaders could face the prospect of being driven out by fire themselves.

In fact, during the night a blaze did break out in the area near Boniface of Montferrat's troops. Villehardouin relates that some unknown men were so worried by a Greek onslaught that they ignited buildings lying between the two sides. Gunther of Pairis names a German count, possibly Berthold of Katzenellenbogen, as the responsible party.[36] This latest conflagration, the third since the crusaders had arrived, spread from near the monastery of Evergetes down towards the Droungarios Gate on the edge of the Bosphorus. Once again the westerners brought destruction to the Queen of Cities, although this was only a prelude to the final act of horror with the sack itself. The new fire lasted all night and through the next day before dying down the following evening. Compared with its predecessors this fire caused the least damage.[37]

For Murtzuphlus the day that had begun with such confidence had now ended in hopeless disaster. The abject collapse of his troops meant that his personal bravery and desperate attempts to motivate his people by threats, offers of reward and simple dedication to their cause were in vain. Like Alexius III, nine months earlier, he concluded that the lack of fortitude shown by his compatriots, together with the strength of his opponents, meant that he could not defeat them. Given his manifest antipathy towards the crusaders, his complicity in Alexius IV's murder and the horrendous execution of the three Venetian knights on the city walls, Murtzuphlus had no wish to be caught. Concerned that he might be handed over to the westerners if the city hierarchy decided to surrender, he resolved to leave.

Near midnight he stole through Constantinople, keeping well clear of the western troops and making his way to the Bucoleon palace. He commandeered a small fishing boat and put on it Empress Euphrosyne, the wife of Alexius III, along with her daughters (one of whom, Eudocia, he was said to be infatuated with). Then, under the cover of night, Murtzuphlus slipped shamefully away across the Bosphorus.

Against this backdrop of high politics, the ordinary inhabitants had three stark choices: they could gather everything they could carry and flee into exile like their emperor; they could try to resist the crusaders at the risk of death and even greater destruction to their beloved city; or they could simply surrender. In the last two cases, there remained the need to safeguard their personal possessions and Niketas tells us that many resorted to burying their valuables.[38]

As the news of Murtzuphlus's flight spread, the remaining clergy, administrators and nobles gathered in the early hours of 13 April to consider their next move. So stubborn was their belief in the strength of their city and so great their fear and loathing of the westerners that they decided to choose a new emperor and to continue the struggle. Two men stepped forward to claim, as Niketas expressed it, 'the captaincy of a tempest-tossed ship'. The candidates were both skilled warriors: Constantine Lascaris and Constantine Ducas. Both men were regarded as possessing equal abilities and so, given the impossibility of holding a full and formal debate on their merits, they drew lots for the prize.

Lascaris was the winner, although, because of the circumstances of his election, he refused to wear the imperial insignia. He urged the populace to resist the westerners and bluntly told the Varangian Guard that if the crusaders triumphed, they would no longer receive the substantial wages or generous treatment to which they were accustomed. The hierarchy of Constantinople was prepared to fight, but similar determination was lacking elsewhere. Nobody among the public at large responded to Lascaris's exhortations, while the Varangians took advantage of the unde-niable need for their services to negotiate a pay rise. When, early in the morning of 13 April, they saw the crusaders gathering themselves, even the inducement of increased remuneration was not enough to convince them to fight and many of the Guard quickly dispersed.[39]

For all his resolve the previous night, like Alexius III and Murtzuphlus, Lascaris concluded that nothing could save Constantinople and he became the third emperor to flee within 10 months.

As they had planned, the western forces formed up into their divi-sions, expecting to fight. Yet no one was there to face them. At first the crusaders were unaware of Murtzuphlus's escape, but very soon it became apparent that there was no opposition anywhere in the city. The news of the emperor's flight quickly emerged and it became clear that Constantinople was at the mercy of the westerners. Those who had held out longest despaired at the fickleness of their leaders and decided that surrender was the only sensible course. Dressed in their ecclesiastical finery, and bearing beautiful crosses and precious icons of Christ, the religious hierarchy came to the crusaders in the belief that showing them sufficient honour would prevent their city from being savaged. They were accompanied by some of the Varangians who presumably hoped to transfer their allegiance yet again, or else, as foreigners, to be spared possible reprisals against the Orthodox population.

Interestingly, the Greek churchmen focused their attention on Boniface of Montferrat. His family connections to the imperial line and his theoretical position as leader of the crusade gave rise to the expectation that he would be their new emperor.[40]

If the Greeks believed that this show of respect would soften the crusaders' hearts they were to be grievously mistaken. Decades of mistrust towards the Byzantines, coupled with the escalating mutual antipathy of recent months, could not be washed away. Niketas wrote that the crusaders' 'disposition was not at all affected by what they saw, nor did their lips break into the slightest smile, nor did the unexpected spectacle transform their grim and frenzied glance and fury into a semblance of cheerfulness'.[41] Once the surrender was formally accepted, the crusaders pushed the Greek clergy aside and started to seize all they could. The sack of Constantinople had begun.

CHAPTER FOURTEEN

'These forerunners of Antichrist'

The Sack of Constantinople, April 1204

A S THE MASS of crusaders started to plunder Constantinople their leaders moved swiftly to secure the city. The first priority was to take control of the main imperial residences, the Bucoleon (the Great Palace) and the Blachernae. Boniface of Montferrat immediately rode down to the former and the gates opened to him, on condition that those inside were spared. Many senior figures from the Byzantine hierarchy had taken shelter in this complex, including members of the various imperial families. The haughty Agnes, sister of King Philip of France, was present, along with Margaret, the widow of Isaac Angelos and sister of the king of Hungary. More importantly to the crusaders, the palace was packed with treasure accumulated over centuries of imperial rule. Villehardouin could hardly describe the riches on display: 'there was such a store of precious things that one could not possibly count them'.[1] Boniface left a garrison of men to hold the palace castle and to guard the fortune within.

In the north of the city, Henry of Flanders entered the Blachernae palace on the same terms and he too discovered magnificent prizes and left men to protect the crusaders' new-found wealth. While the takeover of these two locations seemed relatively orderly, events elsewhere saw an explosion of greed and violence as the crusaders found themselves in a treasure-trove of unimagined proportions. Some accounts pass over this shameful and tragic episode in silence: Villehardouin and Robert of Clari, to name but two. Others, such as Gunther of Pairis, provide some startling revelations but, predictably perhaps, it is from two Byzantine writers,

Niketas Choniates and Nicholas Mesarites, that the most vivid and lurid descriptions of the sack of Constantinople emerge.

In spite of the crusaders' sworn agreements to regulate the behaviour of the western troops, the allure of so much booty – and certain tensions within the crusader force itself – could not be resisted. Fired by a belief that God was rewarding them for fighting the impious and murderous Greeks, the crusaders saw their actions as legitimate and justified. The westerners' lust for wealth drove them to seize and despoil citizens and city alike and, in their righteous zeal, they gave little thought to the feelings of those whom they ravaged or the sanctity of the places they ransacked. As Baldwin of Flanders chillingly observed: 'So those who denied us small things have relinquished everything to us by divine judgement.'[2]

The crusaders spread into the city like a deadly virus running through the veins of a weak old man: they shut down movement and then they ended life. To Niketas they were 'forerunners of Antichrist, the agents and harbingers of his anticipated ungodly deeds'.[3] Churches were an obvious target for the westerners and they gathered hundreds of magnificent icons. Precious reliquaries – containing the remains of saints who had suffered for Christ's sake – were torn from the altars; the bread and wine that signified the body and the blood of Christ were spattered onto the ground. 'Although His [Christ's] side was not pierced by the lance yet once more streams of Divine Blood poured to the earth', as Niketas sadly commented.[4] Nicholas Mesarites wrote of:

> war-maddened swordsmen, breathing murder, iron-clad and spear bearing, sword-bearers and lance bearers, bowmen, horsemen, boasting dreadfully, baying like Cerberus and breathing like Charon, pillaging the holy places, trampling on divine things, running riot over holy things, casting down to the floor the holy images (on walls or on panels) of Christ and His holy Mother and of the holy men who from eternity have been pleasing to the Lord God.[5]

The Hagia Sophia, Constantinople's greatest, most glorious building and the spiritual heart of the Byzantine Empire, was ravaged and defiled. This, above all else, symbolised the collapse of a once-mighty civilisation and the arrival of a new, aggressive power that, in the short term at least, cared little for the majesty of the imperial past. The high altar, an extraordinary piece of craftsmanship made from a blend of precious metals and fused into one multicoloured object, was divided into pieces so as to reward several different claimants. The spiritual value of an item was often ignored in the face of an overpowering need to gain plunder. It was as if the crusaders had the most consuming addiction imaginable – a need that could only be satisfied by jewels and precious metals. Of course, not everything was broken up: a glance in the treasury in St Mark's in Venice, or a view of the four famous horses in the cathedral museum there, is evidence enough that some valuables were simply taken whole.[6]

Within hours, centuries of precious offerings were gathered up. It was not just movable objects that were taken, for the fabric of the Hagia Sophia itself was attacked. For example, as the crusaders stripped the silver overlay from the pulpit gates, the carefully deployed workmanship of years was destroyed. So huge was the haul that the holy thieves had to bring pack animals into the building. The excrement of mules and asses fouled the smooth marble floors of the house of God; men and beasts slipped and fell as they struggled to move their burdens away. The pollution of the great church was absolute.

It was not just the knights and foot-soldiers who seized valuables. Gunther of Pairis gives an astonishingly candid account of the behaviour of his superior, Abbot Martin, during the sack of the city.[7] After Martin had taken part in the mission that sought papal forgiveness for the siege of Zara, he had travelled to the Holy Land (April 1203) before rejoining the crusaders at Constantinople. When Martin saw everyone enriching themselves, he resolved to acquire some of the precious relics for his own church. With two companions he hurried towards the monastery of Christ Pantocrator, the magnificent foundation of the Comnenus dynasty that lay in the centre of Constantinople. In recent months the Greeks had used this as a repository for the wealth of neighbouring monasteries, including those lying outside the city walls, in the hope that it would be a place of safety. Knowledge of this treasure store was spread to the crusaders by those westerners expelled from the city in the weeks before it fell, and so it was, from the start, an inevitable target for the looters. Martin headed for the monastery, not, as Gunther assures us, to take gold and silver, but to find relics; he was only prepared to commit sacrilege in a holy cause. To a modern audience, this may seem a slim distinction, particularly given what followed. Ignoring the main treasury located in the body of the church, Martin sought out the sacristy, the place where the most precious religious objects were kept.

There he found an old man with a long white beard – a priest. Gunther asserts that the abbot took him to be a layman, because western monks were clean-shaven. This may be so, but it is certainly surprising that Martin appears not to have seen a single Orthodox monk in his travels in the eastern Mediterranean. In any case, he roared: 'Come, faithless old man, show me the more powerful of the relics you guard. Otherwise, understand that you will be punished immediately with death.' While the priest could not understand the precise meaning of Martin's guttural bellows, he plainly registered the message. Shaking with fear, he tried to calm the abbot in the few words of Latin that he could muster. Martin clarified what he was seeking. Gunther claims that the priest realised that the abbot was a man of religion and reasoned that it was preferable to surrender the relics to a man of the Church – however violent and intimidating – than to knights whose hands were stained with blood.

The old man led Martin over to an iron chest. The priest opened it and the abbot gazed in wonder at the religious treasures it contained – a sight more 'pleasing and more desirable to him than all the riches in Greece'. The urge to seize these fabulous objects overcame him: 'The abbot greedily and hurriedly thrust in both hands, and, as he was girded for action, both he and the chaplain filled the folds of their habits with sacred sacrilege.' Martin probably made some assessment as to which were the most valuable of the relics, or perhaps he communicated with the old priest as to the provenance of certain pieces. Then, having taken those things that he believed to be most powerful, the 'holy robber' departed. The image of a western abbot towering above an ageing Orthodox monk and threatening him with death is hard to view in anything other than a cynical light. Even for Martin, as the existence of Gunther's text shows, there was a need to explain these actions. The justification he gave reflected divine approval for the capture of Constantinople, encompassed here by the fact that Martin himself shed no blood and that he looked after the relics with great care.

With his robes weighed down with precious artefacts, Martin started to labour back to his ship to deposit the haul. He presented a faintly ridiculous sight, and Gunther acknowledged this. People who met him could tell from his bulging appearance that the abbatial robes concealed more than just a man of God. They cheerfully asked him whether he carried any loot and why he appeared so burdened. With a twinkle in his eye Martin responded: 'We have done well'; to which they responded: 'Thanks be to God'.

The abbot was concerned to escape from the crowds of looters as soon as possible and to store his cargo. Accompanied by only one of his chaplains and the old priest, who probably judged that his own safety was best assured by staying with this important figure, Martin got back to his ship and then remained in his quarters waiting for calmer times. While the chaos of the initial sack subsided, he venerated the holy objects and probably learned the identity of even more of them. In the next day or so, the old priest arranged some suitable accommodation for Martin and his entourage within the city and then, once more bearing his secret treasures, the abbot moved to this house where he concealed his prize. Perhaps Martin was afraid that others might steal such precious objects, or he may have worried that they would be discovered and handed over to the general war chest. In any case, he continued to cherish his collection through the summer of 1204.

It was not only Martin who gathered relics. As the crusaders tore their way through Constantinople, the number of items that they plundered was enormous. Two of the eye-witness accounts, those of Anonymous of Soissons and the *Deeds of the Bishops of Halberstadt*, contain formal lists of the relics that particular churchmen brought back to their home church. This was a unique opportunity to present pieces of inestimable value to institutions that could not have dreamed of such spiritual riches and, after the crusade, certain regions of northern Europe became flooded with holy objects.

Bishop Nivelo of Soissons, whose ship had made the first contact with the walls of Constantinople, was soon sending numerous treasures back to his cathedral church, including the head of the Protomartyr Stephen, a thorn from the Crown of Thorns and the finger of the Apostle Thomas, which he is said to have placed in the Lord's side. Nivello also rewarded the nuns of the abbey of Our Lady of Soissons with a belt of the Virgin Mary, and to the abbey of St John of Vignes he dispatched the forearm of St John the Baptist. When Nivelo himself returned to northern France in 1205 he took with him the head of John the Baptist and the head of the Apostle Thomas, as well as two large crucifixes made from the True Cross — an astonishing haul that demonstrates Nivelo's seniority amongst the crusading clergy.[8]

Bishop Conrad of Halberstadt took home a fine selection of relics, including further parts of the True Cross as well as dozens of relics from the bodies of the apostles (the head of James, Christ's brother) and many other saints. So many objects came back with him that Conrad had to build a new altar to house them and he also contributed gold, silver, purple cloth and two splendid tapestries to decorate his church.[9]

When one adds to these records the information in narratives such as that of Robert of Clari and the evidence in, for example, the treasury of St Mark's in Venice, then one can begin to glimpse the scale of the plunder. Robert wrote of a phial of Christ's blood coming from the church of the Blessed Virgin of the Pharos in the Bucoleon palace, along with the Crown of Thorns and a robe of the Virgin Mary.

So much more material must have gone back to northern Europe than has been recorded. Sometimes it has left a trace, as in the case of the northern French village of Longpré-les-Corps-Saints, near Amiens, which derives its name from the relics brought back to the church by the Fourth Crusader Aleames of Fontaines.[10] In the majority of cases, however, the loot has passed out of sight and was absorbed into the treasure houses, churches or palaces of the West, or was simply melted down at Constantinople and lost for ever. Some items the Greeks managed to take with them. Robert of Clari wrote that the church of the Blessed Virgin of the Pharos in the Bucoleon palace contained the grave cloth in which Christ was wrapped and which clearly displayed His features. The crusaders could have seen this precious relic during their visits to the city in the latter half of 1203, but as an object that was easily transportable it must have been spirited away the following April because, as Robert lamented, no one knew what had become of it.[11]

To Niketas, the most insufferable aspect of the sack of Constantinople was the westerners' utterly uncompromising treatment of the inhabitants. Any attempt to reason with the conquerors provoked a drawn dagger and the prick of cold steel. People who tried to leave the city were stopped and their carts ruthlessly plundered. So focused were the crusaders on the desire for loot that many no longer seemed capable of reason.

The westerners' aggression found an outlet in sexual violence, too. As with so many armies through the ages, the defiling of a defeated enemy's women was both a physical release and another manifestation of victory. With no heed to their victims' screams, and ignoring the anguished cries of fathers, husbands or brothers, the crusaders forced themselves upon women, young and old, married or maiden. Niketas asked: 'Did these madmen, raging thus against the sacred, spare pious matrons and girls of marriageable age or those maidens who, having chosen a life of chastity, were consecrated to God?'[12] Nicholas Mesarites wrote of the westerners 'tearing children from mothers and mothers from children, treating the virgin with wanton shame in holy chapels, viewing with fear neither the wrath of God nor the vengeance of men'.[13]

Some of those spared were taken off as captives to be ransomed. People tried to hide from the crusaders and a few attempted to seek sanctuary in the churches, but 'there was no place that could escape detection or that could offer asylum to those who came streaming in'.[14] Over the next few days the invaders were relentless and thorough in their stripping of the city and rooted out anything of worth, no matter how well hidden it was.

They appropriated houses, turning out the inhabitants or taking them prisoner. Villehardouin's comment on this was very matter-of-fact: 'everyone took quarters where they pleased, and there was no lack of fine dwellings in that city'.[15] Interestingly, for Robert of Clari, the issue of accommodation was far more divisive. As a senior member of the crusade hierarchy, Villehardouin must have been allocated an appropriately sumptuous palace from the many that existed within Constantinople. From Robert's far humbler perspective, the leadership had chosen to look after its own needs and to ignore those of the poor. Robert alleged that the division of the best houses was settled amongst the nobles, without the knowledge or agreement of the lesser men, and he saw this as a sign of future bad faith and betrayal of the common people.[16]

The crusaders seized more than money, relics, precious objects and houses. They paraded around the streets wearing splendid robes. They adorned their horses' heads with fine linen veils and the drum-shaped hats and wigs of curly white hair popular amongst the women of the city. There were enormous alcohol-fuelled celebrations. A western prostitute, quickly returned from her pre-battle exile, straddled the patriarch's throne in the Hagia Sophia and then jumped up to sing and dance around the sacred altar, kicking up her heels and delighting her audience.

The wine cellars of Constantinople were ransacked and such was the westerners' urge to drink that they did not, as was customary at the time, bother to mix in water. Singing and revelry lasted day and night. Some men ate local foods, others commandeered the ingredients needed to make dishes more familiar to them. They stewed the chine (backbone) of oxen in great cauldrons, they boiled chunks of pickled hog with ground beans, flavoured with a powerful garlic sauce. Then they sat and ate their fill, regardless of whether they were using sacred objects as tables, chairs or stools.[17]

Niketas Choniates himself fell victim to the crusaders and from his narrative we get an exceptional insight into the experiences of an individual on the receiving end of the looting. History is often said to be written by the victors; in medieval times this was especially true and so, while bearing in mind the author's understandable prejudices, Niketas's work offers a rare and revelatory perspective. 'On that truly hateful day' (13 April), as he aptly described it, many of his friends gathered at his house. His main residence had been destroyed in the fire of late 1203 and this new property stood near the Hagia Sophia.

As the crusaders spread towards them, Niketas and his companions saw how they grabbed at people, extorted money and goods or committed assaults. The Greeks had to improvise: part of the author's household was a Venetian-born wine-merchant named Dominic and his wife. This man possessed a helmet, armour and weapons, which he donned to pretend that he had just taken the house for himself. When crusaders arrived to take over the property, Dominic beat them away, cursing them in their own language and claiming that the house and those inside were already his. Over the next few hours, more and more men tried to lay claim to the place and Dominic despaired of being able to resist them. During a lull in these events he urged Niketas and his household to depart so that the men could remain free and the women inviolate.

Dominic led the Greeks to the house of another Venetian who had elected to stay in the city despite the recent hostilities. They did not rest there long, but chose to be dragged along by the hands behind Dominic, as if they were his prisoners. Soon, however, the servants in Niketas's household melted away to fend for themselves. They left their master and his friends to carry on their shoulders the children who were too small to walk and left the writer to protect an infant at his own breast. Niketas's wife was heavily pregnant and this, of course, added yet another pressure to the group. This proud, educated man led his entourage around Constantinople for five days before accepting that the situation could only deteriorate further: the crusaders continued to strip the city of all its valuables and to assault its people. Niketas decided that they had to leave.

On 17 April 1204 they began to make their way towards the Golden Gate – the site of so many triumphal returns for the emperors of Byzantium in days gone by. Now it was the exit point for refugees, driven from their homes by the barbarian invaders. As Niketas and his household moved towards the gate they passed many westerners laden with booty. Sometimes crusaders stopped the group to see if they were hiding fine clothes under their dirty tunics or concealing gold or silver on their person. While some of the crusaders looked for money, others were more interested in the young women in the party, and Niketas told his female companions to dirty their faces and to walk where the crowd was thickest so as to attract least attention. The small party of Greeks prayed for their safe passage and implored God that they should pass through the Golden Gate unharmed.

At the church of the Martyr Mokios one particularly predatory crusader grabbed a young girl from the midst of the group and started to drag her away, clearly intending to rape her. The girl's father, an ageing judge, appealed for mercy, but he was thrust aside. He fell into the mud by the side of the road where he lay calling for someone to assist his daughter. He asked Niketas himself to help and, in an act of extraordinary courage, the writer chased after the abductor, imploring him to leave the girl alone. From Niketas's descriptions of the sack of Constantinople one might expect that his efforts would have earned him a dagger in the chest. But such callous treatment of women cannot have been universal amongst the westerners because Niketas managed to convince some passing crusaders that they should prevent this outrage. So great was his agitation that he even pulled some of them along by the hand to encourage them to help.

They followed the thug back to his lodgings, where he locked the girl inside before turning to face his pursuers. Niketas accused the man of ignoring the commands of his leaders – presumably a reference to the oaths concerning the sanctity of women taken before the siege began –

and depicted him as 'braying like a salacious ass at the sight of chaste maidens'. He then turned to the crusaders nearby and challenged them to abide by their own laws and again he implored them to defend the girl. He appealed to the feelings of those who had wives and daughters of their own and he also prayed to Christ for help. His arguments soon struck a chord with his audience and they began to insist on the girl's release. Initially the evildoer tried to ignore these protests, but he soon realised that the men were deadly serious when they threatened to hang him unless he freed her. Finally, reluctantly, he let the girl go, much to the delight and relief of all, and Niketas and his party hurried away and out of the Golden Gate.

Niketas described his anger and sorrow at leaving the city behind. He raged against the walls for remaining upright, yet failing to protect the inhabitants. He wondered when he would see the place again, 'not as thou art, a plain of desolation and a valley of weeping, but exalted and restored'.[18] The writer and his party found their way to Selymbria, a town in Thrace, where they settled. He mentions the ridicule to which the local people subjected the fallen citizens and how they delighted in the great and the good being brought down to their level.

Nicholas Mesarites also witnessed crusader greed, violence and ill-treatment of the Greeks. He related that:

breasts of women were searched [to see] whether a feminine orna-ment or gold was fastened to the body or hidden in them, hair was unloosed and head-coverings removed, and the homeless and money-less dragged to the ground. Lamentation, moaning and woe were everywhere. Indecency was perpetrated, if any fair object was concealed within the recesses of the body; thus the ill-doers and mischief-makers abused nature itself. They slaughtered the new-born, killed prudent [matrons], stripped elder women, and outraged old ladies. They tortured the monks, they hit them with their fists and kicked their bellies, thrashing and rending their reverend bodies with whips. Mortal blood was spilled on the holy altars, and on each, in place of the Lamb of God sacrificed for the salvation of the universe, many were dragged like sheep and beheaded, and on the holy tombs, the wretched slew the innocent.[19]

Palm Sunday and then Easter Day brought a brief pause in the looting as the crusaders gave thanks for the victory that the Lord had granted them. By this point the bulk of the movable plunder had been collected and it was time to share it out according to the agreement made the previous month. Three churches had been earmarked as storehouses for all the spoils of war, and ten Frenchmen and ten Venetians were set the task of guarding them. Day after day, men or carts had drawn up carrying the most incredible riches. Mountains of gold and silver objects, jewels and precious cloth all arrived at these buildings. The scale of the haul was immense and almost impossible to convey. Robert of Clari described the volume of plunder in epic terms: 'Not since the world was made was there ever seen or won so great a treasure or so noble or so rich, not in the time of Alexander nor in the time of Charlemagne nor before nor after. Nor do I think, myself, that in the forty richest cities of the world there has been so much wealth as was found in Constantinople.'[20]

To Villehardouin the volume of treasure was similarly vast: 'Geoffrey of Villehardouin here declares that, to his knowledge, so much booty had never been gained in any city since the creation of the world.'[21] Baldwin of Flanders wrote of 'an innumerable amount of horses, gold, silver, costly silk tapestries, gems and all those things that people judge to be riches is plundered. Such an inestimable abundance . . . that the entire Latin world does not seem to possess as much.'[22]

It is plain, however, that not all the men were scrupulous in submitting the booty to the common purse. All the oaths made beforehand were an indication that the crusade leaders expected people to hold back plunder and to try to keep it for themselves. Their fears were to be entirely justified: faced with the sensational riches they discovered in Constantinople, many found it impossible to surrender everything they had taken. Greed, long portrayed by churchmen as one of the greatest vices of the crusading knight, took firm root in the hearts and minds of the westerners. Tempted by the prodigious wealth that lay in front of them and disregarding any threats of hanging or excommunication, they kept back huge sums of money – possibly as much as 500,000 marks[23] – more indeed than the sum gathered in the official treasury.

Whatever the value of the purloined goods, there was enough in the common purse to pay off the first tranche of debts recorded in the March Pact. In other words, the Venetians received the 150,000 marks owed to them and the French crusaders 50,000. There was then a further 100,000 marks that the two groups divided equally between them, as well as 10,000 horses of various breeds.

The money was distributed amongst the crusaders according to a strict formula: a knight received twice as much as a mounted sergeant, who in turn was given twice as much as a foot-soldier. The *Devastatio Constantinopolitana* provides detailed figures, stating that each knight received 20 marks; clerics and mounted sergeants 10 marks; and foot-soldiers five marks. This matches the ratio noted by Villehardouin and computes fairly neatly to a force of 10,000 men in the combined French, German and northern Italian contingents, with a further 10,000 Venetians, bringing the total crusading army to 20,000 – a figure cited by Geoffrey himself.[24]

Villehardouin was, tacitly at least, disappointed with the amount of spoil collected, although as we have seen, a huge proportion of the booty never reached the official treasuries. But if he was comparatively phlegmatic, Robert of Clari was incandescent. The lesser men had all seen Constantinople's breathtaking wealth with their own eyes and their expectations of personal gain were commensurately high. When the funds were dispensed there was disbelief; foul play was deemed certain and Robert accused the treasury guards and the senior leaders of siphoning off whatever they wished. He denounced them for taking gold ornaments, cloth of silk and gold, and for sharing nothing other than plain silver – the mere pitchers that ladies would carry to the baths, as he complained – with the lesser knights and foot-soldiers. This, Robert believed, was an unjust reward for those who had shared in the sacrifices and struggles of the campaign and he hinted that this unfair treatment had repercussions for the leaders.[25]

There was a notably personal edge to Robert's complaints because his brother Aleaumes – the man who had, arguably, been the bravest of all in the taking of Constantinople – was given only 10 marks as a cleric. Yet Aleaumes wore a chain-mail hauberk and owned a horse, just like a knight, and his martial prowess was conspicuous. He appealed to Hugh of Saint-Pol for parity with the knights and the count gave judgement in his favour: Hugh himself witnessed that Aleaumes had done more than all the 300 knights in his division.[26]

Some attempts were made to track down those known to have hidden valuable objects for their own personal benefit. Villehardouin claims that many men were hanged, including one of Hugh of Saint-Pol's knights who was strung up with his shield around his neck to broadcast his own shame and that of his family.[27]

Throughout the sack of Constantinople the crusader camp had been alive with discussion, rumour and gossip as to the choice of a new emperor. The whole army was summoned to a meeting and a lengthy and vigorous debate ensued. In the end the decision came down to the two most obvious candidates: Boniface of Montferrat and Baldwin of Flanders. Yet to choose between these two fine men was extremely difficult and the other leading nobles worried that whoever lost would depart from the host and take his men with him, leaving the victor in a seriously compromised position. They drew a parallel to the First Crusade when, after the election of Godfrey of Bouillon as the ruler of Jerusalem, his rival, Raymond of Saint-Gilles, was so envious that he induced many others to abandon Godfrey, with the result that hardly any knights remained to hold the fledgling state together. Only through God's protection, they concluded, had the land of Jerusalem survived. In order to avoid a repetition of these events, the leadership in 1204 proposed that the unsuccessful candidate should be rewarded with lands of such scale and value that he would be pleased to remain in the region. This idea was supported by everyone, including the two candidates.

Only the doge of Venice remained uneasy about the potential for serious trouble if the failed candidate reacted badly. He advised that Boniface and Baldwin should vacate their imperial palaces and that the buildings should be placed under a common guard. He argued that whoever was elected emperor should be able to take possession of the palaces as he wished. In other words, he thought that a reluctant loser might choose not to hand over his residence and would then have a powerful base from which to cause trouble. Again, the two nobles involved acceded to the proposal and the election process continued peacefully.

The major challenge that faced the French, German and northern Italian crusaders was how best to select their six electors, as required by the March Pact. Because both the candidates came from this broad group, the identity of the electors could easily load the voting process in one particular direction. Robert of Clari wrote that each man attempted to place his own people into the sextet and there followed days of intense debate as the haggling and arguments dragged on. In the end it was decided that six churchmen should be chosen, on the basis that they would not be swayed by political considerations. As Baldwin himself (unsurprisingly) wrote: 'all partisanship [was] put aside'.[28] The clerics were the bishops of Soissons, Halberstadt and Troyes, the bishop of Bethlehem (a new papal legate), the bishop-elect of Acre and the northern Italian abbot of Lucedio. The worthiness of this group may not be in doubt; whether it was free of bias is less clear: Peter of Lucedio had accompanied Boniface to Soissons when he took the cross, and Conrad of Halberstadt was a partisan of Boniface's overlord, Philip of Swabia. Set against this, John of Noyen, now the bishop-elect of Acre, had been Baldwin of Flanders's chancellor.

The Venetians used a different method of selecting their electors. Familiar as they were with government by committee and council, the doge directed a distinctive process. Dandolo chose the four men he most trusted and made them swear on holy relics that they would select the six people most worthy of the task. As each individual was identified, he was obliged to come forward, not talk to anyone and go into seclusion in a church until the full meeting of the Venetians with the other crusaders.

The crucial assembly took place in the chapel of the palace occupied by the doge himself. A mass of the Holy Spirit was chanted to seek divine guidance for the imminent debate. The chapel doors were shut and the discussion began. There is no extant eye-witness account, and the details of the conference remain secret. In the palace outside, partisans of the two candidates gathered anxiously. The committee was making a decision of quite stupendous dimensions: the elevation of a man to the rank of emperor, and the acquisition of all the status, wealth and lands that came with it, was a staggering responsibility. A Catholic emperor would also represent a massive extension of lands under the authority of the papacy.

The council worked late into the night of 9 May until it made its choice – a unanimous selection, according to Villehardouin. They appointed Bishop Nivelo of Soissons to announce the result. Everyone had assembled in the great hall and the tension was palpable as he stepped forward. Which of the two men would win the imperial crown? As the smoke from candles and braziers drifted slowly upwards, hundreds of eyes fixed upon Nivelo; men crowded around him as they strained to see and hear. A pause for silence and then he spoke:

Lords, by the common consent of all of you we have been dele-
gated to make this election. We have chosen one whom we ourselves
knew to be a good man for it, one in whom rule is well placed and
who is right well able to maintain the law, a man of gentle birth,
and a high man. You have all sworn that the man whom we elect
shall be accepted by you, and that if anyone should dare to challenge his election you will come to his support. We will name him
to you. He is Baldwin, count of Flanders.[29]

A roar of approval echoed around the hall and the news coursed
through the city. The French contingent was jubilant; the marquis's men
were understandably despondent. We do not know Boniface's true feelings, but Villehardouin reports that he nobly acknowledged his opponent's victory and paid him due honour. He drew deeply on the chivalric
ethos of the court of Montferrat and abided by the pre-election agreements: there was none of the divisive friction that had been so feared. In
the short term, at least, it seemed that the consensual, conciliar approach
had paid off and Baldwin was able to enjoy his success to the full.

The churchmen, the leading nobles and the French crusaders proudly
escorted the emperor-elect to the Bucoleon palace, the seat of imperial
power and Baldwin's new home. The next priority was to fix a date for
the coronation ceremony. They chose Sunday 16 May, one week later.

Niketas Choniates gave his own reasons for Baldwin being preferred
to Boniface. The Greek regarded Doge Dandolo as the moving force
behind the Fleming's selection. Niketas hated the doge and regarded him
as a scheming and self-interested man who would have competed in the
ballot himself, had his blindness not rendered him ineligible for the imperial dignity. Niketas neglected to add two other important reasons for
Dandolo not standing: first, the Venetian's advanced years and, second, a
general awareness that by choosing him the crusaders would be open to
accusations that their campaign was motivated by financial considerations.
Notwithstanding his great abilities, it would have been political and diplomatic suicide to choose Dandolo as emperor.

Putting aside Niketas's prejudices, his analysis of why the Venetians
favoured Baldwin is fundamentally plausible. He suggests that the doge
wanted an emperor who would not be too ambitious and whose lands
were some distance from Venice, so that, if the two parties fell out in

the future, Dandolo's home city would not be threatened. Boniface, of course, was based in northern Italy, uncomfortably near Venice; and he had a close association with the Genoese, one of the other major trading powers of the medieval Mediterranean. The possibility of an emperor sympathetic to the Venetians' great rivals, who might threaten the commercial privileges secured through the toil and sacrifice of the present campaign, could not be countenanced: 'thus those things which the many with sight could not clearly perceive, he who was sightless discerned through the eyes of his mind'.[30] On this basis, the six Venetian electors were always likely to vote against Boniface and, as long as a plausible alternative existed – which Baldwin certainly was – then only one of the six churchmen needed to be swayed to deny the marquis the imperial throne. The Flemish candidate's natural supporters – the bishops of Soissons and Troyes and the Flemish bishop-elect of Acre – gave him a comfortable majority. The remaining three churchmen, notwithstanding the northern Italian home of Peter of Lucedio, may well have concluded that Baldwin was the best man anyway, or else they decided to join the winning side and deliver a unanimous verdict.

The week leading up to the coronation saw frantic activity in Constantinople as the westerners prepared for the formalisation of their conquest. The mercers, tailors and clothiers of the city did tremendous business as the crusaders spent some of their new-found wealth on the finest robes available. The need to be seen in the most magnificent attire possible brought out all the ostentatious vanities and competitive instincts of the chivalric courts of the West. Many splendid robes and gowns were made from the famous silk cloth created in the western parts of the Byzantine Empire, and these beautiful garments were adorned with precious stones looted from the city.

Another formal event took place on Saturday 15 May when Boniface married Margaret, the widow of Isaac, to continue the Montferrat dynasty's links to the Angeloi family begun with his brothers Conrad and Renier. The marriage may perhaps have made him a more natural candidate as emperor of the Greeks – had not the decision to crown Baldwin already been taken. On a more sober note, Odo of Champlitte, one of the senior crusader nobles, fell ill and died. He was buried with full tributes in the Hagia Sophia.[31]

On 16 May 1204 an escort of the leading clergy and the senior French, northern Italian and Venetian nobles collected Baldwin from the Bucoleon palace and escorted him with due honour to the Hagia Sophia. Once at the church, dressed in his splendid robes, he was led to the altar by Louis of Blois, Hugh of Saint-Pol, Marquis Boniface and several ecclesiastics. In front of a packed congregation, all dressed in their resplendent new clothes, Baldwin was stripped to the waist, anointed, reclothed and then formally crowned emperor. The crusader conquest of Constantinople was complete. In a hall filled with western adventurers, an expedition that had set out to free the holy places reached a climax that no one could have predicted, as a Flemish count took control of one of the most powerful political entities in the known world.

Baldwin sat upon the imperial throne and listened to mass, in one hand holding a sceptre and in the other a golden globe topped by a cross. Robert of Clari pointedly acknowledged this rarefied level of authority when he wrote that 'the jewels which he was wearing were worth more than the treasure a rich king would make'.[32] After mass the new emperor processed out of the great church, mounted a white horse and was escorted back to his palace to be seated upon the throne of Constantine. There Baldwin sat, at the very epicentre of the imperial dignity and a clear symbol of the westerners' perception of a continuity between themselves and the Greek rulers. Then the knights and churchmen and all the Greek nobles paid homage to him as emperor. With the formalities complete, it was time for the coronation banquet; tables were placed in the hall and a sumptuous feast rounded off the first day of what we know as the Latin Empire of Constantinople.

In the aftermath of the sack, writers from both sides reflected on events and considered how and why they had happened. Baldwin himself wrote a series of letters to prominent figures in Europe to explain the situation in Greece. Letters addressed to the archbishop of Cologne, the abbots of the Cistercian order, to 'all the Christian faithful' and, most importantly, to Pope Innocent III himself survive. As in the case of earlier letters from the crusade leaders, such as that of Hugh of Saint-Pol in the summer of 1203, this missive had to outline and justify the progress and outcome of the expedition. Baldwin was aware that the campaign was open to charges from several different quarters: the crusaders had disobeyed papal commands concerning attacks on the Byzantines; they were motivated purely by money; they had neglected their brethren in the

Holy Land and had discredited their crusading vows. This letter is, therefore, a thoughtful and highly polished piece of writing. In modern terms we would regard it as political 'spin' – putting a positive gloss on events that have provoked controversy or disquiet. The new emperor's close circle, particularly the highly educated clerics, worked hard to support his case by peppering the narrative with an impressive array of biblical and rhetorical apparatus.

The basic thrust of Baldwin's letter was to emphasise divine endorsement for what had taken place: 'Divine Clemency has performed a wondrous turn of events round about us . . . there can be no doubt, even among the unbelievers, but that the hand of the Lord guided all of these events, since nothing that we hoped for or previously anticipated occurred, but then, finally, the Lord provided us with new forms of aid, insamuch as there did not seem to be any viable human plan.'[33] The very success of the expedition had to be God's will. This was the best and strongest argument that the crusaders could muster.

The emperor gave a narrative of events from August 1203 onwards, taking great care to illuminate Alexius IV's lies and perjury and in particular his failure to adhere to the promises in the Treaty of Zara, which had led the crusade to Constantinople in the first instance. He was held responsible for the attack of the fire-ships (perhaps untrue) and for inflicting terrible hardships on his own people. Murtzuphlus was damned as a perjurer for failing to keep his promise to hand over the Blachernae palace in return for crusader support of Alexius. Murtzuphlus was then depicted as a traitor and murderer for his brutal removal of the young emperor. Baldwin was careful to detail the final attempt to make peace when the doge met the Greek usurper, and the letter laid stress upon Murtzuphlus's refusal to submit the Orthodox Church to Rome, a matter of obvious importance to Innocent.

Baldwin consistently ascribed crusader successes, such as the capture of the icon of the Virgin Mary and the lack of damage wrought by the fire-ships, to the blessing of God. This divine approval was, naturally, linked to the crusaders' proper moral purpose, and during the final assault on Constantinople the Fleming portrayed them as attacking the city 'for the honour of the Holy Roman Church and for the relief of the Holy Land'.[34] When he described the storming of the battlements he again chose to explain the crusader victory in divinely ordained terms: 'at the

Lord's bidding a vast multitude gives way to very few'. While Baldwin did not shy away from mentioning the killing of many Greeks, he chose to omit the more unpleasant details of rape, pillage and sack that took place. The scale of the booty ('an inestimable abundance') was noted as he emphasised the triumph of such a small force. Baldwin wrote: 'we might safely say that no history could ever relate marvels greater than these so far as the fortunes of war are concerned'. This was the kind of language and hyperbole that authors used after the capture of Jerusalem by the First Crusade in 1099 and, like the remarkable achievement of that earlier expedition, the campaign of 1204 *had* to be blessed with God's approval. Quoting from Psalms 98 and 118, Baldwin wrote: 'Now however, we do not wrongly lay claim to this victory for ourselves because the Lord's own right hand delivered Himself and His powerful arm was revealed in us. This was done by the Lord, and it is a miracle above all miracles in our eyes.'[35] In other words, the diversion to Constantinople was justified and above reproach.

Further sections of Emperor Baldwin's missive cast the destruction of the perfidious Greeks as a valid crusade in itself. He claimed, correctly, that some churchmen and soldiers from the Holy Land were present at his coronation and that 'above all others their joy was incalculable and unrestrained', and that they gave thanks to God 'just as if the Holy City had been restored to Christian worship'. The reason for their delight was that the crusade had ended the Greeks' enmity towards the holy warriors. Baldwin criticised the Byzantines' alliances with the Muslims, their supplying of the infidel with arms, ships and food, and their disregard for their shared bond of faith with the westerners. He drew attention to their lack of respect for the papacy, to the various liturgical and practical differences of religious observance between the Orthodox and the Catholics, and how the former viewed all westerners as dogs. Baldwin argued that the Greeks had provoked God by their sins and, through the crusaders, He had punished them.

Having portrayed the conquest of Constantinople as a crusade against heathens, Baldwin took care not to forget the expedition to the Levant. He expressed the hope that, once the Byzantine lands were stabilised, he would travel on to the Holy Land. In the meantime he turned to Innocent for support and, making clear that he regarded his new responsibilities as a spiritual matter, Baldwin urged the pope to call for a crusade to help the nascent Latin Empire and promised that those who came would be rewarded with lands and honours according to their station. He also asked for churchmen to come and settle, having first gained the permission of their religious superiors.

Baldwin also appealed to Innocent to summon a General Church Council in Constantinople. This would enable the pope to formally demonstrate the submission of the Orthodox to the Catholics and would act as a public blessing for the capture of Constantinople. The emperor cited earlier popes who had visited the city several centuries before and implored Innocent to follow suit.

Baldwin closed his letter by commending the honest and prudent conduct of the clergy in the course of the crusade and by providing a ringing commendation of the character of Doge Dandolo and all the Venetians, 'whom we find to be faithful and diligent in all circumstances'.[36] The fact that some of the crusader clergy had chosen to suppress papal correspondence at Zara, and that Innocent was one of many who were deeply suspicious of Venetian motives, meant that it was important for the emperor to bolster the credibility of the Italians. The letter was dispatched in the summer and would probably have reached the pope in around September or October 1204.

If Baldwin was in the happy position of explaining the capture of Constantinople from the perspective of the victor, Niketas Choniates had to comprehend the reverse. The loss of Constantinople was a massive personal blow; its devastation provoked pain at the outrages perpetrated against its people and fabric, as well as anger against those who committed such terrible deeds: 'crimes committed against the inheritance of Christ'. To him, the greed, the inhumanity and arrogance of the westerners were unbearable. He constructed a coruscating indictment of their motives. Most particularly he blamed the leadership and mocked their high moral stance: 'They who were faithful to their oaths, who loved truth and hated evil, who were more pious and just and scrupulous in keeping the commandments of Christ than we Greeks.' He claimed that the crusaders had entirely abandoned their vows to cross over Christian lands without shedding blood and to fight the Muslims. He also reviled them for their sexual impurity as men 'consecrated to God and commissioned to follow in His footsteps'.[37]

His conclusion was scathing: 'In truth they were exposed as frauds.

Seeking to avenge the Holy Sepulchre, they raged openly against Christ and sinned by overturning the Cross with the cross they bore on their backs, not even shuddering to trample on it for the sake of a little gold and silver.'[38] Niketas then drew a simple parallel: when the First Crusaders took Jerusalem in 1099 they had shown no compassion to the Muslim inhabitants. When, 88 years later, the Muslims had taken the holy city back they had behaved far better, neither lusting after the Christian women nor 'transforming the entranceway to the life-giving tomb [the Holy Sepulchre] into a passageway leading down into Hades'. By ransoming the defenders cheaply and letting them keep their possessions, the Muslims had dealt magnanimously with the defeated people of Jerusalem.

To draw such a damning comparison with, of all people, the Muslims was, of course, richly ironic. The analogy was also true: Saladin's men did spare the majority of those in Jerusalem, yet the Fourth Crusaders had slaughtered their fellow-Christians. The implication here is obvious: to Niketas, the westerners' behaviour rendered them worse than infidels. For a second time, therefore, the crusaders had been revealed as blood-thirsty barbarians. His analysis ended with a simple observation: 'How differently . . . the Latins treated us who love Christ and are their fellow-believers, guiltless of any wrong against them.'[39]

This devastating analysis of the crusaders' performance was borne out of Niketas's anger at the events of 1203–4 although, as we have seen, the author also believed that the Byzantines contributed much to their own downfall through the lamentable actions of their leaders and the sins of their people.[40]

Nicholas Mesarites, addressing himself to his fellow-Byzantines, condemned the crusaders along broadly similar lines: 'Such was the reverence for holy things of those who bore the Lord's Cross on their shoulders, thus their own bishops taught them to act. Then why designate them as such? Bishops amongst soldiers or soldiers amongst bishops? And why recount many things in this speech? You all know how these dreadful deeds ended, for you were not among those who practised violence, but among those who endured it.'[41]

In the short term, Niketas and Nicholas had to deal with day-to-day survival, but for Emperor Baldwin there was a need to take a longer view. Aside from trying to influence the way in which the crusade was perceived in the West, he had to start the business of government. He appointed

John, bishop-elect of Acre (and former chancellor of Flanders), as his new chancellor and set about gathering the money needed to run his empire.

To produce more cash would require the regime to look beyond the movable treasures already looted. They began to examine the fabric of Constantinople ever more closely and to inflict even greater destruction on the legacy of centuries of Byzantine rule. A few more items remained to be plundered and the westerners' treatment of one of these objects crossed yet another rubicon of propriety.

The church of the Holy Apostles contained a mausoleum holding the tombs of some of the great Byzantine emperors of the past, including Justinian. Not content with pillaging all the church's ornaments and chalices, the crusaders broke open the great imperial tombs. These mighty sarcophagi, made of the purple porphyry marble that signified imperial status, held not just corpses, but also gold, jewels and pearls. Justinian's body was found to be in almost perfect condition; in the 639 years since his death his cadaver had barely decomposed. In medieval terms this was a sign of great sanctity and divine endorsement of a good life. While the crusaders were duly impressed, it did nothing to halt their stealing the valuables lying around the imperial body. As Niketas searingly observed: 'In other words the western nations spared neither the living nor the dead, but beginning with God and his servants, they displayed complete indifference and irreverence to all.'[42]

Precious metals were stripped from public buildings and monuments in order to create wealth: melted down and minted into coins, they allowed the westerners to start paying wages and to finance projects of their own. Many of Constantinople's great statues were callously cast to the ground and consigned to the smelting furnaces. The bronze figure of Hera was pulled down and carted off to the fires; such was its huge size that her head was said to have needed four yokes of oxen to carry it away. Other statues, such as Paris, Alexander and Aphrodite, joined Hera in the dust. The extraordinary wind-vane, the *Anemodoulion*, a mighty equestrian statue from the Forum of the Bull, was also dragged off to feed the insatiable fires.

Constantinople was becoming transformed from the greatest city in the Christian world to a scarred and ragged shadow of its former splendour. Its fine walls were hideously misshapen by the remains of the wooden siege defences; three terrible fires had damaged buildings right across the city; and now the monuments that had commemorated and sustained the Byzantines' cultural identity were being torn down. Pedestals stood shorn of their statues, alcoves lay bare, except where a sad stub of metal marked where finely crafted figures had once stood.

The Hippodrome was stripped of its decorations: a great bronze eagle; representations of charioteers; a massive hippopotamus with a crocodile or basilisk in its jaws; a stunning, shapely figure of Helen of Troy, who 'appeared as fresh as the morning dew, anointed with the moistness of erotic love on her garment, veil, diadem and braid of hair'.[43]

Alongside the crusaders' continued ruination of the Queen of Cities they behaved uncouthly amongst themselves. Enriched by their new-found wealth, the conquerors engaged in endless bouts of gambling and gaming, or else they fought one another, even including their wives as part of the wager. Displaying the rather condescending superiority of a highly educated imperial official, Niketas concluded that one might expect little else of a group of 'unlettered barbarians who are wholly ignorant of their ABCs, [and] the ability to read and have knowledge of . . . epic verses'.[44]

From Emperor Baldwin's perspective, the need to generate money was an imperative that sentiment or aesthetics could not resist; his responsibilities as an anointed ruler required immediate action and it was to the wider issues of government that he now turned.

CHAPTER FIFTEEN

'For a high man – high justice!'

The End of the Fourth Crusade and the Early Years of the Latin Empire, 1204–5

THE STORY OF the Latin Empire of Constantinople (1204–61) is a convoluted and frustrating tale. The crusade had culminated in Baldwin's coronation, but the attempt to consolidate this achievement meant years of warfare, brief periods of progress and peace and, for many of the main actors, a violent death. Yet the impact of the events of April 1204 went far beyond the walls of Constantinople. A change of such magnitude in the landscape of the Christian world had enormous consequences for many different peoples, not just those in and around the Byzantine Empire. The papacy, the Crusader States in the Levant, the families and countrymen of the crusaders back in western Europe, the Italian trading cities and the Muslim world: each had to calibrate and assess a political and religious topography that had never previously been conceived of. A full consideration of these issues would, however, fill another book and the main concern here is with the early years of the nascent Latin Empire.

In the first months of his reign Baldwin experienced two unexpected and agonising difficulties: the challenge of an internal rebellion and the tragedy of personal bereavement. After his coronation the new emperor started to allocate Byzantine lands to his followers, although many of these areas remained under hostile control. Baldwin had to defeat several challengers who included: Murtzuphlus, Alexius III, Theodore Lascaris (leader of a group of the Byzantine exiles and brother of Constantine Lascaris, the man elected emperor on the eve of the crusader conquest) and, most seriously of all, the powerful King Johanitza of Bulgaria. Given this formidable array of contenders there was every likelihood of a protracted and bloody fight to extend and sustain Latin rule in Greece, but before beginning this, the emperor had to confront an issue closer to home.

The March Pact of 1204 had stated that the unsuccessful candidate for the imperial throne would receive the Peloponnese peninsula and lands in Asia Minor.[1] Following Baldwin's coronation, Marquis Boniface wanted to renegotiate this: he wished to exchange the territories origi-nally stipulated for the kingdom of Thessalonica, because the latter lay near the kingdom of Hungary – the royal house of his new wife. Boniface had a further interest in Thessalonica through his deceased brother Renier, who had been granted overlordship of the city by Manuel Comnenus as a part of his marriage gift in 1180.[2] Villehardouin mentioned a 'serious discussion of the pros and cons' of the situation before Baldwin agreed to this proposal. Some of the emperor's men opposed the idea, presumably because they had earmarked it for themselves and viewed it as a better prospect than territory in Asia Minor – land that was under threat from Theodore Lascaris and the Seljuk Turks. Boniface, however, had been the nominal leader of the crusade and, if Baldwin turned him down, he could simply leave for home, thereby depriving the Latins of one of their most powerful nobles. This fear of losing manpower had shaped the crusaders' pre-election discussions and this same concern now surfaced again. The emperor granted Boniface the kingdom of Thessalonica, and amidst much rejoicing the marquis paid homage for the land.[3]

The Latins' first aims were to extinguish the threat of Murtzuphlus and to bring western Thrace under their authority. As Baldwin led a large army out from Constantinople, the aged doge and the infirm Louis of Blois, along with Conon of Béthune and Villehardouin, remained to preserve authority on the Bosphorus. The Latins' initial target was Adrianople, a major city about 100 miles north-west of Constantinople, which soon submitted to an advance force led by Henry of Flanders. Murtzuphlus was known to be in the vicinity, but managed to stay ahead of the Latins to reach the settlement of Mosynopolis, around 160 miles west of Constantinople.

The ruler of this town was Alexius III, who had fled from the crusaders in July 1203. Might the two deposed emperors join forces to confront their mutual enemy? Initial contacts were extremely cordial. Alexius offered to give his daughter in marriage to Murtzuphlus (with whom she was already romantically involved) and suggested a formal alliance.

One day Murtzuphlus and a few companions came into Mosynopolis to dine and bathe. As soon as his principal guest arrived, Alexius took him aside into a private room where his men were waiting. They flung Murtzuphlus to the ground, held him down and tore his eyes out. The gestures of friendship had been a façade because Alexius III had no shred of trust for a man who had so callously murdered a rival, and he now showed similar ruthlessness in eliminating a challenger to his own position. Alexius III had signalled his determination to lead the opposition to the Latins alone. To Villehardouin this brutality was yet more evidence of the inherent duplicity of the Greeks: 'Judge for yourselves, after hearing of this treachery, whether people who could treat each other with such savage cruelty would be fit to hold lands or would deserve to lose them?'[4] Once Baldwin heard of this gruesome act he marched towards Mosynopolis as fast as he could, but Alexius III departed and all the people of the region submitted to Latin rule.

At this moment, after years of close and effective co-operation, a serious rift developed between Baldwin and Boniface. Despite the emperor's promise to give Thessalonica to the marquis, when Boniface asked permission to take control of the region and, at the request of its people, to fight off an incursion from the Bulgarians, Baldwin rejected the idea. The emperor decided to march there and take possession of the lands himself. Boniface was understandably enraged: 'If you do, I shall not feel you are acting for my good. I must tell you clearly that I shall not go with you, but break with you and your army.'[5]

Villehardouin was perplexed by these developments and wrote how ill-advised this breach was. One senses that his sympathies lay with Boniface and that he felt the emperor had taken bad counsel, perhaps from men who wanted parts of Thessalonica for themselves or who felt that the new emperor should assert his authority over the marquis. Baldwin would achieve the latter goal by going to the lands in person and then publicly bestowing them upon Boniface, rather than letting the marquis assume power by himself.

Furious at such shabby treatment, Boniface stormed away towards Demotika, south-west of Adrianople. Many nobles followed him, including the German contingent and warriors of the standing of Jacques of Avesnes and William of Champlitte. As Baldwin took possession of Thessalonica, Boniface made his displeasure clear: he seized the castle of Demotika from the emperor's men and laid siege to Adrianople. Messengers rushed to Constantinople to tell Count Louis and Doge Dandolo of these troubling events. The senior crusaders cursed the people who had fomented this rupture, because they feared such divisions might expose them to the loss of all their hard-fought gains. Diplomacy was called for and once again Villehardouin came forward. He approached the marquis 'as a privileged friend' and reproached him for acting so rashly. Boniface countered by saying that his behaviour was entirely justified and that he had been grievously wronged. Eventually, Villehardouin persuaded him to place the matter in the hands of the doge, Count Louis, Conon of Béthune and himself. This core of men had been at the heart of the crusade throughout, and it is a mark of the respect in which they were held that Boniface agreed to this idea.

When Baldwin heard that the marquis had besieged Adrianople, his first reaction was one of anger and he wanted to rush to the city and confront him. The situation seemed to be spiralling out of control. 'Alas! What mischief might have resulted from this discord! If God had not intervened to put things right, it would have meant the ruin of Christendom,' lamented Villehardouin.[6] During the emperor's stay outside Thessalonica a serious illness had hit the Latin camp. Amongst those who perished were the imperial chancellor, John of Noyon; Peter of Amiens, one of the heroes of the capture of Constantinople; and around 40 other knights. These losses were a grievous blow to the westerners and revealed how easily their numbers could be depleted. Perhaps such sad events brought Baldwin to his senses. When envoys from the crusaders in Constantinople arrived to mediate, some of his nobles decried this as impertinence. Baldwin, however, disagreed and came to see that, in the longer run, he could not alienate the quartet of senior men, as well as Marquis Boniface, and he consented to submit to the judgement of the four nobles.

Back in Constantinople the wise old heads quickly convinced the emperor of his mistake and of the need for reconciliation. Boniface was summoned to the city and many of his friends and allies came to greet him warmly. They organised a conference and decided that Thessalonica and its environs would be given to the marquis as soon as he handed over the castle of Demotika. When this was done, Boniface rode west to take hold of his rightful lands and most people in the region quickly came to recognise his authority.

It was at this point, in September 1204, after the resolution of this wasteful bout of in-fighting, that Villehardouin was able – for the only time in his history – to write of calm in Latin Greece. He said that 'the land of Constantinople to Salonika [Thessalonica] was at peace. The road from one city to the other was so safe that although it took twelve days to cover the distance between them people were able to come and go as they pleased.'[7]

The westerners began to extend their operations into the Greek islands and across the Bosphorus into Asia Minor. The Venetians took the islands of Corfu and Crete, two valuable and fertile areas in their own right, but also vital staging posts on the sea routes to and from the eastern Mediterranean. Louis of Blois planned the annexation of the duchy of Nicaea, although the count's health remained poor and he sent the mighty Peter of Bracieux to make war on the Greeks there.

Around this same time the Latins achieved a genuine coup. The blinded Murtzuphlus had managed to escape from Alexius III and was trying to flee into Asia Minor, but informers betrayed his movements and he was captured and brought to Constantinople. The Latins were elated because at last they held the man who had murdered their candidate for the imperial throne, who had directed the fire-ships against them, and whose virulent anti-western invective had caused them so much suffering.

Murtzuphlus knew that he was going to pay a terrible price for his deeds and he could only hope that the westerners would be marginally less cruel than some of his own predecessors had been. In September 1185 Emperor Andronicus had met a particularly grisly fate. At the end of the coup that removed him from power he was seized by the supporters of Isaac Angelos, cast into prison and grotesquely tortured. One eye was gouged out, his teeth torn out, his beard pulled out and his right hand severed. He was paraded through the streets of Constantinople on the back of a mangy camel to face the spiteful savagery of the mob. Some poured human and animal excrement onto him, others pelted him with stones and a prostitute emptied a pot of her urine over his face. In the forum Andronicus was hung upside down and had his genitals hacked off. A few of the crowd thrust swords into his mouth, others between his buttocks, before finally, mercifully, Andronicus expired – surely one of the most public and hideous deaths of the medieval age.[8] Could Murtzuphlus hope for greater mercy from the Latin 'barbarians'?

Some form of hearing or show-trial was held and Murtzuphlus tried to justify the killing of Alexius IV. He claimed that the young emperor was a traitor to his people and that many others had supported his (Murtzuphlus's) actions. There was, of course, some truth to these arguments, but no heed was paid to the Greek's desperate pleas and he was sentenced to death. The question remained: how should the captive die?

Baldwin consulted with his nobles. Some recommended that Murtzuphlus should be dragged through the streets, others simply wanted him hanged. It was the doge of Venice who came forward with the solution. He argued that Murtzuphlus was too important a man to be hanged. 'For a high man, high justice!' he exclaimed. 'In this city there are two columns . . . let us make him mount to the top of one of them and then have him thrown to the ground.'[9] The match of this play on words and the unpleasantness of the proposal pleased everyone and they agreed on death by precipitation. The form of punishment may also have been known to Baldwin and Henry of Flanders because similar executions had taken place earlier in the twelfth century in the city of Bruges.[10]

In November 1204 Murtzuphlus was taken to the column of Theodosius in the Forum of the Bull. As he was led up the narrow steps inside, the baying of the crowd must have been temporarily muffled by the interior of the pillar. He had, of course, seen the column many times and knew where he stood, although now his lack of sight added a further element of hopelessness to his doomed situation.

Emerging from the narrow, cylindrical stairwell into the clear air on the top of the pillar, the defeated emperor must have sensed the space below him. There is no record of any prayers or speeches; one sharp push and he was propelled into the void, where his body fell feet first, accelerating and plummeting headlong, before twisting sideways to thump violently onto the stone ground, a ruptured and shattered sack of flesh and bone. Villehardouin claimed that the decoration of the column included a representation of a falling emperor and marvelled at the coincidence of this with Murtzuphlus's death.[11]

Within a few weeks the Latins would remove another challenger to their power when Alexius III was captured by Boniface near Thessalonica.

The emperor's scarlet stockings and imperial robes were dispatched to Constantinople to show what had happened and he was imprisoned. Alexius was not a figure so reviled as Murtzuphlus and he was sent to the marquis's homelands in northern Italy.[12]

Towards the end of 1204 the brief period of calm mentioned by Villehardouin was about to come to a close. Serious opposition to Latin rule began to appear: the Byzantine noble Theodore Lascaris led uprisings in Asia Minor, and in northern Thrace King Johanitza stirred tensions near Philoppopolis. The westerners faced the prospect of having to fight a war on two fronts – a task compounded by the failing health of their leaders. The doge found it difficult to leave Constantinople; Louis of Blois remained ill; and Hugh of Saint-Pol became crippled by gout that meant he could not walk. Fortunately, a large group of crusaders led by Stephen of Perche and Reynald of Montmirail, both cousins of Louis of Blois, arrived from Syria.

Stephen had left the main body of crusaders back in the autumn of 1202 when illness prevented him from embarking at Venice with the main fleet, although he had then chosen to sail to the Holy Land rather than Constantinople.[13] Reynald had taken part in a diplomatic mission to the Levant following the capture of Zara but, contrary to his promise, he had failed to return to attack Byzantium.[14] By late 1204, however, both men wished to assist their fellow-crusaders and perhaps hoped for a share in the spoils of victory.

The coming of Reynald and Stephen was not, however, wholly a cause for celebration: they carried the terrible news that Emperor Baldwin's wife, Marie, had died of plague in the Holy Land. Her connections with the crusade were tragic and complex. Her brother, Thibaut of Champagne, had been the original choice to lead the expedition before his death. Marie had taken the cross with Baldwin, but could not accompany him because she was pregnant with their second child (they already had an infant daughter, Joan, born in 1199 or early 1200). Once she had given birth to another girl, Marie set off for Marseille, leaving her babies in the care of one of Baldwin's younger brothers. Sadly, the two girls never laid eyes on either of their parents again. In the spring of 1204 Marie sailed towards Acre, ignorant of her husband's second attack on Constantinople. Almost immediately after she landed, however, messengers told of his success and summoned her to Constantinople as the empress. Marie was delighted, but before she could begin her journey she fell victim to an outbreak of plague that ravaged the Crusader States at that time. She died in August 1204 and her husband's envoys brought only a corpse to Constantinople, rather than the emperor's adored and admired wife. Baldwin's fidelity and devotion, so praised by Niketas Choniates, were cruelly unrewarded and he was crushed by these mournful tidings.[15]

The last few months of 1204 and the early months of 1205 saw an exhausting round of conflicts in Asia Minor, the Peloponnese (where Villehardouin's young nephew fought with distinction) and the lands near Thessalonica. The Greeks realised that the Latins were severely stretched and they proposed an alliance with King Johanitza. They promised to make him emperor, to obey him and to slay all the French and Venetians in the empire. Given the history of serious enmity between the Bulgarians and the Byzantines, this was a strange combination, but it clearly showed Theodore Lascaris's determination to remove the Latins.

In January 1205 the westerners lost Count Hugh of Saint-Pol who succumbed to gout. He was buried in the church of St George of Mangana in the tomb of Sclerene, an eleventh-century imperial mistress, although soon afterwards his remains were transferred back to northern France and laid to rest in the abbey of Cercamp in his home county.[16]

Around the same time the most serious revolt yet broke out when the key city of Adrianople rose in rebellion. The emperor called his principal advisers together. The doge, Louis of Blois and Baldwin agreed to pull in as many men as possible and to concentrate on this deepening crisis.

As the first contingents arrived from Asia Minor, Baldwin was eager to head towards Adrianople with all possible speed. For the first time in months, Louis of Blois was fit to take his place in the army and together they prepared to set out. Henry of Flanders and many other men were still to come, but Baldwin decided to press on with just 140 knights. On 29 March they reached Adrianople to see banners proclaiming allegiance to King Johanitza fluttering from well-defended walls and towers. Despite their lack of numbers the Latins mounted two attacks on the gates. As Baldwin and Louis directed operations they were joined by another familiar figure from the senior hierarchy of the crusaders. To demonstrate the importance of this campaign a force of Venetian knights had joined the northern Europeans, and at their head was Dandolo himself. The doge had ignored his age and apparent infirmity – he had asked the pope for absolution from his vow to allow him to return home – and insisted on commanding his men on this rare, and crucial, inland expedition.

Johanitza learned of the Latins' weakness and hurried south to Adrianople with as large a force as he could muster. Alongside his own knights he had a huge group (numbering 14,000, according to Villehardouin) of mounted Cumans, fierce pagan nomads whose endurance and brutality made them formidable opponents.

The Latins struggled to find supplies and spent Easter 1205 desperately foraging for food and trying to build siege engines and dig mines so that they could break into the city. All the while Johanitza moved closer, until on 13 April an advance force of Cumans raided the westerners' camp. The call to arms was raised and the knights rushed to confront the enemy. The Cumans soon wheeled away and, for once, the Latins' customary discipline eluded them and they carried on the chase, quickly becoming spread out. The Cumans swiftly turned and unleashed volleys of arrows at their opponents, wounding many of the Latins' horses, but killing few. The westerners faced about and retreated – it had been a close escape.

The leadership was furious. A meeting was called to demand much tighter control and orders were issued proclaiming that no one should do more than form up in proper order outside the camp. Nobody was to move unless explicitly ordered. The whole army knew that there would be a major battle the following day and the next morning the men said mass and confessed their sins.

In the early afternoon the Cumans charged forward once more. First out of the camp was Count Louis of Blois. Disastrously, he completely ignored the previous night's agreement and set off in hot pursuit of the enemy, urging Baldwin to follow suit. Perhaps Louis was trying to compensate for his sickness-induced failure to take part in the conquest of Constantinople. If so, his need to perform glorious deeds overcame any sense of discipline at a terrible cost. As the excitement of the pursuit invigorated Louis's men, they harried the pagan warriors for miles before, inevitably, beginning to lose formation and tire – exactly what their opponents hoped for. As the Cumans had shown only the previous day, their tough nomadic ponies and expert riders were skilled in the art of turning on the retreat. Many, many times crusader armies had been defeated by Turkish or Syrian troops performing just such a manoeuvre and the impetuosity of the count of Blois meant that another force of men was doomed to join that sad list. With the strength of the Latin onslaught hopelessly diluted across a broad front, the Cumans swung around and hurtled back towards the westerners, screaming and firing their arrows.

Shocked by this, some of the less experienced men in the Latin army – probably recruits from Constantinople – began to panic and the line rapidly started to disintegrate. Baldwin had been forced to follow the initial charge; he caught up with the fighting and found himself close to Louis. The count had been badly wounded and was soon knocked from his horse. Amidst the churning frenzy of the conflict the Latin knights plunged towards the stricken noble. They drove the Cumans away from Count Louis and, in the vortex of battle, created a small space sufficient to raise him to his feet and examine his wounds. They begged him to go back to camp because of the severity of his injuries, but he refused: 'God forbid that I should ever be reproached for flying from the field and abandoning my emperor.' Regardless of the Latins' bravery, sheer weight of numbers started to tell and one by one they began to fall. Still, however, Baldwin urged his men on. He swore to fight to the last and defended himself with even greater vigour, but on this occasion chivalric loyalty and knightly prowess were not enough. The Cumans closed in on their prey. Inevitably, perhaps, given the number of battles they had fought, the Latins' good fortune had finally run out. 'In the end, since God permits such disasters to occur, the French were defeated,' mourned Villehardouin.[17] Louis was killed and Baldwin was overcome and taken prisoner. The Cumans slaughtered many other veteran knights and, in one devastating engagement, a large part of the crusader elite was ripped away.

Those who escaped rushed back to the camp where Villehardouin was in charge. By now it was mid-afternoon and he gathered together a force of men to try to halt the Cumans' pursuit of his ailing colleagues. Their efforts succeeded and the pagans started to drop back in the early evening. Villehardouin found himself the senior surviving French noble. He sent word of the disaster to the Venetians, whose men had not been involved in the day's conflict. The doge and Geoffrey must have been shattered – their emperor was in captivity and many close friends and brave knights were dead. The only option was to retreat. The canny Dandolo suggested the best way to get a head-start on Johanitza. Even as night fell, he advised

Villehardouin to keep his own troops lined up outside the camp and, at last, the Cumans returned to their base on the far side of Adrianople. The doge himself went around the tents, encouraging the Latins to take heart and telling them to put on their armour and wait for orders. When it was completely dark they marched away as quietly as possible. The fact that the Cumans had withdrawn from the field helped the westerners to leave undetected.

Their target was Rodosto, a three-day march away on the coast, but the wounded hampered any quick progress. One group of Lombards split away and managed to reach Constantinople within two days (16 April), where they broke the awful news to Peter Capuano, the papal legate, and Conon of Béthune, who was in charge of the city.

As the defeated troops struggled back towards Rodosto they met some comrades who had come over from Asia Minor and were heading to join the main force. Many of these men, such as Peter of Bracieux, were vassals of Count Louis and were grief-stricken at the loss of their lord. There was little time for mourning, however: Johanitza had marched up to Adrianople, discovered that the Latins had fled and was now in hot pursuit. Villehardouin urged the new arrivals to take over as the rearguard while the wounded and the weary carried on to Rodosto as swiftly as they could. They managed to reach the town in safety, where they encountered Henry of Flanders and more reinforcements. Had the whole force assembled before riding to Adrianople, the outcome of the campaign – assuming greater discipline – might well have been very different. The Latins were now in a deeply perilous position and they made Henry of Flanders regent of the empire, pending his brother's possible release from captivity. In the meantime, as Johanitza's men ravaged across the region, almost the entire mainland territory of the Latins went over to the Bulgarian king.

Back at Constantinople the remaining leaders resolved to ask for help from Pope Innocent, from Flanders, France and other countries in the West. In doing so they were following a practice long established by the Christian settlers in the Holy Land. Throughout the twelfth century the settlers in the Levant had turned to their fellow-Catholics in Europe seeking military and financial support. Sometimes they had been rewarded with a new crusade; more usually, however, only small groups of knights responded to these appeals because – excepting the most urgent of occasions, such as the fall of Jerusalem in 1187 – the remainder were too occupied in their own affairs to help.[18] In 1205 the Latins chose the bishop of Soissons and two senior French knights to convey these requests while their colleagues remained at Constantinople in fear of their lives.

Around the same time, Doge Dandolo sent a letter to Pope Innocent asking to be absolved from his pilgrim's vow to relieve him of the need to journey to Jerusalem. Perhaps the news of the plague that was affecting Acre, coupled with his age and the prospect of another long voyage to the Levant, caused the Venetian to fear for his survival in the next part of the expedition. He may also have wanted to return home to die and to better assure the succession of his son as doge. Dandolo assured the pope that his departure would not affect the presence of the Venetian fleet and insisted that it would continue to serve the crusade as arranged.

The case for recognising Dandolo's increasing frailty was obvious, yet Innocent politely, but firmly, rejected it. He had abhorred the doge since the siege of Zara and here – gently and, one suspects, with some degree of satisfaction – he turned the other crusader leaders' praise of the old man back against Dandolo. Surely, Innocent argued, on account of the importance that Emperor Baldwin and his colleagues attached to the doge's advice, it would not be prudent to approve the request, lest it caused the army going to the Holy Land to fail. Furthermore, he continued, 'someone or other could fault you' for having been a crusader who had avenged the injuries done to the Venetians at Zara, but who had not avenged the injuries done to Christ by the enemies of the faith. Innocent intimated, therefore, that he was acting in Dandolo's own best interests by protecting him from accusations of wrongful motivation and insisting that he stayed on the crusade.[19]

Innocent's response was, in fact, almost irrelevant because in June 1205 there was yet another heavy – if by now hardly unexpected – blow to the Latin presence in Byzantium when, aged over 90, Dandolo died. He was buried with due honour in the church of Hagia Sophia, where a small memorial to him still stands. The doge was probably the most remarkable of all the crusaders: neither his age nor his blindness prevented his agile mind and unparalleled grasp of strategy from exerting the most powerful influence over the expedition. If his insistence on the campaign at Zara brought him criticism from some quarters, it is noticeable that his standing amongst his fellow-leaders on the crusade remained extremely high; and on many occasions his were the ideas and plans employed by the westerners. His loss meant that only Marquis Boniface (based at Thessalonica), Conon of Béthune, Villehardouin and Henry of Flanders remained alive, and at liberty, from amongst the senior nobility who had set out on the original expedition.

While some knights and nobles from the Fourth Crusade settled in Greece and began to set up flourishing dynasties, many of the other crusaders returned home. A number travelled via the Holy Land where they completed their pilgrimage vows; the others sailed directly back to the West. They had been away for more than three years. Children had grown up, parents and relatives may have died, lordships and abbacies changed hands. The crusaders themselves had endured the most appalling hardships, had seen horrors and wonders beyond imagination, and now they came home, relieved and thankful to have lived through the great ordeal. They carried news of fine deeds, of the forging of new friendships, the loss of companions, the splendour of Constantinople and the perfidy of the Greeks. Many brought back treasure and valuable reliquaries that did much to repay the money they had needed to set out in 1202.

Robert of Clari probably departed for France in the late spring of 1205. The death of his lords, Peter of Amiens (summer 1204) and Hugh of Saint-Pol (March 1205), may well have prompted him to leave shortly before the defeat at Adrianople. Robert brought back various relics, including a part of the True Cross, one of several treasures he gave to his local abbey of Corvey. Aside from this and the writing of his narrative we know nothing more of his fate, other than that he was alive in 1216, the last event mentioned in his work.[20]

For prominent men, such as Bishop Conrad of Halberstadt, there is a record of their journey.[21] Conrad sailed to the Holy Land in August 1204 and his voyage from Constantinople to Tyre took almost seven weeks. Soon after he arrived, the archbishop of Tyre prepared to set sail for Greece, and in the light of Conrad's status as a bishop, he asked the German to look after his flock during his absence. Conrad gladly agreed and took up residence in the archiepiscopal palace where he consecrated various churchmen and conscientiously oversaw the repair of the city walls after an earthquake. He also toured pilgrimage sites, including the church of Our Lady in Tortosa (a beautiful building that still exists today in southern Syria) where the saint cured him of a bout of fever. The following spring Conrad took leave of the people of the Holy Land and, after a two-month voyage, reached Venice on 28 May 1205. News of his return had been sent ahead and the dean of Halberstadt and others from the church travelled down to Venice to meet their superior. The Venetians also paid Conrad great respect and on the day of Pentecost (29 May) he was led by Renier Dandolo, the vice-doge, and the clergy of Venice to St Mark's church where they celebrated mass.

Before travelling north to Germany, Conrad visited the pope. He carried with him a letter from King Aimery of Jerusalem (1197–1205) and the churchmen of the Holy Land, which recommended him as a person worthy of apostolic favour. Innocent duly acknowledged this and, fortified by a papal benediction, Conrad began the last leg of his journey. As he approached Halberstadt, Duke Bernhard of Saxony, his nobles and churchmen came out to meet the bishop and celebrate his homecoming. Conrad obviously had a good eye for public display and he arranged for a bier to be carried before him upon which were shown the relics he had taken from Constantinople. The entire local population flocked to see such a great spectacle and all cried out blessings on the man who had brought such valuable articles back to their land.

On 16 August 1205 Conrad was escorted to the doors of the church of St Stephen where the clerics happily sang the antiphon *Iustum deduxit Dominus* ('The Lord has led forth the just man'). Then Conrad delivered a sermon identifying all of the relics that he had gathered – objects that would now reside in the church. He also proclaimed an annual festival throughout the diocese to honour the day of the relics' arrival and, in one sense, to commemorate his own achievement. These joyful events offer a glimpse of what some returning crusaders could expect. Not all could boast the reception arranged at Halberstadt, but the process of celebration, reception of relics and then storytelling was, in outline at least, repeated widely across western Europe.

If the final destiny of some of the crusaders is relatively clear, the fate of the first Latin ruler of Constantinople was not. As we saw above, Emperor Baldwin had been captured by King Johanitza at the Battle of Adrianople in April 1205. Niketas Choniates reported that the prisoner was taken to Tirnovo, Johanitza's capital, deep in the Balkan mountains, where he was cast into a dungeon with metal bands clamped around his neck.[22] Pope Innocent III wrote to Johanitza to try to convince him to release the emperor, but in vain. By the summer of 1206 it was generally believed that Baldwin was dead, and on 20 August Henry of Flanders was crowned emperor in the Hagia Sophia.

The precise details of his brother's death are elusive and for that reason generated an intense amount of speculation. Niketas reported that when, in the summer of 1205, one of Johanitza's Greek allies, Alexander Aspietes, defected to the Latins, the king was thrown into an uncontrollable rage. He ordered Baldwin to be brought before him and commanded that his legs be chopped off at the knees and his arms be severed at the elbows. In this horrifying, crippled condition, the mutilated emperor was cast into a ravine where he lived for three days before expiring.[23] A sanitised confirmation of Baldwin's fate was to come from Johanitza himself, who replied to Innocent III's request to free the emperor by writing that this was not possible because the prisoner had died. Unsurprisingly perhaps, he did not provide any further details.

Two further accounts offer even more imaginative versions of the Fleming's fate. The Greek writer George Akropolites claimed that Johanitza cut off the emperor's head, hollowed out the skull and used it as a drinking cup. As we saw earlier, Gervaise of Bazoches had claimed the dubious precedent for a crusader's head becoming a posthumous drinking vessel, a fate also shared by the Antiochene noble, Robert fitz-Fulk the Leper, after he died at the hands of Tughtegin of Damascus in 1119.[24] It is also possible that Johanitza was copying one of his own ancestors who had treated enemies in this way; in any case, Akropolites confirms that Baldwin died in captivity.[25]

Alberic of Trois-Fontaines supplies a different story and one that he himself voiced doubts about, although he still chose to include it in his chronicle. He described how a Flemish priest journeying through Tirnovo had heard that Johanitza's wife tried to seduce Baldwin and get him to promise to take her away if she would free him. Given Baldwin's impeccable behaviour thus far, even as a widower, he was unlikely to be tempted by his captor's wife. When he spurned her, the angry queen told Johanitza that Baldwin had promised to marry her if she helped him to escape. The king was furious and started drinking heavily; then, in his drunken rage, he ordered that Baldwin should be executed and had his corpse thrown to the dogs. The truth of this version may be tenuous, but again the end result was the emperor's death in captivity.

Baldwin's disappearance did not just cause problems in Constantinople, but also raised considerable difficulties back in his native Flanders. It seems that some did not believe – or did not choose to believe – that he was dead. The ambiguous status of a prisoner meant that it was hard for families to move on with their lives: some captives died in jail, a few were incarcerated for decades and then returned home, while others simply disappeared. The fact that Count Baldwin had left two infant daughters, and that he ruled over one of the most wealthy and important areas of northern Europe, created conditions ripe for controversy, and various political players tried to exploit the situation for their own ends. The detailed ramifications of this episode are not relevant here, but an historian has drawn attention to a bizarre episode that stemmed from the turmoil in Flanders and the mysterious fate of its crusading emperor.[26]

After Baldwin's death, his daughter Joan steered the county into a closer relationship with the French crown – a policy opposed by some within Flanders. In 1224 a hermit in the village of Mortaigne, near Tournai, was identified as a crusading companion of Baldwin, but this he denied. Within a year, however, as various nobles and clerics came to see him and talk to him, the man eventually stated that he was the count himself. In Holy Week 1225 he showed scars that the real Baldwin had allegedly possessed. Inconveniently, however, he was about a foot shorter than the count, his local geography was hazy and his French was rather more erratic than people remembered. One writer put these factors down to advancing age and time spent in Greek prisons. With this flexible approach to memory and physical likeness, the town of Valenciennes received the individual they called 'emperor' and he took a ceremonial bath and had a shave. Such was their delight at his 'reappearance' that the monks of St John's abbey kept his whiskers and drank his bathwater.

The man now began to tell of his escape from Johanitza, the tortures that he had endured (which included the loss of some toes), his suffering during several periods of captivity at the hands of Muslims, and his final journey back to the West. Joan of Flanders sent her lover to interview the hermit and he was convinced that the man was her long-lost father. More and more towns came out in support of the returned hero – and thereby created a vehicle to assert Flemish independence from France and to turn against Joan's rule. She tried to have him discredited: Baldwin's former chancellor could not recognise him, and the hermit could not remember the old court official. In spite of testimonials by men claiming to have seen Baldwin killed on the battlefield (another error because, as we have seen, all the sources indicated that he was captured), the imposter rallied massive popular support and Joan was forced to flee to Paris. The hermit was taken so seriously that King Henry III of England wrote to him to ask for a renewal of earlier alliances between Flanders and England.

Joan turned to her ally, King Louis VIII of France (1223–6), for help. The king sent his aunt Sibylla, who was also Baldwin's younger sister, to meet the claimant. She did not recognise the man, but hid this from the hermit and convinced him to meet King Louis. Before this, with his confidence now at a peak, the impostor processed through Flanders dressed as an emperor and with his adherents walking ahead, bearing a cross and banners. He even issued charters, knighted ten men and confirmed documents with a seal that described him as the count of Flanders and Hainault and the emperor of Constantinople. The cities of Lille, Courtrai, Ghent and Bruges all welcomed him as he went on to an audience with the king at Péronne.

Louis received the 'emperor' with due courtesy and started to question him. Perhaps the man was by now so assured that he did not anticipate such an interrogation: in any case he was ill-prepared. He could not recall where, and how, he had done homage for Flanders to Louis's father, King Philip; nor was he able to recollect being knighted, or his marriage to Marie of Champagne. His supporters argued that he refused to respond to such questions out of pride; soon, however, he asked for a rest and a chance to eat. Once he had left, several churchmen rushed forward to claim they recognised the man as a jongleur who had once tried to impersonate Count Louis of Blois, another noble killed on the Fourth Crusade. The bishop of Beauvais claimed to have had the man in his prison; he was a professional hoaxer and a charlatan who had lost his toes to frostbite, rather than torture.

Even as he left the interview chamber the impostor realised that he was in trouble and escaped back to Valenciennes, where many of his baronial supporters abandoned him, although the poor continued to proclaim their loyalty and prepared to resist Joan by force. Next, the hermit fled first towards Germany and then southwards into Burgundy where he was captured and sent to Louis. The French king had found the whole affair at Péronne highly entertaining and passed the prisoner on to Joan with a recommendation that she spare his life. Joan was far less amused and had the hermit tried and condemned to death at Lille. He was made to confess his true identity as a jongleur and put in the pillory between two dogs. He was then tortured, hanged and his body impaled upon a pole surrounded by armed guards. The mob, it seems, still refused to accept that he was not Baldwin and accused Joan of parricide. In modern times, DNA testing means that such a hoax could not hope to succeed for so long. In the thirteenth century the fact that no one had seen Baldwin die, coupled with a strong desire by many nobles and lesser people to find a way to oppose Joan's pro-French policies, led to the impostor having such a lengthy career. In reality, Baldwin of Constantinople had died thousands of miles from his homeland at the hands of a violent and unforgiving king of Bulgaria.

While the strange tale of the impersonator of Baldwin of Flanders is one legacy of the Fourth Crusade, perhaps the most intriguing and dramatic reactions to the capture of Constantinople belong to Innocent III. Over the course of the campaign he had watched with growing alarm as his great project – for which, as head of the Catholic Church, he bore full spiritual responsibility – had veered from Zara to Corfu and thence to Constantinople. He had seen how his bull of excommunication, the supreme papal sanction, had been cynically suppressed. Yet still he held firm to the hope that the core of the crusaders could extricate themselves from their paralysing debt to the Venetians and somehow get help to the Holy Land. He had tried to create a balance between his role as leader of the Catholic Church and the need to make allowances for the practical demands of the expedition. There had been times, particularly in the case of the Venetians, when he felt that the proper boundaries had been overstepped, yet he recognised the requirement for a degree of flexibility to prevent the whole enterprise from grinding to a halt. Coupled with these competing tensions were the problems of distance and poor communications. At times, therefore, the pope was only the passive recipient of news and, if the crusaders had acted of their own accord, he could only react to, rather than direct, events.

From the start, Innocent had made plain his opposition to any attacks on Christian lands, yet to the modern reader the inclusion of clauses allowing this in conditions of necessity always leaves a slightly ambiguous feel to his pronouncements. He tried to include safeguards concerning the need to secure the permission of his legate before making such moves, but the churchmen on the expedition did, at times, perform in ways that their master found frustrating. Given this fact, as well as the Venetians' apparent willingness to ignore his threats of excommunication at Zara, it might be thought that creating any potential loophole in the ban on attacking Christian territories left a hostage to fortune.

Such was Innocent's overpowering obsession with regaining the Holy Land that there is no doubt where his ultimate priorities lay, yet one wonders what conflicting emotions he felt on hearing of the capture of Constantinople. He had castigated the Greeks for their failure to support the crusade back in 1198; he knew that they had broken their promises to the westerners and had murdered their emperor (whose case he had earlier declined to support). He was also a pope who, above all others in the medieval period, had a staggeringly high conception of papal authority that stretched across the ecclesiastical and secular worlds and undoubtedly encompassed Rome's supremacy over the schismatic Greek Orthodox Church.[27] With the crusaders achieving victory, surely God had ruled on whose cause was right?

In a letter to Emperor Baldwin of 7 November 1204, Innocent expressed his joy at the capture of Constantinople and described it as 'a magnificent miracle'. In this letter, and one addressed to the clerics with the crusading army (13 November), he portrayed the campaign as God transferring the Byzantine Empire from 'the proud to the humble, from the disobedient to the obedient, from schismatics to Catholics . . .'; this, he concluded, 'was done by the Lord and is wondrous in our eyes'.[28] Innocent was delighted and placed the Latin Empire under papal protection – a mark of special favour – and decreed that the task of preserving the newly conquered lands should be rewarded with the remission of sins (the same as for a crusader to the Holy Land). In other words, he harnessed a fundamental element of the crusading concept – the defence of Christian lands – to the immediate priorities of Emperor Baldwin. At this point, perhaps rather naively underestimating the work needed to consolidate the new conquests, the pope still imagined that the crusade would be able to continue onwards to the Levant.

A swathe of letters from early 1205 shows Innocent's euphoria continuing unabated. He seems to have been totally caught up in this mighty step forward for the Catholic Church. For him, the momentous scale of God's judgement heralded a Golden Age that would see the liberation of the Holy Land, the return of all schismatic Christians to St Peter's see, the conversion of many heathens and the salvation of Israel – the last of which would signify the Second Coming and the End of Time. This was a remarkable agenda, but one evidently conceivable within contemporaneous currents in papal thought.[29] The pope continued to profess his pleasure at the events in Constantinople: 'I am enveloped by great wonder, along with those who are with me, at the novelty of such a miracle that has come to pass in these days.'[30]

So content was Innocent that, for the moment, he overlooked yet another arrogation of papal authority by the Venetians. The March Pact of 1204 had stated that the losing party in the imperial election should have the right to provide a patriarch. Thus it fell to the doge's churchmen to choose a candidate and they elected Thomas Morosini as their head. Unsurprisingly, as a Byzantine, Niketas Choniates found the presence of this man loathsome and he offered a savage pen-portrait of the Venetian: 'He was of middle-age and fatter than a hog raised in a pit; his face was clean-shaven, as is the case with the rest of his race, and his chest was plucked smoother than pitchplaster; he wore a ring on his hand, and sometimes he wore leather coverings which were fitted to his fingers.'[31] Innocent was more concerned with Thomas's spiritual attributes and acknowledged that he was of good character – notwithstanding the fact that the process outlined in the March Pact was a serious transgression of papal prerogatives. The agreement was, after all, a deal concluded between secular parties (the Venetians and the other crusaders), but the relevant clause here concerned election to one of the five patriarchal seats of the Christian Church, something that those enjoined to the contract had no right to decide. For this reason, Innocent had no hesitation in declaring the election void. Yet such was the pope's positive mood at this time that he listened to representations from Baldwin, Boniface and the other crusade leaders that emphasised the huge Venetian contribution to the campaign and argued that this merited a proper reward. In response, Innocent conceded that Thomas was indeed a suitable candidate for patriarch, regardless of his improper election. Then, most realistically of all, 'wishing to show favour to the Venetians in the hope that they might be tied more strongly to the service of the Cross of Christ', he informed the churchmen in Constantinople that he now properly elected and confirmed Thomas as the first Latin patriarch of Constantinople.[32]

By the middle of 1205, however, events in the Holy Land and Constantinople conspired to darken Pope Innocent's mood considerably. The situation in the Levant plunged into a new crisis with the death (from a surfeit of fish) of King Aimery of Jerusalem, followed quickly by the demise of his infant son. War between the Christian states of Antioch and Armenia, along with a fear that the Muslims of Egypt and Damascus were poised to break a treaty made with Aimery, created huge anxieties for the papacy. The Franks were vulnerable enough anyway and these calamities threatened their fragile hold on the Syrian coastline.

To compound these troubles Peter Capuano, the papal legate, had left the Holy Land — against Innocent's wishes — and travelled to Constantinople. There, incredibly, he had released all the westerners from their crusading vows. In other words, they were no longer obligated to go to the eastern Mediterranean, the area that Innocent continued to see as the final destination of the expedition and a region now in urgent need of help. Capuano had, in effect, terminated the Fourth Crusade. His reasoning for this is not explicit, although in the way that he had allowed the expedition to attack Zara in order to preserve its unity, pragmatism was probably at the root of his thoughts. He may have taken the view that the best way to sustain the fledgling Latin Empire was to concentrate the crusaders' efforts in and around Constantinople and that this, rather than an exodus of men to the Holy Land, was in the best interests of the Church. Whatever Capuano's intentions were, Pope Innocent was livid. On 12 July 1205 he wrote a stinging rebuke to the legate: 'We leave it to your judgement as to whether or not it was permissible for you to transform — no, rather to pervert — such a solemn and pious vow.'[33] Ironically, therefore, an agent of the papacy brought the Fourth Crusade to a close. Innocent's grand design had been grounded on the shores of the Bosphorus and, in the short term, his hopes of reclaiming Christ's patrimony were ended.

In conjunction with this disastrous development, the pope's perception of the capture of Constantinople was changing. Stories concerning the evils perpetrated by the crusaders during the sack of the city were growing ever more unpleasant and troubling. As we saw earlier, the letters sent to Rome by the expedition's leadership had chosen to pass over the westerners' brutality. But as the months went by, rumours carried by traders and travellers were supplemented by information from returning crusaders, such as Bishop Conrad of Halberstadt or Bishop Martin of Pairis, and exposed the full horrors of the episode. Innocent was sickened by what he learned – what had seemed a glorious success was in reality a sordid exercise in greed and violence. His letters lamented: 'By that from which we appeared to have profited up to now we are impoverished, and by that from which we believed we were, above all else, made greater, we are reduced.' Innocent questioned why the Greek Church might wish to express its devotion to the papacy – as the crusaders so proudly claimed that it would – when it saw in the Latins 'nothing except an example of affliction and the works of Hell, so that now it rightly detests them more than dogs'. He recounted the crusaders' merciless slaughter of Christians of all ages, men and women alike, 'staining with blood Christian swords that should have been used on pagans'.[34] He grimly recited some of the other atrocities: the rape of matrons, virgins, nuns; the sack of the churches and the violation of sacristies and crosses. Initially Innocent seems to have believed that only the imperial treasuries had been looted, but he was horrified to learn of the plunder of churches across the city.

Innocent had also become aware of the Latins' terrible defeat at Adrianople, yet instead of lamenting the death of so many great knights he described the episode as one of Divine Retribution for the crusaders' deeds – an uncompromisingly harsh judgement on the loss of many genuinely pious warriors. The pope felt that events of April 1204 damaged future calls for a crusade because those who had been on the campaign would be returning home, dispensed from their vows and laden with spoils.

The details of the sack caused Innocent to express doubts as to the true motives of some of the crusaders. He had already been deeply sceptical of the Venetians' aims, but now, in a letter to Boniface of Montferrat, he suggested that the marquis had 'turned away from the purity of your vow when [you] took up arms not against Saracens, but Christians . . . preferring earthly wealth to celestial treasures'.[35] Innocent indicated that 'it is reputed far and wide' that the crusaders had behaved disgracefully towards the people and churches of Constantinople.

Yet alongside this anger there was also a sense of puzzlement. As the contemporary churchman and writer Gerald of Wales stated: 'The judgement of God is never unjust even if it is sometimes hard to understand.'[36] The pope struggled to reconcile the divinely approved outcome of the expedition with news of the crusaders' behaviour during the conquest. In the final analysis Innocent had too much of a pragmatic streak to condemn the crusaders wholeheartedly. He did not, for example, raise the question of excommunicating the army for their deeds, let alone suggest a withdrawal from Byzantium. The pope accepted God's judgement against 'an evil people' (the Greeks) and retreated behind rumination on 'the incomprehensible ways of God'. He concluded: 'For who can know the mind of the Lord?' He also urged Boniface to hold, defend and even extend the lands he now ruled, which shows that Innocent saw the new Latin Empire as a permanent feature of the political and religious landscape. The pope instructed the marquis to do proper penance for his sinful acts and to exert himself for the relief of the Holy Land because 'through this [Byzantine] land, that [the Holy Land] can be easily recovered'.[37]

If Innocent's feelings towards the sack of Constantinople now reflected a more accurate sense of what had really taken place, he could not step back from the fact that the Catholic Church had, through its capture of the patriarchal city of Constantinople, derived an enormous (if unforeseen) benefit from the Fourth Crusade. There now remained the need to reinforce and defend this land – yet another onerous responsibility for the head of the Latin Church and one of the most far-reaching consequences of the campaign.

CHAPTER SIXTEEN

'Nothing is lacking for the achievement of complete victory . . .
except an abundance of Latins'

The Fate of the Latin Empire, 1206–61

O N 15 AUGUST 1261 – fifty-seven years after the Fourth Crusade
had sacked the Queen of Cities – Michael Palaeologus, the ruler
of Nicaea, processed into the Hagia Sophia where he was
crowned emperor of Byzantium. The Greeks had reclaimed
Constantinople. Other spoils of the Latin victories in 1204 – such as the
principality of Achaea and the island of Crete – remained in western
hands but the heart of the conquest had been torn out.[1]

As the first generations of Frankish settlers in the Holy Land had
discovered, large-scale backing from the West was needed to consolidate
their new territories.[2] As early as 1211 Emperor Henry of Constantinople
(1206–16) wrote: 'nothing is lacking for the achievement of complete
victory and for the possession of the empire, except an abundance of
Latins, since . . . there is little use in acquiring [land] unless there are
those who can conserve it'.[3] Yet ultimately, the support of a second
Catholic satellite in the eastern Mediterranean proved too great a demand
on the physical and emotional resources of Europe.

In the course of the thirteenth century the scope of crusading extended
considerably. In 1208 Pope Innocent III launched the Albigensian Crusade
against the Cathar heretics of southern France. There was also, as before,
continuous activity in the Baltic region and periodic campaigns against
the Muslims of the Iberian peninsula. Crusading proved a highly flexible
concept and in the middle of the thirteenth century, as relations between
the papacy and Emperor Frederick II of Germany became hostile, a holy
war was preached against the most powerful secular figure in the West.

From the late 1230s a new and terrifying force began to appear on the borders of eastern Europe and soon threatened the Levant as well. The fearsome Mongol hordes were in the process of creating the largest land empire in the history of the world, stretching from Hungary to the China Sea, and in 1241 the papacy called for a crusade to combat this deadly menace. Given this extraordinary level of crusading activity – not all of which was met with approval or enthusiasm by the knightly classes of Europe – the chances of a new and comparatively distant sphere of holy war attracting widespread support were slim.

Probably the greatest obstacle to the flowering of the Latin Empire was the situation in the Holy Land. By the mid-thirteenth century, after decades of relative stability, the settlers' position had deteriorated sharply. In August 1244 at the Battle of La Forbie, 1,034 out of 1,099 knights from the Military Orders were slain. This prompted the Seventh Crusade (1248–54), a substantial expedition consisting of more than 2,500 knights, properly financed by the French crown and the French Church, and led by the saintly King Louis IX. The resources and motivation demanded by an undertaking of this scale could not be summoned repeatedly, particularly if, as with Louis's crusade, the campaign failed.

The fundamental problem for the Latin Empire was that it lacked the unparalleled cachet of the Holy Places. It could not boast of a biblical past and it had not been seized from the hands of the infidel, but rather from Christians, albeit heretics. Baldwin's lands were in competition with the allure of the Holy Sepulchre, quite apart from the existing regional holy wars in Spain, the Baltic and the new campaigns in southern France, and those against the Mongols and Frederick II of Germany. For this reason the conquests of the Fourth Crusade were always destined to struggle for attention except from those parties directly interested in the area, such as the Montferrat dynasty or the Venetians. The fact that the Latin emperors were not from a royal house of the West, coupled with a decline in the standing of the counts of Flanders, reduced the obvious sources of help even further.[4]

As early as 1204, the Latin Empire and the Holy Land competed with each other for the attention of the Christian world. A letter from the archbishop of Nazareth pleaded for assistance 'for the recovery of the patrimony of the Crucified One'; yet around the same time the papal legate, Peter Capuano, released crusaders at Constantinople from their obligation to go to the Levant so that they could stay to defend the new empire.[5] The appeal sent to the papacy in the aftermath of the Battle of Adrianople was another request for help that reached the West just as the pleas from the archbishop of Nazareth were being considered.

In the early years, the Latin conquerors and the papacy had clung to the belief that their conquests might help the holy war against Islam, but this optimism was utterly misplaced. Even Pope Innocent came to recognise the conflict between consolidating the Latin Empire and liberating the Levant. In 1211 he wrote to Emperor Henry and grumbled, 'since you and other crusaders have striven to capture and keep the empire . . . principally in order that by this means you may bring help more easily to the Holy Land, you have not only failed to provide any assistance in this, but have also brought trouble and damage . . .' to those trying to resist the infidel.[6]

In the aftermath of the conquest, the prospect of land and money had attracted people from – of all places – the Levant. In 1202–3 the Crusader States had experienced a plague, a colossal earthquake and were confronted with a numerically overwhelming enemy. Thus, in the aftermath of the conquest of Byzantium, many inhabitants of the Levant – unwilling to pass up new opportunities to win land and money – eagerly decamped to Constantinople. As we have seen, men such as Stephen of Perche, Reynald of Montmirail and Geoffrey of Villehardouin's nephew (as well as some recent settlers in the kingdom of Jerusalem, such as Stephen of Tenremonde, a Fleming who had remained after the Third Crusade) were quick to abandon the defence of the Frankish East. Defections such as these caused Pope Innocent to complain that the exodus of pilgrims from the Holy Land left it weakened. Of course, given their overall vulnerability, the papacy was obliged to call for support for the Christians in the new empire. Yet every time a crusade set out, or money was sent to Constantinople, it meant less assistance for the Holy Land. Thus, far from preparing a way to liberate Christ's patrimony, the conquests of the Fourth Crusade actually weakened it.

It was not, however, until 1224 that the first crusade preached for the defence of the Latin Empire prepared to set out. This was a northern Italian (Montferrese) expedition focused on the relief of Thessalonica, but the leadership was delayed by illness and lack of funds and by the time the crusade reached the area, the city had already surrendered to the Greeks of Epirus.

Notwithstanding the adverse effects on campaigns to the Holy Land, the papacy tried hard to persuade some potential crusaders that they should fight for the Latin Empire instead of going to the Levant. In 1239 Richard of Cornwall, brother of King Henry III of England, and his companions were asked to commute their vows to Jerusalem in return for a money payment to help Constantinople or to go there in person, but they refused to be diverted and to shed Christian blood. The popes raised direct clerical taxation in Greece for the defence of the empire but the large-scale crusade that was required to defeat the Byzantines never looked like materialising. In fact, by 1262 Pope Urban IV was so desperate to encourage a new expedition to regain Constantinople that he offered free passage to participants (in contrast to the payments to the Venetians required in 1204) and – astonishingly – an indulgence of 40–100 days' penance for simply listening to the crusade sermon in the first instance.[7]

The Latin emperors worked hard to gather men and money and Baldwin II (1228–61) resorted to long tours around the courts of western Europe (1236–9 and 1244–8) in the hope of securing support, but all he received were polite displays of interest, small gifts and open-ended promises. Baldwin himself cut an unimpressive figure and contemporaries described him as 'young and childish' and not the 'wise and vigorous' figure needed.[8]

In 1237 he had to pawn the Crown of Thorns, worn by Christ on the Cross, to a Venetian merchant for 13,134 gold pieces. When he could not redeem the debt, the relic was taken by agents acting for the pious King Louis IX of France, who was so delighted with this treasure that he constructed the magnificent Sainte-Chapelle in Paris especially for it.[9] A year later Louis was involved in a more secular transaction when Baldwin mortgaged him the title to the county of Namur (a region of northern France – a link back to the emperor's Flemish forefathers) for 50,000 livres. By 1257 so impoverished was the empire that Venetian creditors required Baldwin's son Philip as surety for a loan, and even the lead from the palace roof was being sold to generate cash.[10]

In spite of this generally sorry tale on the mainland, the fertility and relative security of the principality of Achaea (in the Peloponnese peninsula), and the Venetian-controlled island of Crete, formed two regions of economic strength. The export of bulk products, including wheat, olive oil, wine and wool, as well as luxury items such as silk, created real wealth for the Italians and the Villehardouin dynasty who ruled Achaea. The latter fostered a flourishing court life and the chivalric traditions of the West blossomed. On one occasion Geoffrey II (1229–46) rode through his lands accompanied by 80 knights wearing golden spurs and the French spoken in Achaea was said to be as good as that in Paris. Frescos depicting chivalric deeds decorated palace walls, and tournaments and hunting were popular pastimes. The capture of Prince William (1246–78) at the Battle of Pelagonia (1259) marked the end of Achaean ascendancy, although the principality did survive through the female line.[11] Crete remained under Venetian rule until 1669 and was by far the most durable manifestation of the Fourth Crusade.

Elsewhere the Latins were less successful. Boniface of Montferrat did not enjoy his hard-won prize of the kingdom of Thessalonica for long. In September 1207 he was killed in battle, and years of pressure from the Greek rulers of Epirus led to their winning Thessalonica in 1224. It was, however, the empire of Nicaea, based in Asia Minor, which posed the most potent threat to the Latins. John III Vatatzes (1222–54), later canonised by the Orthodox Church, pushed the westerners out of Asia Minor, established a bridgehead at Gallipoli on the European side of the Bosphorus and later took over Thessalonica to tighten the noose around Constantinople. John's death meant that the final push to eject the Latins came from his general, Michael Palaeologus, who became regent for John's young son and then seized the imperial title for himself. The boy was, inevitably, imprisoned and blinded.

In July 1261, as the Greeks gathered for a full assault on Constantinople, a sympathiser opened one of the gates and the Byzantine advance party took the city with barely a struggle. Most of the Latin garrison was engaged on a campaign elsewhere and the citizenry were generally pleased to see the return of their natural lords. So unexpected was this turn of events that Michael Palaeologus had yet to cross the Bosphorus. His sister, Eulogia, heard the news early one morning and, as her brother lay sleeping in his tent, is said to have crept in and tickled his feet with a feather. When he awoke she told him that he was now the ruler of Constantinople. Playing along with her lighthearted mood, Michael laughed, but refused to accept what he heard. Only when a messenger entered with the imperial crown and sceptre did he believe it; God had indeed delivered

Constantinople back to the Greeks.[12] The principal achievement of the Fourth Crusade was thus wiped out.

In reality then, the Latin Empire proved to be an unwanted burden that only hindered the cause of the Holy Land. It expired 30 years before the fierce Mamluk dynasty prised the westerners from the city of Acre (1291) to mark the end of Christian power in the Levant until the British general, Edmund Allenby, entered Jerusalem in 1917. By one of history's neater ironies, in later centuries, as the reconstituted Byzantine Empire struggled against the mighty Ottoman Turks, the papacy tried to rouse western Europe for another crusade to help defend the Greeks.[13] The effort failed and, when the Ottomans took the city of Constantinople in 1453, it was finally lost to Byzantium for ever.

'The science of war, if not practised beforehand, cannot be gained when it becomes necessary'

ET AGAINST ITS original aim of the reconquest of Jerusalem, the Fourth Crusade was an utter failure. Yet the sack of Constantinople means that the expedition has achieved lasting notoriety as the crusade that turned against fellow-Christians. The reasons why the campaign followed its tragic path are numerous and overlapping. It is undeniable that – at the cost of some contemporary disquiet – the papacy, the Venetians and many other crusaders all derived enormous, if sometimes short-lived, increases in wealth and authority. Furthermore, an attack on Constantinople helped to settle many old scores. The papacy had watched the Byzantines openly obstruct recent crusading efforts and even form a rapprochement with Saladin. The Venetians had seen their citizens purged from Constantinople in 1171. Boniface of Montferrat, the leader of the crusade, had more personal reasons to dislike the Byzantines: one of his brothers, Renier, was murdered by the Greeks and another, Conrad, had been forced to flee Byzantium in fear of his life.

Several other issues created broader tensions between Byzantium and the West prior to 1204. The long-running schism between the Orthodox and Catholic Churches dated back to 1054. A persistent antagonism between crusading armies and the Greeks had started with the First Crusade, and the savage pogroms against westerners living in Constantinople in 1182 were the most prominent markers along this trail of mutual ill-feeling and mistrust.

Many from each party viewed the other in terms of simplistic and hostile caricatures. The westerners often regarded the Greeks as mendacious, effeminate heretics. Odo of Deuil described them as lacking 'all manly vigour, both of words and of spirit ... they have the opinion that anything done for the holy empire cannot be considered perjury'.[1] To the Byzantines, as Niketas Choniates graphically indicates, the westerners were often just as distasteful:

> Between us and them [the Latins] is set the widest gulf. We are poles apart. We have not a single thought in common. They are stiff-necked, with a proud affectation of an upright carriage and love to sneer at the modesty and smoothness of our manners. But we look upon their arrogance and boasting and pride as a flux of the snivel which keeps their noses in the air and we tread them down by the might of Christ, who giveth unto us the power to trample upon the adder and the scorpion.[2]

All of these feelings lay close to the surface in relations between Byzantium and the West, yet none was exactly a 'live' issue in 1204; in fact there were some indications of a more positive nature. For example, the Greeks had ended their cordial relationship with the Muslims in 1192. Furthermore, although Innocent had urged Alexius III to help the Fourth Crusade and made vague threats against the emperor if he failed to comply, the papal letters of 1202 were far more emollient. The Venetians were again trading with the Greeks (although full compensation for 1171 had yet to be made) and a large western European community existed once more in Constantinople. In spite of this marginally warmer atmosphere, however, the underlying difficulties persisted. The various points of friction could encourage, or provide partial reasons to justify or explain, an attack on Constantinople, but were insufficient to prompt as bold a step as a planned assault on the great city. In consequence, there can be no question of a pre-conceived plot to seize the Byzantine Empire by any of the western powers involved in the crusade.[3]

The reason why the Fourth Crusade went to Constantinople in the late spring of 1203 was, ironically, in response to the invitation of a Greek – the appeal by Prince Alexius to help him and his father secure what they regarded as their rightful position as rulers of the Byzantine Empire. Had this request not been made, there is no convincing evidence to suggest that the expedition would have turned towards Constantinople. To explain why the westerners' fleet sailed down to the Bosphorus, rather than heading towards Egypt and the Holy Land, one has to ask why the prince's offer was accepted.

Herein lay the Achilles heel of the whole enterprise: the lack of men and money. These were hardly new considerations and were, indeed, two prime causes of the collapse of the Second Crusade in 1148. Richard the Lionheart took great care to learn from this experience in preparing for the Third Crusade, but in 1201–2 these same concerns once again lay in ambush. The Fourth Crusade, however, possessed an additional constituent – the contract between the French and the Venetians – and it was the need to make good the terms of this agreement that became a powerful force in driving and shaping the expedition.

Even though, by the spring of 1201, the French negotiators in Venice knew that the rulers of England, France and Germany were unlikely to take part in the campaign, they still committed themselves to an extremely high level of recruitment (33,500 men). But by the summer of 1202, only around 12,000 had gathered at Venice. Consideration as to why this number fell so short of the target must include the erratic preaching of Fulk of Neuilly and, more seriously, the death of Thibaut of Champagne. The loss of the popular and dynamic head of one of the great crusading dynasties of Europe damaged morale at a crucial moment.[4] Leadership and resources from such a powerful figure could convince other nobles to join and help generate the critical mass of men required for an effective war. Equally, his premature death and lack of a mature successor in Champagne could have deterred people from leaving, for fear of a succession struggle.[5] But once the French were contractually bound to the Venetians there was no stepping back – for either party. The scale of the Venetian commitment to the enterprise was massive. Doge Dandolo could not retreat from it, even if his use of the crusaders' debts as a cover for Venice's long-term political and economic aims at Zara was a morally questionable move.

The fact that the crusaders were prepared to risk papal wrath by attacking a city under the protection of King Emico of Hungary, a man signed with the cross (however contentious his use of that status was), shows how obligated the Frenchmen felt towards the Venetians. It also demonstrates that they were determined to prevent the expedition from grinding to a halt: the crusaders' motivation to succeed in their holy war cannot be doubted.

The reasons for a man to take the cross were multi-faceted and over-lapping. By the time of the Fourth Crusade they reflected a combination of powerful contemporary currents and the same basic impulses that prompted the First Crusaders to act in 1095. For some noble families a century of crusading tradition imposed something close to an obligation to take part in holy war.[6] Coupled with this was the chivalric culture that came to dominate the courts of northern Europe (and Montferrat) during the twelfth century and instilled in its devotees an unswerving sense of honour and obligation to one's lord. These principles extended beyond secular ties and fused with the intense religiosity of the age to weigh upon the responsibility of a good Christian knight to show his loyalty to the ultimate authority – God – and to try to regain the Holy Land from the infidel.

The spiritual rewards for crusading dovetailed neatly with the knightly vocation. As warriors who fought and killed, the need to wash away the consequences of sin and thereby escape the torments of hell was paramount, and the remission of all sins offered crusaders a way to achieve this.

A cornerstone of the chivalric ethos was performing feats of valour. A wealth of contemporary literature shows a near-obsession with the importance of displaying knightly prowess. The tournament circuit of northern Europe provided a popular stage, but the crusade offered a setting in which to give these activities a spiritual aspect as well. It was a chance to blend acts of bravery with the ideas of faith and honour, and presented an opportunity to achieve the fame and standing of crusading heroes of the past such as Godfrey of Bouillon and Bohemond of Antioch.

The desire for loot and, in some cases, land was undeniably another of the crusaders' motives. In moderation, these wishes did not contradict the Church's idea of a crusader's proper concerns. But to stay within acceptable boundaries meant taking only what was necessary to survive and paying followers appropriate, but not excessive, rewards. Where this did happen, the sins of greed and envy were aroused and the crusade would incur God's displeasure. In any case, holy warfare was extremely expensive and before one considered the prospect of returning home wealthy, a large amount of money and valuables was needed to set out in the first place. Previous crusaders had hardly laid down an inspiring trail of financial advantage – in fact, if anything, the number who returned penniless indicated quite the reverse. Nonetheless, if the Fourth Crusade did manage to conquer Egypt and then reclaim the kingdom of Jerusalem, material gains were an undoubted possibility.

A combination of all these factors probably motivated the majority of the crusader knights. For the lesser men, the foot-soldiers and the squires, requirements of service to a lord and a desire to escape from the drudgery of the fields replaced the high-level chivalric element. In all cases, it demanded a remarkably strong dynamic to overcome the negative aspects of crusading: a combination of fear of death, captivity and sea travel; high cost; and separation from families, loved ones and homelands. Once the vow was taken, the search for honour, salvation and wealth – along with a fear of excommunication – combined to generate a relentless pressure to complete it.

In August 1202 the overwhelming need to fulfil their vows, coupled with parlous conditions in the Holy Land, led the bulk of the crusaders to accept the diversion to Zara. The siege represented only a brief delay before the invasion of Egypt although, as we have seen, the campaign failed to yield much booty and the financial problems remained. At this point, the embassy from Prince Alexius arrived at the crusader camp.

Even though their master had been rebuffed in his earlier attempts to secure help from rulers in the West, his envoys now offered contributions of men and money – sweetened with possible submission of the Orthodox Church to Rome – needed by the crusaders to help the Franks in the Holy Land. The envoys' portrayal of Prince Alexius and his father, Isaac, as being wrongfully dispossessed connected neatly with the crusading ideal of recovering lands illicitly taken. To secure these rewards the crusaders had to divert the fleet to Constantinople to install Prince Alexius on the imperial throne. While some crusaders left the campaign at this point, a majority of the leadership believed that if the prince's promises were fulfilled, this deal would enhance the crusade's chances of success. In other words, the diversions to Zara and Constantinople were both viewed as stepping-stones to the campaign in Egypt.

When they arrived at Constantinople in June 1203 the crusaders expressed genuine surprise at the hostile reception accorded to Prince Alexius. It was anticipated that a wave of popular support would sweep him back to power without the need for military action. Emperor Alexius

III, however, had worked hard to harness the long-standing Byzantine suspicion towards crusaders to create a groundswell of serious opposition.

By July 1203, however, the westerners' aggressive military operations compelled Alexius III to flee and the Byzantine hierarchy decided to free Isaac and crown the prince as co-emperor. While the installation of Alexius IV seemed a positive development for the crusaders, the simmering enmity of the Byzantines, agitated by the new emperor's need to satisfy his enormous financial obligations, gradually destroyed the young man's chances of keeping his promises. As Alexius became pinned down by his allies' increasingly aggressive demands for funds, the anti-western factions in Constantinople further reduced his room for manoeuvre.

Despite their deteriorating relationship, while Alexius remained in power the crusaders probably had a chance to leave Byzantium in good order. The ascendancy of Murtzuphlus and the murder of the emperor changed this irrevocably. It was at this point, and not before, that a crusader conquest of Constantinople became the aim of the expedition. They were camped outside an implacably hostile city with hardly any food or money; they were enraged by months of broken promises; they had faced aggressive enemy sorties (especially the fire-ships); and they were appalled by the killing of Alexius. These grievances ignited the long-standing religious and political grudges, and the westerners' accumulated anger and fear burst into flame with the ferocity of a coniferous forest fire. Helping the Holy Land remained the long-term goal of the crusade, but immediate survival took priority – and this meant an assault on the Queen of Cities.

Given Constantinople's redoubtable defences and the small numbers in the crusade army, the westerners' achievement was, by their own admission, quite incredible. The city had resisted several large-scale invasions over the centuries, so why did the crusaders succeed? The most important reason for the Greeks losing Constantinople was the chronic instability that took root at the heart of Byzantine politics following the death of Emperor Manuel Comnenus in 1180. In the two decades after Manuel's passing, a series of rebellions and revolts broke out as the leading families of Constantinople sought to gain ascendancy over each other and to create their own dynastic power base.[7] At the same time the Byzantines' military strength declined sharply. The army shrank in size and skill and, more crucially, the navy withered close to extinction. The contrast between the proud fleet of more than 230 ships sent to invade Egypt in 1169 and the dismal array of rotting hulks and fishing vessels that lined up across the Golden Horn in June 1203 could not be more stark. Small wonder that, with the centre of the empire so inwardly focused, some of the provinces saw an opportunity to break away. In 1184 Isaac Comnenus took authority for himself on Cyprus; in 1185 the Bulgarians revolted; and in 1188 the city of Philadelphia in Asia Minor seceded. Outside powers also sought advantage. The Greeks' long-term rivals from Sicily invaded the Balkans (again in direct response to an invitation from a claimant to the imperial crown) and brutally sacked the empire's second city, Thessalonica, in August 1185. Likewise, Frederick Barbarossa bullied his way past the Greeks during the Third Crusade in 1190.[8] These episodes were all symptomatic of a chronic malaise at the core of the empire.

As the twelfth century drew to a close, Alexius III was beginning to settle into power, but his failure to close off the potential challenge of his nephew (the prince) left open the possibility of further unrest. The frenetic interchange of men at the head of the Byzantine Empire did nothing to produce competent leadership. Niketas Choniates, our main source, was fiercely critical of those in power for bearing much of the responsibility for the fall of Constantinople, and the general tenor of his comments is borne out by other observers. Alexius III, Isaac and Alexius IV possessed few inspiring qualities. Their ability to assess a broad strategic picture was, at times, disastrously limited and they often seemed far more concerned with self-indulgent luxuries, such as Isaac's obsession with building projects, than with offering direction to the mighty Byzantine Empire. In the case of Alexius IV, he simply lacked the maturity and experience to carve out the requisite political and administrative platform. The military capabilities of successive emperors were particularly feeble. Only Murtzuphlus showed genuine talent, although by the time he took power the position was already critical.

The arrival of the Fourth Crusade added more ingredients to an already turbulent situation. It imposed intolerable pressures upon the volatile Byzantine hierarchy and the imperial system convulsed as never before. In the eleven months from June 1203 to April 1204 no fewer than six men – Alexius III, Isaac, Alexius IV, Nicholas Kannavos, Murtzuphlus and Constantine Lascaris – held the imperial title: indication enough of rampant and chronic instability.

Even so, up to the early afternoon of 12 April, when a change in wind direction brought the crusaders' ships up to the battlements of Constantinople, the city had successfully defied the crusaders. Until this moment, exploited by the bravery of Peter of Bracieux and Aleaumes of Clari, the fall of the Byzantine capital was by no means assured. The walls of Constantinople constituted a massive barrier, the Varangian Guard was a small but lethal body of men, and the Greeks held a substantial advantage through sheer weight of numbers. Had the westerners been beaten back for the second time in four days, their will to fight – already stretched to near breaking point – might have snapped. Combined with a lack of food, this could have forced them to seek terms with the Greeks or simply to melt away in humiliating defeat.

The fact that, after 11 months outside Constantinople, the crusader army was still in a condition to exploit the fortuitous winds is a testimony to their grim tenacity and military prowess. The amphibious landing at Galata in June 1203, the facing down of Alexius III's army outside the Theodosian walls 12 days later, the two seaborne assaults along the Golden Horn (June 1203 and April 1204), the courage of the men crossing from the flying bridges suspended high above the Venetians' ships – these were all indicative of courage and fighting skills of the highest order.

The groundwork for many of these great deeds was laid on the tournament fields of western Europe, a factor generally underestimated in earlier accounts of the Fourth Crusade. Roger of Howden, a cleric who took part in Richard the Lionheart's crusade, observed: 'The science of war, if not practised beforehand, cannot be gained when it becomes necessary. Nor indeed can the athlete bring high spirit to the contest who has never been trained to practise it.'[9] The relentless training of men and horses offered the very finest practice in a dangerous and competitive environment. The need to work as a team, as well as honing individual skills, was drilled into the knights. They were not, in the modern sense, a professional army that rehearses on the parade-square, but the chivalric ethos had instilled the skills, the discipline and the mentality to drive them onwards. As various contingents of crusaders departed during the campaign, the expedition slimmed down to a tough central core. The longer the crusade continued, the more familiar the remaining men became with working as a group, until their co-ordination and mutual confidence added another valuable weapon to their armoury. The siege of Zara provided a form of training ground and this was built upon through the first attack on Constantinople, the expedition to Thrace in the autumn of 1203, and the numerous skirmishes with the Greeks in the winter and spring of 1204. Once the crusaders established their battle order after the landings at Galata, they maintained these divisions for the remainder of the campaign: every man – from count to knight to foot-soldier – knew his place. A sense of shared responsibility, mutual reliance and teamwork is evident throughout the eye-witness accounts.

The crusader army was not, however, a faultless military machine – witness the temporary loss of formation outside the Theodosian walls in June 1203 and Louis of Blois's reckless charge at Adrianople in 1205, both ironically caused by a chivalric desire for glory. Nevertheless, they formed a truly formidable fighting force.

The horsemanship of the knights was complemented by the unparalleled seafaring capabilities of the Venetians. Centuries of maritime experience meant that the Italians were amongst the elite of medieval sailors. The Venetian shipyards had more than a year to prepare for the campaign and their vessels and equipment were in excellent condition. The huge fleet sailed from the Adriatic to Constantinople with barely any losses and then, in the heat of battle, the Venetians proved themselves fully committed and courageous. The amphibious landing at Galata and the fabrication of the extraordinary siege machinery at the top of their vessels in June 1203 and April 1204 showed their improvisational skills, while bringing and holding their ships to the shore to deliver these attacks demonstrated their remarkable prowess as mariners. The quality of the Venetian fleet and its contribution to the crusade's success dramatically highlighted the decline of the Byzantine navy.

Finally, again in contrast to the Greeks, the crusaders had effective commanders. The leadership was a mix of younger men, such as Baldwin of Flanders and Louis of Blois, and more experienced warriors. In July 1203 Hugh of Saint-Pol wrote to a friend in the West who had expressed concern about some of the knights: 'you were exceedingly upset because I had undertaken the pilgrimage journey with such men who were young in age and maturity and did not know how to render advice in such an arduous affair'.[10] As time went on, however, this worry must have faded as everyone became battle-hardened. Generally, Baldwin of Flanders, Boniface of Montferrat, Louis of Blois, Hugh of Saint-Pol, Conan of

Béthune and Geoffrey of Villehardouin, along with Doge Dandolo, worked in close harmony. Their determination to keep the campaign moving impelled the crusade onwards and ensured that it did not completely fragment. This broad co-operation also represented a stark contrast to the destructive bickering and tension that marked earlier expeditions, particularly the relationship between Richard the Lionheart and Philip of France during the Third Crusade.

Throughout the crusade Enrico Dandolo proved a monumentally influential figure – an unrivalled source of advice and encouragement for the other leaders. His demand to be thrust to the forefront during the assault on the walls of the Golden Horn in July 1203 was a moment of genuine inspiration and appealed perfectly to the crusaders' sense of honour and mutual competitiveness. Baldwin of Flanders too emerged as a man of sufficient standing and integrity to be the popular choice as the first Latin emperor of Constantinople.

While the martial qualities of the crusader warriors cannot be disputed, nothing can excuse the excesses perpetrated during the sack of Constantinople, although their behaviour can, perhaps, be explained. The combination of decades of ill-feeling between the Greeks and Latins, coupled with the tensions of months of conflict outside Constantinople, exploded in an appalling wave of violence and greed. Horrific events following sieges or battles were by no means new – witness the aftermath of the capture of Jerusalem in 1099. The western 'barbarians' were, however, not the sole perpetrators of such acts in the medieval world and this simple label should not obscure the fact that the Byzantine Empire's institutionalised duplicity and considerable capacity for violence did not always give them a clear position on the moral high ground. The savagery of the Greeks towards the Europeans in Constantinople in 1182 was one example of this. Nor were atrocities the exclusive province of warfare in the eastern Mediterranean as the 1258 sack of Baghdad by the Mongols, and the Norman invaders' terrible ravaging of northern England in 1068–9, demonstrate.

To the contemporary Byzantines, as much as modern commentators, it was the crusaders' stated purpose as holy warriors that made the episode especially hard to understand. While an appreciation of the values of medieval society does much to illuminate events of the time, even Pope Innocent had to acknowledge that, with regard to the Fourth Crusade, at least, sometimes even he could not fathom the ways of God. The crusaders, elated at overcoming the most enormous odds, had no doubt that they had received a divine blessing. Once the expedition had ended and the longer-term problems of establishing and running an empire emerged, delight at the capture of Constantinople soon became a distant memory and this new Catholic outpost became a distraction from the relief of the Holy Land.

The legacy of the sack of Constantinople is most acute in the Greek Orthodox Church where a deep-rooted bitterness at the perceived betrayal of Christian fraternity has long lingered.[11] The full story behind the conquest is, as we have seen, more complicated than this allows. Even so, whether in its morality or its motivation, it remains one of the most controversial, compelling and remarkable episodes in medieval history.

In the immediate aftermath of the conquest the troubadour Raimbaut of Vaqueiras, an eye-witness, acknowledged the crusaders' misdemeanours and set out the task that faced them if they were, in their own terms at least, to make good their misdeeds:

> For he [Baldwin] and we alike bear guilt for the burning of churches and the palaces, wherein I see both clerics and laymen sin; and if he does not succour the Holy Sepulchre and the conquest does not advance, then our guilt before God will be greater still, for the pardon will turn to sin. But if he be liberal and brave, he will lead his battalions to Babylonia and Cairo with the greatest ease.[12]

By this time it was a challenge the crusaders could never hope to meet.

Chronology

1202, December	Envoys from Prince Alexius at Zara
1203, 24 May	Crusade sails from Corfu
1203, 23 June	Arrival of the crusaders at Constantinople
1203, 5 July	Landing at Galata
1203, 17 July	Attack on Constantinople, retreat of Alexius III
1203, 18 July	Flight of Alexius III, reinstatement of Isaac Angelos
1203, 1 August	Coronation of Alexius IV
1203, August–October	Alexius IV and crusaders tour Byzantine Empire
1203, December	Growing tensions between Alexius IV and the crusaders
1204, January	Attack of the fire-ships
1204, 27–8 January	Imprisonment of Alexius IV by Murtzuphlus
1204, 8 February	Murder of Alexius IV
1204, March	Agreement between French and Venetian crusaders for division of the Byzantine Empire
1204, 9 April	Initial assault on Constantinople
1204, 12 April	Capture of Constantinople
1204, 13–15 April	Sack of Constantinople
1204, 16 May	Coronation of Emperor Baldwin and start of the Latin Empire
1205, 14 April	Battle of Adrianople, death of Louis of Blois and capture of Emperor Baldwin
1205, June	Death of Enrico Dandolo
1206, 20 August	Coronation of Emperor Henry
1216	Death of Pope Innocent III
1224	Crusade for the defence of the Latin Empire
1261	Capture of Constantinople by Michael Palaeologus and end of the Latin Empire
1291	Fall of Acre, end of Frankish presence in the Levant

Notes

ABBREVIATIONS

DBH   'Deeds of the Bishops of Halberstadt', *Contemporary
               Sources for the Fourth Crusade*, tr. A. J. Andrea, Leiden,
               2000, 239–64

DC   'Devastatio Constantinopolitana', *Contemporary Sources for
               the Fourth Crusade*, tr. A. J. Andrea, Leiden, 2000, 205–21

GP   Gunther of Pairis, *The Capture of Constantinople: The
               'Hystoria Constantinopolitana'*, ed. & tr. A. J. Andrea,
               Philadelphia, 1997

GV   Geoffrey of Villehardouin, 'The Conquest of
               Constantinople', *Chronicles of the Crusades*, tr. M. R. B.
               Shaw, London, 1963, 29–160

Innocent III   'Letters', *Contemporary Sources for the Fourth Crusade*, tr.
               A. J. Andrea, Leiden, 2000, 7–176

NC   Niketas Choniates, *O City of Byzantium: Annals of Niketas
               Choniates*, tr. H. J. Magoulias, Detroit, 1984

RC   Robert of Clari, *The Conquest of Constantinople*, tr. E. H.
               McNeal, New York, 1936

Sources   *Contemporary Sources for the Fourth Crusade*, tr. A. J. Andrea,
               Leiden, 2000

INTRODUCTION

1 NC, 314–15.
2 The most detailed narrative of the expedition is by Queller and Madden,
  Fourth Crusade, whose perspective is as historians of Venice. Another
  good account of the campaign is Godfrey, *1204. The Unholy Crusade*.
3 Vehemently anti-western accounts of the crusade written by Byzantine
  historians include: Runciman, *History of the Crusades*, III; Norwich,

Byzantium: The Decline and Fall, 156–213. For more balanced and scholarly views, see: Harris, Byzantium and the Crusades; Angold, The Fourth Crusade.

4 Constable, 'The Historiography of the Crusades'.

5 Siberry, 'Images of the Crusades in the Nineteenth and Twentieth Centuries', The Oxford Illustrated History of the Crusades, 314.

6 Runciman, History of the Crusades, III, 469, 480.

7 Cited in Bartlett, Medieval Panorama, 12–13.

8 Runciman, History of the Crusades, III, 474.

9 Riley-Smith, 'Islam and the Crusades in History and Imagination', 164–7.

10 Phillips, 'Why a Crusade will lead to a jihad'.

11 Innocent III, Sources, 107.

12 Innocent III, Sources, 173–4.

13 See especially the comments by Harris, 'Distortion, Divine Providence and Genre in Niketas Choniates' Account of the Collapse of Byzantium'.

14 Jackson, 'Christians, Barbarians and Masters: The European Discovery of the World Beyond Islam'.

15 Bull, 'Origins'.

16 Guibert of Nogent, cited in and translated by Bull, Knightly Piety and the Lay Response to the First Crusade, 3.

17 William of Tyre, I, 372–3.

18 The best account of this is Hillenbrand, The Crusades: Islamic Perspectives.

19 See Phillips and Hoch, Second Crusade: Scope and Consequences, 1–14.

20 Harris, Byzantium and the Crusades, 116–20.

21 Eustathios of Thessaloniki, The Capture of Thessaloniki, 35.

22 William of Tyre, II, 465.

23 Hamilton, The Leper King and His Heirs: King Baldwin IV and the Crusader States.

CHAPTER ONE

THE ORIGINS AND PREACHING OF THE FOURTH CRUSADE, 1187–99

1 Gregory VIII, Audita tremendi, 64–5.

2 Beha ad-Din, The Rare and Excellent History of Saladin, 146, 150.

3 Chronicle of the Third Crusade, 382.

4 This period is expertly analysed by Gillingham, Richard I, 155–301.

5 A good, modern biography of Innocent is: Sayers, *Innocent III*. Also important are the essays collected in: *Innocent III: Vicar of Christ or Lord of the World?*, ed. Powell; *Pope Innocent III and his World*, ed. Moore.

6 Sayers, *Innocent III*, 10–27; Peters, 'Lothario dei Conti di Segni becomes Pope Innocent III', in: *Innocent III and his World*, 3–24.

7 Sayers, *Innocent III*, 2.

8 Innocent III, *Sources*, 7–9.

9 Innocent III, *Sources*, 9, n.4.

10 Ross, *Relations between the Latin East and the West, 1187–1291*, 58–60.

11 Innocent III, *Sources*, 10–11.

12 Innocent III, *Sources*, 12.

13 Innocent III, *Sources*, 14.

14 On this papal appeal, see also: Cole, *Preaching the Crusades*, 80–5.

15 Gillingham, *Richard I*, 316.

16 There is an excellent translation of the first 10,000 lines of the *History*. See: *History of William Marshal*, ed. Holden, tr. Gregory. The remainder of the text is forthcoming.

17 Translations from: Crosland, *William the Marshal*, 78–81. For William's life see: Crouch, *William Marshal*; for this period of Richard's reign, see: Gillingham, *Richard I*, 318–20.

18 Gillingham, *Richard I*, 323–5.

19 The most accessible modern account of Philip's life is: Bradbury, *Philip Augustus*; for his marital difficulties, see 173–94.

20 Joinville, *Life of Saint Louis*, 196.

21 France, 'Patronage and the First Crusade'.

22 Riley-Smith, 'Casualties and Knights on the First Crusade', 17–19; Phillips, *Second Crusade*.

23 Fulcher of Chartres, *History of the Expedition to Jerusalem*, 85.

24 Albert of Aachen, *Historia*, 329.

25 Raymond of Aguilers, in: Peters, *First Crusade*, 212–13.

26 Odo of Deuil, *Journey of Louis VII*, 123.

27 Guibert of Nogent, *The Deeds of the Franks*, 165. For the subject of crusader captives in general, see: Friedman, *Encounters between Enemies*.

28 *Gesta Francorum*, 3–4.

29 *Gesta Francorum*, 89.

30 *Gesta Francorum*, 62.

31 *Chronicle of the Third Crusade*, 232-3.

32 Orderic Vitalis, *Ecclesiastical History*, V, 17.

33 For Raymond and Eleanor, see: William of Tyre, *History*, II, 179–81. For women as guardians of property, see: Riley-Smith, *First Crusaders*, 135-43.

34 *Chronicle of the Third Crusade*, 48.

35 Gerald of Wales, *Journey through Wales*, 76.

36 *Conquest of Lisbon*, 73.

37 Peters, *First Crusade*, 287–9.

38 *Cartulaire de l'abbaye de Saint-Père de Chartres*, II, 646.

39 Fulcher of Chartres, *History of the Expedition to Jerusalem*, 139.

40 *Conquest of Lisbon*, 131.

41 Riley-Smith, *First Crusaders*, 120.

42 Robinson, *The Papacy, 1073–1198: Continuity and Innovation*, 336–9.

43 De Hemptinne, 'Les épouses des croisés et pèlerins flamands aux XIe et XIIe siècles'.

44 Hugh of Saint-Pol, *Sources*, 186–7.

45 William of Malmesbury, *History of the Kings of England*, 655.

46 Orderic Vitalis, *Ecclesiastical History*, V, 5.

47 Lambert of Ardres, *History*, 164–5.

48 Suger, *Deeds of Louis the Fat*, 41.

49 For Bishop Ortleib, see: Frolow, *Relique de la vraie croix*, 349; for Gouffier, see: Riley-Smith, *First Crusaders*, 235.

50 Odo of Deuil, *The Journey of Louis VII*, 115, 123.

51 Albert of Aachen, *Historia*, 626.

52 Herman of Tournai, *The Restoration of the Monastery of Saint Martin of Tournai*, 47.

53 Suger, *Deeds of Louis the Fat*, 40.

54 See also: Kenaan-Kedar and Kedar, 'Significance of a Twelfth-Century Sculptural Group'.

CHAPTER TWO

ABBOT MARTIN'S CRUSADE SERMON, BASEL CATHEDRAL, MAY 1200

1 For Fulk's career see: O'Brien, 'Fulk of Neuilly'. Note also: McNeal, 'Fulk of Neuilly and the Tournament of Ecry'.

2 Ralph of Coggeshall, *Sources*, 278–9.

3 GV, 29.

4 Ralph of Coggeshall, *Sources*, 280.

5 Cole, *Preaching the Crusades*, 89–90.

6 Maier suggests 3 May as the most likely date for the sermon in 'Kirche, Kreuz und Ritual', 101–4.

7 For sermons in general, see: Maier, *Crusade Propaganda and Ideology: Model Sermons for the Preaching of the Cross*; Cole, *Preaching the Crusades*.

8 There is an excellent translation with a full introduction and analysis of Gunther's writings in: Gunther of Pairis, *The Capture of Constantinople*, ed. Andrea. For the Basel sermon, see also: Cole, *Preaching the Crusades*, 92–7; Maier, 'Kirche, Kreuz und Ritual'.

9 Spicher, *Geschichte des Basler Münsters*.

10 For a discussion of this with regard to an earlier expedition, see: Phillips, 'Holy War', 133–4.

11 Cole, *Preaching the Crusades*, 45.

12 GP, 68.

13 GP, 69.

14 Maier, 'Kirche, Kreuz und Ritual'.

15 GP, 70. On the True Cross, see also: Riley-Smith, *First Crusade and the Idea of Crusading*, 23–5, 31–2, 150–1; Murray, 'Mighty Against the Enemies of Christ'.

16 For translations of excerpts from Urban's sermon, see: Riley-Smith, *Crusade: Idea and Reality*, 40–3.

17 On the need to atone for sin, see: Bull, 'Origins'; Bull, *Knightly Piety*, 155–249.

18 GP, 71.

CHAPTER THREE
THE TOURNAMENT AT ÉCRY, NOVEMBER 1199

1 On tournaments generally, see: Keen, *Chivalry*, 20–3; Barber and Barber, *Tournaments*, 13–27; Strickland, *War and Chivalry*, 149–53.

2 Roger of Howden, *Chronica*, II, 166–7. Translated in: *The Annals of Roger of Hoveden*, I, 490.

3 *History of William Marshal*, I, 309.

4 *History of William Marshal*, I, 173.

5 Lambert of Ardres, *History*, 126.

6 *History of William Marshal*, I, 177, 181.

7 Geoffrey of Monmouth, *History of the Kings of Britain*, 229.

8 Keen, *Chivalry*, 21.

9 On the difficult relationship between romantic literature and historical reality, see: Keen, *Chivalry*, 102–24; Bouchard, *Strong of Body*, 105–9.

10 Chrétien de Troyes, *Érec et Énide*, 63–4.

11 *History of William Marshal*, I. 175–9.

12 Lloyd, *English Society and the Crusade*, 199–200.

13 *Decrees of the Ecumenical Councils*, I, 199–200. This decree of the 1139 Lateran Council reiterated earlier statements from the 1130 Council of Clermont and the 1131 Council of Reims.

14 Keen, *Chivalry*, 22. For Flanders, Champagne and the crusades generally, see the references in Phillips, *Defenders*.

15 Humbert of Romans, *De predicatione Sancte crucis*.

16 Gillingham, *Richard I*, 19; Hillenbrand, *The Crusades: Islamic Perspectives*, 336.

17 Gillingham, *Richard I*, 19.

18 Keen, *Chivalry*, 56.

19 GV, 29.

20 Longnon, *Les compagnons de Villehardouin*, 11–13.

21 Longnon, *Les compagnons de Villehardouin*, 79–84.

22 GV, 29.

23 GV, 57.

24 Morris, 'Geoffroy de Villehardouin and the Conquest of Constantinople', 34. For a concise overview of the debate over Villehardouin's writings, see: Andrea, 'Essay on Primary Sources', 299–302; note also Noble, 'The Importance of Old French Chronicles'. For a remarkably hostile assessment of the text, see: Archambault, 'Villehardouin: History in Black and White'. For Villehardouin's treatment of the Champenois contingent, see: Dufournet, 'Villehardouin et les Champenois dans la Quatrième croisade'.

25 Longnon, *Les compagnons de Villehardouin*, 18, 20, 113.

26 GV, 30; Wolff, 'Baldwin of Flanders and Hainault'.

27 NC, 328.

28 GV, 30–1; RC, 32–3. On Robert as a source, see: RC, 3–27, and the comments in Andrea's 'Essay on Primary Sources' in Queller and Madden, *Fourth Crusade*, 302–3; also Noble, 'The Importance of Old French Chronicles'.

29 GV, 31.

30 *Conquest of Lisbon*, 12–26.

31 Pryor, *Geography, Technology and War*, 3–4, 36, 51–3.

32 Marshall, 'The Crusading Motivation of the Italian City Republics in the Latin East, 1096–1104', 60–79.

33 For Genoa, see: *La cattedrale di Genova nel medioevo secoli VI–XIV*, ed. Di Fabrio, 188–91. For Venice, see: Cerbani Cerbani, 'Translatio mirifici martyris Isidori a Chio insula in civitatem Venetem', 323–4; Marshall, 'The Crusading Motivation of the Italian City Republics in the Latin East'.

34 Caffaro, in: Williams, 'The Making of a Crusade', 38–9.

35 Ibn Jubayr, *The Travels*, 300–1.

36 Innocent III, *Sources*, 22.

37 Innocent III, *Sources*, 16.

38 GV, 31.

CHAPTER FOUR

THE TREATY OF VENICE, APRIL 1201

1 Lane, *Venice*, 1–21; Zorzi, *Venice, A City, A Republic, An Empire*, 10–20, 102–8; Howard, *Architectural History of Venice*, 2–41.

2 Tafel and Thomas, *Urkunden*, I, 51–4; Jacoby, 'The Chrysobull of Alexius I to the Venetians'.

3 Madden, *Enrico Dandolo and the Rise of Venice*. Madden's book was published as this present work was being completed. I have, therefore, been unable to include any of its detailed ideas.

4 Madden, 'Venice and Constantinople in 1171 and 1172', 169–70.

5 Madden, 'Venice and Constantinople in 1171 and 1172', 179–84.

6 For Innocent III see: *Sources*, 60–9, 95–8; 145–51. For later historians hostile to Venice, see: Queller and Madden, *Fourth Crusade*, 318–21; Runciman, *History of the Crusades*, III.

7 GP, 97.

8 Innocent III, *Sources*, 112.

9 RC, 40.

10 Stahl, 'The Coinage of Venice in the Age of Enrico Dandolo'.

11 GV, 32–3.

12 Riley-Smith, *First Crusaders*, 19, 29.

13 GV, 33.

14 Tafel and Thomas, *Urkunden*, I, 362–73. See also: Queller and Madden, *Fourth Crusade*, 11, 217, n.23.

15 GV, 33–4.

16 For concise details on the construction of St Mark's, see: Howard, *Architectural History of Venice*, 17–28. For the most complete survey of the church's mosaics, see: Demus, *Mosaic Decoration of San Marco, Venice*.

17 Demus, *Mosaic Decoration of San Marco*, 20–3.

18 GV, 34–5.

19 GV, 35.

20 Queller and Madden, *Fourth Crusade*, 12; Mack, *The Merchant of Genoa*, 28–43.

21 Lane, *Venice*, 37.

22 For the First Crusade, see: France, *Victory in the East*, 142; for the Third Crusade, see: Johnson, 'The Crusades of Frederick Barbarossa and Henry VI', 89–94.

23 GV, 35.

24 Phillips, *Crusades*, 95–6.

25 William of Tyre, *History*, II, 313.

26 William of Tyre, *History*, II, 408.

27 Phillips, *Crusades*, 95–101, 146–50.

28 GV, 35.

29 GP, 77.

30 Hillenbrand, *The Crusades: Islamic Perspectives*, 557.

31 Queller and Madden, 'Some further arguments in defence of the Venetians', 438. See also: Lane, *Venice*, 70–3.

32 Madden, 'Venice, the Papacy and the Crusades before 1204'.

33 Innocent III, *Sources*, 23–4.

34 William of Tyre, *History*, II, 335.

35 Ibn Jubayr, *The Travels*, 32.

36 Lane, *Venice*, 88; Howard, *Architectural History of Venice*, 17–19.

37 GV, 35.

38 Martin da Canal, *Les Estoires de Venise*, 46–7.

39 McNeill, *Venice*, 5–6; Zorzi, *Venice: A City, A Republic, An Empire*, 38–9.

40 The dimensions of all vessels discussed here are taken from: Pryor, 'The Naval Architecture of Crusader Transport Ships'. See also: Martin, *The Art and Archaeology of Venetian Ships and Boats*.

41 Pryor, 'Transportation of Horses by Sea during the Era of the Crusades'.

42 Pryor, 'The Venetian Fleet for the Fourth Crusade', 119–22.

43 GV, 35–6.

CHAPTER FIVE

FINAL PREPARATIONS AND LEAVING HOME,
MAY 1201–JUNE 1202

1 For a full and stimulating discussion of the Jews in Europe at this time, see: Abulafia, *Christians and Jews*. For usury in particular, see 58–62.

2 Peter the Venerable, *Letters*, I, 327.

3 Bernard of Clairvaux, *Letters*, 466.

4 GV, 37.

5 Jubainville, *Histoire des ducs et des comtes de Champagne*, 4, 96. For the full description of the tomb, see the same work, 90–9.

6 Jackson, 'Crusades of 1239–41 and their aftermath', 32–60.

7 GV, 37.

8 Evergates, 'Aristocratic Women in the County of Champagne', 79–85.

9 William of Tyre, *History*, II, 416.

10 William of Tyre, *History*, II, 450–1.

11 NC, 97.

12 Brand, *Byzantium Confronts the West*, 19.

13 NC, 210.

14 *Continuation of William of Tyre*, 53.

15 *Continuation of William of Tyre*, 54.

16 *Chronicle of the Third Crusade*, 40.

17 Jacoby, 'Conrad of Montferrat and the Kingdom of Jerusalem, 1187–92'.

18 *Continuation of William of Tyre*, 114–15. The account in *Chronicle of the Third Crusade* gives another account of the murder, differing in minor details, such as that Conrad did eat with the bishop of Beauvais before meeting his fate en route home. *Chronicle of the Third Crusade*, 305–7.

19 Raimbaut de Vaqueiras, *Poems*, 312.

20 Queller and Madden, *Fourth Crusade*, 25–6.

21 RC, 35.

22 Brundage, 'Cruce signari: The Rite for taking the Cross in England'.

23 Raimbaut of Vaqueiras, *Poems*, 218–20.

24 Morris, *Papal Monarchy*, 245.

25 Ralph of Coggeshall, *Sources*, 281.

26 Ralph of Coggeshall, *Sources*, 281.

27 Cole, *Preaching the Crusades*, 90.

28 Longnon, *Les compagnons de Villehardouin*, 209–10, 212–13.

29 For Alexius's age, see: Brand, *Byzantium Confronts the West*, 96–7.

30 RC, 84.

31 NC, 305.

32 See the arguments put forward by Winkelmann and Riant, reproduced in: Queller, *Latin Conquest of Constantinople*, 26–9, 32–8.

33 The point is made by Queller and Madden, *Fourth Crusade*, 45–6.

34 NC, 242–3.

35 Johnson, 'Crusades of Frederick Barbarossa and Henry VI', 92–109.

36 Angold, *Byzantine Empire*, 303–11, 318–19.

37 NC, 248.

38 NC, 242–3.

39 'Novgorod Account of the Fourth Crusade', 306.

40 Powell, 'Innocent III and Alexius III: a Crusade Plan that Failed', 96–100.

41 Tafel and Thomas, *Urkunden*, I, 241–6; Angold, *Byzantine Empire*, 319. See also: Brand, *Byzantium Confronts the West*, 225–9.

42 Innocent III, *Sources*, 32–4.

43 Innocent III, 'Solitae', from: Andrea, *Medieval Record*, 321.

44 Translation from Slack, *Crusade Charters, 1138–1270*, 145.

45 Translated from *Cartulare de Notre-Dame de Josaphat*, I, 358. For Geoffrey of Beaumont, see also: Longnon, *Les compagnons de Villehardouin*, 107.

46 Riley-Smith and Riley-Smith, *Crusades: Idea and Reality*, 147.

47 *Continuation of William of Tyre*, 68.

48 Fulcher of Chartres, *History of the Expedition to Jerusalem*, 74.

49 RC, 39.

50 Conon of Béthune, *Les Chansons de Conon de Béthune*, 6–7.

51 GV, 40.

52 Joinville, *Chronicles of the Crusades*, 195.

53 GV, 40. The *Devastatio Constantinopolitana* recorded that crusaders began to arrive in Venice from 1 June, *Sources*, 214.

54 Spufford, *Power and Profit*, 140–69.

CHAPTER SIX

THE CRUSADE AT VENICE AND THE SIEGE OF ZARA, SUMMER AND AUTUMN 1202

1 GV, 40.

2 GV, 40.

3 Villehardouin records that Pope Innocent III endorsed the agreement between the Venetians and the crusaders, but he does not mention any papal instructions for the crusaders to meet at Venice. Had the pope done so, it is odd that neither Innocent nor Villehardouin himself (who was always ready to apportion blame for the shortfall in men at Venice) chose to mention such an important point. This argument is contra to the view of Madden, 'Venice, the Papacy and the Crusades before 1204'.

4 Spufford, *Power and Profit*, 152–5; 169–70.

5 GV, 41.

6 *Gesta Innocenti*, col. 138.

7 GV, 42.

8 RC, 42.

9 Hugh of Saint-Pol, *Letter*, 191; NC, 295–6.

10 For Conrad's career in full, see: Andrea, 'Conrad of Krosigk, Bishop of Halberstadt, Crusader and Monk of Sittichenbach'.

11 GV, 42.

12 RC, 40.

13 DC, *Sources*, 205–12.

14 DC, *Sources*, 214.

15 RC, 40.

16 DC, *Sources*, 214.

17 GV, 42.

18 GV, 42–3.

19 GV, 43; RC, 41.

20 GV, 43.

21 RC, 41.

22 GV, 43.

23 DBH, *Sources*, 251.

24 GV, 44.

25 GV, 44.

26 Phillips, *Second Crusade*.

27 RC, 42.

28 RC, 42.

29 The treaties are reproduced in: Tafel and Thomas, *Urkunden*, I, 386, 396.

30 DBH, *Sources*, 250–1.

31 Innocent III, *Sources*, 43; *Gesta Innocenti*, translated in: *Sources*, 44.

32 GV, 48.

33 RC, 44.

34 GV, 48.

35 Peter of Vaux-Cernay, *History of the Albigensian Crusade*, 58.

36 France, *Western Warfare in the Age of the Crusades*, 117–20; Bradbury, *Medieval Siege*, 254–70.

37 DC, *Sources*, 215.

38 *Conquest of Lisbon*, 143, 145. A cubit is a medieval measurement equivalent to a forearm.

39 DBH, *Sources*, 251.

40 GP, 80; Innocent III, *Sources*, 43.

41 Innocent III, *Sources*, 129.

42 GP, 78–9.

43 GP, 78.

44 GP, 79.

45 DC, *Sources*, 215.

46 GV, 49.

47 RC, 44.

48 Innocent III, *Sources*, 41.

49 Innocent III, *Sources*, 42–3.

50 Innocent III, *Sources*, 43.

CHAPTER SEVEN

THE OFFER FROM PRINCE ALEXIUS,
DECEMBER 1202–MAY 1203

1 GV, 50.

2 GP, 90.

3 GV, 50.

4 GV, 51.

5 GV, 51.

6 GV, 51.

7 Innocent III, *Sources*, 35.

8 RC, 45.

9 RC, 59, 66.

10 GP, 91.

11 For this complex subject, see: Nicol, *Byzantium and Venice*, 50–123; Martin, 'Venetians in the Byzantine Empire before 1204'; Madden, 'Venice and Constantinople in 1171 and 1172: Enrico Dandolo's attitudes towards Byzantium'; Angold, *Byzantine Empire*, 226–33.

12 Tafel and Thomas, *Urkunden*, I, 179–203, 206–11.

13 GP, 91.

14 GV, 51; RC, 66.

15 RC, 66.

16 GV, 51.

17 GV, 52.

18 Longnon, *Les compagnons de Villehardouin*, 114–15.

19 GV, 52.

20 GV, 52–3; Longnon, *Les compagnons de Villehardouin*, 149–50.

21 Innocent III, *Sources*, 48.

22 Innocent III, *Sources*, 52–4.

23 Innocent III, *Sources*, 54–7.

24 Innocent III, *Sources*, 57–9.

25 DBH, *Sources*, 253.

26 Hugh of Saint-Pol's Letter, *Sources*, 188.

27 Hugh of Saint-Pol's Letter, *Sources*, 189.

28 GV, 55.

29 GV, 55.

30 GV, 56.

31 DBH, *Sources*, 254.

CHAPTER EIGHT

THE CRUSADE ARRIVES AT CONSTANTINOPLE, JUNE 1203

1 GV, 57.

2 GV, 57.

3 GV, 57.

4 GV, 58.

5 Pryor, 'Winds, Waves and Rocks: the Routes and the Perils Along Them', 85.

6 GV, 58.

7 Jacoby, 'La population de Constantinople à l'époque Byzantine: Un problème de démographie urbaine', 107.

8 GV, 58–9.

9 RC, 67.

10 Alexander, 'The Strength of Empire and Capital as Seen Through Byzantine Eyes', 345.

11 Baynes, 'The Supernatural Defenders of Constantinople'.

12 Van Millingen, *Byzantine Constantinople*, 4.

13 Sarris, 'The Eastern Empire from Constantine to Heraclius (306–641)', 21.

14 For a full discussion of all these interpretations, see: Angold, 'Road to 1204: the Byzantine background to the Fourth Crusade'.

15 Van Millingen, *Byzantine Constantinople*, 40–58.

16 Van Millingen, *Byzantine Constantinople*, 59–73.

17 RC, 108–9.

18 Mango, 'Constantinople', 66.

19 NC, 358.

20 Magdalino, 'Manuel Komnenos and the Great Palace', 101–14; Van Millingen, *Byzantine Constantinople*, 284.

21 William of Tyre, *History*, II, 381–2.

22 RC, 103.

23 Nicholas Mesarites, translation from: Mango, *Art of the Byzantine Empire, 312–1453*, 229.

24 Maguire, 'Medieval Floors of the Great Palace'.

25 Benjamin of Tudela, *Itinerary*, 70–1; NC, 160; Magdalino, *Manuel I Komnenos*, 111.

26 RC, 107.

27 Many books have been written on the Hagia Sophia. See particularly: Mainstone, *Hagia Sophia: Architecture, Structure and Liturgy of Justinian's Great Church*.

28 Mango, *Art of the Byzantine Empire*, 74–5.

29 RC, 106.

30 Alberic of Trois-Fontaines, 'Chronicle', *Sources*, 298.

31 Odo of Deuil, *Journey of Louis VII*, 65–7

32 RC, 108.

33 Ousterhout, 'Architecture, Art and Komnenian Ideology at the Pantokrator Monastery', *Byzantine Constantinople*, 133–50; Megaw, 'Notes on Recent Work of the Byzantine Institute in Istanbul', 333–64.

34 For details of the running of the hospital, see: *Byzantine Monastic Foundation Documents*, II, 725–74.

35 Phillips, *Crusades, 1095–1197*, 58.

36 Mango, 'Three Imperial Byzantine Sarcophagi', 397–404.

37 Runciman, 'Blachernae Palace and Its Decoration', 277–83.

38 Odo of Deuil, *Journey of Louis VII*, 65.

39 William of Tyre, *History*, II, 450.

40 Benjamin of Tudela, *Itinerary*, 72.

41 Odo of Deuil, *Journey of Louis VII*, 65.

42 Cited by Magdalino, *Manuel I Komnenos*, 121.

43 NC, 132.

44 Ralph of Coggeshall, *Sources*, 285.

45 NC, 296.

46 NC, 296–7.

47 Innocent III, *Sources*, 35–8.

48 William of Tyre, *History*, II, 361.

49 Pryor notes that, given the Venetians' knowledge of the weakness of the Byzantine navy, if Constantinople was always the planned target for the crusade, then the provision of 50 war galleys was superfluous. By contrast, the Egyptian navy was known to be more of a danger, hence the provision of war galleys to fight them. This is further proof that the crusade intended to go to Egypt from its inception. Pryor, 'The Venetian Fleet for the Fourth Crusade', 108–11, 119–22. See also Sesan, 'La flotte Byzantine à l'époque des Comnenes et des Anges'.

50 Birkenmeier, *The Development of the Komnenian Army, 1081–1180*, 231–5.

51 Benjamin of Tudela, *Travels*, 71.

52 For the expedition of King Sigurd, see: Snorri Sturlusson, *Heimskringla: History of the Kings of Norway*, 689–99; for the Varangian guard, see: Birkenmeier, *Development of the Komnenian Army*, 62–6, 90–7.

53 Innocent III, *Sources*, 82.

54 Cheyet, 'Les effectifs de l'armée byzantine aux x–xii s.', 333.

55 GV, 59.

56 GV, 59.

57 Stephenson, 'Anna Comnena's *Alexiad* as a source for the Second Crusade', 41–54.

58 GV, 60.

CHAPTER NINE

THE FIRST SIEGE OF CONSTANTINOPLE, JULY 1203

1 Hugh of Saint-Pol, *Sources*, 190.

2 GV, 63.

3 GV, 63.

4 RC, 67.

5 Innocent III, *Sources*, 81.

6 Hugh of Saint-Pol, *Sources*, 190.

7 GV, 64.

8 RC, 67.

9 GV, 64.

10 Innocent III, *Sources*, 82.

11 This had become very apparent during the First Crusade. See France, *Victory in the East*, 369–73.

12 GV, 65.

13 RC, 68.

14 RC, 68.

15 Hugh of Saint-Pol, *Sources*, 191.

16 Hugh of Saint-Pol, *Sources*, 191.

17 RC, 68.

18 RC, 68.

19 Hugh of Saint-Pol, *Sources*, 191.

20 Van Millingen, *Byzantine Constantinople*, 228–9.

21 Hugh of Saint-Pol, *Sources*, 191.

22 GV, 67.

23 RC, 70.

24 Alberic of Trois-Fontaines, *Sources*, 298.

25 Van Millingen, *Byzantine Constantinople*, 174–7.

26 Hugh of Saint-Pol, *Sources*, 194.

27 RC, 70.

28 GV, 68.

29 RC, 70; Hugh of Saint-Pol, *Sources*, 194.

30 GV, 69.

31 NC, 298.

32 NC, 298.

33 NC, 298.

34 Hugh of Saint-Pol, *Sources*, 196.

35 GV, 71.

36 Alberic of Trois-Fontaines, *Sources*, 299.

37 NC, 298.

38 NC, 298–9.

39 RC, 71.

40 GV, 72.

41 NC, 299.

42 Hugh of Saint-Pol. *Sources*, 197; RC, 71.

43 GV, 72.

44 RC, 72.

45 RC, 74.

46 RC, 75.

47 RC, 75.

48 RC, 75.

49 Hugh of Saint-Pol, *Sources*, 197.

50 NC, 299.

51 Innocent III, *Sources*, 83.

52 Hugh of Saint-Pol, *Sources*, 197.

53 Anna Comnena, *Alexiad*, 342.

54 NC, 299.

55 NC, 299–301.

56 NC, 299.

57 NC, 301.

58 NC, 299–301.

59 GV, 73.

60 GV, 73.

CHAPTER TEN
TRIUMPH AND TENSIONS AT CONSTANTINOPLE, JULY–AUGUST 1203

1 John Kinnamos, *Deeds of John and Manuel Comnenus*, 69.

2 GV, 75.

3 GV, 75.

4 Hugh of Saint-Pol, *Sources*, 198; NC, 302.

5 See Jackson, 'Early Missions to the Mongols: Carpini and His Contemporaries'.

6 RC, 78–9.

7 Agnes was the sister of King Philip of France and was the widow of Emperor Alexius II (1180–3) and Andronicus I (1183–5). Theodore Branas was her third husband.

8 RC, 79.

9 RC, 79–80.

10 GV, 76.

11 RC, 80–1.

12 Innocent III, *Sources*, 63.

13 Innocent III, *Sources*, 68.

14 Innocent III, *Sources*, 72.

15 Hugh of Saint-Pol, *Sources*, 198–9.

16 Hugh of Saint-Pol, *Sources*, 201.

17 The link between tournament imagery and the crusades was not new and can be seen in an anonymous Old French *trouvère* song from the Second Crusade. See: Phillips, *Crusades*, 182–3.

18 Innocent III, *Sources*, 95–8.

19 Innocent III, *Sources*, 80–5.

20 Innocent III, *Sources*, 80–5.

21 RC, 81. See also RC, 41. Villehardouin gives a slightly lower figure: GV, 43.

22 NC, 302.

23 GV, 76–7.

24 GV, 77.

25 GV, 78.

26 DC, *Sources*, 218.

27 NC, 304.

28 GV, 78.

29 Angold, *Byzantine Empire*, 304–7.

30 NC, 304.

CHAPTER ELEVEN
THE GREAT FIRE OF AUGUST 1203

1 NC, 302.

2 NC, 303.

3 NC, 303.

4 NC, 303.

5 NC, 304.

6 DC, *Sources*, 218.

7 NC, 304.

8 NC, 305.

9 NC, 305.

10 NC, 305.

11 NC, 305.

12 For the Boar of Kalydon, see the novel by Lawrence Norfolk, *In the Shape of a Boar.*

13 NC, 305.

14 NC, 306.

15 Oration in: Brand, 'Byzantine Plan for the Fourth Crusade', 464–72.

16 RC, 83. For more on Murtzuphlus, see: Hendrickx and Matzukis, 'Alexios V Doukas Mourtzouphlus: His Life, Reign and Death'.

17 GV, 81.

18 GV, 82.

19 Van Millingen, *Byzantine Constantinople*, 174–5.

20 GV, 82.

21 GV, 82.

22 GV, 82.

23 GV, 83.

24 GV, 83.

25 RC, 83–4.

26 RC, 84.

27 NC, 307.

28 GV, 83.

29 GV, 83.

30 GV, 84.

31 GV, 84.

CHAPTER TWELVE

THE MURDER OF ALEXIUS IV AND THE DESCENT INTO WAR, EARLY 1204

1 DC, *Sources* 219; NC, 307.

2 DC, *Sources*, 219–20.

3 NC, 307–8.

4 NC, 308.

5 Innocent III, *Sources*, 102.

6 NC, 308–9.

7 RC, 86.

8 NC, 311.

9 NC, 311.

10 France, *Western Warfare in the Age of the Crusades*, 119.

11 Alberic of Trois-Fontaines, *Sources*, 302.

12 RC, 84.

13 Alberic of Trois-Fontaines, *Sources*, 302.

14 Alberic of Trois-Fontaines, *Sources*, 302.

15 NC, 312.

16 Alberic was not, of course, an eye-witness to these events and his account of this battle may well have been embroidered. He also refers to Patriarch John by the name 'Sampson', another error. For Greek clergy not fighting, see: Anna Comnena, *Alexiad*, 256–7.

17 RC, 89.

18 RC, 90–1.

19 Innocent III, *Sources*, 105.

20 NC, 312.

21 NC, 312.

22 GV, 84; RC, 85.

23 Innocent III, *Sources*, 105.

CHAPTER THIRTEEN
THE CONQUEST OF CONSTANTINOPLE, APRIL 1204

1 Anonymous of Soissons, *Sources*, 234.

2 RC, 92.

3 RC, 92.

4 RC, 92; Innocent III, *Sources*, 103.

5 William of Tyre, II, 227.

6 For the March Pact, see: Innocent III, *Sources*, 140–4; Tafel and Thomas, *Urkunden*, I, 445. Also GV, 88.

7 RC, 92.

8 RC, 92.

9 NC, 312.

10 GV, 89.

11 RC, 93.

12 RC, 93.

13 Innocent III, *Sources*, 105.

14 GV, 89.

15 *Conquest of Lisbon*, 153.

16 Bradbury, *Medieval Siege*, 278.

17 RC, 95.

18 Innocent III, *Sources*, 106.

19 NC, 313.

20 Innocent III, *Sources*, 106.

21 GP, 104.

22 RC, 96.

23 Innocent III, *Sources*, 106.

24 Longnon, *Les compagnons de Villehardouin*, 204.

25 RC, 97.

26 RC, 98.

27 NC, 313.

28 NC, 313.

29 RC, 91.

30 NC, 313.

31 GV, 91.

32 Innocent III, *Sources*, 106.

33 DC, *Sources*, 221.

34 GP, 106.

35 GV, 91.

36 GP, 105.

37 Madden, 'Fires of Constantinople', 84–5.

38 NC, 313.

39 NC, 314.

40 DC, *Sources*, 221.

41 NC, 314.

CHAPTER FOURTEEN
THE SACK OF CONSTANTINOPLE, APRIL 1204

1 GV, 92.

2 Innocent III, *Sources*, 107.

3 NC, 315.

4 NC, 315.

5 Nicholas Mesarites, translated in: Brand, *Byzantium Confronts the West*, 269.

6 Buckton, *Treasury of San Marco, Venice*.

7 GP, 109–12.

8 Anonymous of Soissons, *Sources*, 235–7.

9 DBH, *Sources*, 261–3.

10 Longnon, *Les Compagnons de Villehardouin*, 179–80; *Michelin Green Guide – Northern France and Paris Region*, 351.

11 RC, 112.

12 NC, 315.

13 Nicholas Mesarites in: Brand, *Byzantium Confronts the West*, 269.

14 NC, 316.

15 GV, 92.

16 RC, 100–1.

17 NC, 327.

18 NC, 325.

19 Nicholas Mesarites in: Brand, *Byzantium Confronts the West*, 269.

20 RC, 101.

21 GV, 92.

22 Innocent III, *Sources*, 107.

23 For these figures, see the detailed analysis in Queller and Madden, *Fourth Crusade*, 294–5.

24 DC, *Sources*, 221; GV, 93–5.

25 RC, 102.

26 RC, 117–18.

27 GV, 94.

28 Innocent III, *Sources*, 107.

29 This is a conflation of the reports of Villehardouin and Robert of Clari. RC, 115; GV, 96.

30 NC, 328.

31 GV, 96–7.

32 RC, 117.

33 Innocent III, *Sources*, 100.

34 Innocent III, *Sources*, 105.

35 Innocent III, *Sources*, 107.

36 Innocent III, *Sources*, 112.

37 NC, 316.

38 NC, 316.

39 NC, 317.

40 Harris, 'Distortion, Divine Providence and Genre in Niketas Choniates's Account of the Collapse of Byzantium, 1180–1204'.

41 Nicholas Mesarites, in: Brand, *Byzantium Confronts the West*, 269.

42 NC, 357.

43 NC, 360.

44 NC, 360.

CHAPTER FIFTEEN

THE END OF THE FOURTH CRUSADE AND THE EARLY
YEARS OF THE LATIN EMPIRE, 1204–5

1 GV, 92.

2 Brand, *Byzantium Confronts the West*, 19; Tafel and Thomas, *Urkunden*, I, 513.

3 GV, 97.

4 GV, 99.

5 GV, 101.

6 GV, 104.

7 GV, 107.

8 NC, 192–3.

9 RC, 124.

10 Galbert of Bruges, *Murder of Count Charles the Good*, tr. Ross, 251–2.

11 GV, 109; NC, 334; RC, 124.

12 In 1209 or 1210 Alexius III was ransomed by Michael, the Greek ruler of Epirus, who sent him to the Seljuk court at Konya. Theodore Lascaris, the Byzantine ruler of Nicaea, captured him in 1211 and had him placed in a monastery until his death a year or so later. Lock, *The Franks in the Aegean*, 70, n.4.

13 Longnon, *Les compagnons de Villehardouin*, 105.

14 Longnon, *Les compagnons de Villehardouin*, 114.

15 GV, 110–11; NC, 328.

16 GV, 115; NC, 336; Longnon, *Les compagnons de Villehardouin*, 195–7.

17 GV, 122.

18 Phillips, *Defenders of the Holy Land*, passim.

19 Innocent III, *Sources*, 147.

20 RC, 628.

21 DBH, *Sources*, 256–64.

22 NC, 337.

23 NC, 353.

24 Walter the Chancellor, *The Antiochene Wars*, 161.

25 In 811 Krum of Bulgaria had executed Nicephorus I of Byzantium and used his skull as a drinking vessel.

26 Wolff, 'Baldwin of Flanders and Hainault', 289–301.

27 Sayers, *Innocent III*, 91–3, 185–6.

28 Innocent III, *Sources*, 114, 116–17.

29 Daniel, 'Joachim of Fiore: Patterns of History in the Apocalyse'; Andrea, 'Innocent III, the Fourth Crusade and the Coming Apocalypse'. See also: McGinn, *Visions of the End: Apocalyptic Traditions in the Middle Ages*, 126–41.

30 Innocent III, *Sources*, 135.

31 NC, 357.

32 Innocent III, *Sources*, 139.

33 Innocent III, *Sources*, 166.

34 Innocent III, *Sources*, 166.

35 Innocent III, *Sources*, 173.
36 Gerald of Wales, *Journey through Wales*, 170.
37 Innocent III, *Sources*, 176.

CHAPTER SIXTEEN
THE FATE OF THE LATIN EMPIRE, 1206–61

1 The best accounts of the history of the Latin Empire are: Lock, *The Franks in the Aegean, 1204–1500*; Jacoby, 'The Latin Empire of Constantinople and the Frankish States of Greece', *New Cambridge Medieval History, c.1198–c.1300*, V, ed. Abulafia, 525–42; Harris, *Byzantium and the Crusades*, 163–82; Setton, *The Papacy and the Levant*, I, 1–105. The most important primary sources are: GV, 98–160; Henry of Valenciennes, *Histoire de l'empereur Henri de Constantinople*, ed. Longnon.
2 Phillips, *Crusades, 1095–1197*, 40–51.
3 From Barber, 'Western Attitudes to Frankish Greece', 122.
4 Nicholas, *Medieval Flanders*, 150–61.
5 The archbishop's letter is in: Röhricht, 'Amalrich I, König von Jerusalem (1162–74)', 489–91.
6 Innocent III, from: Barber, 'Western Attitudes to Frankish Greece,' 113.
7 Barber, 'Western Attitudes to Frankish Greece', 116.
8 Barber, 'Western Attitudes to Frankish Greece, 123–4.
9 Weiss, *Art and Crusade in the Age of Saint Louis*, 11–74.
10 Harris, *Byzantium and the Crusades*, 170.
11 Jacoby, 'Knightly Values and Class Consciousness in the Crusader States of the Eastern Mediterranean', 158–86.
12 Harris, *Byzantium and the Crusades*, 173–4.
13 Housley, *The Later Crusades*, 80–117.

AFTERWORD

1 Odo of Deuil, *Journey of Louis VII*, 57. On closer examination, even Odo can display a more rounded view of the Greek character. See: Phillips, 'Odo of Deuil's *De profectione Ludovici VII in Orientem* as a Source for the Second Crusade'.

2 NC, 167, although this more flowing translation is from Hussey, *Cambridge Medieval History*, IV, Pt ii, 81.

3 Queller, *Latin Conquest of Constantinople*, 19–54.

4 GV, 36–9.

5 Evergates, 'Aristocratic Women in the County of Champagne', 80–5.

6 For some of the early stages of this, see: Riley-Smith, 'Family Traditions and Participation in the Second Crusade'.

7 Angold, 'The Road to 1204: The Byzantine Background to the Fourth Crusade'.

8 Harris, *Byzantium and the Crusades*, 129, 147–8.

9 Roger of Howden, *Chronica*, II, 166. Translation from: *Annals of Roger de Hoveden*, I, 490.

10 Innocent III, *Sources*, 187.

11 Siberry, *New Crusaders*, 161–74.

12 Raimbaut of Vaqueiras, *Poems*, 228.

Bibliography

FOR REASONS OF accessibility, the emphasis throughout this book is on material translated into English. For texts in the original language, consult the references for each particular work below.

PRIMARY SOURCES

Alberic of Trois-Fontaines, 'Chronicle', *Contemporary Sources for the Fourth Crusade*, tr. A. J. Andrea, Leiden, 2000, 291–309

Albert of Aachen, 'Historia', *Recueil des historiens des croisades: Historiens occidentaux*, 5 vols. Paris, 1844–95, IV, 265–713

Anonymous of Soissons, 'Concerning the Land of Jerusalem and the Means by Which Relics were Carried to This Church from the City of Constantinople', *Contemporary Sources for the Fourth Crusade*, tr. A. J. Andrea, Leiden, 2000, 223–38

Archbishop of Nazareth, letter of 1204, in 'Amalrich I, König von Jerusalem (1162–74), *Mittheilungen des Instituts für Oesterreichische Geschichtsforschung* 12 (1891), 432–93

Beha ad-Din, *The Rare and Excellent History of Saladin*, tr. D. S. Richards, Aldershot, 2001

Benjamin of Tudela, *The Itinerary of Benjamin of Tudela*, tr. M. N. Adler, London, 1907

Bernard of Clairvaux, *Letters*, tr. B. S. James, 2nd edn, new introduction B. M. Kienzle, Stroud, 1998

Byzantine Monastic Foundation Documents, ed. & tr. J. Thomas & A. C. Hero, 5 vols, Washington, 2000

Caffaro, '*Ystoria captionis Almerie et Turtuose*', tr. J. B. Williams, in 'The Making of a Crusade: The Genoese Anti-Muslim Attacks in Spain, 1146–8', *Journal of Medieval History* 23 (1997), 29–53

Cartulaire de l'abbaye de Saint-Père de Chartres, ed. B. E. C. Guérard, 2 vols, Paris, 1840

Cartulaire de Notre-Dame de Josaphat, ed. C. Metais, 2 vols, Chartres, 1912

Cerbani Cerbani, 'Translatio mirifici martyris Isidori a Chio insula in civitatem Venetem', *Recueil des historiens des croisades: Historiens occidentaux*, 5 vols, Paris, 1844–95, V, 321–34

Chrétien de Troyes, 'Érec et Énide', in *Arthurian Romances*, tr. W. W. Kibler & C. W. Carroll, London, 1991

Chronicle of the Third Crusade: A Translation of the Itinerarium Peregrinorum et Gesta Regis Ricardi, tr. H. Nicholson. Aldershot, 1997

Conon of Béthune, *Les Chansons de Conon de Béthune*, ed. A. Wallensköld, Les Classiques Français du Moyen Age 24, Paris, 1921

Conquest of Lisbon – De expugnatione Lyxbonensi, tr. C. W. David, new introduction J. P. Phillips, New York, 2001

Contemporary Sources for the Fourth Crusade, tr. A. J. Andrea, Leiden, 2000

Continuation of William of Tyre: The Conquest of Jerusalem and the Third Crusade, tr. P. W. Edbury, Aldershot, 1996

Crusade Charters, 1138–1270, ed. C. K. Slack, tr. H. B. Feiss, Arizona, 2001

Decrees of the Ecumenical Councils, ed. N. Tanner, 2 vols, Washington, 1990

'Deeds of the Bishops of Halberstadt', *Contemporary Sources for the Fourth Crusade*, tr. A. J. Andrea, Leiden, 2000, 239–64

'Devastatio Constantinopolitana', *Contemporary Sources for the Fourth Crusade*, tr. A. J. Andrea, Leiden, 2000, 205–21

Eustathios of Thessaloniki, *The Capture of Thessaloniki*, tr. J. R. Melville Jones, Byzantina Australiensia 8, Canberra, 1988

Fulcher of Chartres, *A History of the Expedition to Jerusalem, 1095–1127*, ed. H. S. Fink, tr. F. R. Ryan, Knoxville, 1969

Galbert of Bruges, *The Murder of Charles the Good*, tr. J. B. Ross, New York, 1959

Geoffrey of Monmouth, *The History of the Kings of Britain*, tr. L. Thorpe. London, 1966

Geoffrey of Villehardouin, *La Conquête de Constantinople*, ed. & tr. E. Faral, Les

Classiques de l'histoire de France au Moyen Age 18–19, 2 vols, Paris, 1938–9

Geoffrey of Villehardouin, 'The Conquest of Constantinople', *Chronicles of the Crusades*, tr. M. R. B. Shaw, London, 1963, 29–160

Gerald of Wales, *The Journey through Wales*, tr. L. Thorpe, 1978

Gesta Francorum et aliorum Hierosolimitanorum: The Deeds of the Franks and the Other Pilgrims to Jerusalem, ed. R. Mynors, tr. R. M. T. Hill, Oxford, 1962

'Gesta Innocenti Papae', *Patrologia Latina*, ed. J. P. Migne, 221 vols., Paris, 1844–64, CCXIV, cols. 17–227

Gregory VIII, *Audita tremendi*, translated in L. Riley-Smith & J. S. C. Riley-Smith, *The Crusades: Idea and Reality, 1095–1274*, London, 1981, 63–7

Guibert of Nogent, *The Deeds of God through the Franks: Gesta Dei per Francos*, tr. R. Levine, Woodbridge, 1997

Gunther of Pairis, *The Capture of Constantinople: The 'Hystoria Constantinopolitana'*, ed. & tr. A. J. Andrea, Philadelphia, 1997

Henry of Valenciennes, *Histoire de l'empereur Henri de Constantinople*, ed. & tr. J. Longnon, Documents Relatifs à l'histoire des croisades, Vol. II, Paris, 1948

Herman of Tournai, *The Restoration of the Monastery of Saint Martin of Tournai*, tr. L. H. Nelson, Washington, DC, 1996

History of William Marshal, ed. B. Holden, tr. J. Gregory, London, 1960

Hugh of Saint-Pol, 'Letter', *Contemporary Sources for the Fourth Crusade*, tr. A. J. Andrea, Leiden, 2000, 177–201

Humbert of Romans, *De predicatione Sancte crucis*, Ms Vat. Lat. 3847, later printed in Nuremberg, 1495

Ibn Jubayr, *The Travels*, tr. R. J. C. Broadhurst, London, 1952

Innocent III, 'Solitae', from A. J. Andrea, *The Medieval Record: Sources of Medieval History*, Boston, 1997, 317–22

Innocent III, 'Letters', *Contemporary Sources for the Fourth Crusade*, tr. A. J. Andrea, Leiden, 2000, 7–176

John of Joinville, 'Life of Saint Louis', *Chronicles of the Crusades*, tr. M. R. B. Shaw, London, 1963, 163–353

John Kinnamos, *Deeds of John and Manuel Comnenus*, tr. C. M. Brand. New York, 1976

Lambert of Ardres, *The History of the Counts of Guines and Lords of Ardres*, tr. L. Shopkow, Philadelphia, 2001

Mango, C. (ed.), *The Art of the Byzantine Empire, 312–1453: Sources and Documents*, Toronto, 1986

Martin da Canal, *Les Estoires de Venise: Cronaca veneziana in lingua francese dalle origini al 1275*, ed. A. Limentani, Civiltà Veneziana Fonti e testi 12, serie terza 3, Florence, 1972

Nicephorus Chrysoberges, 'A Byzantine Plan for the Fourth Crusade', tr. C. M. Brand, *Speculum* 43 (1968), 462–75

Nicholas Mesarites, extracts translated in C. M. Brand, *Byzantium Confronts the West, 1180–1204*, Cambridge, MA, 1968, 269

Niketas Choniates, *O City of Byzantium: Annals of Niketas Choniates*, tr. H. J. Magoulias, Detroit, 1984

'Novgorod Account of the Fourth Crusade', tr. J. Gordon, *Byzantion* 43 (1973), 297–311

Odo of Deuil, *The Journey of Louis VII to the East: De profectione Ludovici VII in orientem*, ed. & tr. V. G. Berry, New York, 1948

Orderic Vitalis, *The Ecclesiastical History*, ed. & tr. M. Chibnall, 6 vols, Oxford, 1969–80

Peter of Vaux-Cernay, *The History of the Albigensian Crusade*, tr. W. A. Sibly & M. D. Sibly, Woodbridge, 1998

Peter the Venerable, *Letters*, ed. G. Constable, 2 vols, Cambridge, MA, 1967

Raimbaut of Vaqueiras, *The Poems of the Troubadour Raimbaut de Vaqueiras*, ed. & tr. J. Liniskill, The Hague, 1964

Ralph of Coggeshall, 'Chronicle', *Contemporary Sources for the Fourth Crusade*, tr. A. J. Andrea, Leiden, 2000, 277–90

Raymond of Aguilers, in *The First Crusade: The Chronicle of Fulcher of Chartres and other Source Materials*, 2nd edn, ed. E. Peters, Philadelphia, 1998

Robert of Clari, *The Conquest of Constantinople*, tr. E. H. McNeal, New York, 1936

BIBLIOGRAPHY

Roger of Howden, *Chronica*, ed. W. Stubbs, 4 vols, Rolls Series 51, London, 1868–71, translated as *The Annals of Roger de Hoveden*, tr. H. T. Riley, 2 vols, London, 1853

Snorri Sturlusson, *Heimskringla: History of the Kings of Norway*, tr. L. M. Hollander, Austin, 1964

Suger, *The Deeds of Louis the Fat*, tr. R. C. Cusimano & J. Moorhead, Washington, DC, 1992

Tafel, G. L. & Thomas, G. M. (eds), *Urkunden zur älteren Handels- und Staatsgeschichte der Republik Venedig*, 3 vols, Vienna, 1856–7, reprinted Amsterdam, 1967

Walter the Chancellor, *The Antiochene Wars*, tr. T. S. Asbridge & S. B. Edgington, Aldershot, 1999

William of Malmesbury, *Gesta Regum Anglorum: The History of the English Kings*, ed. & tr. R. A. B. Mynors, R. M. Thomson & M. Winterbottom, 2 vols, Oxford, 1998–9

William Marshal, *History of William Marshall*, ed. A. J. Holden, tr. S. Gregory, notes by D. Crouch, Vol. 1, lines 1–10031, Anglo-Norman Text Society Occasional Publications Series 4, London, 2002

William of Tyre, *A History of Deeds Done Beyond the Sea*, tr. E. A. Babcock & A. C. Krey, 2 vols, New York, 1943

William of Tyre, *Chronicon*, ed. R. B. C. Huygens, Corpus Christianorum Continuatio Mediaevalis 63/63A, 2 vols, Turnhout, 1986

SECONDARY MATERIAL

Alexander, P. J., 'The Strength of Empire and Capital as Seen Through Byzantine Eyes', *Speculum* 37 (1962), 339–57

Andrea, A. J., 'Conrad of Krosigk, Bishop of Halberstadt, Crusader and Monk of Sittichenbach: His Ecclesiastical Career, 1184–1225', *Analecta Cisterciensia* 43 (1978), 11–91

Andrea, A. J., 'Essay on Primary Sources', *The Fourth Crusade: The Conquest of Constantinople*, D. E. Queller & T. F. Madden, 2nd edn, Philadelphia, 1997, 299–344

Angold, M., *The Byzantine Empire 1025–1204: A Political History*, 2nd edn, London, 1997

Angold, M., 'The Road to 1204: the Byzantine Background to the Fourth Crusade', *Journal of Medieval History* 25 (1999), 257–68

Angold, M., *The Fourth Crusade: Event and Context*, Harlow, 2003

Archambault, P.,'Villehardouin: History in Black and White', *Seven French Chroniclers. Witnesses to History*, Syracuse, 1974, 25–39

Barber, M., 'Western Attitudes to Frankish Greece in the Thirteenth Century', *Latins and Greeks in the Eastern Mediterranean After 1204*, ed. B. Arbel, B. Hamilton & D. Jacoby, London, 1989, 111–28

Barber, R. & Barber, J. R. V., *Tournaments: Jousting, Chivalry and Pageants in the Middle Ages*, Woodbridge, 1989

Bartlett, R., *Medieval Panorama*, London, 2001

Baynes, N. H., 'The Supernatural Defenders of Constantinople', *Analecta Bollandiana* 67 (1949), 165–77

Birkenmeier, J. W., *The Development of the Komnenian Army, 1081–1180*, Leiden, 2002

Bouchard, C. B., *Strong of Body, Brave and Noble. Chivalry and Society in Medieval France*, Ithaca, 1998

Bradbury, J., *The Medieval Siege*, Woodbridge, 1992

Bradbury, J. *Philip Augustus, King of France 1180–1223*, London, 1998

Brand, C. M., *Byzantium Confronts the West, 1180–1204*, Cambridge, MA, 1968

Brundage, J. A., '*Cruce signari*: The Rite for taking the Cross in England', *Traditio* 22 (1966), 289–310

Buckton, D., *The Treasury of San Marco, Venice*, New York, 1984

Bull, M. G., *Knightly Piety and the Lay Response to the First Crusade. The Limousin and Gascony, c.970–c.1130*, Oxford, 1993

Bull, M. G., 'Origins', *The Oxford Illustrated History of the Crusades*, ed. J. S. C. Riley-Smith, Oxford, 1995, 13–33

Cheyet, J.-C., 'Les effectifs de l'armée byzantine aux x–xii s.', *Cahiers de Civilisation Médiévale X–XII Siècles* 38 (1995), 319–35

Cole, P. J., *The Preaching of the Crusades to the Holy Land, 1095–1270*, Cambridge, MA, 1991

Constable, G., 'The Historiography of the Crusades', *The Crusades from the Perspective of Byzantium and the Muslim World*, ed. A. E. Laiou & R. P.

Mottahedeh, Washington, DC, 2001, 1–22

Crosland, J., *William the Marshal: the Last Great Feudal Baron*, London, 1962

Crouch, D., *William Marshal: Knighthood, War and Chivalry, 1147–1219*, 2nd edn, London, 2002

Daniel, E. R., 'Joachim of Fiore: Patterns of History in the Apocalypse', *The Apocalypse in the Middle Ages*, ed. R. K. Emmerson & B. McGinn, Ithaca, 1992, 72–88

De Hemptinne, T., 'Les épouses des croisés et pèlerins flamands aux XIe et XIIe siècles: L'exemple des comtesses de Flandre Clémence et Sibylle', *Autour de la première croisade*, ed. M. Balard, Byzantina Sorboniensia 14, Paris, 1996, 83–95

Demus, O., *The Mosaic Decoration of San Marco, Venice*, ed. L. Kessler, Chicago, 1988

Di Fabrio, C., *La cattedrale di Genova nel medioevo secoli VI–XIV*, Genoa, 1998

Dufornet, J., 'Villehardouin et les Champenois dans la Quatrième croisade', in *Les Champenois et la croisade*, ed. Y. Bellenger & D. Quéruel, Paris, 1989, 55–69

Evergates, T., 'Aristocratic Women in the County of Champagne', *Aristocratic Women in Medieval France*, ed. T. Evergates, Philadelphia, 1999, 74–110

France, J., *Victory in the East: A Military History of the First Crusade*, Cambridge, 1994

France, J., 'Patronage and the Appeal of the First Crusade', *The First Crusade: Origins and Impact*, ed. J. P. Phillips. Manchester, 1997, 5–20

France, J., *Western Warfare in the Age of the Crusades, 1000–1300*, London, 1999

Friedman, Y., *Encounters between Enemies: Captivity and Ransom in the Latin Kingdom of Jerusalem*, Leiden, 2002

Frolow, A., *La Relique de la Vraie Croix: recherches sur le développement d'un culte*, 2 vols, Paris, 1961–5

Gillingham, J. B., *Richard I*, New Haven, 1999

Godfrey, J., *1204: The Unholy Crusade*, Oxford, 1980

Hamilton, B., *The Leper King and his Heirs: Baldwin IV and the Crusader Kingdom of Jerusalem*, Cambridge, 2000

Harris, J., 'Distortion, Divine Providence and Genre in Niketas Choniates's Account of the Collapse of Byzantium, 1180–1204', *Journal of Medieval History* 26 (2000), 19–31

Harris, J., *Byzantium and the Crusades*, London, 2003

Hendrickx, B. & Matzukis, C., 'Alexios V Doukas Mourtzouphlus: His Life, Reign and Death (?–1204), *Hellenika* 31 (1979), 108–32

Hillenbrand, C., *The Crusades: Islamic Perspectives*, Edinburgh, 1999

Housley, N., *The Later Crusades: From Lyons to Alcazar, 1274–1580*, Oxford, 1992

Howard, D., *The Architectural History of Venice*, revised edn, New Haven, 2002

Hussey, J. M., *Cambridge Medieval History* IV, Pt ii, Cambridge, 1967

Jackson, P., 'The Crusades of 1239–41 and their Aftermath', *Bulletin of the School of Oriental and African Studies* 50 (1987), 32–62

Jackson, P., 'Early Missions to the Mongols: Carpini and His Contemporaries', *Hakluyt Society Annual Report* (1995), 14–32

Jackson, P., 'Christians, Barbarians and Monsters: The European Discovery of the World Beyond Islam', *The Medieval World*, ed. P. Linehan & J. L. Nelson, London, 2001, 93–110

Jacoby, D., 'La population de Constantinople à l'époque Byzantine: Une problème de démographie urbaine', *Byzantion* 31 (1961), 81–109

Jacoby, D., 'Knightly Values and Class Consciousness in the Crusader States of the Eastern Mediterranean', *Mediterranean Historical Review* 1 (1986), 158–86

Jacoby, D., 'Conrad of Montferrat and the Kingdom of Jerusalem, 1187–92', *Atti del Congresso internazionale 'Dai feudi monferrine e dal Piemonte ai nuovi mondi oltre gli Oceani', Alessandria, 2–6 aprile 1990*, Biblioteca della Società di storia arte e archeologia per le province di Alessandria e Asti, no. 27, Alessandria, 1993, 187–238

Jacoby, D., 'The Chrysobull of Alexius I Comnenus to the Venetians: the Date and the Debate', *Journal of Medieval History* 28 (2002), 199–204

Jacoby, D., 'The Latin Empire of Constantinople and the Frankish States of Greece', *New Cambridge Medieval History, c.1198–c.1300* V, ed. D. Abulafia, Cambridge, 2002, 525–42

Johnson, E. N., 'The Crusades of Frederick Barbarossa and Henry VI',

A History of the Crusades, ed. K. M. Setton, 6 vols, Wisconsin, 1969–89, II, 87–122

Jubainville, H. de, *Histoire des ducs et des comtes de Champagne*, 7 vols, Paris, Troyes, 1859–69

Keen, M., *Chivalry*, New Haven, 1984

Kenaan-Kedar, N. & Kedar, B. Z., 'The Significance of a Twelfth-Century Sculptural Group: Le Retour du Croisé', *Dei gesta per Francos: Crusade Studies in Honour of Jean Richard*, ed. M. Balard, B. Z. Kedar & J. S. C. Riley-Smith, Aldershot, 2001, 29–44

Lane, F. C., *Venice: A Maritime Republic*. Baltimore, 1973

Lloyd, S. D., *English Society and the Crusade, 1216–1307*, Oxford, 1988

Lock, P., *The Franks in the Aegean, 1204–1500*, Harlow, 1995

Longnon, J., *Les compagnons de Villehardouin: Recherches sur les croisés de la quatrième croisade*, Geneva, 1978

Mack, M., *The Merchant of Genoa*, unpublished Ph.D. thesis, Cambridge University, 2003

Madden, T. F., 'The Fires of the Fourth Crusade in Constantinople, 1203–4: A Damage Assessment', *Byzantinische Zeitschrift* 84/85 (1992), 72–93

Madden, T. F., 'Venice and Constantinople in 1171 and 1172: Enrico Dandolo's attitudes towards Byzantium,' *Mediterranean Historical Review* 8 (1993), 166–85

Madden, T. F., *Enrico Dandolo and the Rise of Venice*, Baltimore, 2003

Madden, T. F., 'Venice, the Papacy and the Crusades before 1204', *The Crusades: New Perspectives*, ed. S. Ridyard, Sewanhee, 2004

Magdalino, P., 'Manuel Komnenos and the Great Palace', *Byzantine and Modern Greek Studies* 4 (1978), 101–14

Magdalino, P., *The Empire of Manuel I Komnenos, 1143–1180*, Cambridge, 1993

Maguire, H., 'The Medieval Floors of the Great Palace', *Byzantine Constantinople: Monuments, Topography and Everyday Life*, ed. N. Necipoglu, Leiden, 2001, 153–74

Maier, C. T., 'Kirche, Kreuz und Ritual: Eine Kreuzzugspredigt in Basel im Jahr 1200', *Deutsches Archiv für Erforschung des Mittelalters* 55 (1999), 95–115

Maier, C. T., *Crusade and Propaganda: Model Sermons for the Preaching of the Cross*, Cambridge, 2000

Mainstone, R. J., *Hagia Sophia: Architecture, Structure and Liturgy of Justinian's Great Church*, London, 1988

Mango, C., 'Three Imperial Byzantine Sarcophagi Discovered in 1750', *Dumbarton Oaks Papers* 16 (1962), 397–404

Mango, C., 'Constantinople', *The Oxford History of Byzantium*, ed. C. Mango, Oxford, 2002

Marshall, C. J., 'The Crusading Motivation of the Italian City Republics in the Latin East, 1096–1104', *The Experience of Crusading: Western Approaches*, ed. M. G. Bull & N. Housley, Cambridge, 2003, 60–79

Martin, L. R., *The Art and Archaeology of Venetian Ships and Boats*, Rochester, 2001

Martin, M. E., 'The Venetians in the Byzantine Empire before 1204', *Byzantinische Forschungen* 13 (1988), 201–14

McNeal, E. H., 'Fulk of Neuilly and the Tournament of Écry', *Speculum* 28 (1953), 371–5

McNeill, W., *Venice: The Hinge of Europe, 1081–1797*, Chicago, 1974

Megaw, A. H. S., 'Notes on Recent Work of the Byzantine Institute in Istanbul', *Dumbarton Oaks Papers* 17 (1963), 333–64

Michelin Green Guide – Northern France and Paris Region, Watford, 2001

Moore, J. (ed.), *Pope Innocent III and His World*, Aldershot, 1999

Morris, C., 'Geoffroy de Villehardouin and the Conquest of Constantinople', *History* 53 (1968), 24–34

Morris, C., *The Papal Monarchy: The Western Church from 1050 to 1250*, Oxford, 1989

Murray, A. V., 'Mighty Against the Enemies of Christ: The Relic of the True Cross in the Armies of the Kingdom of Jerusalem', *The Crusades and their Sources: Essays Presented to Bernard Hamilton*, ed. J. France & W. G. Zajac. Aldershot, 1998, 217–38

Nicholas, D., *Medieval Flanders*, London, 1992

Nicholas, K. S., 'Countesses as Rulers in Flanders', *Aristocratic Women in Medieval France*, ed. T. Evergates. Philadelphia, 1999, 111–37

Nicol, D. M., *Byzantium and Venice: A Study in Diplomatic and Cultural Relations*. Cambridge, 1988

Noble, P., 'The Importance of Old French Chronicles as Historical Sources of the Fourth Crusade and the Early Latin Empire of Constantinople', *Journal of Medieval History* 27 (2001), 399–416

Norfolk, L., *In the Shape of a Boar*, London, 2000

Norwich, J. J., *Byzantium: The Decline and Fall*, London, 1995

O'Brien, J., 'Fulk of Neuilly', *Proceedings of the Leeds Philosophical Society* 13 (1969), 109–48

Ousterhout, R., 'Architecture, Art and Komnenian Ideology at the Pantokrator Monastery', *Byzantine Constantinople: Monuments, Topography and Everyday Life*, ed. N. Necipoglu, Leiden, 2001, 133–50

Peters, E., 'Lothario dei Conti di Segni becomes Pope Innocent III', in *Pope Innocent III and His World*, ed. J. C. Moore, Aldershot, 1999, 3–24

Phillips, J. P., *Defenders of the Holy Land: Relations between the Latin East and the West, 1119–87*, Oxford, 1996

Phillips, J. P., 'Ideas of Crusade and Holy War in *De expugnatione Lyxbonensi* (The Conquest of Lisbon)', *The Holy Land, Holy Lands, and their Christian History*, ed. R. N. Swanson, Studies in Church History 36 (2000), 123–41

Phillips, J. P., 'Why a Crusade will lead to a *jihad*', *The Independent*, 18 September 2001

Phillips, J. P., *The Crusades, 1095–1197*, London, 2002

Phillips, J. P., 'Odo of Deuil's *De profectione Ludovici VII in Orientem* as a Source for the Second Crusade', *The Experience of Crusading: Western Approaches*, ed. M. G. Bull & N. Housley, Cambridge, 2003, 80–95

Phillips, J. P., *The Second Crusade: Extending the Frontiers of Christianity*, Yale, (forthcoming)

Phillips, J. P. & Hoch, M., *The Second Crusade: Scope and Consequences*, Manchester, 2001, 1–14

Powell, J. M. (ed.), *Innocent III: Vicar of Christ or Lord of the World?*, 2nd edn, Washington, 1994

Powell, J. M., 'Innocent III and Alexius III: A Crusade Plan that Failed', *The Experience of Crusading: Western Approaches*, ed. M. G. Bull & N. Housley, Cambridge, 2003, 96–102

Pryor, J. H., 'Transportation of Horses by Sea during the Era of the Crusades: Eighth Century to 1285 A.D.', *Mariners' Mirror* 68 (1982), 9–27, 103–25

Pryor, J. H., 'The Naval Architecture of Crusader Transport Ships: A Reconstruction of Some Archetypes for Round-Hulled Sailing Ships', *Mariners' Mirror* 70 (1984), 171–219, 275–92, 363–86

Pryor, J. H., *Geography, Technology and War: Studies in the Maritime History of the Mediterranean, 649–1571*, Cambridge, 1988

Pryor, J. H., 'Winds, Waves and Rocks: the Routes and the Perils Along Them', *Maritime Aspects of Migration*, ed. K. Fiedland, Cologne, 1989, 71–85

Pryor, J. H., 'The Venetian Fleet for the Fourth Crusade and the Diversion of the Crusade to Constantinople', *The Experience of Crusading: Western Approaches*, ed. M. Bull & N. Housley, Cambridge, 2003, 103–23

Queller, D. E. (ed.), *The Latin Conquest of Constantinople*, New York, 1971

Queller, D. E., Compton, T. K. & Campbell, D. A., 'The Fourth Crusade: The Neglected Majority', *Speculum* 49 (1974), 441–65

Queller, D. E., & Madden, T. F., 'Some Further Arguments in Defence of the Venetians on the Fourth Crusade', *Byzantion* 62 (1992), 433–73

Queller, D. E. & Madden, T. F., *The Fourth Crusade: The Conquest of Constantinople*, 2nd edn, Philadelphia, 1997

Riant, P., 'Innocent III, Philippe de Souabe et Boniface de Montferrat', reproduced in D. E. Queller, *Latin Conquest of Constantiniple*, New York, 1971, 32–8

Riley-Smith, J. S. C., *The First Crusade and the Idea of Crusading*, London, 1986

Riley-Smith, J. S. C., 'Family Traditions and Participation in the Second Crusade', *The Second Crusade and the Cistercians*, ed. M. Gervers, London, 1992, 101–8.

Riley-Smith, J. S. C., *The First Crusaders, 1095–1131*, Cambridge, 1997

Riley-Smith, J. S. C., 'Casualties and Knights on the First Crusade', *Crusades* 1 (2002), 13–28

Riley-Smith, J. S. C., 'Islam and the Crusades in History and Imagination, 8 November 1898–11 September 2001', *Crusades* 2 (2003), 151–67

Riley-Smith, L. & Riley-Smith, J. S. C., *The Crusades: Idea and Reality, 1095–1274*, London, 1981

Robinson, I. S., *The Papacy, 1073–1198: Continuity and Innovation*, Cambridge, 1990

Ross, L. R., *Relations between the Latin East and the West, 1187–1291*, unpublished Ph.D. thesis, University of London, 2003

Runciman, S., *A History of the Crusades*, 3 vols, Cambridge, 1951–4

Runciman, S., 'Blachernae Palace and Its Decoration', *Studies in Memory of David Talbot Rice*, Edinburgh, 1975, 277–83

Sapir Abulafia, A., *Christians and Jews in the Twelfth-Century Renaissance*, London, 1995

Sarris, P., 'The Eastern Empire from Constantine to Heraclius (306–641)', *The Oxford History of Byzantium*, ed. C. Mango, Oxford, 2002, 19–59

Sayers, J. E., *Innocent III: A Leader of Europe, 1198–1216*, London, 1994

Sesan, M., 'La flotte Byzantine à l'époque des Comnenes et des Anges (1081–1204)', *Byzantinoslavica* 21 (1960), 48–53

Setton, K. M. (ed.), *The Papacy and the Levant, 1204–1571*, 4 vols, Philadelphia, 1976–84

Siberry, E., 'Images of the Crusades in the Nineteenth and Twentieth Centuries', *The Oxford Illustrated History of the Crusades*, ed. J. S. C. Riley-Smith, Oxford, 1995, 365–85

Siberry, E., *The New Crusaders: Images of the Crusade in the 19th and Early 20th Centuries*, Aldershot, 2000

Spicher, E., *Geschichte des Basler Münsters*, Basel, 1999

Spufford, P., *Power and Profit: The Merchant in Medieval Europe*, London, 2002

Stahl, A. H., 'The Coinage of Venice in the Age of Enrico Dandolo', *Medieval and Renaissance Venice*, ed. E. E. Kitell & T. F. Madden, Urbana, 1999, 124–40

Stephenson, P., 'Anna Comnena's *Alexiad* as a Source for the Second Crusade', *Journal of Medieval History* 29 (2003), 41–54

Strickland, M., *War and Chivalry: The Conduct and Perception of War in England and Normandy, 1066–1217*, Cambridge, 1996

Van Millingen, A., *Byzantine Constantinople: The Walls of the City and Adjoining Historical Sites*, London, 1899

Winkelmann, E., 'Phillip von Schwaben und Otto IV von Braunschweig', reproduced in D. E. Queller, *Latin Conquest of Constantinople*, New York, 1971, 26–9.

Wolff, R. L., 'Baldwin of Flanders and Hainault, First Latin Emperor of Constantinople: His Life, Death and Resurrection, 1172–1225', *Speculum* 27 (1952), 281–322

Zorzi, A., *Venice 697–1797: A City, A Republic, An Empire*, Woodstock, NY, 1999

Index